Latin American
Male Homosexualities

With additional contributions by

Clark L. Taylor
Manuel Arboleda G.
Paul Kutsche
Karl J. Reinhardt
Peter Fry
Luiz Mott
Frederick L. Whitam
Richard G. Parker
Wayne R. Dynes
Beverly N. Chiñas

Latin American Male Homosexualities

STEPHEN O. MURRAY

University of
New Mexico Press
Albuquerque

LIBRARY OF CONGRESS CATALOGING-IN-PUBLICATION DATA

Murray, Stephen O.
Latin American male homosexualities / Stephen O. Murray ; with additional
contributions by Manuel Arboleda G. . . . et al.".
    p.   cm.
Includes bibliographical references (p.).
ISBN 0-8263-1646-8 (cl)   ISBN 0-8263-1658-1 (pa)
    1. Gays—Latin America.
    2. Homosexuality—Latin America.
1. Title.
HQ76.2.L29M87 1995
305.38'9664'098—dc20   95-4349
                                                         CIP

for

JOSEPH M. CARRIER
who blazed the trail for such research

❦

Contents

Part 3
Brazil

Part 4
Indigenous Societies

❦

Tables

Introduction

Changes and Variations in Male Homosexuality in Latino and Indigenous Societies

Stephen O. Murray

This book focuses on the halting and obstructed transformation from gender-defined to egalitarian (gay) organization of male homosexuality in Latin America. The first chapter explains these types. It briefly discusses examples from outside Latin America of these and other types, and of changes from one type to another.[1] The following two chapters discuss two long-enduring obstacles to gay self-identification and gay community-building in Latin American societies: the centrality of family and the cult of masculinity that is called *machismo*. Continued residence with their natal family limits the flamboyance of those inclined to gender variance as well as nearly precluding same-sex couples living together. It also eliminates the possibility of the kind of residential concentration that in the United States and Canada preceded (and enabled) the development of gay institutions and a sense of gay community. In my discussion of machismo, I suggest that some Anglo anthropologists, suffused with the vision of human sexual potentiality unencumbered by roles and identities, have over-generalized from the margins of experimentation available to young Latinos—particularly in relations with aliens such as Anglo anthropologists—to fantasies that "anything goes" and that fucking men enhances Latino men's masculine status. Representations of what Latino men do sexually with other Latino men provided in this volume by native and alien

---

1. Ancient Athens is a special focus of attention because of its importance in the development of "Western civilization," because it is the prototype of age-stratified homosexuality, and because it has been the major site for recent analysis of social construction of homosexuality before the "modern"/"Western"/"gay" construction.

anthropologists are supplemented by consideration of representations by native writers who are not social scientists.

I think that the first chapter in the section on Spanish-speaking societies, discussing non-genetic reasons for clusterings in "homosexual occupations," also applies to Brazil and Spanish-speaking South America, although the data are from Guatemala and México. The co-existence of acceptance by some and virulent, often violent, homophobia by others that Clark Taylor finds among Mexicans also seems to me of wider applicability. His chapter pays considerable attention to indigenous peoples, past and present. If his point was not one of syncretism between pre-Columbian and Spanish Catholic official intolerance and de facto ignoring of what is officially condemned and of floral homosexuality, I would have split his contribution into two chapters in different sections of the book.

In the following pair of chapters, the natives (Manuel Arboleda and Jacobo Schifter, the latter the proponent of the model contradictory to Kutsche's) stress the structuring of homosexual encounters by the *activo/ pasivo* dichotomy of roles (most fully described by Carrier 1972, 1995). No one contends that there are no departures from the "ideal norms." The native analysts (including Mott) also call attention to the diffusion of the model of egalitarian homosexuality from prestigious northern (American and European) societies. Nevertheless, role-dichotomization seems much more durable in the natives' view than in that drawn by enthusiastic alien analysts such as Kutsche and Parker. Mott focuses on the violence perpetrated against those labeled *homosexual*, a phenomenon addressed more briefly by Taylor and in my chapter on machismo.

Given the marxist roots of (allegedly "social") constructionist dogma, I find it interesting that the constructionists here (who, I hasten to add, are not notably marxist) pay much less attention to the economic structuring of homosexual relations (and constraining of gay institutional development) than do those (Arboleda, Mott, Murray, Whitam) who stress the enduring role-dichotomization conception/organization of Latin American homosexual relations. Arboleda and Whitam stress that such "gay" venues as exist are too expensive for most of the men who would like to frequent them. I stress that finding a place to have sex is very difficult; living together is generally unimaginable.

Manuel Arboleda and I document the diffusion of non–role-defined homosexuality along with the assimilation of the new word *gay* to the old model as a euphemism for *pasivo*. Mott and Parker also discuss changes in how Brazilians live and conceive homosexuality, along with impediments to changes. Karl Reinhardt and I show the persistence of macho definitions of effeminate, weak *maricones* in Mexican-American fiction from the United States. I discuss a break with much of this tradition in the series of suspense novels by Michael Nava in which a Mexican-American *activo* publicly identifies himself as gay and Chicano. I suggest cautions about interpreting some Mexican and Peruvian HIV-test data indicating middle class men's homosexual behavior not particularly constrained by role fixation to the larger population of men who have sex with men.[2]

Both the Spanish and Portuguese sections close with collections of baroque arrays of terms used to refer to homosexual roles (especially for *pasivo* males, but also terms for *activos*, role-switchers, and women who have sex with women).

This volume aims to remind us of what earlier observers wrote about some South and Mesoamerican cultures (critically reviewing material and making it accessible) and to add some new descriptions and analyses of homosexuality in contemporary Latin American societies.[3]

---

2. Moreover, that a man has taken both the *pasivo* and *activo* role over time, does not establish that his relations with any particular partner are not structured by being cast in one role or the other (often at the point of initial contact).

3. I would have liked to have reviewed and included ethnographic work on female homosexualities in urban Latin America, but such work does not exist. Although there are more female than male anthropologists of prime fieldwork age (i.e., graduate students and new Ph.D.s), and many of these are lesbian, there is nothing in the way of published ethnographic literature on "lesbians" in Latin America for me to have discussed or included in this book. Lesbian invisibility is sustained (reproduced) by the unwillingness of female ethnographers (the only ones who can gain entry to Latinas at home) to undertake research on Latina lesbians. Female ethnographers such as Fernea (1965), el-Messiri (1974), Nelson (1974), Wikan (1980, 1982), and Ginat (1982), who studied Arab women more severely constrained from public participation than Latinas are, showed an extensive women's culture in the homosocial Arab women's sphere— and showed that ethnography of women's worlds in officially patriarchal societies is possible. For now, there are glimpses of home from some Latina lesbians living in the United States in some of the anthologies of Latina lesbian writings listed in the second bibliography in "Gay Latinos and Latinas in the USA" in this volume, Ferguson's (1991) essay on lesbians during the Sandinista era in Nicaragua, and Randall's (1993) discussion with cosmopolitan Nicaraguan lesbians, but no ethnographies. I hope that women will undertake the research to find, describe, and analyze women who have sex with women in mestizo/criollo Central and South America. Meanwhile, this book critically sorts through research and writing that have been done on changing conceptions of male homosexuality in Latin American cultures. Chiñas and I discuss masculine roles for women in Zapotek and "traditional" Araucanian cultures along with feminine male roles. The sexuality(-ies?) of these women's roles is unclear.

The (perversely?) last section of this volume attempts to read through biased "descriptions" of age- and gender-stratified homosexualities in indigenous South American cultures. Its first chapter focuses on attempts by ethnographers to explain away homosexuality in Amazonian tribes. The second deals with the opposite bias: a traveler overeager to find his fantasies (of cannibalism and ubiquitous homosexual preference) organizing a remote people's society. Crossing the Andes to the west side and down to the Pacific coast, I review the confusing early accounts of sodomy along what is now the southern Ecuadorian and northern Peruvian coast,[4] extensive 17th-century vocabulary for gender-variant roles among the Aymara on the northern shores of Lake Titicaca, and gender-variant shamans among the Araucanians of Chile.

Just as the Inkas, who had conquered/assimilated many tribes and city-states into a South American empire, condemned and punished sodomy, so did the more tenuously established Aztek overlords of México. As Clark Taylor shows in his chapter (in the Spanish-speaking section) in México, as in Peru/Ecuador, coastal peoples were regarded by the native and then by the Spanish conquerors as dedicated sodomites. This was a basis for highland rulers' contempt before serving as a rationale for horrified Spanish Christians to save their souls. The early Spanish chroniclers wrote about "the nefarious sin" among peoples of the Pacific coast of South America and the lowlands (Gulf of Mexico and Pacific coasts) of Mesomerica. Early on, Spaniards regularly argued that acceptance of such "outrages" was a reason that Christian Spain needed to take charge of "depraved heathens" and save their souls from abominable practices. As suspectly ideological as this litany was, because the Spaniards did not attribute the "sin not to be named among Christians" to **all** New World peoples, there is reason to suppose that there was variation in openness/public acceptance. Given that there were major coastal cities in Peru, not just mountain citadels like Quito and Cuzco, I do not think a rural/urban contrast (as in Boswell 1980) can account for the differences between *altiplano* puritanism and coastal "licentiousness" (presuming there were differences in behavior and public acceptance between coastal and serrano groups, not just regional/ethnic slurs).

Clark Taylor's chapter shows a syncretism between Azteks and Span-

---

4. Arboleda's chapter on contemporary Lima mentions his own study of ceramic evidence on homoeroticism among the Moche, a pre-Inka kingdom in what is now northwestern Peru.

iards in condemning "sodomites" alongside some acceptance of transvestites and of homosexuality, especially among coastal (lowland) peoples in Mesoamerica. As in his chapter, most of the section on indigenous
homosexualities interprets biased sources, ranging from the 16th century into the 1970s. For many cultures, including major urban ones that
had collapsed or been overthrown before the Spanish incursions, very
little is known about sexual attitudes and roles.[5] Beverly Chiñas's discussion of a respected gender-variant role, the *muxe*, in one contemporary lowland people—the Zapoteks of the isthmus of Tehuantapec,
with whom she has worked for more than two decades—is a rare example
of sympathetic investigation of an extant positively valued role. Interestingly, at least some of the positive valuation derives not from tradition but from the *muxe* successes in mediating with Spanish-speaking
Mexican officials.[6]

In that it focuses on a gender-variant role with some positive valuation (even a sacred status), Peter Fry's fascinating account of possession
cults in Bahia is closer to the phenomena discussed in the last section
than to the gender-to-gay focus of the rest of the volume. The African
strand in Brazilian culture is important,[7] and especially prominent in

---

5. Coe (1992:238) characterized the walls of the recently discovered Mayan cave
at Naj Tunich (near the Belize border in the southeast of Petén, in Guatemala) as
containing drawings of "realistic homoerotic encounters." Drawing 18 contains an
embrace between a figure with a phallus as thick as his thigh and another figure
wearing a male headdress, a (female) long braid of hair, with substantially larger hips
and no discernible anatomical clues of sex (Coe interprets a smudge as testicles).
Andrea Stone (24 Sept. 1993 letter), the archeologist in charge of deciphering Naj
Tunich, believes "that the right figure may be a female impersonator in the context of
ritual performance. Even today, some Maya groups perform bawdy dances and such
with men playing women's roles. That is what I think is going on and I don't consider
this kind of acting homosexual per se." Insofar as the figure on the right is dressed
(which is only above the forehead), his dress is male. Insofar as the large phallus of the
figure on the left defies gravity (somewhat), this has to be considered a representation
of desire. Although homoerotic, it is stylized, not "realistic." The artist could easily
have made the figure on the right more clearly male or more clearly female. Because
the Maya principalities collapsed centuries before Europeans arrived on the scene, it is
difficult to know what to make of this drawing or of groups of Maya men standing in
a circle with a cord threaded through their penises recorded by a Spanish priest and
depicted in a pre-Columbian codex.

6. For Southwestern United States analogs to this, see Roscoe (1988, 1991).

7. It is strikingly and puzzlingly absent from Parker's (1991) book on Brazilian
sexual culture(s), particularly in that earlier Parker (1986) had written about Fry's
work. See Murray (1992).

northeastern Brazil. Though a deep stratum, African possession religions are not indigenous to South America, so Fry's chapter is with
other discussions of modern Brazil.

REFERENCES

Boswell, John
    1980 *Christianity, Social Tolerance and Homosexuality*. Chicago: University of
        Chicago Press.
Carrier, Joseph M.
    1995 *Mexican Male Homosexual Encounters*. New York: Columbia University
        Press.
Coe, Michael D.
    1992 *Breaking the Maya Code*. New York: Thames and Hudson.
el-Messiri, Saswan
    1978 Self-images of traditional urban women in Cairo." In *Women in the
        Muslim World*. L. Beck and N. Keddie, eds. Pp. 522–40. Cambridge, MA:
        Harvard University Press.
Fernea, Elizabeth Warnock
    1965 *Guests of the Sheik*. Garden City, NY: Doubleday.
Ginat, Joseph
    1982 *Women in Muslim Rural Society*. New Brunswick, NJ: Transaction Books.
Murray, Stephen O.
    1992 Review of Parker (1991). *Journal of the History of Sexuality* 2:679–82.
Nelson, Cynthia
    1974 Public and private politics: women in the Middle Eastern world. *Amer-
        ican Ethnologist* 1:551–63.
Parker, Richard G.
    1986 Masculinity, femininity, and homosexuality: on the anthropological in-
        terpretation of sexual meaning in Brazil. *Journal of Homosexuality* 11:155–63.
    1991 *Bodies, Pleasures, and Passions: Sexual Culture in Contemporary Brazil*.
        Boston: Beacon.
Randall, Margaret
    1993 To change our own reality and the world: a conversation with lesbians
        in Nicaragua." *Signs* 18:907–24.
Roscoe, Will
    1988 We'wha and Klah: the American Indian berdache as artist and priest.
        American Indian Quarterly 12:127–50.
    1991 *The Zuni Man-Woman*. Albuquerque: University of New Mexico Press.
Wikan, Unni
    1980 *Life among the Poor in Cairo*. London: Tavistock.
    1982 *Behind the Veil in Arabia: Women in Oman*. Baltimore: Johns Hopkins
        University Press.

Latin American
Male Homosexualities

1

Homosexual Categorization in Cross-Cultural Perspective

Stephen O. Murray

Homosexual behavior probably occurs everywhere. Defining persons by their sexual behavior or preference does not. That is, sexual identity is not a domain for everyone—even in societies that have sexual identity categories.[1] The modern, northern European and American notion that everyone who engages in homosexual behavior is "a homosexual," a distinct "species" with unique features, is far from being universally credited.[2] Indeed, the concept of "the homosexual" does not very well explain behavior, life, or categorization even in the society that created the model. On the one hand, those involved in homosexual behavior do not all consider themselves (and are not considered by others) as *homosexual*,[3] even in a city such as contemporary San Francisco in which *gay* is clearly recognized as a category of persons who even are alleged to be an organized political force. On the other hand, no single type with a unique set of characteristics exists.[4] In the compact (seven-mile by seven-mile) city in which I live, there is an enormous—and frequently con-

---

1. Indeed, "nothing automatically translates itself for the child into sexual meaning" (Plummer 1990:237). Over time, children learn to conceive of feelings and behavior as "sexual." Although it sometimes seems that this can vary without limits, there are certainly regularities. Defining a self out of "sexual" feelings and behavior is a later (ontogenic) development, one that not all individuals necessarily make.

2. Wayne Dynes (1990, personal communication) suggests that it is a late 20th-century concoction, that no one before Michel Foucault (1980) treated "the homosexual" as "a species," so that this is a "straw man," nowhere credited.

3. Humphreys (1975); Miller (1978); Weinberg (1983); Murray (1979a,b, 1984, 1992b); Goodwin (1989).

4. Hooker (1957); Bell and Weinberg (1978); Roscoe (1988a); Murray (1992a: 363–86).

3

flicting—range of homosexual behaviors, typifications, self-identifica-
tions, and meanings; just as there are ranges of "Latino" or "Chinese" or
"Italian," "working class" or "capitalist" behaviors, typifications, self-
identifications, and meanings.

Avoiding the Scylla of labeling everyone anywhere who engages in
homosexual behavior a *homosexual* or a *gay person* (as Boswell 1980 followed psychoanalysts in doing), exposes one to the opposite danger, the
Chardybdis of arguing that there is no category at all except in modern,
(north-)western societies (Faderman 1978, 1991:37–61; Weeks 1981;
Halperin 1990). To be sure, there is diversity, intraculturally as well as
interculturally, but conceptions do not vary endlessly. Relatively few of
the imaginable mappings of cognitive space recur in the panorama of
known cultures, despite the anthropological tradition of stressing "ex-
otic" differences and ignoring what is familiar to observers.[5] There are
not hundreds or even dozens of different social organizations of homosexual relations in human societies (Murray 1984:19–21). Relatively few
of the imaginable patternings of homosexuality have been attested from
anywhere in the world. As for other cultural domains, only a few categorization systems recur across space and time.[6]

---

5. This is a genre convention going back to Herodotus, "the father of anthropology" (Redfield 1985), and also characteristic of non-western writers about different
cultures (Murray 1994a). On the European tradition, see Hodgen (1964), Murray
(1981), Roscoe (1995).

6. Ethnosemanticists have studied the domain of color more extensively than any
other, since for color there is an organization of data (the spectrum with its equal
interval calibration of wavelengths) other than that provided by one language with
which to contrast the seeming immense diversity of color lexicons in different languages (Lenneberg 1953; Kay and McDaniel 1978). Berlin and Kay (1969) demonstrated that there is a great deal of order in this seeming diversity; indeed, that the
elaboration of color lexicon occurs in a nearly invariant order. If there is a third
category (after light/dark), it is red. After red, the order of elaboration is yellow-green-
blue, or green-yellow-blue, and so on. All categorization systems overlook and ignore
some perceived differences (Goodenough 1990:598–99), and cultural novices (mostly
children) learn categories from instructors pointing out prototypical examples, not
from exhaustive labeling of all possible shades. For instance, instead of trying to define
"red" in terms of a set of wavelengths that is a segment of the spectrum of light, or a
checklist of essential/"defining" features of "redness," good examples of "red" are
labeled, often in a "not orange, but red" form (Goodenough 1990:606, following upon
the discussion of foci in Berlin and Kay 1969). Universals in ordering of categories for
plants and animals were suggested by Berlin (1972, 1973), substantiated by Brown
et al. (1976), Hunn (1976), Boster and D'Andrade (1989), Boster and Johnson (1989),
and others. Kay (1978) applied the method of analyzing categories to such contentious

Barry Adam (1979, 1986)[7] proposed a fourfold typology of social structuring of homosexuality: (1) age-structured, (2) gender-defined, (3) profession-defined, and (4) egalitarian/"gay" relations.[8] One of these ideal types tends to figure most prominently as "the dominant discourse" about homosexuality in any one society. While relationships structured by age, gender, profession, and by comradeship may coexist in a society, one of them predominates both among those who are native to the society and in explanation to aliens who ask about same-sex relations.[9] For instance, age-graded male homosexuality was the norma-

social categories as "race" and "class" in Tahiti. Regularities in both synchronic and developmental orders of categorization schema for "nature" and for "culture" exist cross-culturally. On the extreme selectivity of nominalism in work on "the social creation of homosexuality," see Murray (1983, 1984:18–21), and Dynes (1990:226–30). Readers of creationist discourse are "left with the impression that other diachronic [and cross-cultural] abstractions are accurate as commonly applied, while this one alone is singularly inaccurate" (Boswell 1990:139; also see 142–44).

7. Trumbach (1977) demarcated the age/gender distinction, but Adam told me that he was unaware of Trumbach's paper in 1979. Similarly, Trumbach told me that he was unaware of Geoffrey Gorer's earlier age/gender dichotomy, which, in turn, seems to me to derive from Richard Burton's "Terminal Essay" to his translation of *The Thousand and One Nights,* first printed privately in 1886.

8. Donaldson and Dynes (1990) proposed a triaxial typology with a gender axis, a role/reciprocity axis, and a time axis (temporary/permanent) that encompasses gender, and egalitarian organizations, but not the profession-defined type. Moreover, it includes age-stratified homosexuality only uncomfortably. Murray (1992a) moved towards splitting age-structured homosexuality (not on the temporary/permanent basis but on the amount of disparity in ages of partners: a few years versus "trans-generational") and toward folding "profession-defined" into being part of "gender-defined," since the professional roles are markedly gender-variant. Roscoe (1988a) suggested six dimensions (sexuality, subjectivity, gender, social roles, economic roles, and spirituality). Given the high correlation of these dimensions, this typology seems over-elaborate at the same time that it lacks principles to order the dimensions. Moreover, it ignores age-structured homosexuality, and I am not sure that it encompasses egalitarian organization of homosexuality (although the subjectivity dimension might). Roscoe (1991 personal communication) suggests that cross-cultural comparison needs to use polytypic classes, and not expect to be able to specify in advance what will be the combinations of "significant features."

9. "Of course, any single set of cultural institutions never completely contains the full range of human experience and innovation. Social coding practices may be uneven, incomplete, or in transition. Even where sexuality has a culturally specific complex of meanings, there remains a larger universe of experience, maladjustment, and emigrations from prescribed interpretive frameworks. The dominant sexual codes of one place take on subterranean aspects elsewhere as a 'little tradition'"(Adam 1986: 20). The same cultural categories may be variously interpreted and lived by individ-

tive form in ancient Athenian discourse. Gender-defined and comradely homosexuality also occurred, and at least the former was lexicalized with a term for such a kind of person, *kinaidos* (Winkler 1990:45–54; on comradely relations see Halperin 1990:225, 47, 76–87). Similarly, many indigenous North American peoples had terms for the "two-spirit"/"third gender" or "gender-mixing" ("berdache") role, while sexual relationships between two braves or between two women often lacked labels.

Whether the typology applies to female homosexuality has been little discussed. Those interested in "social construction" of sexualities cannot (consistently with their theory, or with the distinct constraints on women's movement and associations in various societies) take a similarity between male homosexuality and female homosexuality as pre-given and "natural." Yet, there has been a marked reluctance to deconstruct this particular equation—even though it is this linkage that seems to be what is most unique to the modern, "western" (northern European and American) conception of homosexuality (Dynes 1990:229; Halperin 1990:24). An equation of male and female homosexuality is very alien to those men involved in recurrent homosexuality in the societies I have studied (México, Guatemala, Peru, Taiwan, and Thailand). Adam (1986:21,24) rejected a parallel for age-structured female homosexuality, because a period between puberty and marriage (bachelorhood) exists only for males in the gerontocratic and/or polygynous societies with age-structured male homosexual relations. However, I think there is evidence of at least rudimentary age-stratified female-female relationships.[10] Clearly, no body of writings exists by women celebrating the charms of budding girls to parallel those by men on the charms of budding boys. The extent to which this is an epiphenomenon of the lack of female representations of female desire is hard to gauge. What has survived of Sappho is extremely fragmentary, and there have been very few women whose writings (or paintings, etc.) have survived at all. Although the representations of it are mostly from males, female gender-stratified homosexuality occurs (Adam 1986:35). It seems less likely to be exclusive and life-long than is the case for male gender-

---

uals. Over time, shared new meanings may move even the cultural categories. Moreover, traditions that are overshadowed (by dominant discourses) may nonetheless persist (see Morris 1994).

10. An interesting study of institutionalized roles in a southern African milieu was provided by Gay (1986).

stratified homosexuality. Similarly, involvement in egalitarian female-female sexuality seems to me more episodic and less enduringly self-defining than is typical of men's engagement with egalitarian (gay) male-male sexuality.

The typology seems to encompass the observed empirical variance in societal/cultural schemata of male-male sexual relations and, insofar as any exist, cultural models of female-female sexual relations as well. It is important to remember that expressed norms are very inadequate descriptions of behavior. In particular, the only acts that laws bother to forbid are those that some people would like to do—such as "coveting" a neighbor's wife, "lying with a man as with a woman," eating pork, or smoking crack. Those concerned about their society's image may deny that proscribed acts occur, or, if they admit that such acts do occur, may attribute them to foreign influences, whether cocaine from Colombia, or homosexuality from "infidels" (e.g., Arabs), or "heretics" (e.g., Bulgarians) or some other antagonist (e.g., "the French vice"). One should be careful about accepting claims that behavior stigmatized in the questioner's culture is unknown or alien to the culture observed. One should be even more wary about assuming that no one anywhere at any time was aware of same-sex sexual preferences or sexual behavior just because a language seems to lack a term for *homosexual* (Murray 1988:471; Roscoe 1988a:25; Dynes 1990:225). Rather a lot of the homosexual behavior in Anglo North America, and even more of it in Latin America, is not between persons who consider themselves (or their sexual partners) to be *homosexuales*. Homosexual behavior occurs outside the often-simplistic roles recognized (with labels) in a society. This is true even where, as in contemporary urban North and Latin America, there are multiple labels used in self-reference.

As with almost all cross-cultural work dealing with homosexuality, the contributors to this volume focus on cultural/social categories. Discussion of individual manipulation of and maneuvering within the categories is not altogether absent, but should be a priority in future work. The following sections of this chapter review the types and suggest their historical succession.[11]

---

11. The major attempts at synthesis to date are Bullough (1976) and Greenberg (1988). I think that discussion of the correlates to and possible explanations of observed organizations of homosexuality should be deferred until the variations have been better mapped. Work in "the history of sexuality" and "gay studies" seems to me

Age-Stratified Organization of Homosexuality

Indigenous sub-Saharan Africa included both societies in which young males were sexual objects for other young males,[12] and societies in which the elite had boy wives who did women's work as well as providing sexual outlets for their "husbands."[13] The boys, accustomed to exclusive receptive homosexuality, graduated to "husband" roles when they were older, and themselves took "boy wives" from a new generation.[14]

A number of Australian and the better documented Melanesian cultures "share the belief that boys do not become physically mature men as a result of natural processes. Growth and attainment of physiological maturation is contingent on the cultural process of initiation, and this entails insemination, because it is semen which ensures growth and development" (Kelly 1976).

As Herdt (1984:39) explained, Melanesian homosexuality masculinizes both participants. Indeed, it is a central part of a cult of masculinity. In these cultures, growing up male and a warrior requires several years of exclusive homosexual receptivity towards physically mature males. By "physically mature," I mean post-pubescent. Generally, those playing the insertor role in the sexual portions of Melanesian initiation are not socially fully mature. Specifically, they are not married. Among Herdt's Sambia, a penis that has entered a woman is too polluted to be a suitable source of semen for growing young boys. There are four Sambian male age grades: the pre-initiated boy with no sexual activity, the initiate who receives semen, the initiated but unmarried

---

to have been over eager for all-encompassing theories, too impatient to examine diverse conceptions and organizations of sex, gender, and sexualities or to explore the salience of these modern, western analytic grids for other peoples. I find Adam's (1986:31) suggestion that the societies with "profession-defined" homosexual niches (viz. shamans) have more complex divisions of labor particularly puzzling. Surely the Chukchi and Iban of ethnographic record (which is to say the late 19th century) or the Araucanians (discussed in this volume) had less complex divisions of labor than Tokugawa Japan, medieval Islamic states, or ancient Greece.

12. E. g., the Nyakyusa described by Wilson (1951:196–97).

13. E. g., the Azande described by Evans-Pritchard (1937, 1970, 1971).

14. Lindenbaum's (1984:344) suggestion that pederasty is a functional alternative to brideprice in Melanesia would seem to apply to Africa and elsewhere, as well. The bride and her brother receive semen from the same man—or the boy stands in for a non-existent or too-young sister "owed" his sexual partner('s clan). See the Chapter 19 in this volume for some Amazonian analogs and Murray (1992a:6–7) for some aboriginal Australian ones.

young men who provide semen to their juniors, and married men. The age difference between receptive and insertive youths is not sufficient to warrant "trans-generational," nor (because the insertors are not fully adult) "man-boy" love.[15] Similarly, in medieval Japan, age-structured samurai homosexuality often involved slight (and in some cases only nominal) age differences.[16]

The case of ancient Greece (see Dover 1978) demonstrates that adolescent "submission" to sexual relations with one's elders does not necessarily foster lifelong effeminacy, nor prevent later siring of children. Some European classicists interpret ancient Greek pedagogical pederasty as a residue of an earlier proto–Indo-European male initiation complex, and, therefore, masculinizing in the same way as Melanesian ritualized pederasty.[17] British and American classicists who are critical of linking 5th-century B.C. pederasty to male initiation do not consider the boys whose compassion (never, in their view, desire![18]) motivated them to permit men access to between their thighs to have been masculinized by such behavior and relationships.[19] Although temporarily in an inferior position of submission—so long as he avoided penetration, payment, and any public indications of sexual desire to be penetrated, and also ceased passive intercrural intercourse when he reached

---

15. However, in some other Melanesian societies—e.g., the Marind-Anim described by Van Baal (1984)—adult males provide semen to initiates. I doubt whether there is a single "Melanesian type" of age-structured homosexuality (Adam 1986; Bleibtreu-Ehrenberg 1990) to compare with "ancient civilizations." If the age-stratified type is subdivided, it seems to me that intergenerational relationships should be distinguished from those in which contiguous age-classes are paired.

16. Contrast the evidence discussed by Murray (1992a:111–50) and Leupp (in press) with the assertion of Adam (1986:25).

17. E. g., Dumézil (1969, 1986), Patzer (1982), Sergent (1986).

18. Theognis (Second Book 1251, 1261, 1270, 1301, 1377) clearly attributed sexual desires to those he regretted were not faithful *eromenos*. Reproaches of infidelity are far more common in ancient Greek (and Roman) poetry than are references to specific erogenous zones (see Bing and Cohen 1991). In Greek vase paintings, "it is the *erastes* who must stoop [or sit] so as to have sex intercrurally [or to fondle the boy's genitals], while the *eromenos* stands modestly upright" (Bing and Cohen 1991:9), indifferent—or feigning indifference (and thereby, through the power of the least interest, enhancing his power over his ardent suitors). The beloved in Islamic mystical poetry also withheld his favors (or, at least, there was a genre convention of complaining that he did). In ancient, medieval, or modern literature, the beautiful beloveds are rarely heard from. It is the frustrated or courting lovers who write.

19. See Dover (1978, 1988), Greenberg (1988), Halperin (1990), Bleibtreu-Ehrenberg (1990:20–23).

maturity (made generally visible by the growth of a beard)—the free-born youth remained distinct from the socially inferior, penetrable cate-gories of women and slaves. In this view, although playing the *eromenos* (beloved) role did not masculinize the boys, neither did it stigmatize or effeminize them. In his turn, an *eromenos* was expected quickly to join the ranks of the *erastes* (lover/phallic insertor).[20] The transitoriness of young male beauty and the power the beloved had over the yearning adult lover are leitmotifs (often expressed in set formulae) in medieval Islamic and Japanese literatures (Murray 1992a:111–50, and forthcom-ing; Leupp in press; Schalow 1990; for a Greek precursor, see The-ogonis's Second Book 1305–34).[21]

Without doubt, the norm in societies in which homosexuality is age-defined—even in the African ones in which the boywives do women's work—is for men to "graduate" to insertor roles, ceasing altogether to play receptor. Not all behavior conforms with any ideal norm, and not everyone in societies with age-defined structures of homosexuality "grad-uates" from the homosexual "phase." Dover (1978) supplied evidence (though without grasping its import) of bearded adults in ancient Greece who continued to enjoy sexual receptivity to other males.[22] Herdt's contribution to Murray (1992a:33–68; also see Herdt and Stoller 1990) relates the life history of a Sambian who preferred to continue supply-

---

20. The *erastes* was not conceived as effeminized by transitory homosexual behav-ior, or even by a preference for boys. See Winkler (1990:114), where he translates *phusei paiderastês* as "naturally a lover of young men."

21. The most vivid representation in European art of the adult literally overcome by a beautiful boy is Michelangelo's statue "Victory." Donatello's "David" can be read that way almost as easily, especially if it is the sculptor's head on the vanquished men in both sculptures. The great classical exemplar of the transitoriness of the young male beloved, Antinous, did not tie up or decapitate Hadrian, but in avoiding aging he provoked grief and a (popular, not just court) cult of his adolescent beauty. Also recall the early deaths of such not particularly macho figures as Adonis, Attis, Osiris, and Jesus, and the murder of the great Persian mystic poet Rumi's beloved, Shamsuddin.

22. In a startling addendum to his very doctrinaire book, Halperin (1990:225) disavowed his categorical statements throughout his writings on Athenian pederasty, admitting that there are representations (on black-figure ceramics) of reciprocal erotic contacts between adult males and reversals of roles between man and boy. Winkler (1990) was much more cautious of cultural determinism, treating the norms upheld in discourse about masculinity as "loose-fitting hand-me-downs that do not reveal the shape of individual behavior" and as "strongly articulated but only very selectively enforced," and going so far as to write that "the standards of rigor had virtually nothing to do with actually regulating men's sexual behavior" (45, 64, 11; also see Halperin 1990:58, 68; Boswell 1990:152,n.21, 144; Bing and Cohen 1991:9).

ing boys with semen instead of settling down into the roles of husband and father, as expected in and demanded by his culture. There are also Islamic instances of lifelong homosexual preferences (discussed in Murray, forthcoming), and representations of Japanese adult *wakashu*, including a 63-year-old continuing the "boy" role (Schalow 1990:96, 182).

Gender-Stratified Organization of Homosexuality

Unlike age-stratified organizations in which the natives regard homosexual receptivity as masculinizing, and, in some cultures, even as necessary to the development of masculinity; the natives of cultures with gender-stratified organizations of homosexuality expect the sexually receptive partner to enact some other aspects of the feminine gender role: usually, to behave and/or sound and/or dress in ways appropriate to women in that society.[23] The relative importance of sexuality, dress, and occupation to the natives of the cultures is often unclear in accounts by missionaries, anthropologists, and other kinds of travelers (and even of natives other than those enacting the gender-subordinate role). While alien observers generally do not observe actual sexual behavior, they are especially likely to notice a man wearing clothing distinctively different from that worn by most men or one who does what is regarded there as "women's work."

The prototypical gender-defined role is the *pasivo* role widespread in the Mediterranean and Latin American culture areas. The "active" male in homosexual copulation is an unmarked male, not officially regarded (and especially not by himself) as "homosexual." One of the pleasures that must be forborne by adult males in such cultures is sexual receptivity. Winkler (1990:67ff.) shows that the ancient Greeks conceived such pleasure. Exactly the fear of coming to enjoy being penetrated recurs in Muslim societies as a reason not to try the behavior (Schmitt 1985; Murray, forthcoming). In Mesoamerica, I have also heard *activos* say that if they got fucked they might want it all the time, so the safest course for their masculinity is to avoid trying it. Thus, although the

---

23. Roscoe (1988a:28) cautions that those engaged in what he typifies as "sociosexual specialization" may mimic female stereotypes. These may have little to do with how most women in a society usually behave.

penetrator may have little concern about whether the penetrated person has a pleasant time, he conceives the possibility that someone biologically male can enjoy being penetrated.

Whether enjoying being penetrated or performing a duty to provide the masculine partner with pleasure, the sexually receptive partner is expected to conform in some ways to the female social role. This applies to persons born into what we call either "biological sex." However, ("biological") men in female roles and occupations generally retain some male prerogatives[24] and/or are said to be better at "women's work" than mere women are.[25] Because of the distinction of men doing women's work from women doing it, and because dress mixes what is typically male with what is typically female or is not typical of either, some Anglo North American theorists have suggested (with little established basis in native enumeration of sex or of genders) that various cultures have three genders (male, female, berdache) rather than two. Meso-americans I have asked insist that a *pasivo* is "a kind of a man," definitely not "a kind of woman" (Murray 1980, 1987a:129–38). Baduddrin Khan (1993, personal communication) insists that the South Asians conceive of *gandu*, and even *hijra* as kinds of men (albeit inadequate specimens), not a third gender or third sex (cf. Nanda 1990). Similarly, Vinson Sutlive (1990, personal communication) reports the northern Borneo Iban similarly regard their gender-crossing shamans as men, not a third kind of person. Nonetheless, native views of the number of genders deserve empirical investigation in other cultures before the "third gender" categorization is dismissed as just an analysts' imposition on other cultures.[26]

---

24. See Fry (this volume); Jackson (1989); Murray (1987a:159–64, 1992a:341–52); Roscoe (1987, 1988b, 1990, 1991, 1994); Whitehead (1981); Williams (1986).

25. For a long time I thought this was just male ideology, i.e., whatever men do, they must do better. Although I remain unconvinced that blind evaluation of men's and women's work would be unequivocal, I now believe that men doing women's work frequently command the best raw materials. They can also concentrate on their crafts with less interruption from children than craftswomen typically can.

26. Cf. Williams (1986:76–86); Murray (1987a:159–64, 1993); Roscoe (1987, 1991, 1994); Herdt (1990). In ancient Athens, "*kinaidos* was a category of person, not just of acts" (Winkler 1990:46), and I would hazard the guess that so was a *binoumenos* ("a fucked male" in Winkler's [1990:61] translation), but as with the Polynesian *mahu* and the North American berdache, describing someone as "womanly" or "like a woman" does not establish whether there are two or more genders, or whether the type is a kind of man or a kind of woman if there are only two. The salient distinction in Halperin

Latin Americans generally stigmatize the *pasivos*. Afro-Brazilian cults, however, provide a niche in which some *pasivo* males exercise spiritual powers and claim the attendant prestige (Landes 1940; Fry, this volume). Important powers also attached to transvestite shamans along both sides of the North Pacific (Williams 1986; Roscoe 1987; Murray 1992a:293–352), and even down into Borneo and Indochina (Heimann and Cao 1975; Murray 1992a:171–92, 257–84). Those playing the role commanded awe—an admittedly ambivalent emotion. The Catholic priesthood is also a niche for those boys who do not seem "normally" masculine to wear colorful robes and to avoid marriage.[27]

In Mediterranean and Mediterranean-influenced societies, people take for granted (regard as "natural") that some men won't attain masculinity. Attempts to extirpate homosexuality are not traditional, but violence—sexual (rape) and other kinds (beatings)—is the "fate" of effeminate men (cross-dressed or not) in cultures (including those of Latin America and the Philippines) influenced during colonial domination by the Iberian code of male honor and Catholicism. This is also the case in the prototype of "acceptance of homosexuality," contemporary Thailand (Jackson 1989:224–28; also see Manalansan 1990, 1991, 1993; Arenas 1993:97–99, 108). Although family members may give up on their children marrying and producing more children, they often make major efforts to discourage public gender non-conformity of children or of siblings. In that unmarried children continue to live in the natal home indefinitely, families often demand ongoing decorum even from those whose gender and sexual "abnormality" they have ceased trying to alter.

As will be discussed more extensively in this volume, in Latin America, even before the diffusion of *gay* models, behavior was far less clearly dichotomized than the simple *activo/pasivo* contrast would suggest. Over time (in an individual's sexual "career") or with different partners, behavior(al repertoire) diverged from the ideally clear dichotomy. Thus, Carrier (1976:120–21) noted that

---

(1990) and Winkler (1990) is between citizens and non-citizens, so that gender might be considered incidental, along with sexuality, to the most salient schema of Greek thought. Non-citizens could be penetrated with relative impunity. Also see Dynes (1983) and Richlin (1993) on ancient Rome; Murray (forthcoming) on the analog of non-believers in Islamic societies.

27. For many Latin American men, priests' manhood is suspect. Respect for them is frequently little; jokes about their "dresses" and lack of *cojones* (testicles properly bursting with semen that must out) are common.

while there is a low probability that both active and passive anal intercourse are practiced by both participants in a given homo-sexual encounter . . . a little over forty percent of those playing the anal passive sex role and close to one-fourth of those play-ing the anal active sex role during their first sustained year, over time, incorporated the other sex role into their sexual repertoire. [See also Taylor 1978; Murray 1980, 1987a]

In a 1986 sample of 2,400 men tested for HIV antibodies in Gua-dalajara, México, 74 percent reported engaging in both insertive and receptive anal intercourse (Carrier 1989:132),[28] and other studies of men tested for HIV antibodies in México have reported even less rigid role separation. (I discuss these data in more detail in chapter 9 below.)

Profession-Defined Organization of Homosexuality

Whether a profession-defined organization exists, distinct from the gender-defined one deserves consideration. I began, but by no means concluded, this consideration in Murray (1992a:257–352). What is most questionable is whether there is self-selection by those seeking a niche for homosexual desire and/or gender deviance, as Alfred Kroeber (1940) and his student George Devereux (1937) suggested among California Indians, Ashworth and Walker (1972), and Whitam and Mathy (1986) in industrialized societies; or whether there is sexual resocialization of "heterosexuals" in roles such as shamans, dancing boys, transvestite singers and prostitutes (see my discussion of the Araucanian case in Chapter 21; Allyn and Collins 1988).

Such concern about the cultural primacy of gender, sexuality, and occupation is bootless according to Roscoe (1988a), who proposes to include these (along with self-identity, social role, and spirituality) as dimensions of "sociosexual specialization." His essay is an interesting attempt to delineate an object of study, but begs the question of the relative importance and empirical inter-correlation of the dimensions.[29] In the Indonesian and Siberian cases reviewed in Murray (1992a), desire for same-sex copulation was secondary, though highly correlated for

---

28. Carrier (1990, personal communication) believes that those being tested for HIV antibodies are better educated than the norm, so that this is a biased sample.

29. Like Boswell (1980), Roscoe (1988a, et seq.) downplays age-stratified homosex-uality to the point of invisibility.

those called to service by spirits. A predisposition for gender-crossing is far from invariable, and resistance to the call is conventional in African, Afro-Brazilian, Siberian, and West Pacific cultures in which spirit possession is valued highly. In the prototypical case, among the Siberian Chukchi studied by Vladimir Bogoraz (1904:418), men especially resisted calls from the spirits that included demands for sexual transformation.

Convincing evidence about motivation is missing from the historical literature and the question is unasked in such more-or-less contemporary anthropological literature as exists on gender-variant shamans (e.g., Fry 1974; Wafer 1991). Cultures in which spirit possession is positively valued do not consider possession a choice made (even unconsciously) by the person possessed.[30] "Shamans" routinely deny learning and training (Bogoraz 1904; Estrada 1981; Samarin 1972; Murray and Hong 1994). Agnostic questions about predispositions, psychopathology, training, and rewards that might be sought by those whom the gods/spirits have chosen to borrow are not just rude, but blasphemous. Generally, those living in a cosmology that includes beliefs in the reality of spirit possession (1) do not view their ideas as arbitrary, conventional, dependent upon local consensus, or dependent on the imagination, desire, or will of individuals; (2) believe that their reality-posits express significant insights into reality and illuminate/explain real experiences; (3) remain convinced that their reality-posits constitute knowledge about the world, even after alien observers "explain" that the beliefs are individual or collective delusions, wishful thinking, false consciousness, etc., and, (4) within presuppositions alien to atheistic ones, reason rationally.[31]

Professions other than spirit healers attested elsewhere (such as dancing boys and actors playing female roles) are uncommon in the indigenous Americas. In a paper reprinted as Chapter 4 of this volume (Murray 1991), I question whether particular occupational specializations rest on biological predispositions. I argue that concentrations are, instead, a function of occupations becoming niches. Communication of information about job opportunities within particular networks keeps the occupation filled with the "same kind" (*pasivos* in the instance of hairdressers and interior decorators).

---

30. This contrasts with cultures, such as North American Plains ones, in which visions (but not possession) were/are quite clearly sought.

31. This list derives from a generalization from orthodox Hindu conceptions of karma and reincarnation to witchcraft by Shweder (1991:58). For an attempt to discuss spirit possession from inside a non-Western belief system, see Murray and Hong (1994).

Egalitarian Organization of Homosexuality

More recently, "gay" organization of homosexuality has become prominent in Western Europe and North America and, at least incipiently, in Latin America and industrialized Asian and Pacific societies. What is distinctive about this mode is (1) a group consciousness of comprising a distinct kind, (2) a separate subculture based on (3) egalitarian (not gender-role-bound or involving the submission of the young) and (4) the possibility of exclusive (not bisexual) same-sex relations (Adam 1979; elaborated in Adam 1987:6). Readily available sources sufficiently well describe the genesis and organization of "gay" communities so as not to require discussion here.[32]

A number of chapters in this volume discuss the influence of North American models and the ambivalence of Latin Americans to taking such models as goals. I discuss my own skepticism of unilinear gender-to-gay evolution in Chapter 2 and will not anticipate that argument here. Parker's chapter on Brazil, Arboleda's on Peru, and the one by Murray and Arboleda drawing on semantic data from several times and places all focus on the changing conception/organization of homosexual behavior. I also discuss whether behavioral data collected in HIV-test sites in México and Peru show the emergence of "modern, gay" homosexuality in those countries.

Changes in Organization

For most cultures, data on homosexual behavior and societal reaction to it are so rare, recent, and incomplete, that little can be said about changes. Even for much-written-about Western Europe, controversy rages about whether there were significant changes in conception (self or societal) of homosexuality and reactions to it in the millennium and a half between the fall of Rome and the rise of Napoleon (or later, with the coining of the word *homosexuality* and medical discourse about it).

---

32. See Adam (1987), Bérubé (1990), Chauncey (1994), D'Emilio (1983), Grube (1986, 1987, 1991), Humphreys (1972), Humphreys and Miller (1980), Marotta (1981), Murray (1979b, 1984, 1992b), Newton (1993), Plummer (1981), Steakley (1975) on the genesis; Harry and Devall (1979), Herdt (1992), Lee (1978, 1979a,b), Levine (1979, 1986), Leznoff and Westley (1956), Murray (1979a, 1984, 1992b), Plummer (1992), Weinberg (1983), Weston (1991), D. Wolf (1979) on the organization.

The repressive weight of triumphant sex-negative Christianity is widely believed to have crushed the somewhat-effeminized pederastic silver age of imperial Rome, heir to the masculinist golden age of pederasty in Greek city-states.[33]

In the Foucaultian view, only with the supposed epistemic break of the Enlightenment and later replacement of clerical with medical "knowledge" did an inter-sexed homosexual "species" come into existence.[34] Within this view or (more appropriately) behind these theoretical blinders, between the time of Justinian and that of Magnus Hirschfeld (i.e., between the middle of the 6th and end of the 19th centuries), there were homosexual acts but no homosexual roles for homosexual selves to enact (as, similarly, there were crimes but no criminals, and deranged behavior without madmen and madwomen). At the end of the medieval period, traces of a pederastic subculture were still somewhat visible.[35] Before the recent emergence of gay people rejecting gender and age roles, a subculture organized by cross-gender assumptions flourished with varying degrees of covertness.[36]

Thus, in terms of self-conception, northwestern European culture exemplifies a succession of age, gender, and gay subcultures, with a gap in the late-17th century between the age-stratified and gender-stratified eras (Trumbach 1990; Rousseau 1990), and a rapid shift during the 1970s of gender distinctions or "variance" from being normative to being stigmatized (Humphreys 1972; Levine 1986).

The transformation from gender to gay is usually treated as a revolution, while no one seems to realize that an earlier transformation from age to gender occurred—in Europe, in Japan, and possibly also in China and the Roman Empire.[37] During the period commonly glossed as "the

---

33. Boswell (1980), unlike social creationists who did not look beyond the late-19th century before proclaiming it the point of origin of homosexual categorization/identity, dissents from this view. I think that he goes too far to the opposite extreme. On the *sodomite* as a cultural category beyond "random" acts of sodomy, see Murray (1988). On the effeminization of the sexually receptive "boys" during the Roman Empire, see Dynes (1983) and Richlin (1993).

34. Foucault (1980), Weeks (1981). Cf. note 2 above and Thorp (1992:58–60).

35. See Goodich (1979) and the tantalizing document discussed by Johansson (1984) from 12th-century London.

36. See Bérubé (1990), Chauncey (1994), Leznoff and Westley (1956), Newton (1972), Humphreys (1972, 1975), Humphreys and Miller (1980), Vacha (1985), Grube (1986, 1987, 1991). For Latin American exemplars, see Taylor (1978), Bao (1993).

37. As I noted elsewhere (Murray 1992a:145–46), the usual monk-samurai-kabuki

Renaissance" in Europe, there was a homosexual role, "the sodomite," which did not entail crossing gender patterns for dress, public demeanor, or sexual receptivity. Sexual receptivity to one's social inferiors seems to have been a serious affront to the social order, and violations of taboos against such unbecoming behavior seem to have occasioned the disgrace of the Earl of Castlehaven in 1631, the most discussed case of an English Renaissance sodomy conviction.[38] Everyone took for granted that the older and richer would sexually use the younger and poorer. Ancient Greeks and Romans made the same assumption. In medieval and early modern Europe the catamite or his family received gifts or sponsorship in exchange for providing the sodomite patron's pleasures. Some people may have noticed homosexual preferences, but the archetype of the libertine had his wench on one arm and his catamite (boy) on the other. Fucking a boy, even preferring to fuck boys, does not appear to have been the basis for an identity, despite the label for a role "sodomite" (and, possibly, also that of "libertine"). We do not know how those playing either sodomite or catamite role felt about the sex they

---

order of discussing homosexuality in Japanese history obscures the increased salience of gender in the 17th century, both for kabuki and for demobilized samurai. A parallel transformation of the dominant social organization of homosexuality from age-stratified to gender-stratified occurred somewhat later, around the beginning of the 18th century, in a Great Britain similarly recently unified after civil war (and subsequent naval warfare with the Dutch), and with similarly ascendant prosperous merchants and a similarly destabilized aristocracy (see Murray 1984:43; 1988; Rousseau 1990; Trumbach 1990). That is—despite the widespread equation of effeminacy and aristocracy (reviewed by Dynes 1985:14–15; 1990:74)—in both Japan and Great Britain it was a rising, mercantile bourgeoisie in which effeminate homosexuality displaced military/masculinist/aristocratic age-graded homosexuality. The popularity of boys on stage preceded the mid–17th-century closing of theaters in (Puritan revolutionary) England (see Smith 1991), whereas it increased after the mid–17th-century elite attempts to close Japanese theaters. With the Ching dynasty replacing the Ming in mid–17th-century China, a parallel replacement of pederastic patronage and comradely homosexual relations with gender-crossing actor-prostitutes occurred (Xiaominxiong 1984:173–91, 209; Ng 1989). Explaining this process of increasing feminization of the boys involved in age-graded homosexual relations, and especially the near-simultaneity in societies not in contact, seems a fascinating task for historical/comparative gay studies. The decline in importance of military aristocracies is an obviously significant component, but not the whole explanation. As amorphous as the category "capitalism" frequently is, it seems singularly inapplicable to Tokugawa Japan or to early Ching China.

38. Also see Perry (1980: 143) on the 1597 burning of Alonso Telles Girón in Seville.

had together, or what kind or degree of variance from the ideal-type "cultural script" those performing those roles ad-libbed or rewrote, or how much egalitarian homosexuality occurred outside the pederastic script (see Murray 1988).

Given that pederastic relationships continue to exist even today in cities with generally recognized gay neighborhoods and institutions, caution is in order in assuming that the rates of behavior changed as attention (and the dominant cultural representation) shifted to the "mollies" (in England and analogous gender-crossing men elsewhere). Perhaps the dominant culture's equation of homosexuality and visible effeminacy camouflaged persisting and clandestine egalitarian and age-graded homosexuality, as Whitehead (1981), Williams (1986), Callender and Kochems (1983) argue was the case for "berdaches" in native American cultures. Trumbach (1977:17–18) noted, "Descriptions of the [molly] subculture which were intended for the general public always emphasized its effeminacy." This public appearance certainly does not prove that in late-17th-century London everyone involved in homosexuality, or even most of those who were, enacted the "molly" role. The public focus on "mollies" may have kept invisible other non–gender-stratified homosexualities and may even have been manipulated by those whose conduct was so camouflaged.

After the mysteriously swift and total shift in emphasis from age-graded to gender-defined homosexuality during the 17th century (at least in England), expectations of gender deviation were provided with spurious causal explanations by the conventional wisdom of medical taxonomizing in the late 19th century. Chauncey (1982, 1985, 1994; also see Murphy 1984, 1988; Bérubé 1990) convincingly showed that medical experts codified popular prejudices rather than inventing a wisdom that trickled down to the masses. It would be ludicrous to suppose that medical discourse created the "mollies" of 17th-century England, given the low prestige of medicine in that time and place and the lack of physicians' interest in theorizing about homosexuality. Whether the Society for the Reformation of Manners discovered or crystallized a "molly" role is a more interesting question for labeling dialecticians to consider. No one has yet suggested that medical discourse "constructed" *wakashu* of feudal Tokugawa-era Japan (see Leupp, in press) or caused an increasing feminization of the role during the 17th century or the seemingly-simultaneous feminization of "the love of the cut sleeve" in Ching China (Xiaominxiong 1984:157–240; Ng 1989).

The Limits of Explanation in Terms of Cultural Roles

In all cultures, not just in our own, individuals adapt what Simon and Gagnon (1986) call "cultural scripts" for generating interactional and intrapsychic sexual meaning.[39] While normative models may channel perception of others and conception of self, they do not determine these. Observers should not assume that everyone in a culture shares the normative models—even unconsciously or inarticulately. During the 1950s, Anthony F. C. Wallace demonstrated that tribal societies are not homogeneous (1952a,b) and went on to suggest that "culture" should be conceived as "the organization of diversity," rather than a replication of normative uniformity, so that even small, low-technology, ethnically homogeneous societies are "plural societies" (1961, 1970:110). Individuals not only may fail to share cultural understandings, but may not seek to explain what their own patterns of sexual behavior mean. As Eric Wolf (1990:592–93) recalled Wallace's breakthrough,

> He pointed out that participants in social action do not need to understand what meanings lie behind the behavior of their partners in interchange. All they have to know is how to respond appropriately to the cues signalled by others. Issues of meaning need not ever rise into consciousness. This is often the concern only of certain specialists, whose specific job or interest it is to explore the plenitude of possible meanings: people such as shamans, *tohunga,* or academics.

Those living their lives in the culture of which the analyst is trying to make sense may never reflect upon what seems inconsistent or anomalous to an analyst. For everyday, practical purposes, people can and do operate quite well with fuzzily bounded categories, even if some analysts cannot. Adjudicating border disputes among arcane combinations of features that normally do not occur together is not how people usually use their (language's) categories. Fixing classification schema into writing can create anomalies from what is usually ignored, rarely or

---

39. I am less sure than they that except in "post-modern" societies, "the content and significance of the intrapsychic is limited, at best accounting for minor variations in performance [of culturally scripted roles]" (Simon and Gagnon 1986:99). Evidence for conceptions of "self" *(personnage)* in the purportedly "modern" sense across time and space is marshaled against Mauss (1938) in Carrithers et al. (1985) and Spiro (1993). Their critiques bear directly on the Durkheimian schema of the evolution of "the self" elaborated by Simon and Gagnon.

never reflected upon by those living with and using the category. Formalizing native classifications may even generate culturally nonsensical problems.[40]

The texts touching upon indigenous conceptions of sex and gender and/or homosexual behavior in various American cultures that are reviewed in this volume are fragmentary[41] and generally fail to answer the questions our current theories pose, especially about intracultural diversity, individual meaning, the individual or shared salience of categories, and what (if any!) the relationship is between what people do and what they say. As Winkler (1990:69) cautioned in regards to another fragmentary corpus of data, "Behind sentences that begin 'The Greeks believed———' there lies a fairly small set of elite canonized texts. Many of them are what I would broadly call legislative rather than descriptive." The "native views" about gender-crossing and homosexuality recorded by explorers, missionaries, travelers, and allegedly "objective" anthropologists similarly tend to mistake elite prescriptions and rationalizations for adequate descriptions of usual behavior. Official accounts, especially for outsiders, may have little to do with statistical behavioral regularities, let alone with showing the range of intracultural variation. What the "natives" think that the alien "analysts" want to hear and what the natives think the alien observer approves (based in part on what the "natives" know about the observer's culture) shape even unofficial accounts and explanations. Repeatedly, throughout the missionary, travel, and ethnography literatures, "unfortunately, the object of many of these reports seems to have been to stress the moral abomination so that little or no space was left to describe the reprehensible conduct itself" (Bleibtreu-Ehrenberg 1990:14; see Murray, forth-

---

40. See Murray (1983, 1987b, 1993:430–33, building on Goody 1977:52–73), Nachman (1984), Rumsey (1989:353–54), Goodenough (1990:598–59).

41. Few members of my generation (or of later ones) think that a holistic ethnography of a discrete culture is possible, and many reject it as even an aspiration. Fragmentation is currently very chic in anthropology. Although by no means do I aspire to produce an authorless text, I have sought to produce a polyvocal one, quoting earlier observers (and wherever possible, native informants) verbatim and at length, rather than abstracting the sources or coding their contents (following the prescriptions of Kluckhohn (1943:268; see Murray 1986:261–64). I have also included antagonistic perspectives (especially about Brazilian homosexualities). To ascertain other features in accounts of the cultures herein considered, the reader may turn to the original texts cited or to Human Relations Area File codings of the features of particular correlative interest.

coming). I show that this continues to be true for alleged social "scientists" in Chapter 19 below.

Historians have barely scratched the surface of reports in Spanish and Portuguese archives on the behavior of conquered tribes. What was the nature of homosexuality in indigenous South America at the time of European invasion is largely *terra incognita*, but we can hope that more knowledge of the early European representations will be explored as a byproduct to work on the Inquisition.[42]

Alas, even if they are, there will still be few cultures in which data are available on the interactional negotiation—let alone individual meanings!—of homosexual behavior. Most ethnographies (e.g., 114 of the 190 cultures surveyed by Ford and Beach 1951) fail even to mention what is the dominant normative/societal view of homosexuality. Despite the confident assertions of creationists such as Halperin (1990:32) and Plummer (1990:237), we are far from having enough evidence about what desires are (or were) in settings other than modern Europe, Anglo North America, Sambia (Herdt 1981, 1987; Herdt and Stoller 1990), Japan (Leupp, in press; Schalow 1990), and Thailand (Jackson 1989; Allyn 1992) to discuss the relative impact of social construction of sexual desire. We know something about how types of homosexuality were conceptualized (represented in public) in a few societies, but practically nothing about how desire or homosexual behavior are/were experienced (represented by/to those actually involved).

Descriptions and analyses of lived experience should follow the surveys of prescriptive norms and distributions of behavior that are necessary beginnings but often raise more questions than they answer. Unfortunately, we are unlikely ever to learn what homosexual behavior meant in most of the cultures of the world before the massive incursions and disruptions of European colonialism and neocolonialism. We can continue to ask questions of documents from early periods of contact,[43] but salvage anthropology of memory cultures was late on the scene, and even salvage anthropology is no longer possible for many of the world's cultures.

Of course, contemporary cultures, not just "traditional forms," deserve study—preferably both more intensive than most sociological work

---

42. See Parker (1982) and work in Gerard and Hekma (1988), especially that by Mott and Assunçao, and by Perry.

43. See Murray (1994b). Roscoe (1995) shows that new questions can be asked even of the often-examined literature on native North America, however.

and more systematic than the casual sampling, unexplained data selection, and over-generalizing that anthropologists have repatriated as they have been driven increasingly out of the rest of the world. Even if the diversity of organizations of homosexuality (and of other phenomena) has been reduced in what is still very far from being a culturally homogeneous world, very little is known about the meaning of homosexuality for those involved or for those not involved in it in the societies of the 1990s, even the United States. We know too little about what was, but we also know too little about what is![44]

REFERENCES

Adam, Barry D.
    1979 Reply. *Sociologists' Gay Caucus Newsletter* 18:8.
    1986 Age, structure and sexuality. *Journal of Homosexuality* 11:19–33.
    1987 *The Rise of a Gay and Lesbian Movement.* Boston: Twayne.
Allyn, Eric
    1992 *Trees in the Same Forest: Thailand's Culture and Gay Subculture.* Bangkok: Bua Luang.
Allyn, Eric, and John P. Collins
    1988 *The Men of Thailand.* Bangkok: Bua Luang.
Arenas, Reinaldo
    1993 *Before Night Falls.* New York: Viking.
Ashworth, A. E., and W. M. Walker
    1972 Social structure and homosexuality. *British Journal of Sociology* 23: 146–58.
Bao, Daniel
    1993 *Invertidos sexuales, tortileras,* and *maricas machos*: the construction of homosexuality in Buenos Aires, Argentina, 1900–1950." *Journal of Homosexuality* 24 (3/4):183–219.
Bell, Allen P., and Martin S. Weinberg
    1978 *Homosexualities.* New York: Simon & Schuster.
Berlin, Brent
    1972 Reflections on the growth of ethnobotanical nomenclature. *Language in Society* 1:51–86.
    1973 Folk systematics in relation to biological classification and nomenclature. *Annual Review of Ecology and Systematics* 4:259–71.
Berlin, Brent, and Paul Kay
    1969 *Basic Color Terms.* Berkeley: University of California Press.

---

44. This is even more so for female homosexuality. I have already expressed my puzzlement about this continuing lack in note 3 of the introduction.

Bérubé, Alan

    1990 *Coming Out Under Fire*. New York: Macmillan.

Bing, Peter, and Rip Cohen

    1991 *Games of Venus*. New York: Routledge.

Bleibtreu-Ehrenberg, Gisela

    1990 Pederasty among primitives. *Journal of Homosexuality* 20:13–30.

Bogoraz, Vladimir (Bogoras, Waldemar G.)

    1904 *The Chukchee*. American Museum of Natural History Memoir II, 2.

Boster, James S., and Roy D'Andrade

    1989 Natural and human sources of cross-cultural agreement in ornitho-
logical classification. *American Anthropologist* 91:132–42.

Boster, James S., and Jeffrey C. Johnson

    1989 Form or function? *American Anthropologist* 91:866–89.

Boswell, John

    1980 *Christianity, Social Tolerance and Homosexuality*. Chicago: University of
Chicago Press.

    1990 Concepts, experience and sexuality. In *Forms of Desire*. E. Stein, ed.
Pp. 133–73. New York: Garland.

Brown, Cecil H., et al.

    1976 Some general principles of biological and non-biological folk classi-
fication. *American Ethnologist* 3:73–86.

Bullough, Vern L.

    1976 *Sexual Variance in Society and History*. New York: Wiley.

Callender, Charles, and Lee Kochems

    1983 The North American berdache. *Current Anthropology* 24:443–70.

Carrier, Joseph M.

    1976 Cultural factors affecting urban Mexican homosexual behavior. *Ar-
chives of Sexual Behavior* 5:103–24.

    1989 Sexual behavior and the spread of AIDS in México." In *The AIDS
Pandemic*. R. Bolton, ed. Pp. 37–50. New York: Gordon & Breach.

Carrithers, Michael, Steven Collins, and Steven Lukes

    1985 *The Category of the Person*. New York: Cambridge University Press.

Chauncey, George

    1982 From sexual inversion to homosexuality. *Salmagundi* 58:114–46.

    1985 Christian brotherhood or sexual perversion? Homosexual identities
and the construction of sexual boundaries in the World War One era.
Journal of Social History 19:198–211.

    1994 *Gay New York . . . 1890–1940*. New York: Basic Books.

D'Emilio, John

    1983 *Sexual Politics, Sexual Communities*. Chicago: University of Chicago
Press.

Devereux, Georges

    1937 Institutionalized homosexuality of the Mohave. *Human Biology* 9:
498–527.

Donaldson, Stephen, and Wayne R. Dynes

    1990 Typology of homosexuality. In *Encyclopedia of Homosexuality*. W. Dynes,
ed. Pp. 1332–37. New York: Garland.

Dover, Kenneth J.
1978 *Greek Homosexuality*. Cambridge: Harvard University Press.
1988 *The Greeks and their Legacy*. New York: Basil Blackwell.
Dumezil, Georges
1969 *Heur et malheur de guerrier*. Paris: Payot.
1986 Preface *in* Sergent (1986).
Dynes, Wayne R.
1983 Homosexuality in ancient Rome. In *Cultural Diversity and Homosexualities*. S. Murray, ed. Pp. 27–44. San Francisco: Instituto Obregón.
1985 *Homolexis*. New York: Gay Academic Union.
1990 Wrestling with the social boa constructor. In *Forms of Desire*. E. Stein, ed. Pp. 209–38. New York: Garland.
el-Messiri, Saswan
1978 Self-images of traditional urban women in Cairo. In *Women in the Muslim World*. L. Beck and N. Keddie, eds. Pp. 522–54. Cambridge, MA: Harvard University Press.
Estrada, Alvaro
1981 *María Sabina: Her Life and Chants*. Santa Barbara: Ross-Erikson.
Evans-Pritchard, E.E.
1937 *Witchcraft, Oracles, and Magic among the Azande*. Oxford: Clarendon Press.
1970 Sexual inversion among the Azande. *American Anthropologist* 72:1428–34.
1971 *The Azande*. Oxford: Clarendon Press.
Faderman, Lillian
1978 The morbidification of love between women by nineteenth-century sexologists. *Journal of Homosexuality* 4:73–90.
1991 *Odd Girls and Twilight Lovers: A History of Lesbian Life in Twentieth-Century America*. New York: Columbia University Press.
Ferguson, Ann
1991 Lesbianism, feminism, and empowerment in Nicaragua. *Social Review* 21(3/4):75–97.
Ford, Clellan S. and Frank A. Beach
1951 *Patterns of Sexual Behavior*. New York: Harper.
Foucault, Michel
1980 *The History of Sexuality*. New York: Pantheon.
Fry, Peter
1974 Male homosexuality and Afro-Brazilian possession cults. Paper presented at the American Anthropological annual meetings in Mexico City. Published in Murray (1987:55–91); reprinted in this volume.
Gay, Judith
1986 'Mummies and babies' and friends and lovers in Lesotho." *Journal of Homosexuality* 11:97–116.
Gerard, Kent, and Gert Hekma
1988 *The Pursuit of Sodomy: Male Homosexuality in Renaissance and Enlightenment Europe*. New York: Haworth Press. [*Journal of Homosexuality* 16(1/2)]
Ginat, Joseph
1982 *Women in Muslim Rural Society*. New Brunswick, NJ: Transaction Books.

Goodenough, Ward H.
  1990 Evolution of the human capacity for beliefs. *American Anthropologist* 92:597–612.
Goodich, Michael
  1979 *The Unmentionable Vice.* Santa Barbara: Ross-Erikson.
Goodwin, Joseph P.
  1989 *More Man then You'll Ever Be!: Gay Folklore and Acculturation in Middle America.* Bloomington: Indiana University Press.
Goody, Jack.
  1977 *The Domestication of the Savage Mind.* Cambridge: Cambridge University Press.
Greenberg, David F.
  1988 *The Construction of Homosexuality.* Chicago: University of Chicago Press.
Griffin, Jasper
  1990 Greek love. *New York Review of Books* 37(7):60.
Grube, John
  1986 Queens and flaming virgins. *Rites* 2(9):14–17.
  1987 Are you now or have you ever been an essentialist? Paper presented at the Homosexuality/Which Homosexuality conference in Amsterdam.
  1991 Natives and settlers: an ethnographic note on early interaction of older homosexual men with younger gay liberationists. *Journal of Homosexuality* 20:119–35.
Halperin, Daniel
  1990 *One Hundred Years of Homosexuality.* New York: Routledge.
Harry, Joseph, and William Devall
  1979 *The Social Organization of Gay Males.* New York: Praeger.
Hart, Donn V.
  1968 Homosexuality and transvestism in the Philippines. *Behavior Science Notes* 3:211–48. (Reprinted in Murray 1992:193–230.)
Heimann, Elliott, and Cao Van Lê
  1975 Transvestism in Vietnam. *Archives of Sexual Behavior* 4:89–96.
Herdt, Gilbert H.
  1981 *Guardians of the Flute.* New York: McGraw-Hill.
  1982 *Male Initiation in New Guinea.* Berkeley: University of California Press.
  1984 *Ritualized Homosexuality in Melanesia.* Berkeley: University of California Press.
  1987 *The Sambia.* New York: Holt.
  1990 Mistaken gender. *American Anthropologist* 92:433–46. (Revised as "Mistaken Sex" in Herdt 1994:429–45.)
  1991 Representations of homosexuality: an essay on cultural ontology and historical comparison. *Journal of the History of Sexuality* 1:481–50, 603–32.
  1992 *Gay Culture in America.* Boston: Beacon.
  1994 *Third Sex, Third Gender.* New York: Zone Books.
Herdt, Gilbert H., and Robert J. Stoller
  1990 *Intimate Communications.* New York: Columbia University Press.

Hodgen, Margaret T.
1964 *Early Anthropology in the Sixteenth and Seventeenth Centuries*. Philadelphia: University of Pennsylvania Press.

Hooker, Evelyn
1957 Adjustment of male overt homosexuals. *Journal of Projective Techniques* 21:18–31.

Humphreys, Laud
1972 *Out of the Closets*. Toronto: Prentice-Hall.
1975 *Tearoom Trade*. Chicago: Aldine.

Humphreys, Laud, and Brian Miller
1980 Identities in the emerging gay culture. In *Homosexual Behavior*. J. Marmor, ed. Pp. 142–56. New York: Basic Books.

Hunn, Eugene S.
1976 Toward a perceptual model of folk biological classification. *American Ethnologist* 3:508–24.

Jackson, Peter A.
1989 *Male Homosexuality in Thailand*. Amsterdam: Global Academic Publishers.

Johansson, Warren
1984 London's medieval sodomites. *Cabirion* 10:5–7.

Kay, Paul
1978 Tahitian words for 'race' and 'class.' *Publications de la Société des Océanistes* 39:81–91.

Kay, Paul, and Chad McDaniel
1978 The linguistic significance of the meaning of basic color terms. *Language* 54:610–46.

Kelly, Raymond
1976 Witchcraft and sexual relations. In *Man and Woman in the New Guinea Highlands*. P. Brown & G. Burchinder, eds. Pp. 36–53. Washington, DC: American Anthropological Association.

Kluckhohn, Clyde
1943 Review of *Sun Chief* by Leo Simmons. *American Anthropologist* 45:267–70.

Kroeber, Alfred L.
1940 Psychosis or social sanction? *Character and Culture* 8:204–15.

Landes, Ruth.
1940 A cult matriarchate and male homosexuality. *Journal of Abnormal and Social Psychology* 35:386–97.

Lee, John Alan
1978 *Getting Sex*. Toronto: General.
1979a The gay connection. *Urban Life* 8:175–98.
1979b The social organization of sexual risk. *Alternative Lifestyles* 2:69–100.

Lenneberg, Eric H.
1953 Cognition in ethnolinguistics. *Language* 29:463–71.

Leupp, Gary P.
in press *Nanshoku*. Berkeley: University of California Press.

Levine, Martin P.
1979 *Gay Men*. New York: Harper & Row.

    1986 *Gay Macho.* Ph.D. dissertation, New York University.
Levy, Robert I.
    1973 *The Tahitians.* Chicago: University of Chicago Press.
Leznoff, Maurice, and William A. Westley
    1956 The homosexual community. *Social Problems* 2:257–63.
Lindenbaum, Shirley
    1984 Variations on a sociosexual theme in Melanesia. In Herdt (1984:
        337–61).
Manalansan, Martin F. IV
    1990 Tolerance or struggle?: Homosexuality in the Philippines. Paper pre-
        sented at the American Anthropological Association meetings in New
        Orleans.
    1991 Neo-colonial desire. *Society of Lesbian and Gay Anthropologists Newsletter*
        13:37–40.
    1993 (Re)locating the 'gay' Filipino: resistance, postcolonialism and iden-
        tity. *Journal of Homosexuality* 26(2):53–72.
Marotta, Toby
    1981 *The Politics of Homosexuality.* New York: Houghton Mifflin.
Mauss, Marcel
    1938 Une Catégorie de l'Ésprit Humain: la Notion de Personne, Celle de
        'Moi.' *Journal of the Royal Anthropological Institute* 68. (An English version
        constitutes 1–25 in Carrithers et al. 1985.)
Miller, Brian
    1978 Adult sexual resocialization. *Alternative Lifestyles* 1:207–34.
Morris, Rosalind C.
    1994 Three sexes and four sexualities: redressing the discourses on gender
        and sexuality in contemporary Thailand. *Positions* 2:15–43.
Mott, Luiz, and Aroldo Assunçao
    1988 Loves labors lost: five letters from a seventeenth-century Portuguese
        sodomite. *Journal of Homosexuality* 16:91–101.
Murphy, Lawrence R.
    1984 Cleaning up Newport. *Journal of American Culture* 7:57–64.
    1988 *Perverts by Official Order.* New York: Harrington Press.
Murray, Stephen O.
    1979a Institutional elaboration of a quasi-ethnic community. *International*
        Review of Modern Sociology 9:165–78.
    1979b The 'species homosexual' as an aberration of late capitalism? *Sociolo-*
        gists' Gay Caucus Newsletter 18:7–8.
    1980 Lexical and institutional elaboration: the 'species homosexual' in Gua-
        temala. *Anthropological Linguistics* 22:177–85.
    1981 Die ethnoromantische Versuchung. *Der Wissenschaftler und das Irra-*
        tionale 1:377–85.
    1983 Fuzzy sets and abominations. *Man* 19:396–99.
    1984 *Social Theory, Homosexual Realities. Gai Saber Monograph* 3.
    1986 Edward Sapir in the 'Chicago School' of sociology. In *New Perspectives in*
        Language, Culture, and Personality. W. Cowan, M. Foster, & K. Koerner, eds.
        Pp. 241–91. Amsterdam: John Benjamins.

1987a *Male Homosexuality in Central and South America. Gai Saber Monograph* 5.

1987b Snowing canonical texts. *American Anthropologist* 89:443–44.

1988 Homosexual acts and selves in early modern Europe. *Journal of Homosexuality.* 16:457–78.

1991 'Homosexual occupations' in Guatemala? *Journal of Homosexuality* 21: 57–64. (A revised version is included in this volume.)

1992a *Oceanic Homosexualities.* New York: Garland.

1992b Components of *gay community* in San Francisco. In Herdt (1992: 107–46).

1993 *Theory Groups in the Study of Language in North America: A Social History.* Amsterdam: John Benjamins.

1994a A thirteenth-century imperial ethnography. *Anthropology Today,* 10(5): 15–18.

1994b Subordinating native cosmologies to the empire of gender. *Current Anthropology* 35:59–61.

1995 Male homosexuality in Guatemala: possible insights and certain confusions from obtaining data by sleeping with the natives. (To appear in *Lesbian and Gay Ethnography.* E. Lewin and W. Leap, eds. Urbana: University of Illinois Press.)

Forthcoming *Islamic Accommodations of Homosexuality.* MS.

Murray, Stephen O., and Keelung Hong

1994 A Taiwanese woman who became a spirit medium. MS.

Nachman, Steven R.

1984 Lies my informants told me. *Journal of Anthropological Research* 40: 536–55.

Nanda, Serena

1990 *Neither Man Nor Woman: The Hijra of India.* Belmont, CA: Wadsworth.

Nelson, Cynthia

1974 Public and private politics: women in the Middle Eastern world. *American Ethnologist* 1:551–63.

Newton, Esther

1972 *Mother Camp.* Toronto: Prentice-Hall.

1993 *Cherry Grove.* Boston: Beacon.

Ng, Vivien W.

1989 Emblems of anomie: homoerotic literature in 17th-century China. *American Journal of Semiotics* 6:3–11.

Parker, Geoffrey

1982 Some recent work on the Inquisition. *Journal of Modern History* 54: 519–32.

Patzer, Harald

1982 *Die griechische Knabenliebe. Sitzungsberichte der Wissenschaftlichen Gesellschaft an der Johann Wolfgang Goethe-Universität* 19(1).

Perry, Mary E.

1980 *Crime and Society in Early Modern Seville.* Hanover, NH: University Press New England.

1988 The 'nefarious sin' in early modern Seville. *Journal of Homosexuality* 16:67–89.

Plummer, Ken
    1981 *The Makings of the Modern Homosexual.* London: Hutchinson.
    1990 Understanding childhood sexualities. *Journal of Homosexuality* 20: 231–49.
    1992 *Modern Homosexualities.* London: Routledge.
Redfield, James
    1985 Herodotus, the tourist. *Classical Philology* 80:97–118.
Richlin, Amy
    1993 Not before homosexuality: the materiality of the Cinædus and the Roman Law against love between men. *Journal of the History of Sexuality* 3:523–73.
Roscoe, Will
    1987 Bibliography of berdache and alternative gender roles among North American Indians. *Journal of Homosexuality* 14:81–171.
    1988a Making history: the challenge of gay and lesbian studies. *Journal of Homosexuality* 15(3/4):1–40.
    1988b We'wha and Klah: the American Indian berdache as artist and priest. *American Indian Quarterly* 12:127–50.
    1990 The life and times of a Crow berdache. *Montana: The Magazine of Western History* (Winter) 46–55.
    1991 *The Zuni Man-Woman.* Albuquerque: University of New Mexico Press.
    1994 How to become a berdache: toward a unified analysis of gender diversity. In Herdt (1994:329–72).
    1995 Was Whe'wha a homosexual? *GLQ* 2: in press.
Rousseau, George S.
    1990 An introduction to the *Love Letters. Journal of Homosexuality* 19:47–91.
Rumsey, Alan
    1989 Wording, meaning, and linguistic ideology. *American Anthropologist* 92:345–61.
Samarin, William J.
    1972 *Tongues of Men and Angels.* New York: Macmillan.
Schalow, Paul G.
    1990 *The Great Mirror of Male Love.* Stanford: Stanford University Press.
Schmitt, Arno
    1985 *Klein Schriften zu zwischmeannlicker sexualitat und Erotik in der muslimischen Gesellschaft.* Berlin: privately printed.
Sergent, Bernard
    1986 *Homosexuality in Greek Myth.* Boston: Beacon Press.
Shweder, Richard A.
    1991 *Thinking Through Cultures.* Cambridge, MA: Harvard University Press.
Simon, William, and John H. Gagnon
    1986 Sexual scripts. *Archives of Sexual Behavior* 15:97–120.
Smith, Bruce R.
    1991 *Homosexual Desire in Shakespeare's England.* Chicago: University of Chicago Press.

Spiro, Melford E.
1993 Is the western conception of the self 'peculiar' within the context of world cultures? *Ethos* 21:107–53.

Steakley, James
1975 *The Homosexual Emancipation Movement in Germany.* New York: Arno.

Taylor, Clark L.
1978 *El Ambiente.* Ph.D. dissertation, University of California, Berkeley.

Thorp, John
1992 The social construction of homosexuality. *Phoenix* 46:54–61.

Trumbach, Randolph
1977 London's sodomites. *Journal of Social History* 11:1–33.
1990 Sodomy transformed: aristocratic libertinage, public reputation and the gender revolution of the 18th century. *Journal of Homosexuality* 19: 105–24.

Vacha, Keith
1985 *Quiet Fire.* Trumansburg, NY: Crossing Press.

Van Baal, J.
1984 The dialectics of sex in Marind-Anim culture. In Herdt (1984:128–76).

Van Gulik, Robert H.
1961 *Sexual Life in Ancient China.* Leiden: Brill.

Wafer, Jim
1991 *The Taste of Blood: Spirit Possession in Brazilian Candomblé.* Philadelphia: University of Pennsylvania Press.

Wallace, Anthony F. C.
1952a *The Modal Personality Structure of the Tuscarora Indians, As Revealed by the Rorschach Test. Bureau of American Ethnology Bulletin* 150.
1952b Individual differences and cultural uniformities. *American Sociological Review* 17:747–50.
1961, 1970 *Culture and Personality.* New York: Random House.

Weeks, Jeffrey
1981 Discourse, desire and sexual deviance. In Plummer (1981:76–111).

Weinberg, Thomas S.
1983 *Gay Men, Gay Selves.* New York: Irvington.

Weinberg, Thomas S., and G. Levi Kamel
1983 *S&M.* Buffalo: Prometheus.

Weston, Kath
1991 *Families We Choose.* New York: Columbia University Press.

Whitam, Frederick L., and Robin Mathy
1986 *Male Homosexuality in Four Societies.* New York: Praeger.

Whitehead, Harriet
1981 The bow and the burden strap. In *Sexual Meaning* S. Ortner and H. Whitehead, eds. Pp. 80–115. New York: Cambridge University Press.

Wikan, Unni
1980 *Life among the Poor in Cairo.* London: Tavistock.
1982 *Behind the Veil in Arabia: Women in Oman.* Baltimore: Johns Hopkins University Press.

Williams, Walter L.
    1986 *The Spirit and the Flesh.* Boston: Beacon.
Wilson, Monica
    1951 *Good Company.* Boston: Beacon.
Winkler, John J.
    1990 *The Constraints of Desire: The Anthropology of Sex and Gender in Ancient Greece.* New York: Routledge.
Wolf, Deborah G.
    1979 *The Lesbian Community.* Berkeley: University of California Press.
Wolf, Eric
    1990 Facing power. *American Anthropologist* 92:586–96.
Xiaominxiong
    1984 *History of Homosexuality in China.* Hong Kong: Pink Triangle Press. (In Chinese with English chapter summaries.)

2

❦

Family, Social Insecurity, and the Underdevelopment of Gay Institutions in Latin America

Stephen O. Murray

One major difference between North American and Latin American men engaged in recurrent homosexual relations is that Latin Americans live with their family of origin until they marry. Whatever their sexual orientation may be, and regardless of class, Latin American men who do not marry continue to live at home indefinitely. In Carrier's sample of fifty-three homosexually involved men in Guadalajara in 1970–71, 85 percent still lived in their childhood home.[1] And

> of the ten homosexual couples I knew, or heard about, that were living together in Guadalajara, only two had families living in the city . . . A partner in one of these pairs—in his early thirties— still had to return each evening to his family home to sleep. It was the consensus of my informants that leaving the city or marrying were the only ways open to leave the family and establish a separate household. [Carrier 1972:121]

In my 1980 sample of homosexually active men in Guatemala City, the only men who did not live with their parents lived with wives of their own. In Argentina, aside from the economic impossibility of finding and buying an available apartment, Rafael Freda told Miller (1992: 201), "if an unmarried child left home, the implication was that the family was not getting along. There would be no other conceivable reason one would leave." In Cuba, state allocations reinforce this pattern: "Housing is in short supply and top priority is given to couples,

---

1. Four percent (all *activo*) lived with wives. Fifty-three percent of *pasivos* planned to live with their natal family indefinitely, with another 27 percent uncertain (Carrier 1972:211).

especially those with children, so that stable relationships between homosexuals are inhibited" (Salas 1979: 171). Residence with families scattered throughout cities precludes the development of gay neighborhoods and is a considerable obstacle to the formation of gay consciousness, culture and community as these have developed in Anglo North America. This chapter will explore some of the not necessarily conscious motivations for this residential pattern and its consequence of inhibiting the development of gay institutions.

Temporal constraints on homosexual activities supplement spatial ones: "Three quarters of the families require their sons, even in their twenties, to return home at a 'reasonable' hour. During weekdays, a reasonable hour is defined as around 10:00 to 11:00 P.M.; on weekends this might be relaxed to before the sun comes up, but the son is definitely expected to return home" (Carrier 1972:100–101). Ninety-three percent of pasivos' parents said that their parents required them to return home to sleep every night (p. 213). Buslines in Guadalajara (and elsewhere) cease running at midnight, which imposes a de facto curfew on any place that is farther than walking distance from the family home.

Bases for Continuing to Reside with One's Natal Family

Familial orientation

Of those Carrier (1972:212) interviewed in Guadalajara living with their families, "64% said they were living at home because they wanted to; 18% said it was because parents insisted; 6% said it was for financial reasons; and 11% said it was a combination of parents insisting and finances." In their own view, Latin Americans are more devoted to their families than are other people: "that's just how we are." Idealist[2] social scientists offer the same non-explanation in fancier garb as "familial orientation." In either guise, the "explanation" itself requires explanation. The explanation is that the contemporary Latin American family has more "functions" than does the contemporary family in Anglo

---

2. Although the penchant for proclaiming ideas and value explanations of social patterns is characteristic of functionalists, particularly Parsonian ones, not all functionalist explanation is necessarily idealist.

America or in Northern Europe (see Ogburn 1928). Much less socialization of children in Latin America stems from school and peer group
than in fully industrialized societies (McGin 1966; Peñalos 1968;
Kinger 1973).

Besides greater centrality in socialization, the Latin American family
retains economic functions. The family as a production unit[3] exists to a
considerable extent in Latin America, and not just in traditional Indian
cultures. In countries far from being welfare states, even urban families
that are not production units provide social security. In societies experienced by most as capricious and heartless, the family provides more
than merely psychological shelter. If an individual is struck down by
illness or injury and has no family to provide support, s/he will be
reduced to begging in the streets. Examples of this horrific danger are
readily visible (Fabrega 1971). Thus, the fear that if one is alone in the
world—which is to say, without relatives nearby—such a fate might
befall one is not irrational. Although no one ever told me he lived with
his family because of fear of being reduced to beggary, the fear was
obviously salient in the combination of shock and concern expressed in
questions about how I dared venture so far from my family and who
would take care of me if I fell ill or had an accident (see Muñoz 1989:
82). Such concerns express more than ingrained fear of the (hostile)
outside world. Latin Americans cannot and had better not take for
granted minimum security being supplied against disability, as citizens
of welfare states can.

The insurance against disability offered by the family is an economic
system, not any perverse, pathological passivity deriving from an obsession with fertility on the part of individuals, the culture, or the Roman
Catholic Church.[4] "Familial orientation" as well as high Latin American fertility can better be explained by examining the family as an
economic unit than by looking to individual-level values.

---

3. "Cottage industry" is the traditional Anglocentric gloss.

4. Latin American men "tend to wear their Catholicism lightly . . . [and] simply
do not tend to take priests or church doctrine terribly seriously," as Lacey (1983:13)
observed, mostly leaving piety to women. Also see Kutsche's comments in Chapter 7.
The Catholic Church continues to have the power to curb publication of "immoral"
literature (Lacey 1983:9), and, concomitant with the inroads of fundamentalist Protestant mission in the countryside, is increasingly intolerant of even covert homosexuality.

Mother Identification

Though homosexually active Latin Americans who do not build their own families live at home longer than those who start families of their own and also show somewhat greater concern about maintaining the support of relatives, these relations often involve no intimacy. The popular psychoanalytic obsession with mothers, projected onto the etiology of homosexuality, is useless in explaining homosexuality in Latin America, because the veneration of martyr (Madonna/saintly) mothers is ubiquitous, while homosexuality is not. Regardless of sexual orientation, everyone continues to live at home, not just "mother-fixated" homosexual men.

Premiums Homosexuals Pay for Such Insurance

Because revelation of homosexuality is a basis for expulsion from the home (Carrier 1976a; see Arboleda 1987; examples were also given by my informants in the capitals of México and Guatemala) and because of the economic as well as psychological security provided by the family, homosexually active Latin Americans cultivate family relations to a greater extent than do those who can take them for granted. Many exercise the right of males who have reached sexual maturity to come and go from home at will less than do their brothers.

"Impersonal social relations" (Tax 1941:33) are characteristic, especially of the Mesoamerican highlands. In Guatemala City, a Cuban-born informant observed, "People in the highlands are very private. They don't talk about personal affairs, even if they do have real friends outside the family [which they often do not have], and they can't talk about sex within the family either." A general reserve is further exaggerated when it comes to stigmatizing information. "One's behavior must be especially circumspect in the presence of one's siblings," Peñalosa (1968: 687) observed, "There must be no looseness of act or word, particularly in the sexual area." As Argentine-American psychologist Alex Carballo-Diéguez (1989:28) noted:

> It is not unusual for relatives of young gay Hispanic men to haunt them with questions and commentaries about girlfriends or marriage plans. A gay Hispanic man may feel it is a lack of respect toward a family member not to answer such questions, and he may resort to evasive answers that, in the end, make him feel badly about himself.

Similarly, Parker's (1988:296) primary informant, Joao told him. "The *casa* is where the name of the family has to be respected. . . . It's the place of good conduct and exemplary morality. The preservation of the traditional family environment is the duty of everyone." Miller (1992:205) tells of an Argentine who lived with a lover, but obeyed "an unstated rule that he was not to talk to or otherwise interact with his nephews, nieces, or cousins." Not only could he not mention same-sex love, he was not even permitted to talk to younger kin who are presumed to be impressionable.[5]

Many people live in a small space. However, they endeavor to live *juntos pero no revueltos* (together, but not scrambled). The lack of intrafamilial intimacy is exemplified by one of my México City friends who was unaware that his brother, who slept in the same room he did, was also much involved in homosexual behavior. It is easy to elicit that young men have never discussed their homosexual behavior with family members. It is more difficult to elicit an estimate of whether family members know of it. Some would say, "I think so-and-so knows, but we never talk about it." Many others refused even to speculate about this potentially anxiety-producing topic.

As Lacey (1983:7) noted

the universal tendency of Latin American writers to use euphemistic language in the description of sexual organs and activities, even when these activities are described with disarmingly complete

---

5. Ana Castillo, who is a native of Chicago, challenged as

a misconception of people who have not really lived among "traditional Mexicans" to think that they are so sexually repressed that they do not ever discuss sexuality, and that they forbid women to do so in mixed company. Men and women do talk and there is even sexual talk, at times, in the presence of your children. I believe it is at the very moment when an adolescent's sexual consciousness emerges, however, that the "censorship" begins. [1991:26]

Since she shows that it is intense, I don't know why Castillo places *censorship* between quotation marks. The editor of the volume in which Castillo's essay appeared, (New Mexico–born) Carla Trujillo (1991:186), wrote, "As Chicanas, we are commonly led to believe that even talking about our participation and satisfaction in sex is taboo. Moreover we (as well as most women in the United States) learn to hate our bodies and usually possess little knowledge of them." In that Trujillo is writing about postpubescence, she is not contradicting Castillo. I think that Castillo underestimates the tact (if that is the word for not bringing up personal concerns) of highland southern Mexico and Guatemala, though sex(uality) is not always entirely tabooed a topic even in heterosocial family setting.

frankness and when the themes are bold, modern and sophisticated: generations of practice in linguistic hypocrisy, in "saying
what one does not say," are evidently not effaced overnight—

even by the avant garde in print, and still less in family circles in
daily life!

A direct relationship between the gay institutional elaboration and
security about healthcare within Latin America is demonstrated in Table 2.1. The number of gay facilities in a country is a function of the
population size (r = .95). Controlling for population, there is a significant correlation between the provision of social security (percentage
covered) and the number of gay facilities per capita. The threshold of an
effect seems to be around coverage of one-fifth of the population. There
is an even stronger correlation between life expectancy and profusion of
gay facilities. Life expectancy is positively correlated to the provision
of social security and strongly negatively correlated to the percentage of
the national population categorized as "Indian." Affluence and security
are not easily distinguished, but there does seem to be a relationship
between greater security about health and the development of gay bars
and clubs that is not a function merely of urban growth. Neither the
size of the nation's largest city nor the concentration of that nation's
population in its largest city has a significant effect on the number of
gay facilities per capita. Values for these values for each country are
summarized in Table 2.2.

Poverty and Lack of Housing

Lack of economic resources to maintain a place of one's own and the
general lack of available housing should not be ignored. The crowding
of dwelling units results more from economic necessity than from family feeling.[6] While many would have liked to have more space, none of
my friends who had been born in Latin America wished to live apart
from his family. "I would be lonely!" each protested at the prospect.
That this is not exclusively rationalization of necessity is demonstrated
by the extension of the pattern of living with the family while single to
the very top of the stratification system. Upper-class informants may

---

6. See Arenas (1993:37). After moving to Havana, Arenas stayed with an aunt.
Even migration does not end living under some extent of family supervision.

Table 2.1
Correlations between Per Capita Gay Listings and Demographic Variables

	Gay Places Listed	Male Life Expectancy	Percent Covered by Social Insurance	Percent Indian	Percent in Largest City
Life-Expectancy	.66**				
Insurance-Covered	.43*	.49*			
Indian %	−.35	−.61**	−.32		
Urban-Concentrated	−.19	.10	.58**	−.16	.09

*p<.10   **p<.05

Table 2.2
Number of Gay Listings and Healthcare Indicators by Country

	Per Capita Health Expenditures	Percent Insured	Per Capita Gay Places	Male Life Expectancy	Percent Indian	Percent Living in Largest City
Costa Rica	51	82	7.14	68.7	00.6	20
Panama	74	47	6.84	68.5	06.8	20
Venezuela	59	30	2.38	65.1	01.5	18
Colombia	49	10	2.34	61.4	02.2	11
Argentina	46	80	2.30	66.7	01.5	34
Dominican Republic	73	4	2.00	60.7	00.0	14
Uruguay	14	50	1.43	67.1	01.8	40
México	49	56	1.24	63.9	12.4	20
El Salvador	52	5	1.14	59.7	02.3	7
Brazil	23	83	1.04	61.6	00.2	4
Peru	36	12	.98	57.6	36.8	26
Honduras	48	7	.91	58.2	03.2	12
Ecuador	89	5	.86	60.6	33.9	14
Guatemala	25	14	.78	51.2	59.7	10
Chile	36	50	.75	62.6	05.7	37
Paraguay	20	13	.65	62.8	02.3	15
Bolivia	52	26	0.00	48.6	59.2	15

Sources: Palmero et al. (1981), Stamford (1982), Wilkie et al. (1988), Zschock (1986)

maintain *putería* (more politely called *leonera*) apartments for assignations and parties,[7] while continuing to dwell with their families. Carrier (1976a: 359) also noted that "even in the upper-income strata of the
society, a majority continue to live with their family while single."

Consequences

Sex and Ignorance about HIV Transmission

Taking prospective sexual partners to where one lives is rarely possible
in Latin America. For the affluent, there are visits to resorts, hotels in
their own city, automobiles, and trysting apartments *(puterías)*. For those
who are not affluent, there is the dark. There are also public baths,
varying in how predominantly they are patronized by those in search of
homosexual encounters (Carrier 1972; Taylor 1978). These are not "gay
baths" in the Northern European and American sense. With no acknowl-
edgment that sex is occurring, they also are not venues for AIDS education.
    In Mérida, which one alien (Ness 1992) claims is "Mexico's gayest
city," a native man with AIDS related the lack of public gay life to his
ignorance about how to avoid HIV transmission:

> There is no public, organized gay community there. Under-
> ground, informal communities revolve around the one bar and
> private friendship networks, especially among men old enough
> and well off enough to have their own homes or apartments. Like
> nearly all younger men who aren't married, I lived at home. . . .
> My awareness of SIDA or AIDS was very vague, based only on
> word-of-mouth rumors. I did not see any pamphlets, posters, or
> flyers about AIDS and HIV until Walt sent me some from the
> United States in early 1989. ["J" in Likosky 1992:368–69]

Relationships

As elsewhere in the world, secure privacy for lovemaking is a luxury.
The pattern of residence pushes pre- and extra-marital intercourse (heterosexual as well as homosexual) into the streets. This does not prevent

---

7. A group of friends all of whom live with their families sometimes acquire one
(Taylor 1978; see Novo 1979; Carrier 1972:122–23). The more affluent can also afford
to rent hotel rooms for assignations.

quick sexual encounters (*fichas*), but it is a major obstacle to ongoing relationships. Those who wish "to walk in the plan of love" (*amblar en el plan del amor*) do not have the easy path—moving in together—open to *norteamericanos*. Even families that accept a relationship within the family circle (treating the *amante* as another son) do not want outsiders to know that they have produced and are harboring *un raro* (a queer one). In gratitude for this (far-from-certain) minimum of acceptance, few couples are willing to demand more, such as the chance to be alone together sometimes. Some couples do manage to carry on long-term relationships without any place in which they can be together in private, but this is quite a difficult achievement.[8]

The arrangements portrayed in the Mexican film "Doña Herlinda y Su Hijo" are more wish-fulfillment (a fairy tale?) than representative, even of the upper class.[9] What does seem to me typical is that nothing is said about the homosexual relationship, even by the mother who arranges to co-opt it within her plans to ensure the manufacture of grandchildren. That is, even when homosexuality is known, it is not discussed. "No one wants you to explain [a relationship]. . . . No one wants to know what is going on" (Hugo to Miller 1992:209–10). Monteagudo (1991:16) wrote of what he considers "a system of repression and hypocrisy":

> Little Havana, like big Havana, is a family-oriented society that expects its sons and daughters to reside with their parents until they get, heterosexually a means of escape. . . . *La familia* comes first. . . . In the Cuban community a façade of heterosexuality must be maintained while living at home. If one's sexual orienta-

---

8. Miller (1992:201) suggested that younger Argentine "gays and lesbians tended to become involved in relationships with someone older and more established who might have his or own place to live." Adam (1993:175) noted that "there are some male couples who have succeeded in living together in [Sandinista-era] Managua, even though they may present themselves as cousins to their neighbors." In a horrific representation of small-town homophobia, "The Siege," the Nicaraguan writer (and later Sandinista vice-president) Sergio Ramirez (1986 [1967]) imagined the attacks (including a rape) of a couple of men who set up house together, countenanced by a police captain who would not tolerate any "indecency" in his town.

9. The mother trying to shoot her son when she finds him with another boy in Arenas's *Old Rosa* may be extreme, but paternal rejection of sons interested in art and books (long before they engage in homosexuality) is fairly typical among the Mexicans, Mexican Americans, and Guatemaltecos I know, and also in such fictional representations as Muñoz (1989:23, 1991:35, 67, 134–35), and Islas (1984:94).

tion is known it is treated as, at best, an unfortunate vice that should only be indulged elsewhere.

Similarly, Muñoz's (1989:61) Cuban-American protagonist's Colombian-American girlfriend knew he was also having sexual relations with a man: "She'd give me this look of disapproval. But we never talked about it. It was as if we had mutually agreed not to discuss the issue. If we spoke about it, everything would end, my relationship with her, with him. Everything."

In such cases, silence is certainly not consent. Rather, silence is the upper limit of "tolerance" for individual desires (Muñoz 1989:147). What Khan (1990:12) wrote about the impossibility of gay life in Pakistan applies directly, suggesting that the same familial incompatibility with gay life occurs in other cultures so long as the structural basis of a welfare society "safety net" is lacking:

> Families are like organisms that extend themselves by absorbing their young, and grow stronger or weaker based on the contributions of the new entrants. This is not just one model of life in Pakistan; it is not a choice; it is the only way of life . . . If a husband takes care of his family's security needs and produces many children, what he does for personal sexual satisfaction is quite irrelevant—and so long as it is kept a private matter—tolerated. . . . The most successful gay relationships in Karachi are quiet and heavily compromised. They are almost never the most important relationship for either partner; the family occupies that position. [Also see Murray 1992 on Thailand.]

The ongoing liaison between the head of the family and a servant in Mario Vargas Llosa's (1969) novel *Conversación en la Catedral* certainly fits with this characterization.[10]

For less easily hidden gender deviation, exhaustion rather than acceptance is probably more common, as for the small-town families that (mysteriously to itself) spawned a pair of dancer/hustlers in Zapata (1983:100):

---

10. While accepting this representation of Latino homosexuality viewed from outside, I find Vargas Llosa's attempt to write a gay character from the inside, specifically the title character in *La Historia de Mayta* (1984), completely implausible. It provides more data on the cultural model of homosexuality, but I have never met anyone who experienced his homosexuality as the character Alejandro Mayta does. Vargas Llosa (1991) wrote elsewhere of not being able to write from inside characters alien to his experience, although he did not mention Mayta as an example. (He also did not discuss *Conversación* in this regard.)

We had real bad times with our families, specially when they found out about what they called our "unnatural behavior." We fought with them, they tried to punish us, they slapped us around sometimes. Other times they almost seemed to give up and realize there wasn't anything they could do about it.

Many families indefinitely manage to deny that they could have produced a homosexual son or daughter.[11]

Collective Consciousness

Gay consciousness is no more automatic a product of homosexual behavior than class consciousness is of "objective class position" or ethnic consciousness of genealogy. In a population of persons with such a characteristic, some will not consider themselves defined in any way by it, and others will deny the characteristic altogether. The existence and importance of a characteristic must be realized if there is to be a consciousness of kind: characteristics are only potential bases (Murray 1979).

In Anglo America such a realization was facilitated by the congregation into "gay ghettoes" after World War II. Recreational facilities concentrated in already gay neighborhoods, drawing non-residents to these areas for socializing (including, but not confined to cruising). In time a full range of separate facilities and services sprang up in these areas (Lee 1978, 1979; Levine 1979; Murray 1979, 1984). Such residential concentration of homosexually inclined men is precluded where the unmarried indefinitely continue to live at home. The specific pattern of historical development of gay communities in Anglo America need not be assumed to constitute the only possible route to the rejection of pariah status.

On the other hand, sex does not automatically produce a sense of peoplehood. Cruising areas and social networks of homosexually inclined men partying together exist and have existed with varying degrees of visibility in cities everywhere,[12] while a sense of belonging to a

---

11. See Islas (1990), Muñoz (1991) for representations. Fathers' attempts to toughen up sons "to save them from a fate they believed to be worse than death" are recalled bitterly by Monteagudo (1991:15) and Nava (1990:77). Monteagudo recalled that "many a Cuban boy of uncertain sexuality was subjected to hormone shots, a practice that led to a crop of hirsute, deep-voiced gay men who walk the streets of Miami today." Nito in Muñoz (1989:23–24) received hormone shots.

12. See Murray and Gerard (1983).

community of those whose identity is based on shared sexual preferences has not. Something more than sexual acts in "the city of night" is
needed to provide a conception of a shared fate. Where individual sexual acts are ignored and discretion is the rule of social life, homosexuality may not be conceived as constituting a shared fate.[13]

A Latin American cannot learn about the common experiences of
those with homosexual desires from print media,[14] any more than s/he
can discuss them with those with whom s/he lives. Material on homosexuality available in Latin America is mostly caricature, with gruesome
murders of transvestites especially prominent (Carrier 1972, 1976b; Taylor 1978). There is de facto censorship of anything remotely interpret-
able as legitimating homosexuality. Police have considerable discretion
in making their own judgments of what is contrary to public interest,
and judges have similar discretion in labeling printed material dealing
with homosexuality as "apologies for vice" or "offending public morality" (e.g., see Green 1994:44–46). What Fuskóva-Komreich (1993:84)
wrote of Argentina applies to gay men and to all of Spanish America:
"We appeared either in the gutter press or nowhere at all. Any photo [or
text] showing women happy and proud to be lesbians was intolerable to
the system."

Sociation with like others is also limited. For fear of having their
reputation "burned" (quemada) and their security thereby endangered,
many persons involved in homosexual behavior avoid being seen with or
being acknowledged by males who might be judged effeminate and
also avoid places where homosexuals are known to congregate (cf. Carrier 1976a: 365; Arboleda 1981). The same pattern existed among homosexual Anglo Americans in the mid-1960s, although then and there
it was fear of losing jobs more than Latin Americans' fear of the family
learning of stigmatizing association. The lack of positive literature and
the fear of guilt by association were obstacles overcome by gay liberation movements in Anglo America, so there is evidence that such obstacles are surmountable. Indeed, the demonstration that change is

---

13. Those shaken down by police or fag-bashed still may not conceive of a shared
situation. Similarly, many norteamericano casualties did not (and, in some cases and
places, do not).

14. On the importance of group-affirming (indeed, group-defining) literature in
combating stigma, see Humphreys (1972:130–34) and Goffman (1963:25). On the
seriousness with which Latin American regimes take publications, see Lacey (1979:24;
1983:8).

possible is an advantage gay movements in their early development today have. In post-war North America, without any known historical precedent, the possibility of change was difficult to conceive.[15] On the other hand, living in a welfare state in which there is not the economic necessity of staying with one's family, a critical mass developed in a visible territory. The growth and metamorphosis of recreational facilities within an area of increasing residential concentration of homosexuals facilitated the sense of shared experience that led gay North Americans to reject stereotypes of homosexuality and to demand full acceptance. Whether there are functional alternatives to residential concentration is at this point open to question. Even though Latin American homophile organizations seem to be repeating the struggles over tactics and goals characteristic of the era of homophile organizations in the United States (see Marotta 1981; D'Emilio 1983), we need not assume history will repeat itself elsewhere in all its details or that there is only a single possible path of development.[16] A sense of community is easier to instill if there is a visible territory. Nevertheless, distinct gay facilities and services might develop without a residential concentration. Continued residence with families scattered throughout cities is a considerable obstacle to the formation of gay consciousness, culture and community as these have developed in Anglo North America. Only time will tell if there are other routes to similar—or other—developments.[17]

---

15. "Latin American gays are in many ways in approximately the same social and psychological situation from which Anglo Saxon gays, especially in North America, began to emerge 25 years ago" (Lacey 1979:31; 1983:8–12), including the trade/queen (*activo/pasivo, mayate/loca*) distinction. Humphreys (1972), following Toch (1965), emphasized that the "feeling that the status quo is not inevitable and that change is conceivable" is a precondition of social change movements.

16. Only time will tell if there are other routes to similar—or to other—developments. The "four little dragons" (Hong Kong, Singapore, South Korea, Taiwan) have shown that economic modernization (i.e., industrial production that is competitive in the world market) may occur without modernization theory's vaunted values, so sociologists are quieter about proclaiming a singular, universal path to any sort of development.

17. It is difficult to forecast the effect of AIDS on the development of "gay" homosexuality in Latin America. Some officials advocate repressing increasingly public homosexuality because of the specter of AIDS, although to date it has, if anything, provided a basis for increased and increasingly visible gay organization combating AIDS, as in Anglo North America (Lumsden 1991). Moreover, globalization of "safe sex" campaigns (pushing condoms manufactured in the United States) may further disseminate "modern" homosexuality.

REFERENCES

Adam, Barry D.
   1993   In Nicaragua: homosexuality without a gay world. *Journal of Homosexuality* 24:171–81.
Arboleda G., Manuel A.
   1987   La vida entendida en Lima. In Murray (1987:101–17). Revised version in this volume.
Arenas, Reinaldo
   1989   *Old Rosa*. New York: Grove Press.
   1993   *Before Night Falls*. New York: Viking.
Carballo-Diéguez, Alex
   1989   Hispanic culture, gay male culture, and AIDS: counseling implications. *Journal of Counseling & Development* 68:26–30.
Carrier, Joseph M.
   1972   *Urban Mexican Male Homosexual Encounters*. Ph.D. dissertation, University of California, Irvine.
   1976a Family attitudes and Mexican male homosexuality. *Urban Life* 5:359–75.
   1976b Cultural factors affecting urban Mexican male homosexual behavior. *Archives of Sexual Behavior* 5:103–24.
Castillo, Ana
   1991   La macha: toward a beautiful whole self. In Trujillo (1991:24–48).
D'Emilio, John
   1983   *Sexual Politics/Sexual Communities*. Chicago: University of Chicago Press.
Fabrega, Horacio
   1971   Begging in a southeastern Mexican city. *Human Organization* 20:277–87.
Fuswhile-Komreich, Ilse
   1993   Lesbian activism in Argentina: a recent but very powerful phenomenon. In *The Third Pink Book*. A. Hendriks, R. Tielman, and E. van der Veen, ed. Pp. 82–85. Buffalo, NY: Prometheus Books.
Goffman, Erwing
   1963   *Stigma*. Toronto: Prentice-Hall.
Green, James N.
   1994   The emergence of the Brazilian gay liberation movement, 1977–1981. *Latin American Perspectives* 21:38–55.
Humphreys, Laud
   1972   *Out of the Closets*. Toronto: Prentice-Hall.
Islas, Arturo
   1984   *The Rain God*. Palo Alto, CA: Alexandrian Press. (Reprinted, New York: Avon, 1991.)
   1990   *Migrant Souls*. New York: Morrow. (Reprinted, New York: Avon, 1991, the edition quoted herein.)
Khan, Badruddin
   1990   Not-so-gay life in Karachi. *Society of Lesbian and Gay Anthropologists' Newsletter* 12(1):10–19.
Kinger, Nora S.
   1973   Priests, machos and babies. *Journal of Marriage & the Family* 35:300–311.

Lacey, E. A.

1979 Latin America. *Gay Sunshine* 40:22–31.

1983 Introduction in *My Deep Dark Pain is Love*. Winston Leyland, ed. Pp. 7–13. San Francisco: Gay Sunshine Press.

Lee, John A.

1978 *Getting Sex*. Toronto: General.

1979 The gay connection. *Urban Life* 8:175–98.

Levine, Martin P.

1979 *Gay Men*. New York: Harper & Row.

Likosky, Stephan

1992 *Coming Out: An Anthology of International Gay and Lesbian Writing*. New York: Pantheon.

Lumsden, Ian

1991 *Homosexuality, Society and the State in Mexico*. Toronto: Canadian Gay Archives.

McGin, Noel F.

1966 Marriage and the family in middle-class Mexico. *Journal of Marriage and the Family* 28:305–13.

Marotta, Toby

1981 *The Politics of Homosexuality*. Boston: Houghton-Mifflin.

Miller, Neil

1992 *Out in the World*. New York: Random House.

Muñoz, Elías Miguel

1989 *Crazy Love*. Houston: Arte Publico Press.

1991 *The Greatest Performance*. Houston: Arte Publico Press.

Monteagudo, Jesse G.

1991 Miami, Florida. In *Hometowns*. John Preston, ed. Pp. 11–20. New York: Dutton.

Murray, Stephen O.

1979 The institutional elaboration of a quasi-ethnic community. *International Review of Modern Sociology* 9:165–78.

1984 *Social Theory, Homosexual Realities*. Gai Saber Monograph 3.

1987 *Male Homosexuality in Central and South America*. Gai Saber Monograph 5.

(1992) The 'underdevelopment' of 'gay' homosexuality in Mesoamerica, Peru, and Thailand. In *Modern Homosexualities*. Ken Plummer, ed. Pp. 29–38. London: Routledge.

Murray, Stephen O., and Kent Gerard

1983 Renaissance sodomite subcultures? *Onder Vrouwen, Onder Mannen* 1:182–96.

Nava, Michael

1990 *How Town*. New York: Harper & Row.

Ness, Kristian

1992 Merida: Mexico's gayest city is still a well-kept secret. *Christopher Street* 186 (31 Aug.):17–18.

Novo, Salvador

1979 [1973] Memoir. In *Now the Volcano*. W. Leyland, ed. Pp. 11–47. San Francisco: Gay Sunshine Press.

Ogburn, William F.
  1928 *Family Life Today.* Boston: Houghton-Mifflin.
Palmero, Olga, Manuel Millor, and Margarita Elizondo
  1981 *Financiamiento y extension de la seguridad social en America Latina.* México: Instituto Mexicano del Seguro Social.
Parker, Richard G.
  1988 *'Within Four Walls': the Cultural Construction of Sexual Meaning in Contemporary Brazil.* Ph.D. dissertation, University of California, Berkeley.
Peñalosa, Fernando
  1968 Mexican family roles. *Journal of Marriage and the Family* 30:680–89.
Ramirez, Sergio
  1986 The siege. In *Stories.* Pp. 27–35 London: Readers International.
Salas, Luis
  1979 *Social Control and Deviance in Cuba.* New York: Praeger.
Stamford, John
  1982 *Spartacus Gay Guide.* Amsterdam: Spartacus.
Tax, Sol
  1941 World view and social relations in Guatemala. *American Anthropologist* 39:423–44.
Taylor, Clark L.
  1978 *El Ambiente.* Ph.D. dissertation, University of California, Berkeley.
Toch, Hans
  1965 *The Social Psychology of Social Movements.* Indianapolis: Bobbs-Merrill.
Trujillo, Carla
  1991 *Chicana Lesbians.* Berkeley: Third Woman Press.
Vargas Llosa, Mario
  1969 *Conversación en la Catedral.* Barcelona: Editorial Siex Barral. Translated by Gregory Rabassa as *Conversation in the Cathedral.* San Francisco: Harper & Row, 1975.
  1984 *La Historia de Mayta.* Barcelona: Editorial Siex Barral. Translated by Alfred MacAdam as *The Real Life of Alejandro Mayta.* New York: Farrar, Straus and Giroux, 1986.
  1991 *A Writer's Reality.* New York: Houghton-Mifflin.
Wilkie, J. W., B. E. Lorey, and E. Ochoa
  1988 *Statistical Abstract of Latin America, Volume 26.* Los Angeles: UCLA Latin America Center.
Zapata, Luis
  1983 The red dancing shoes. In *My Deep Dark Pain is Love.* W. Leyland and E. A. Lacey, eds. Pp. 98–102. San Francisco: Gay Sunshine Press.
Zschock, Dieter
  1986 Medical care under social insurance. *Latin American Research Review* 21:99–122.

3

Machismo, Male Homosexuality, and Latino Culture*

Stephen O. Murray

The former Iberian colonies in the New World provide the most often described example of the gender-defined organization of homosexuality. Across a number of Caribbean, South and Mesoamerican culture areas (and around the Mediterranean Ocean, as well), ideal (cultural) norms distinguish masculine insertors (*activos*) who are not considered *homosexuales* from feminine insertees (*pasivos*) who are. The queen, as vividly represented in the work of the Argentine writer Manuel Puig

---

*My disbelief of the revisionist image of freewheeling Latino homosexuality represented in a 1986 session of the American Anthropological Association annual meetings led me to add a critical postscript to the book on Central and South American male homosexuality I had completed (Murray 1987). It seems to me that Latin Americans (such as Reinaldo Arenas, Isaac Chocron, Jaime Manrique, Miguel Munoz, Manual Puig, Jacobo Schifter and Unites States–born Mexican Americans like Arturo Islas, Michael Nava, and Richard Rodriquez) offer more credible representations of their cultures than those of *norteamericanos* (e.g., Richard Parker, Erskine Lane, Paul Kutsche and Joseph Itiel), seeking and even finding tropical paradises of sexual behavior unconstrained by sexual identities and other "hangups." Finding the latter's writings on Latino male homosexuality ethnographically thin, and not having had the opportunity to undertake fieldwork in Latin America after the recognitions of SIDA (AIDS), I have drawn extensively on native representations. With my preference for considering what the natives of a culture say in their own forms, I follow Phillips (1987:3–4, 61) in the view that fiction provides a "noetic expression of a social and cultural milieu . . . [that] provide[s] source of indigenous meanings, assumptions, and purposes." As Smith (1991:25) noted, "Poems, plays, and fiction speak from the inside." In contrast, as I suggest in this chapter, the sexual behavior with aliens is a more dubious basis for characterizing intracultural behavior and assumptions. I have discussed the methodological problems elsewhere (Murray 1991, 1995) and focus here on the substantive conclusions that I think are mistaken. Manuel Arboleda, Ralph Bolton, Wayne Dynes, Badruddin Khan, Paul Kutsche, John Lee, Luiz Mott, Luis Paloma, and Pablo Tellez

(see 1979[1976]:203, 243; 1983:76) and the Cuban writer Reinaldo
Arenas (1984, 1992),

> has accepted and bowed to the macho ethic,[1] abandoned the im-
> possible and forbidden "partial masculinity" of bisexuality, and
> become a woman—a "fallen" one at that. The reward for this
> ideological obedience is like the Roman Catholic church's absolu-
> tion of sins of the flesh (so much less important than those of
> doctrine), forgiveness, and even a degree of social acceptance. . . .
> Queens work frequently alongside whores in Latin-American red-
> light districts, which are usually officially known as "zonas de
> tolerancia." [Lacey 1983:10; see Puig 1976; Arenas 1984, 1992;
> Abreau 1983a:276; Monteagudo 1991:18]

Whether the complementary role is a "gay macho" *(bujarrón)* indifferent to what he penetrates is a matter of some controversy among
observers—and also one of dissensus among natives. On the way to
generalizing an essential connection between effeminacy and homosexuality, Fred Whitam eliminated *activos* from the category "homosexual." Constructionists enamored by an "anything goes in private" ethic
(e.g., Kutsche and Parker in this volume) similarly exclude publicly
masculine men from any special "homosexual" category. In their view
males who penetrate males are just ordinary men. Usually, the category
is linguistically unmarked *(hombre-*man) although Schifter and Madrigal (1992) reported *hombres de verdad* (true men), Lancaster (1992)
attested the reduplicated (hence, highly marked) *hombre-hombre,* and
Tierno (1961:74–76) listed *muy hombre* and *mucho hombre* (very man and
much man). The masculine partner, then, at least sometimes is referred
to with linguistically marked forms and is, thereby, distinguished from
men in general.

Parker, Kutsche, and Lancaster also tend to confuse the men with the
boys. Specifically, homosexual experimentation is more acceptable among

---

made useful comments on earlier versions of this chapter. My analysis depends upon
insights shared with me in verbal and non-verbal self-presentations by *activo, pasivo,*
and *internacional* "natives" of Latino culture(s), especially by Luis and Victor in Guatemala; Eduardo, Guillermo, José, and Victor in México; Danilo and Manuel in Peru;
Jesús, Sergio, Vladimir in the United States.

Page citations are from English translations, though the Spanish or Portuguese
original is listed first in the references.

1. Given the expected sexual aspect of the role, bowed away from the macho (i.e.,
offering his *culo* to the macho) would be a more appropriate spatial metaphor.

the unmarried young, but is increasingly threatening to masculine reputation with age and for those whose status is above the working class. As Gombrowicz (1988 [1955]) wrote after a decade and a half in Buenos Aires, "The healthiest and most ordinary boys from the lower classes sometimes give themselves up to this for lack of women—and this, as it turns out, does not distort them at all and does not interfere with the most conventional marriage." There is an age limit, albeit a fuzzily bounded one,[2] on "anything goes in private!"

Drawing on the representations by Latin American writers such as Gasparino Damata, Mario Vargas Llosa, and Luis Zapata, Lacey (1983:10) insisted upon the existence (and native conceptualization) of masculinist/misogynist *activos* with homosexual preferences:

> Influenced by the social reality he inhabits, he has accepted and bowed to the macho ethic, in a different way from the queen, by completely internalizing and assimilating its code of rules, and attempting to live by them. He is no closet case: he openly pursues and beds down boys, and he appears to recognize and condone, even to trumpet, his own homosexuality, but only to the extent that he is the active partner. He is unable psychologically to abandon his cherished masculine orientation. Intimately, moreover, he despises his sexual tendencies, despises all other gays, especially effeminate ones, despises his own sexual partners and despises himself.[3]

Joto and *hombre-hombre* or *veado* and *bofe* are ideal types—native ideal types, not just the model of non-native observers. The typological system is very simple. Behavior and identity are more complex in messy reality. Over time (in a "sexual career") or with different partners, a man's behavioral repertoire may diverge from the clear-cut dichotomy.

---

2. I would hazard the hypothesis that the age has been increasing along with the age of marriage.

3. Particularly in the case of the Brazilian non-commissioned officers portrayed in Damata's (1983) "The Volunteer," it seems to me that homosexuality is age-stratified. They label themselves (in Lacey's translation) as "boy-lovers," and accept that their "nature" is to prefer boys to women (see 217–19 on Henrique and marriage; also the monologue in Abreu 1990 [1988]:81–82). Moreover, they pay the younger enlisted men they fuck, departing from the schema of queens paying studs for sexual services rendered. And the "nature" of the boys (at least Ivo, the central object of desire in "The Volunteer") is to grow up and escape to women and marriage. Also see the representation of Mexican boys seeking sex with the narrator in Ceballos (1969), the variegated career of the narrator of Zapata (1979), and Miller's (1992:201) discussion of the economic bases for age-differentiated lesbian and gay relationships in Argentina.

Indeed, the anal sexual behavior reported by Mexican men tested for HIV status has been less role-dichotomized than for United States samples, as I discuss in chapter 12 of this volume.

The imaginary undifferentiated phallic supremacy of the *hombre*—supposedly common to Mediterranean cultures and to former Iberian colonies in the New World—is too neat. Certainly there are individuals who impersonate these ideal types. However, the sexually omnivorous *hombre* who doesn't have any preferences in "object choice"—the man for whom "meat on the hook is meat on the hook, no reason to be choosy; no opportunity should be allowed to slip by and it doesn't matter who or what you fuck as long as you fuck" (Lane 1978:84)—is more a *maricón* fantasy than a plausible empirical observation. As one veteran observer suggested,

> The mirage of the *hombre* who doesn't care where his prick goes is a consoling rationalization of the macho-adoring *maricón* [or foreigner]. He probably does care and have preferences. He just can't get into his girlfriend often enough, or at all, and you're there as a temporary substitute or relief. [V. Cervantes 1987, personal communication]

Echoing the quotation from Gombrowicz above, the Argentine writer Lucio Ginarte (1983 [1960]:19) wrote (specifically of Recife),

> The sexual problem of the young men is acute. They're poor, and love is expensive. They don't have enough money to pay for a girl [still less to marry and set up a household], so they turn to homosexuals. But even though they come, and feel pleasure and normalise the functioning of their glands, they want money.[4]

Accepting money for sex does not make them *putos,* although projection of what I call "the blind phallus fantasy" (Murray 1987:196) is undoubtedly flattering to young men who are insecure about their masculinity (as to some extent is any Latino male who has not fathered children[5]). They are very unlikely to contradict flattering *maricón* claims

---

4. Even one who "earns a good salary" (and gives the money back once he's received it) insists on payment: "he must maintain the privileges of virility intact" (Ginarte 1983:49).

5. According to Gilmore (1990:41), paternity is the key test in the circum-Mediterranean machismo complex:

> In those parts of southern Europe where the Don Juan model of sexual assertiveness is highly valued, a man's assigned task is not just to make endless con-

about how masculine they are.[6] Increasingly in Latin American cities, men tend to marry a decade or more after puberty. With no farm to inherit, marriage in the mid-twenties "if I can accumulate some money" is a hope of many men. The possibilities of sexual contact with the "good girls" who are the only candidates for future wives are virtually nil, so "bad girls"—a category that for some includes effeminate men— provide culturally expected, quasi-legitimate sexual outlets for unmarried youths.

Penetrating the *huecos* (holes) of *putos* is not as (culturally) valued or desirable as penetrating those of women. Latinos with whom I have discussed claims that masculinity can be enhanced by fucking a *maricón* vociferously disagree with Lancaster's (1992:242) assertion that fucking men enhances "male honor." They also question the extent of banter about homosexual exploits among adults in Latino cultures. The only

---

quests but to spread his seed. Beyond mere promiscuity, the ultimate test is that of competence in reproduction. . . . The Mediterranean emphasis on manliness means results: it means procreating offspring (preferably boys). At the level of community endorsement, it is legitimate reproductive success, more than simply erotic acrobatics—a critical fact often overlooked by experts on Mediterranean honor.

Nineteen is not too young for this ultimate test to be considered in México or Puerto Rico. Also, in both places "one or more women" might be substituted for "wife" in Gilmore's statement.

6. The efforts that consumers of young male phalluses devote to propping up fragile male egos are visible in Ceballos Maldonado (1969), Ginarte (1983 [1960]), Lane (1978), Penteado (1983), et al. In United States cases in which the "homosexual panic" defense has been used, the killers generally acknowledge that they agreed to insert their penis, but when the dead man (allegedly—this formulation says more about cultural assumptions than about what really happened) tried to "rape" them, what could they do but defend their male honor? The same panic (about being penetrated and at any desire for penetration they feel) occurs in Latin America. It sometimes leads to beatings and stabbings, some of which are fatal. It is not in realizing "that he is capable of performing a homosexual act" but in finding pleasure in the thought or act of being penetrated that leads men in Latin and in Anglo America to brutalize what one inwardly, secretly, or subconsciously desires but cannot accept within one's impenetrable masculine self-image. Such panic and concomitant striking-out against those who occasion it occur in other Latin American cultures, and I greatly doubt it is "impossible in Nicaragua," as Lancaster (1992:248) claims in one of many instances of exaggerating (exoticizing) and essentializing differences between Nicaraguan and Anglo North American cultures. Contrast the *activo* panics represented in Zapata (1983), Ribondi (1983), and Marchant Lazcano (1983); and Gombrowicz's (1988 [1955]:142– 46) discussion of "panic-stricken fear at the woman in themselves of Argentinean 'manly' men."

evidence Lancaster adduced that men gain status in boasting about fucking *cochones* is as follows:

> I once heard a Nicaraguan youth of nineteen boast to his younger friends: "I am very sexually experienced. I have had a lot of women. . . . I have done everything. I have even done it with *cochones.*" No one in the group thought this a damning confession, and all present were impressed with their friend's sexual experience and prowess. [p. 241, emphasis added]

He does not tell readers how he knew that all present were impressed. Moreover, the "even" suggests that women and *cochones* are not equally desirable and empowering to those who "use" them. One may reasonably wonder if the youth could have bragged about fucking *cochones* if he hadn't established that he'd fucked "a lot of women" and preferred women. This anecdote is not very convincing evidence of the irrelevance of the sex fucked by the *hombre-hombre.* Lancaster does not appear to have asked direct questions of the residents of the working class barrio in Managua, Nicaragua, among whom he lived about whether one gains honor from using a *pasivo* (*cochón* in the local lexicon), or (as I think is the case), whether, under certain circumstances that include established heterosexual prowess and preference, the man who thrusts the hard synecdoche of masculinity up the available orifice of the weak, less-than-masculine (and therefore penetrable) man neither loses nor gains any macho reputation/honor. Lancaster's eager followers, Alonso and Korceck (1988:111), also fail to present even a passing anecdote in support of their fantasy that fucking males enhances male prestige.

More sensibly, in my view, only two pages after asserting that "one is either a *cochón* or one is not," Lancaster (1992:243) argues that "in its broadest sense," the *pasivo/cochón* stigma threatens all men, so that "although the system of stigma produces certain distinct categories, its operation is never entirely categorical, for stigma is necessarily 'sticky.'" From this, I would infer (especially since Latinos have told me so) that boasting about fucking men is risky to all but the most solidly established macho reputations. Too-frequent forays into this kind of *Banco de Inversiones* undercut a macho reputation, as does emotional investment in those he uses sexually. As one longtime participant observer put it,

> For an *hombre* to boast of fucking men, he must be perceived as having a substantial surplus balance in the *Banco (Hembra) del Macho* before he can publicly invest in this kind of *Banco de Inversiones* [i.e., *maricones, cochones*]. At no time must the two accounts

be equal, and he must loudly proclaim that he prefers women. This is not the happy-go-lucky phallic maniac who doesn't care—or even notice!—where he plants his stalk . . . Further evidence against what you label "the blind phallus" [a hole is a hole] assumption is that when money or gifts are exchanged, the flow is from the *hombre* to the girl, but from the *maricón* to the *hombre*. The first pattern may (if rarely) be reversed, but the *hombre* never pays the *maricón*. [V. Cervantes 1987, personal communication; Lancaster (1992:239) less categorically states that it is only "most typically" that the pasivo pays.]

Topping other men (usually verbally or symbolically, but occasionally physically) is central to machismo, perhaps as important as maintaining the subordination of women. As Lancaster (1992:236–37) explained, machismo

is not exclusively or primarily a means of structuring power relations between men and women. It is a means of structuring power among men. Like drinking, gambling, risk taking, asserting one's opinions, and fighting, the conquest of women is a feat performed with two audiences in mind: first, other men, to whom one must constantly prove one's masculinity and virility; and second, oneself, to whom one must also show all the signs of masculinity. Machismo, then, is a matter of constantly asserting one's masculinity by way of practices that show the self to be "active," not "passive" (as defined in a given milieu . . .). As a gestural system, machismo has a steep temporal dimension, and yesterday's victories count for little tomorrow.[7]

Any variation (or, more correctly, anything that anyone chooses to consider a variation) from (elastic) norms of masculinity risks loss of face, even though direct public criticism is exceedingly rare. Gossip is pervasive, and, therefore, a predominant concern in urban—as well as in rural—Latin America. As in other Mediterranean-influenced cultures, one's "reputation" is important, but it is difficult to be sure how others regard one:

. To be a man in a society where sanctions are discreetly expressed, if at all, and everyone is provided with a "public" that in a sense

---

7. The conquest of men without masculine honor *(cochones)* is rarely performed for the approval of other machos. That Lancaster excluded conquering quasi-men from the list suggests to me that he doesn't really believe that this is a route to enhancing honor and masculine status.

"honours" him, does not make life all that easy. The man must steer a deft and elegant course with very few signals from that public who are his judges. He can never be sure that his value is what he thinks it is, as he observes his bland reflection in his polite spectators. [Wikan 1984:646]

Whether what is called machismo is inner-directed, or other-directed approval-seeking performance, there are elaborate collusions to avoid questioning appearances that could easily be challenged, and not to see deviance (in gender, sexual behavior, or other sites of deviance). What Schmitt (in Schmitt and Sofer 1992:7) wrote of the circum-Mediterranean line between gossip and openly challenging someone's "face" seems to me to have been carried to the New World:

A man should not allow others to bugger him. Otherwise he loses his name, his honor, that is if others know it and are known to know. The decisive line is not between the act kept secret and the act known by many, but between only talking behind one's back and saying it in your presence, between rumors and public knowledge. There is always room for manoeuvre, you can always ignore what everybody knows. As long as nobody draws public attention to something everybody knows, one ignores what might disrupt important social relations. There is a clear rule: You cannot be fucked. But what this really comes down to is: Saying of somebody that he has been fucked disturbs social relation.

Those who have dropped out of the machismo competition generally have the sense not to rattle the fragile masculinity of the macho, who is all too likely to lash out at anyone who questions his (sacred) masculinity. Just as it takes a slave to be a master, the *pasivo* invents, persuades, polishes, and maintains his fantasy of the "real man" *(hombre-hombre)*.[8] This species feels entitled to beat those it sexually uses. Just

---

8. The individual *pasivo* "requires ordinary men, and his activity and identity can never be quite independent of them" (Lancaster 1992:243), but (as Lancaster might have learned had he studied those who call themselves *cochones* rather than picking up tidbits of *hombre-hombres'* views of *cochones), pasivos* are also "marginalized subjects" scripting sexual scenarios. I doubt that they are only objects (mattresses) in the scripts of *activos.* There is also a (Durkheimian) sense in which the culture (or economy) of machismo requires visible specimens of spoiled/failed masculine socialization. Negative role models serve the moral order by providing visible warnings (to which one's elders literally can point) of what boys must strive to avoid resembling and are in danger of becoming if they don't "measure up" to the standards of machismo. See Fry's

like the *bakla'* in the Philippines (Manalansan 1990, 1991), and the *gà'tuhy* in Thailand (Jackson 1989:227–28)—two places in which some have seen paradises of "tolerance for homosexuality" and for gender non-conformity—the *maricón* in México, Cuba, and Peru, the *veado* in Brazil, and (I am confident) the *cochón* in Nicaragua get beaten up after sexually servicing "real men" or just for the hell of it if there's nothing better to do and one comes into the view of "real men," or (frequently, in the case of policemen) because effeminacy and/or homosexuality are affronts to public morality (whether that morality is revolutionary or reactionary).[9] Generally, lower-class men do not share the middle-class view of effeminacy as sickness:

> One of them says you should see a doctor. Or a priest. But a doctor for sure, because you need help . . . because you look and act too much like a woman. . . . And a man says that you don't need no doctor, that he's going to make you normal with his fists. [Muñoz 1991:142]

Besides the *pasivo's* stroking of male vanity, the *activo* maintains his "stud" self-image/self-presentation by an endless stream of sexual remarks meant to signal to interlocutors an insatiable sexual appetite. Such remarks may not signify any actual sexual expectations or even any genuine interest in the targets of the remarks, but those who are no

---

chapter in this volume for an extended (neo-Durkheimian) analysis of a gender anti-exemplar and Murray (1984:10–11) for a review of this kind of interpretation.

9. Carrier (1972:242) found that 53 percent of *pasivos* (in contrast to 12 percent of *activos*) had a great deal of anxiety about police harassment. These anxieties are quite reasonable: 59 percent of the *pasivos* (in contrast to 19 percent of the *activos*) reported having experienced it. The late Brazilian activist Herbert Daniel told Braiterman (1990:299):

> Our society is extremely antidemocratic and authoritarian in its workings and does not allow the exercise of difference. Violence explodes with great ease. Many homosexuals are victims of violence—a permanent situation in Brazil, which is regarded almost with pleasure by the police, almost with delight by the most reactionary sectors of society.

Police discretion to decide that someone is an outrage to public morality (committing, or being a "public scandal") elsewhere in Latin America is available to Cuban police, and is supplemented by neighborhood Committees for the Defense of the Revolution monitoring everyday life for a flexible range of "counter-revolutionary" offenses not enumerated in laws (see Boogard and Kammen 1985:91–93; Salas 1979:157, 296–329; Arenas 1989 [1984]:65–71, 1993 [1992]:69, 133, 151–54; Leiner 1994:28–38).

longer *niños* (babies) and not yet *viejos* (old men) must continually exhibit an interest in phallic activity—especially if they do not have regular sexual opportunities—by talking about what they would like to do to any imaginably penetrable object. Relatively few urbanites have physically demanding occupations. Generally in contemporary cities, there are not many ways to demonstrate "traditional" masculinity.

The lack of women who are available for actual sex and the general lack of privacy for sex with willing partners—along with the cultural pressure on men to have sex regularly and the cultural pressure on women to maintain the honor of their fathers, brothers, or husbands by resisting sexual involvement with anyone except a husband—drives males to flamboyant verbal sexual posturing. Foreign observers may mistakenly interpret such talk as indicating that Latino men are hypersexual. It is easy to play the role of a *lobo listo* (literally, ready wolf) when few demands are likely to be made: the Latino male is rarely if ever going to be pressed to demonstrate that he really is ready.

According to Brandes (1981:223), in everyday Latino conversation, claims to phallic supremacy over women coincide with "a constant attempt to force masculine rivals into the feminine role, in a never-ending quest to avoid adopting the role themselves."[10] I do not think that Latino men talking obsessively about "tomarlo por culo" expect those they tell "¡Baja los pantalones!" actually to drop their pants and take it up the ass, any more than they expect the women they leer at and sling *piropos* at are going to stop and give themselves to their "suitors."[11]

---

10. Brandes was writing about Andalusia. Lumsden (1991:22) makes a similar claim about México, and Reinhardt (1981:42–43) about Chicanos in the United States. Pablo Tellez (personal communication) questions the extent of banter in Latin America about homosexual receptivity. He argues that although young children (into early adolescence) may fling the *maricón* label around (and parents and older siblings may also taunt boys with the label and urge them "¡No sea maricón!"—don't be a *maricón*), such charges are too serious to be used by older adolescents or by adults, except with a grave intent to insult another and to provoke a fight (e.g., see Andrade 1983 [1947]:155).

11. Remarks about women's desirability may express aesthetic appreciation, as claimed by some acculturated Chicanos. The sexual explicitness of most instances makes me doubt that much sublimation occurs in such behavior, however. Gardner (1980) suggests that men are desensitized to sexual rejection by such (very unequal) "exchanges," while women learn to ignore male importuning. Also see Kramarae (1986). Carrier (in press) noted that

the guys who were really interested in having sex with me and Alberto [both publicly known to be sexually available] would also enter into the joking and be

Both kinds of talk seem to me to be ritualistic. To label them "ritualistic" doesn't mean that the behavior lacks motivation. Indeed, it doesn't take much depth psychology to suspect insecurity about masculinity in those who incessantly parade their interest in sexual conquests.[12] Similarly, masculine ideology has consequences, especially for those who believe in it. Kutsche and Parker to the contrary notwithstanding, the (internalized) cultural model of masculinity does keep men in their proper roles, even between four silent walls (see Muñoz 1989:46, for example).

Some observers (e.g., Brandes 1981:232–34) have claimed that a fear of enjoying being anally penetrated is a salient concern for Latino males. "If I let him fuck me I'd probably like it and then I'd do it again, and then I'd be queer," a young Guatemalteco told Lane (1978:56). For Hermes that fear is realized: "I knew that once it had been awakened, it wouldn't sleep again" (Abreu 1983a:277).[13] Schmitt (in Schmitt and Sofer 1992:8) reported that the danger of coming to find being penetrated desirable, indeed, irresistible is a part of (transcontinental) Islamic cosmology: "To most Muslims anal lust is not really unnatural. One has to avoid getting buggered precisely in order not to acquire a taste for it and thus become addicted. It is like an infectious disease: once infected it is difficult to get rid of it" (also see Schmitt 1985:54–55).[14] Such a belief seems to have a circum-Mediterranean diffusion and to have been carried to the New World by Iberian *conquistadores*. In México, "there is even a term, *hechizos* [made ones], for former *mayates*

---

quite crude, but when they wanted to negotiate a sexual encounter it would be done discreetly, out of earshot from the others. They never wanted any of their friends to know for sure that sex had taken place, so some non-sexual pretext was always made for going off alone with either of us.

12. John Rechy (1967:17) wrote that the "femaleness" of one of his ostentatiously *activo* alter egos, Johnny Rio, "has to do with the fact that he moves sensually, that his eyes invite, that he is constantly flirting (although this is not conscious) and that he is extremely vain." (Tight clothes could well be added to this list, and also the denial of being in any way "feminine" on the previous page.)

13. Also see Domingos (1983:313). For a 19th-century representation of this conception, see Caminha (1979 [1895]:89). It is notable that Aleixo left passivity behind after "surrendering" and spending a year as a beloved.

14. The anxiety that one may like getting fucked if he tries it parallels the anxiety about one's women (especially wife) getting to like sex and slipping from the Madonna to the *puta* (or, at least, *chingada*) role, a nagging concern of those living by the particularly acute double standard of Latin American culture. Only Santa María was able to be both a mother and a virgin (see LaFaye 1976, Taylor 1987, Martin 1990).

[hustlers] who have become complete homosexuals over time" (Lumsden 1991:45). Still, the feared anal penetration does not turn everyone who has experienced it into a *maricón*. Similarly, even insertee homosexual activity does not inevitably compromise masculine deportment and/ or end masculine self-conception, especially if the stigmatized behavior occurs with aliens—including ethnographers whose own sexual adventures may have confused them about what Latinos do with each other (see Murray 1991, 1995).

The same bases of sexual scarcity that fuel heterosexual and homosexual verbalizations (in particular, a lack of places in which to fuck) probably contribute to the readiness of young Latin American males to bed foreign males with apartments or hotel rooms. The foreigner is very unlikely to tell the young male's peers who did what to whom. The luxury of some privacy for sex and of removal from scrutiny by family, neighbors, and friends probably loosens the usual constraints on behavior. From experiences with young men experimenting outside their usual world, foreigners may overestimate the sexual role flexibility in the culture, not realizing that their sexual partners in a significant sense are outside their own culture. The seemingly empirical generalization by a traveler (or an ethnographer) that "they're all available" may be mistaken for evidence of bisexual or undifferentiated desire,[15] if no consideration is given to the lack of genuine options for sexual release or for sexual experimentation. That a foreigner has fucked a native does not mean that the native prefers men or prefers getting fucked. Curiosity, xenophilia, hopes for and expectations of material rewards, and confidence that peers won't find out may influence sexual behavior more than deep, "true" desire. From experiences with young males experimenting outside their usual world, foreigners easily overestimate the sexual role flexibility in a culture. Being in a foreign society, and in "intimate contact" with one or more natives, alien observers may not realize that their sexual partners in a significant sense are not playing by the usual rules of their sexual culture. Rather than penetrating the

---

15. "Sexual anarchy," according to Kutsche (in this volume, 1986, Kutsche and Page 1991). "The categories that seem most fixed, most absolute, can always be transformed," according to Parker (1987:163). I would substitute "sometimes may" (or "during Carnaval may") for "always are." Those *bichas* and *maricones* who are beaten or even killed for daring to usurp the *hombre* role vividly demonstrate the salience to some of the *activo/pasivo* ideology. (See Murray 1991, challenging Itiel 1991. Also see Lumsden 1991: 27, 36, 77.)

mysteries of another culture's sexual lifeways, both may be outside their own cultures in a (liminal?) interculture.[16] Almost as much as the foreigner, the native who has sex with the foreigner is "away from home" and, therefore, released to some extent from the cultural constraints that affect intracultural sexual behavior.[17]

Within the culture, among natives, sexual receptivity does not necessarily lead to enacting a *maricón* role or building a gay identity. Other natives are just more likely to hear what happened from the native conquistador, who doesn't move away, and whose secret knowledge remains a threat to the masculine reputation of the insertee. The insertee's honor may be *quemado* (singed) at any time by reports or rumors of receptivity. Moreover, even when obtainable, the luxury of privacy is not as safe with peers as with foreigners. Thus, to say that it doesn't matter what a Latino male does as long as no one finds out (Lacey 1979; Parker 1991) doesn't say much, because of the necessary caveat "hardly ever does no one find out." Some things remain hidden (*escondido*), but guarantees of eternal silence are dubious. Anyone especially concerned about his reputation is not all that safe getting fucked under the sheets or between four silent walls ("entre quatro paredes") when "no one is watching" or even during Carnaval when, supposedly, "anything goes" (Parker 1987:163–216, 1991:100).[18] In the words of José, Parker's primary informant,

---

16. Sexual conduct is far from being the only aspect about which anthropologists are prone to overestimate their participation and their ability to represent another culture from inside, ignoring the extent to which those who choose to interact with the alien are innovating or recurrently acting as "culture brokers" (Crick 1992:180, 188; Caplan 1992:71, 80; Hendry 1992). Designation as an "honorary chief" seems especially likely to go to anthropologists' heads and make them believe that they can continue fieldwork intrapsychically. Contrast Dumont's (1978:164) tortured recognition that he "was playing both within and without the system" with Bloch's (1990:194) smug recommendation of introspection following participant observation.

17. This is not to say that prior socialization (including culturally shaped fantasies about Latins, Americans, et al.) is irrelevant. Foreigners' assumption that they have participated directly in a foreign sexual culture, however, is suspect.

18. Contrast the native (Brazilian) view of Herbert Daniel: "There is a very easy relationship between men sexually, as long as one of them is sexually active and the other sexually passive" (quoted in Braiterman 1990:299). "Tudo": (everything) in "Tudo pode acontecer" (Parker 1987:164, 1991:100) is hyperbole, although Parker in his eagerness to overthrow any rigid sexual orthodoxy (especially recurrent sexual roles) takes it literally. "Todos" in the Spanish formula "Todos hecho, nada dicho" (Everything is done, nothing is said) is similarly hyperbolic (more so than is "nada"!).

Sometimes one gives (*dá*) first, or sucks or jacks off the other, and then when it is the turn of the one who received pleasure first, he doesn't want to do it for the other. There are some times when this same first person goes about telling others that the second did this or that with him. . . . The active defames the passive, giving rise to fights and shame, if not blows and serious punishments coming from family members. The game can sometimes get complicated. [1991:128]

The walls may not speak, but those cavorting between them tend to do so—sooner or later. The ending of Hecker Filho's (1951) novella *Internato* provides an excellent example (of sooner).[19]

Latinos (and others) can compartmentalize homosexuality—in space or time. According to Goode (1960), compartmentalization of roles is a common response to role strain; by no means is it unique to managing masculine self-presentation while engaged in homosexual behavior in Latin America. In Latin America, as in Anglo North America, there is "a traditional difference between that which people know and that which they agree to admit that they know, that which they see and that which they speak of" (Henry James, quoted by Halperin 1990:58; for an Argentine example, see Miller 1992:209–10). Homosexual involvement of some persons is an open secret; that of others is not discussed, and some homosexual involvement is genuinely *escondido* (hidden). Despite the reticence about discussing one's own homosexuality or that of one's friends or family,[20] there is essentializing pressure to bundle sex-(uality) and gender, even though the nuances of technical distinctions of sex, sexuality, gender (and possible variations of each) can be illustrated. For instance, one East Oakland barrio Chicano maintained that "a *maricón* isn't necessarily homosexual. It's someone who can't take care of himself." This distinction from sexual expectations didn't last, however. One of his friends completed the cultural syllogism immediately: "And therefore gets fucked." I asked, "You mean he gets 'fucked over'?" The

---

19. For examples of such "news" trickling out more slowly, but very damagingly, see Abreu (1983b:283), Damata (1983:210), Domingos (1983:313), Donoso (1966:87), Penteado (1979:241), Zapata (1983:97). On the perils of threatening to reveal a married man's homosexual dalliances see Ribondi (1983:339–40) and the film by Zuleica Porto based on it. In contrast, see Penteado (1983:243) for at least the fantasy of escaping having one's masculine reputation singed.

20. Indeed, the reticence extends to discussion of masturbation and prostitutes, or speculating about close friends and family members as discussed above in Chapter 2.

second Chicano speaker answered, "Sure he does, and he takes it up the ass." (The first then agreed with this reformulation.)

It seems to me that in labeling boys and men *cochón, joto, maricón, veado,* etc., gender non-conformity is primary. Since the cultural assumption is that gender and sexuality will be consonant, the natives do not make the (alien) analytical distinction between gender and sexuality: the less-than-masculine by local standards get fucked (and beaten up, too) and those who are known to get fucked are less than masculine. There are certainly masculine-appearing males who are insertees and effeminate-appearing males who are mostly or exclusively insertors, but the clear, simple masculine/feminine division is paramount in Latino views of gender and sex—insofar (which, I think, is not very far) as sex and gender are conceived to be distinct.[21] Behavioral variance is irrelevant to this organizing principle. The actual (considerable) flux and uncertainty of sexual expression are ignored "by the culture," or, rather, by Latino males who don't want to know, talk about, or think that masculine appearances do not necessarily validate untainted masculine essence.

Silva (1979) provided an especially powerful representation. Also see the Venezuelan family in Chocrón (1972): one brother settles comfortably into the *pasivo* role, while another one is a seagull trapped on the land (the *pájaro de mer por tierra* of the title). Braiterman (1992:10) discusses a relatively safe-to-masculine-reputation way to get fucked: hire a hyper-feminine prostitute (who is unlikely to be believed if "she" reported the behavior to those whose opinion matters to the client):

> Stories about the trick's desire "to get fucked like women," repeated endlessly, become as tiresome to hear as the act must be for the queens to perform. . . . The night can be cruel for those who must constantly act like men in bed when they've worked so hard to look like women in the street.

The "Queen of the Night" in Abreu's (1990 [1988]:82) *Dragons* proclaims that "all young men like to get fucked, some are even queer." Reinaldo Arenas (1992) similarly recalled many masculine men eager to be fucked by a queen (along with scores of young Cubans eager to find an available orifice to fuck). The insistence on *activo* identity even by

---

21. Hence the obsessive concern about sartorial detail (e.g., Montero 1993:24). Murray (1994) criticizes the projection of distinctions between sex and gender and sexuality from the elite discourse of feminist theorizing to cosmologies elsewhere.

someone who has just engaged in *pasivo* behavior is exemplified by the
following recollection by Arenas of picking up a muscular adolescent:

> Once inside my home, [he] surprisingly asked me to play the role
> of the man. . . . I fucked him and he enjoyed it like a convict.
> Then, still naked, he asked me, "And if anybody catches us here,
> who is the man?" He meant who fucked whom. I replied, perhaps
> a little cruelly, "Obviously, I am the man, since I stuck it into
> you." This enraged the young man, who was a judo expert, and he
> started to throw me against the low ceiling; thank God, he would
> catch me in his arms on the way down, but I was getting an awful
> beating. "Who? Who is the man here?" he repeated. And I, afraid
> to die on this one, replied, "You, because you are a judo expert."
> [p. 103; also see 113–14, 152]

Behavioral variance to some limited extent corrodes certainty in the
ideal norms, though less than Anglos expect. Variance from roles (queens
taking the activo role, masculine men taking the pasivo role) seems not
to be cognized (see Bolton 1991:126, 151–52; Arenas 1993: 281). As
Arenas learned, it is better not to press too hard as reality even what one
knows from direct involvement happened. I have also been told by
young Latinos with semen inside their rectums that they never get
fucked, which I take to mean that they are not the kind of person who
takes women's roles (see Murray 1995). Loyalty to and credence in the
ideal norms are considerable. They are constantly reiterated in many
media, especially in primary socialization. The *machismo* complex may
not be a *sui generis* reality, but belief in and approval of it channel
behavior to conformity. As Lancaster (1992:236) wrote, machismo is
"more than an 'effect' produced by other material relations. It has its
own materiality, its own power to produce effects, . . . its own economy." How and what sexual norms and behaviors mean for natives are
only beginning to be explored. At this point we know something of
behavioral variety and rather more of official/cultural definitions and
ideologies, theories and norms of sexuality, and far too little of the lived
experiences of men involved in homosexuality.[22]

---

22. Rogers (1975), Martin (1990), and Lancaster (1992) provide vivid accounts of
how women live with, manipulate, and reproduce machismo; Parker (1991) and Lancaster (1992) signally fail to show how *pasivos* do, substituting description of (majority
culture) normative structures of belief for descriptions or analyses of human practices
of such men. Arenas (1992) left an important document (including his own typology
on pp. 77–78 that might be extended to authoritarian states that are not communist;

References

Abreu, Caio Fernando
  1983a [1980] Sergeant Garcia. Translated by E. A. Lacey in Leyland (1983: 267–77).
  1983b [1982] Those two. Translated by E. A. Lacey in Leyland (1983:278–84).
  1988 *Os Dragoes Nao Conhecem O Paraiso*. São Paulo: Companhia das Letras. Translated by David Treece as *Dragons*. London: Boulevard, 1990.
Alonso, Ana Maria, and Maria T. Koreck
  1988 Silences: 'Hispanics,' AIDS and sexual practices. *Differences* 1:101–24.
Andrade, Mário de
  1983 [1947] Frederico Paciência. Translated by E. A. Lacey in Leyland (1983:241–44).
Arenas, Reinaldo
  1984 *Arturo, la estrella mas brilliante*. Barcelona: Montesinos. Translated by Ann Slater and Andrew Hurley in *Old Rosa: A Novel in Two Stories*, New York: Grove Press, 1989.
  1989 *El portero*. Malaga, Spain: Dador. Translated by Dolores M. Koch as *The Doorman*. New York: Grove Weidenfeld, 1991.
  1992 *Antes que Anochezca*. Barcelona: Tusquets Editores. Translated as *Before Night Falls*. New York: Viking, 1993.
Bloch, Maurice
  1990 Language, anthropology and cognitive science. *Man* 26:183–98.
Boogard, Henk van den, and Kathelijne van Kammen
  1985 We cannot jump over our own shadow. In *Coming Out*. S. Likosky, ed. Pp. 82–101. New York: Pantheon, 1992.
Bolton, Ralph
  1991 Mapping terra incognita: sex research for AIDS prevention—an urgent agenda for the 1990s. In *The Time of AIDS*. Gilbert Herdt and Shirley Lindenbaum, eds. Pp. 124–58. Newbury Park, CA: Sage.
Braiterman, Jared
  1990 Fighting AIDS in Brazil. *Gay Community News* 17(39). Quoted from its reprinting, in *Coming Out*. S. Likosky, ed. Pp. 295–307. New York: Pantheon.
  1992 Beauty in flight: Rio and beyond. *Whorezine* 15:9–11.
Brandes, Stanley
  1981 Like wounded stags: male sexual ideology in an Andalusian town. In *Sexual Meaning*. S. Ortner and H. Whitehead, eds. Pp. 216–39. New York: Cambridge University Press.
Caminha, Adolfo
  1979 [1895] *Bom-Crioulo*. Translated by Erskine Lane in Leyland (1979:

---

and an explanation of why he preferred gender-stratified Cuban homosexuality practiced everywhere to egalitarian ghettoized American homosexuality on pp. 106–8).

82–96). [E. A. Lacey translated the whole novel, San Francisco: Gay Sunshine Press, 1982.]

Caplan, Pat
  1992 Spirits and sex: a Swahili informant and his diary. In *Anthropology and Autobiography*. J. Okely and H. Callaway, eds. Pp. 64–81. London: Routledge.

Carrier, Joseph M.
  1972 *Urban Mexican Male Homosexual Encounters*. Ph.D. dissertation, University of California, Irvine.
  In press *Mexican Male Homosexual Encounters*. New York: Columbia University Press.

Ceballos Maldonado, José
  1969 *Después de todo*. México: Premiá.

Chocrón, Isaac
  1972 *Pájaro de mar por tierra*. Caracas: Tiempo Nuevo.

Crick, Malcolm
  1992 Ali and me: an essay in streetcorner anthropology. In *Anthropology and Autobiography*. Judith Okely and Helen Callaway, eds. Pp. 175–92. London: Routledge.

Damata, Gasparino
  1983 [1976] The volunteer. Translated by E. A. Lacey in Leyland (1983: 151–63).

Domingos, Jorge
  1983 The wedding for the king of spades. Translated by E. A. Lacey in Leyland (1983:297–313).

Donoso, José
  1966 *El jugar sin límites*. México: Joaquín Mortiz. Translated by Suzanne Levine as *Triple Cross*. New York: Dutton, 1972.

Dumont, Jean-Paul
  1978 *The Headman and I: Ambiguity and Ambivalence in the Fieldworking Experience*. Austin: University of Texas Press.

Foster, David William
  1991 *Gay and Lesbian Themes in Latin American Literature*. Austin: University of Texas Press.

Gardner, Carol Brooks
  1980 Passing by: street remarks, address rights and the urban female. *Sociological Inquiry* 50:328–56.

Gilmore, David D.
  1990 *Manhood in the Making: Cultural Concepts of Masculinity*. New Haven, CT: Yale University Press.

Ginarte, Lucio
  1983 [1960] Orgy. Translated by E. A. Lacey in Leyland (1983:15–52).

Gombrowicz, Witold
  1988 [1953–56] *Diary: Volume One*. Evanston, IL: Northwestern University Press.

Goode, William J.
  1960 Role strain. *American Sociological Review* 25:483–96.

Gunn, Rufus

1985 *Searching for Sergio.* London: Gay Men's Press.

Halperin, David M.

1990 *One Hundred Years of Homosexuality and Other Essays.* New York: Routledge.

Hecker Filho, Paulo

1951 *Inernato.* Rio de Janeiro: Ediçao Fronteira. Translated by E. A. Lacey as "Boarding School" in Leyland (1983:245–66).

Hendry, Joy

1992 The paradox of friendship in the field. In *Anthropology and Autobiography.* J. Okely and H. Callaway, eds. Pp. 163–74. London: Routledge.

Itiel, Joseph

1991 *De Onda: A Gay Guide to Mexico and Its People.* San Francisco: International Wavelength.

Jackson, Peter A.

1989 *Male Homosexuality in Thailand.* Amsterdam: Global Academic Publishers.

Kramarae, Cheris

1986 Linguistic crimes which the law cannot reach, or compliments and other insulting behavior. In *Proceedings of the First Berkeley Women and Language Conference,* 84–95.

Kutsche, Paul

1986 Gay male identity in Costa Rica. Paper presented at the American Anthropological Association meetings in Philadelphia.

Kutsche, Paul, and J. Bryan Page

1991 Male sexual identify in Costa Rica. *Latin American Anthropological Review* 3:7–14.

Lacey, E. A.

1979 Latin America. *Gay Sunshine* 40:22–31.

1983 Introduction. In Leyland (1983:7–13).

LaFaye, Jacques

1976 *Quetzalcoatl and Guadalupe: The Formation of Mexican National Consciousness, 1531–1813.* Chicago: University of Chicago Press.

Lancaster, Roger N.

1992 *Life is Hard: Machismo, Danger, and the Intimacy of Power in Nicaragua.* Berkeley: University of California Press.

Lane, Erskine

1978 *Game-Texts: A Guatemalan Journal.* San Francisco: Gay Sunshine Press.

Leiner, Marvin

1994 *Sexual Politics in Cuba: Machismo, Homosexuality, and AIDS.* Boulder: Westview Press.

Leyland, Winston

1979 *Now the Volcano: An Anthology of Latin American Gay Literature.* San Francisco: Gay Sunshine Press.

1983 *My Deep Dark Pain Is Love: A Collection of Latin American Fiction.* San Francisco: Gay Sunshine Press.

Lumsden, Ian
 1991 *Homosexuality, Society and the State in Mexico.* Toronto: Canadian Gay Archives.
Manalansan, Martin F. IV
 1990 Tolerance or struggle: male homosexuality in the Philippines. Paper presented at the American Anthropological Association meetings in New Orleans.
 1991 Neo-colonial desire. *Society of Lesbian and Gay Anthropologists Newsletter* 13:37–40.
Manrique, Jaime
 1992 *Latin Moon in Manhattan.* New York: St. Martin's Press.
Marchant Lazcano, Jorge
 1983 Killing the lady of the Camellias. Translated by E. A. Lacey in Leyland (1983:122–26).
Martin, JoAnn
 1990 Motherhood and power: the production of a women's culture of politics in a Mexican community. *American Ethnologist* 17:470–90.
Miller, Neil
 1992 *Out in the World.* New York: Random House.
Monteagudo, Jesse G.
 1991 Miami, Florida. In *Hometowns.* John Preston, ed. Pp. 11–20. New York: Dutton.
Montero, Oscar
 1993 Before the parade passes by: Latino queers and national identity. *Radical America* 24(4):15–26.
Muñoz, Elías Miguel
 1984 *Los viajes de Orlando Cachumbambé.* Miami: Ediciones Universal.
 1987 *El discurso utopico de la sexualidad en Manuel Puig.* Madrid: Pliegos.
 1989 *Crazy Love.* Houston: Arte Publico Press.
 1991 *The Greatest Performance.* Houston: Arte Publico Press.
Murray, Stephen O.
 1984 *Social Theory, Homosexual Realities.* New York: Gay Academic Union (= *Gai Saber Monograph* 3).
 1987 Postscript. In *Male Homosexuality in Central and South America.* Pp. 192–99. New York: Gay Academic Union (= *Gai Saber Monograph* 5).
 1991 Sleeping with natives as a source of data. [Review of Itiel (1991).] *Publications of the Society of Lesbian and Gay Anthropologists Newsletter* 13: 49–51.
 1994 Subordinating native cosmologies to the empire of gender. *Current Anthropology* 35:59–61.
 1995 Male homosexuality in Guatemala: possible insights and certain confusions from obtaining data by sleeping with the natives. To appear in *Lesbian and Gay Ethnography.* E. Lewin and W. Leap, eds. Urbana: University of Illinois Press.
Parker, Richard G.
 1987 AIDS in urban Brazil. *Medical Anthropology Quarterly* 1:155–75.

1991 *Bodies, Pleasures, and Passions: Sexual Culture in Contemporary Brazil.* Boston: Beacon.
Penteado, Darcy
1979 Snow White revisited. Translated by Erskine Lane in Leyland (1979: 237–45).
1983 Part-time hustler. Translated by E. A. Lacey in Leyland (1983:241– 44).
Phillips, Herbert P.
1987 *Modern Thai Literature with an Ethnographic Interpretation.* Honolulu: University of Hawaii Press.
Puig, Manuel
1976 *El Beso de la Mujer Arana.* Barcelona: Seix Barral. Translated by Thomas Colchie as *The Kiss of the Spider Woman.* New York: Knopf, 1979.
1983 Classical Farrah. Translated by E. A. Lacey in Leyland (1983:75–76).
Rechy, John
1967 *Numbers.* New York: Grove Press.
Reinhardt, Karl J.
1981 The image of gays in Chicano prose fiction. *Explorations in Ethnic Studies* 4(2):41–55. (Reprinted in this volume.)
Ribondi, Alexandre
1983 The blue crime. Translated by E. A. Lacey in Leyland (1983:331–42).
Rogers, Susan C.
1975 Female forms of power and the myth of male dominance: a model of female/male interaction in peasant society. *American Ethnologist* 2: 727–56.
Salas, Luis
1979 *Social Control and Deviance in Cuba.* New York: Praeger.
Schifter Sikora, Jacobo
1990 *La formación de una contracultura: homosexualismo y sida en Costa Rica.* San José, Costa Rica: Guayacán.
Schifter Sikora, Jacobo, and Johnny Madrigal Pana.
1992 *Hombres que Aman Hombres.* San José: Ediciones Ilep-SIDA.
Schmitt, Arno
1985 *Kleine Schriften zu zwisemchmännlicher Sexualität und Erotik in der muslimischen Gesellschaft.* Berlin: Schmitt.
Schmitt, Arno, and Jehoeda Sofer
1992 *Sexuality and Eroticism Among Males in Moslem Societies.* Binghamton, NY: Harrington Park Press.
Silva, Aguinaldo
1979 [1977] Greek love. Translated by Erskine Lane. In Leyland (1979:190– 218).
Smith, Bruce R.
1991 *Homosexual Desire in Shakespeare's England: A Cultural Poetics.* Chicago: University of Chicago Press.
Soto, Francisco
1991 Reinaldo Arenas's literary legacy. *Christopher Street* 156:12–16.

Taylor, William B.
    1987 The Virgin of Guadalupe in New Spain: an inquiry into the social
    history of Marian devotion. *American Ethnologist* 14:9–33.
Tierno Galván, Enrique
    1961 Los toros, acontecimiento nacional. In *Desde el Espectáculo a la Trivi-
    lización*. Pp. 53–77. Madrid: Taurus.
Wikan, Unni
    1984 Shame and honour: a contestable pair. *Man* 19:635–52.
Zapata, Luis
    1979 *Los Aventuras, Descenturas y Sueños de Adonis García*. México: Grijalbo.
    Translated by E. A. Lacey as *Adonis García*. San Francisco: Gay Sunshine
    Press, 1981.
    1983 My deep dark pain is love. Translated by E. A. Lacey in Leyland
    (1983:89–97).
    1985 *En Jirones*. México: Posada.
    1990 *De Cuerpo Entero*. México: Ediciones Corunda.

4

🌿

"Homosexual Occupations"
in Mesoamerica?*

Stephen O. Murray

Paradoxically, having rejected "role" as a heuristic category in the sociology of homosexuality (Whitam 1977), Whitam and his collaborators (Whitam and Dizon 1979; Whitam and Mathy 1986) propounded homosexual occupational roles. They apparently regard occupational position as genetically determined by whatever determines sexual desire rather than being products of occupational "choice" and the vicissitudes of job opportunities, job discrimination, and the availability of information about possible jobs. They marshaled data from a series of Iberian-influenced cultures (Phoenix, Arizona; São Paulo, Brazil; Guatemala City; and Cebu City in the Philippines) to proclaim the universality of homosexuality as a predictive variable for non-sexual social behavior, including occupational position (and preference?).

Even in this biased sample of locales, the representativeness of Whitam's samples is questionable. Since I did fieldwork in Mesoamerican capitals in the late 1970s at about the same time Whitam was doing research in one of them (Guatemala City), I was surprised by the claims Whitam and Mathy (1986) made about stereotypical occupational concentrations. They claimed that "social scientists have often assumed, presumably out of egalitarian motivation, that the occupational interests of homosexuals are identical to those of heterosexuals,"—citing novelist Gore Vidal, rather than any social scientists (pp. 84–85). After

*Reprinted with permission from the *Journal of Homosexuality* 21:57–64. Haworth Press, 1991. An earlier version of this paper was presented at the 1987 annual meetings of the American Sociological Association in Chicago. The author gratefully acknowledges helpful criticisms from Manuel Arboleda, the late Phil Blumstein, Hubert Kennedy, and Fred Whitam.

noting that many men who are hairdressers or interior designers are homosexual, they produce the non sequitur, "While such occupations are frequently dismissed by social scientists as stereotypes, it is assumed in homosexual circles that hairdressers and interior decorators are a legitimate part of the homosexual world" (p. 85). Even if there were some exemplifications of the stereotyping social scientists rejecting hairdressers and interior decorators, skepticism about the ubiquity or necessity of cross-gender occupations for those engaged in and/or identified with homosexuality would remain justifiable. It is Whitam and Mathy (1986) who mistook a part for the whole. Again, they failed to list any examples of "social scientists [who] deny that homosexual hairdressers and decorators exist in greater frequency within the homosexual subculture than within the heterosexual society" (p. 86). Their positive data were as unconvincing as the strawmen they manufactured.[1] They enumerated the occupational distributions at three "probably typical" gay male parties in the United States—in which one of 42 men was an interior designer, and none was a hairdresser. They did not present any actual data on the occupational distribution of their Guatemalan sample.

Although my research did not focus on occupational distributions (see Murray 1980), data recoverable from my fieldnotes permit identification of the occupations of thirty-two men reporting a homosexual preference—as many as Whitam's samples from three of four societies. Except for three men whom I met in Pandora's Box, a gay disco in Guatemala City, my sample was drawn to me in Guatemala's purportedly "cruisiest" park (Central) or several Mexico City areas widely known as places to meet men. So far as I could tell, there was no folk model of whether bearded *norteamericanos* are *activo* or *pasivo*. Many of those with whom I spoke had never spoken to one before: especially in the Guatemalan park, circa 1979, nocturnal appearance of a solitary

---

1. Subsequent to the publication of Whitam and Mathy (1986), Neuringer (1989) challenged any disproportionate homosexual concentration in one occupation on which Whitam and Dizon (1979) had focused: actors. Kinsey et al. (1948:361) reported lower incidence of homosexuality among United States white men employed as skilled labor (e.g., bakers, barbers, cooks, as well as bricklayers, plumbers and welders) than among those employed in lower white-collar (often clerical) jobs, or in semi-skilled jobs (e.g., bartenders, blacksmiths, firemen, policemen, and truck drivers). The incidence was highest among day laborers. Kinsey et al. (1948:77–79) laid out their occupational status categories. Today the schema applies better to Latin America than to the United States.

norteamericano was a novelty. I think that the novelty was sufficient to draw more men into conversation than just those who found my "type" sexually attractive. Given the conventional cultural wisdom that *activos* travel singly to such locales (see Arboleda 1987:108), however, there is reason to suspect that those who approached me presumed (before asking "¿Eres activo o pasivo?") me to be an *activo*. Thus, my sample, like Whitam's, might be biased towards *pasivos* (who took the risk of rejection in making approaches).

I encountered one *activo* hustler and one effeminate *pasivo* designer. The hairdresser and ballet dancer in my sample did not seem to be notably effeminate or narcissistic. Both were *internacional* (versatile) in their sexual repertoire. Just as those in the stereotypically gay occupations were not necessarily *pasivo,* those in the stereotypically masculine occupations (truck driver, telephone lineman, construction worker) were not necessarily *activo*. Indeed, although two of the latter were married (in contrast to none of those in the stereotypically gay occupations), two labeled themselves as *pasivo,* and one as *activo,* although all four engaged in at least occasional *pasivo* sexual behavior.

In less markedly homosexual occupational niches were two accountants, an art curator, two hotel clerks, two store clerks, a priest and a travel agent. These are occupations in which perhaps a disproportionate percentage of men are gay in North America. Most of the men who mentioned their occupation to me, however, engaged in ones not particularly noted for concentrations of homosexual men. These included one agronomist, a bus driver, a truck driver, a civil engineer, an oilfield engineer, two government middle managers, a professor of geology, a geography student, a medical student, two bank workers (one in credit, one in investment appraisal), a telephone lineman, two construction workers, two business owners (a bookstore and an import-export firm, not the most macho of enterprises, admittedly), and a lawyer.

Within my coding of a trichotomy of effeminate, disproportionately homosexual, and masculine occupations, four times more homosexual men worked in "masculine" occupations than in "effeminate" ones. If one substitutes the highly aggregated codings of official occupational categories, there are three in which substantially higher percentages of employed women than men are concentrated: clerical, sales, and service workers. 1981 data from Guatemala report that 52.3 percent of employed women work in these three categories, in contrast to 9.5 percent of employed men, or 62.1 percent of the classified non-agricultural female workers in contrast to 26.8 percent of the males (Wilkie, Lorey and Ochoa 1988: Table 1313). With this blunt indicator (and including the ballet dancer and the designer in "service") fourteen (41 percent) of the homosexually involved Guatemaltecos are in "feminine occupations."[2] Only 10 percent of this sample of men are in "production and related workers, transport equipment operators and laborers," whereas 60 percent of the Guatemalan men not working in agriculture (or unclassified) are. Perhaps there is a sense in which this occupational category is more masculine (*duro*—hard) than the professional and administrative categories (nearly half the sample, in contrast to 13 percent of Guatemalan non-agricultural workers), but it seems to me that this disparity is a function more of class bias in my non-random urban sample than a function of sexual orientation.

I think that these data suffice to undercut Whitam's view of any necessary connection between sexual orientation and occupation. I am far from denying that there are occupations with disproportionate numbers of men with homosexual preference. Indeed, it is the intermediate category in this coding. However, I do not think there need be any recourse to genetics,[3] or even to "gay sensibility" to explain homosexual concentrations in occupational slots. This is especially so for occupations in which few succeed in securing an income sufficient to support a family, especially the performing arts (see Ashworth and Walker [1972] for this structural explanation). In Guatemala, as in the United States, working in the prototypically masculine occupation of construction worker more or less requires knowing someone to get into the union or hired by a patron (foreman or employer) at a non-unionized site. Obtaining a position in what hairdressers consider a good salon similarly depends upon personal sponsorship from inside. In any field, there is routine insider trading of information about job vacancies and even

---

2. United States data are available on the sex composition of some more specific occupations. For instance, in 1986, 89 percent of hairdressers were women, and 69 percent of sales workers. At the other extreme, 4 percent of truck drivers, 6 percent of engineers, 18 percent of lawyers and physicians were women (United States Bureau of Labor Statistics 1987; I can safely add o percent of Catholic priests). Insofar as people conceive of "homosexual occupations" as kinds of "women's work," and there is some parallel between sex distributions in the United States and in Guatemala, these rates fit the order of my assignment of the sample's occupations into masculine, less masculine, and feminine categories.

3. There are other kinds of biology besides genetics. Ecology is one other important perspective for social science work dealing with homosexuality. See, for instance, Lee (1979).

secrecy about them (Spector 1973; Granovetter 1974; Wegener 1989, 1991). Therefore, any concentration (of any category of employees) is likely to be replicated and reinforced over time. That is, getting jobs for those whom one knows best and with whom one most wants to work is a common motivation. Those who possess job information transmit it first to their intimates. Moreover, they are likely to "put in a good word" for them as well (Murray, Rankin, and Magill 1981a, b).

Furthermore, there is discrimination against persons viewed as homosexual and/or gender-deviant.[4] Havens or niches developing over time need not reflect genetically intrinsic occupational correlates of homosexuality, as Whitam and Mathy (1986) suppose.[5] They are not unaware that not everyone secures the kind of job s/he wants, noting, "Some ambitions, given the nature of the economic, educational, and stratification structures of these countries, are unlikely to be fulfilled" (p. 88). Some ambitions, childhood or adult, are more impossible than others. There is certainly no reason to suppose that discrimination against those known as homosexuals is invariant from occupation to occupation, firm to firm, or workplace to workplace within a company. Similarly, there is no reason to suppose that information about job openings spreads randomly. Specific concentration in service sectors may also stem from more meritocratic (i.e., less paternalistic) evaluation of candidates than in other occupational sectors.

As I discussed in more detail in the previous chapter, although in the view of self-identified Latino *pasivos,* "real men" *(hombres)* are indifferent to the sex of the orifice into which they thrust, "the sexually omnivorous *hombre* who doesn't have any preference in 'object choice'—the man who 'fucks anything that moves'—is more a *maricón* fantasy than a plausible empirical observation" of Latin American men. Latino men who assert that they have never engaged in homosexuality do not share this *maricón* fantasy. Indeed, those I have asked consider suspect the masculinity of men who make sexual use of *maricones.* Economic advan-

---

4. See Bell and Weinberg (1978); Levine (1979); Adam (1982); Levine and Leonard (1984); Salas (1979:160–61, 172); Schneider (1987).

5. Even were one to take Whitam and Mathy's (1986:101; also see Whitam and Dizon 1979:141–47) childhood recollection data as free of retrospective bias and knowledge of social stereotypes (especially by those reporting themselves to be heterosexual), and as a valid indicator of something important to adult occupation, a "universal" drive to be a hairdresser seems to vary substantially among their transvestitic homosexuals—from 22 percent in Phoenix to 80 percent in Cebu.

tages (stressed by Whitam and Mathy 1986:134–35) do not entirely ameliorate this suspicion, but it is certainly a major prop to maintaining a view of one's self as not implicated by homosexual behavior in private, as in other cultures.[6] Whitam and Mathy (1986) take the *pasivo's* fantasy of *activos* as reality, and do not explore problematic self-conceptions of *activos entendidos,* at least some of whom do express a preference for sex with men, or of the gay *internacionales.*

Like many observers of many cultures, Whitam and Mathy (1986) over-identify with the views of one group that provided them information, and assume that others share these views. Specifically, I would suggest that Whitam has been over-influenced by the most visible (hence most easily found) transvestitic homosexuals and reproduces rather than analyzes their sexual ideology. Anyone who labels himself a *loca* (literally, crazy one) is deviant within a Latin American *ambiente* (the world of those in the know about homosexuality, *los entendidos*), as well as in straight *(buga)* society. There are clearly Mesoamerican men who consider themselves homosexual, while differentiating themselves from the flamboyant *locas. Locas* are highly stigmatized within *de ambiente,* as well as within the majority society. Whitam has done nothing to establish that homosexuality matters in self-definition only to transvestitic homosexuals in Guatemala (or to their analogs elsewhere). Rather, he assumes this, and confines his sample to *las locas,* excluding from consideration those who present themselves as *activo* in public (whatever they may do in private). He thus over-estimates the relationship between male homosexuality and effeminacy in cultures with a complex collusion by *pasivos* to maintain the social masculinity—heterosexuality even—of their partners. This also reinforces the gender idiom for conceiving of sexuality in Latino culture, and, by the time Whitam finishes, "universally."

It seems to me that it is for the natives to label themselves *gay* or *entendido*, not for the researcher to restrict the sample to *pasivos* and then conclude that only *pasivos* consider homosexual desire a salient part of their self-identity. In a personal communication (August 1987) Whitam wrote, "My work in Guatemala is based on people with a homosexual orientation." It is not clear how he assessed the latter, since, as he also noted, quite correctly,

---

6. See Reiss (1961) and Grube (1987, 1990) on Anglo North America; Allyn and Collins (1988) and Jackson (1989) on Thailand; Whitam (1992) on the Philippines.

Straight men will say "I'm *activo*," meaning they are straight and will fuck a man. Gay men may also say "I'm *activo*," meaning they are gay, but like to fuck. In conversation these meanings are implicit, so when a guy says "I'm *activo*," you cannot tell from this what his sexual orientation is.

Although it is conceivable that some of my informants simulated a sexual orientation they did not have, I know that their sexual repertoires included *pasivo* behavior (just as that of most of the self-identified *pasivos* in my sample included *activo* sexual behavior).[7] This would seem to exclude the *activos* in my sample from Whitam's category "straight *activo*, who fucks men but does not get fucked." Although my sample is clearly not random either, I believe that it is drawn from the population of gay-identified Mesoamericans without the bias of excluding gay-identified *activos*. Obviously, neither of these small, opportunistic samples offers solid ground for generalizations about occupational frequencies of the entire population of homosexually involved men in Guatemala and México (the cities, let alone the countries). Nevertheless, the divergent findings (and suggested sampling bias) undercut confidence in Whitam's posited pre-social connection between homosexuality and occupation.

References

Allyn, Eric, and John P. Collins
    1988 *Men of Thailand*. San Francisco: Bua Luang.
Adam, Barry D.
    1981 Stigma and employability. *Canadian Review of Sociology and Anthropology* 18:216–21.
Arboleda G, Manuel.
    1987 Social attitudes and sexual variance in Lima. In Murray (1987). (Revised version in this volume.)
Ashworth A. E., and W. M. Walker
    1972 Social structure and homosexuality. *British Journal of Sociology* 23: 146–58.
Bell, Alan, and Martin S. Weinberg
    1978 *Homosexualities*. New York: Simon & Schuster.

---

7. Caution is in order for extrapolating what people try with aliens to what they usually do with fellow natives. See Murray (1995).

Granovetter, Mark S.
  1974 *Getting a Job*. Cambridge, MA: Harvard University Press.
Grube, John
  1987 Mentors and protégés in the homophile world. Paper presented at the
         Homosexuality/Which Homosexuality? Conference in Amsterdam.
  1990 Natives and settlers: an ethnographic note on early interaction of older
         homosexual men with younger gay liberationists. *Journal of Homosexuality*
         20:119–35.
Jackson, Peter A.
  1989 *Male Homosexuality in Thailand*. Amsterdam: Global Academic Pub-
         lishers.
Kinsey, Alfred C., Wardell B. Pomeroy, and Clyde E. Martin
  1948 *Sexual Behavior in the Human Male*. Philadelphia: W. B. Saunders
         Company.
Lee, J. A.
  1979 The gay connection. *Urban Life* 8:175–98.
Levine, Martin P.
  1979 Employment discrimination against gay men. *International Review of
         Modern Sociology* 9:151–63.
Levine, Martin P., and Robin Leonard
  1984 Discrimination against lesbians in the work force. *Signs* 8:700–710.
Murray, Stephen O.
  1980 Lexical and institutional elaboration: the 'species homosexual' in Gua-
         temala. *Anthropological Linguistics* 22:177–86.
  1987 *Male Homosexuality in Central and South America*. New York: Gay Aca-
         demic Union.
  1995 Male homosexuality in Guatemala. To appear in *Lesbian and Gay Eth-
         nography*. Ellen Lewin and William Leap, eds. Urbana: University of Illi-
         nois Press.
Murray, Stephen O., Joseph H. Rankin, and Dennis W. Magill
  1981a Strong ties and academic jobs. *Sociology of Work and Occupations* 8:119–36.
  1981b Informelle Rationalität in wissenschaftlichen Gemeinschaften. In *Der
         Wissenschaftler und das Irrationale*. Vol. 2. Hans-Petter Duerr, ed. Pp. 219–
         25. Frankfurt/m: Syndikat.
Neuringer, O.
  1989 On the question of homosexuality in actors. *Archives of Sexual Behavior*
         18:523–29.
Reiss, Albert J.
  1961 The social integration of 'queers' and 'peers.' *Social Problems* 9:102–20.
Salas, Luis
  1979 *Social Control and Deviance in Cuba*. New York: Praeger.
Schneider, Beth E.
  1987 Coming out at work. *Work and Occupations* 15:463–87.
Spector, Malcolm
  1973 Secrecy in job seeking among government attorneys. *Urban Life and
         Culture* 2:211–29.

United States Bureau of Labor Statistics

1987   *Employment and Earnings.* Washington, D. C.: Government Printing Office.

Wegener, Bernd.

1989   Soziale Verwandschaften em Karrierprogress. *Kölner Zeitschrift fur Soziologie* 41:270–97.

1991   Job mobility and social ties. *American Sociological Review* 56:60–71.

Whitam, Frederick J.

1977   The homosexual role revisited. *Journal of Sex Research* 13:1–11.

1992   Bayot and callboy: heterosexual/homosexual relations in the Philippines. In *Oceanic Homosexualities.* Stephen O. Murray, ed. Pp. 231–48. New York: Garland.

Whitam, Frederick J., and Mary-Jo Dizon

1979   Occupational choice and sexual orientation in cross-cultural perspective. *International Review of Modern Sociology* 9:137–49.

Whitam, Frederick J., and Robin Mathy

1986   *Male Homosexuality in Four Societies.* New York: Praeger.

Wilkie, J. W., Lorey, B. E., and Ochoa, E.

1988   *Statistical Abstract of Latin America, Volume 26.* Los Angeles: UCLA Latin America Center.

5

❦

Legends, Syncretism, and Continuing Echoes of Homosexuality from Pre-Columbian and Colonial México*

Clark L. Taylor

This chapter provides a sample of the early historical chronicles, folklore and traditions that Mexicans draw upon to explain and understand contemporary values and attitudes concerning male homosexuality. This mosaic of information does not pretend to recover the past as it really was. Most information on homosexuality, its meaning and social structuring either went unrecorded, or was lost, destroyed, distorted, or suppressed. However, though we may never know much about the true nature of homosexuality in early México, the few data and folk traditions which are "remembered" are extremely important. Factual or not, they come together to form a persistent Mexican viewpoint of homosexuality. Ties to the past and to tradition have tremendous importance for Mexicans, a significance that is often difficult for those outside the culture to understand. What they consider tradition (regardless of historical warrant) shapes their lives and the meaning of their conduct. In this chapter I have tried to use this typically Mexican approach to highlight the ways in which ties to the past come together to influence attitudes about homosexuality today.

PreColumbian México

The Setting

At the point of European contact, the area we now call México (along with parts of Guatemala and Honduras) was inhabited by numerous di-

---

*The material presented in the first two sections here draws upon my 1978 Ph.D. dissertation, *El Ambiente: Male Homosexual Social Life in Mexico City*. Research for it was

verse societies. Despite variations between cultures of the region—Maya, Zapotec, Mexica (Nahuatl-speakers, notably Aztecs) and others—there were also important similarities: stone cities, highways, ceremonial pyramids, advanced agricultural and hydraulic systems, considerable social stratification, elaborate communication systems, and a very sophisticated calendar. These resemblances have led anthropologists to refer to the region as a single culture area: Mesoamerica.

When the Spaniards arrived early in the 16th century, some parts of Mesoamerica—particularly the eastern lowlands—were in a state of urban decline. However, the Central Highlands of México were experiencing a cultural florescence. In the Valley of México, the Aztecs lived in urban centers such as Texcoco, Tlatelolco, and México Tenochitlán (all now part of the federal district). Dating back to the founding of Teotihuacan, about 300 B.C., large-scale urban living characterized the central valley. At the time of the conquest, the largest Aztec city, México Tenochitlán, is said to have been surpassed in size only by Paris (Hardoy 1973:154–62).

From the Valley of México, the Aztecs politically dominated most of Mesoamerica and extracted a heavy tribute of raw materials, finished products, slaves and sacrificial victims. However, they usually allowed a considerable degree of home rule and the continuance of local traditions—including sexual practices—within their empire. Indigenous pluralism persists: a rich diversity of customs and attitudes (including attitudes about sexuality) still exists today.

Homosexual Eroticism

The Aztecs exhibited a profound duality in their approach to sexual behavior. They held public rituals which were at times very erotic, but they were extremely prudish in everyday life. As Quesada (1974:9) wrote of eroticism in Aztec religion: "To let oneself go orgiastically in eroticism at the level of ritual was to bring oneself close to the deities of love, but in everyday life, it was to choose the path of an early old age and impotence." This type of extreme dualism between ritual life and ordinary life was very typical of the Aztecs and must be kept in mind in considering their attitudes toward homosexuality.

In their pantheon, the Mexicans worshipped a deity, Xochiquetzal (feathered flower of the maguey), who was the goddess of non-pro-

made possible by grants from the Department of Anthropology and Center for Latin American Studies at the University of California, Berkeley and the Tinker Foundation.

creative love and sexuality. Since the juice of the maguey plant was fermented to make pulque (the native beer) the deity's name alluded to the mind- and mood-altering ability of Xochiquetzal, specifically to her power to make humans drunk with passion, desire, and love.

Originally the consort of Tonacatecutli, a creator god, Xochiquetzal lived in the heaven of Tamaoanchan, where she gave birth to all human-kind. However, subsequently she was abducted by Tezcatlipoca, a war god, and raped. This event mystically redefined her character from the goddess of procreative love to the goddess of non-reproductive activities (Quesada 1974:8; Seler 1902:188–89).

Aztec deities often had dualistic aspects, such as male and female, and good and evil. Thus, Xochiquetzal was male and female at the same time, and in her male aspect (called Xochipilli), s/he was worshipped as the deity of male homosexuality and male prostitution. In Xochi-quetzal's positive aspect, s/he was the deity of loving relationships and the god/dess of artistic creativity; it was said that non-reproductive love was like a piece of art—beautiful and unique.

In her dualistic opposite, as the deity of sexual destruction, s/he incited lust and rape, and inflicted people with venereal disease and piles. At the same time, in yet another aspect, Xochiquetzal/Xochipilli was known as Tlazolteotl (the Divine Eater of Filth) a deity of great compassion to whom the Aztecs said their last confession at death. Because s/he had incited the people to lust and sexual sin, s/he was the one who could take away their guilt, i.e., eat their filth (Seler 1902:189; Requena 1945:44–46; Soustelle 1961:193).

Because of Xochiquetzal's name, homosexuality was often associated with flowers. For example, one name for both male and female homo-sexuals was *xochihuan*, literally "flower owner" and the verb *te-xocihuia* (to use flowers on someone) meant "to convert someone to homosex-uality" (Kimball 1993:11).[1]

There were many other words for homosexuality, but one—*cuiloni*—is still in use today. It had/has a wider meaning than "homosexual," something like "queer." It was applied to people caught having sex in private, cowards, thieves and others under Xochiquetzal's malevolent influence. The term was even used to insult gods. Kimball points out that Tezcatilpoca, the war god who raped Xochiquetzal, was called *Cui i lonpole* (O great faggot) and *Cui i lontepole* (O faggot penis) for such

---

1. To bolster the point Kimball calls attention to two homosexual males depicted with a flower growing between them in the Florentine Code.

misdeeds in his aspect as the trickster as letting a warrior's prisoners escape (p. 19).

In a partly mythical, partly historical account of their past, the Aztecs asserted that there had been four worlds before their own and that the world immediately preceding the present was one of much homosexuality. This "fourth world," called "the Age of Flowers, of Xochiquetzal," may refer to the Toltec empire. The Toltecs were living in the Valley of México when the Aztecs arrived, and were related to the Aztecs by language and custom. The Aztecs conquered them around 1050 and forced them to move south. Aztecs believed that the fourth world was destroyed by the gods because the people supposedly gave up the "manly virtues of warfare, administration and wisdom," and pursued the "easy, soft life of sodomy, perversion, the Dance of the Flowers, and the worship of Xochiquetzal" (Requena 1945:46).

Other than the enigmatic "Dance of the Flowers," the behavior of the Aztecs seem to have found so horrible was the spread of "perversions," including homosexual life, into secular domains where only sobriety, decorous behavior and restrained, procreative marital sex were allowed. While the Toltecs may have permitted the "vices" listed in the text above to flourish, it is also likely that the Aztecs simply attributed these characteristics to the Toltecs, since they tended to call all conquered people *cuiloni*.

Another possibility is that, as legend has it, the barbarous Aztecs, an austere hoard of hunters and gatherers, were scandalized when they first entered the Valley of México and discovered the opulent, urban lifestyle of the Toltecs. If this was the case, their course of reform was strange, since they drove the Toltecs out of their homes, expropriated their wealth, and made slaves from the cultures they conquered in order to support even more luxurious cities.

Other evidence that the "Fourth World" refers to the empire of the Toltecs is a similar statement referring to Toltec invaders in the historical records of the Maya in Yucatan. The writings of the Chilam Balam of Chumayel state, for example, "Their hearts are submerged, they are shrouded beneath the weight of the sins of the flesh. Abundant are the sodomites and abundant the homosexuality of the followers of Naxcit and his companions . . ." (Requena 1945:47).[2] The Maya of the Yucatan

---

2. At first glance, the reference to "sodomy" and "homosexuality" may seem redundant. However, sodomy between men and women is a common form of birth control in México. To be going steady in Mexican heterosexual slang is to be *enculado* or "entwined by the anus." Therefore, the quotation could be referring to Mexican sexual rites in general as well as to homosexual behavior.

peninsula held large private sexual parties, which included homosexuality. However, according to J. Eric Thompson (1966:113–27), a leading Maya scholar, they were aghast at the public sexual rites of their Toltec conquerors. To bolster this interpretation, Roys (1967:83–85) notes that "Naxcit" was one of the Mexican names for Quetzalcoatl—the mythical conqueror of the Maya in the 11th century, high priest of the Toltec Mexican dynasty of Chichen Itza, and a major Highland Mexican deity. Furthermore, Thompson (1970:46) relates, "as to the Itza who moved from Chichen Itza to Lake Peten [Guatemala], the missionary Avedano y Loyola . . . appears to accuse them of widespread homosexuality."

It is wise to be leery of early missionary and traveler accounts of sexual behavior, since they tended to attribute "sodomy" and a long list of other vices to every native culture (Keen 1971). However, along with fabulous tales which came from the New World, there are very good accounts that have held up through time. Bernal Diaz del Castillo, Hernán Cortes, Lopez de Gomara and Bernardo Sahagún are outstanding examples of this latter kind. Below are some of their observations.

In the Yucatan, Diaz del Castillo noted, "There were clay idols made of pottery, with the faces of demons or women and other evil figures that showed Indians committing acts of sodomy with each other" (Idell 1956:21), and de Gomara wrote, "Among some trees, we came upon an idol of gold and many of clay; formed in the position of two men mounted one over the other in the act of sodomy" (Requena 1945:45).

As already noted, the Aztecs allowed the people they conquered to maintain their own customs. Thus, although the Aztecs were publicly sexually exuberant and privately prudish, their subjects (and tributaries) varied greatly in their sexual customs—as the Maya example illustrates. In some Mesoamerican cultures, it appears homosexuality was quite prominent. For example, the area that is now the state of Vera Cruz was very well known for this activity. When Castillo reached Vera Cruz with Cortes, he wrote of the native priests, "the sons of chiefs, they did not take women, but followed the bad practices of sodomy" (Idell 1956:87). When the conquistadors reached Cempoala, near the present city of Vera Cruz, Cortes felt compelled to make a speech in which he stated, "Give up your sodomy and all your other evil practices, for so commands Our Lord God . . ." (quoted in Idell 1956:8). As well, Cortes wrote his sovereign, the Hapsburg Emperor Carlos V: "We know and have been informed without room for doubt that all (Veracruzanos) practice the abominable sin of sodomy" (Morris 1928:25).

Lopez de Gomara wrote of the people living in the delta of the Rio

Panuco just north of Vera Cruz that they were "Grandisimos Putos" (totally "queer") holding public orgies in which huge numbers of men had sex together under the light of the full moon (Requena 1945:51). Diaz del Castillo wrote of the Indians in general, "Most of them were sodomites and especially those who lived along the coast and in the hot lands. . . . were dressed as women, boys went about to make money by this diabolical and abominable vice" (Idell 1956:87).

As pointed out in the beginning, it would be folly to accept all the statements about homosexuals at face value. For example, Spaniards of the time also claimed that homosexuality had been introduced into Spain by the Moors (Lea 1907:363); and it attributed sodomy to new enemies as well. It would also be unwise to reject all the Spaniards' statements, especially when there is corroborating evidence. For example, Scholes and Roys (1948:91) note that a place where Chontal Mayas of Campeche defeated a raiding band of Mexicans was named "Cuylonemiquia," which means "where we killed the Mexican homosexuals." Further, quoting Blom and La Farge, they indicate the place may be the town of Cuilonia (literally, "the place of the homosexuals"), which was once an Aztec garrison. Quite possibly, the Chontal Maya were as scandalized by public Aztec orgiastic rituals as they were by those of the Toltecs. However, it is also possible that there were a lot of *cuiloni* going on in the Mexican garrison that had nothing to do with rituals.

How rigorously Aztecs enforced their prohibitions against private homosexual behavior is impossible to know. Kimball (1993:17–18) interprets the Florentine Codex as indicating that there was a relatively obvious homosexual subculture, since one method of mutual identification, chewing a particular gum, "was commonly known to the non-homosexual population." Considering the highly visible homosexual world of the United States, even in states with draconian sodomy laws, it would be ethnocentric to conclude from Aztec laws that homosexual behavior did not occur. It could be that the Aztecs, like many people in the United States, tolerated homosexuality in private.

Relative tolerance of private homosexuality in a culture that strongly condemned this form of behavior would explain an enduring legend in México that says the Spaniards were more easily able to capture the Aztec emperor, Montezuma, because they sent a blond page to seduce him. When the emperor had fallen thoroughly in love, they threatened to separate the two if the emperor did not place himself in the hands of the Spaniards. While the Spaniards' allies, the Tlaxcalans asserted the story was true, the Spaniards denied it, and we will never know what really happened. However, the tale may help us to understand why the Aztecs, who were so blatant in public but puritanical in private, shouted "Cuiloni! Cuiloni!" ("Queer! Queer") from their canoes at the Spaniards during the "Noche Triste" (1 July 1520), when Cortes was forced to retreat from México City losing many soldiers (Novo 1972:43). The warriors' epithets, of course, may only have been another example of labeling one's enemies homosexual.

A very important source of Aztec society are the questionnaires gathered by Father Sahagún at the Colegio de Santa Cruz in Tlatelolco some thirty years after the conquest. Sahagún had established the college for Aztec nobility and intellectuals in an effort to create a Spanish-speaking, Christianized native elite to help govern the New World. Though the college failed, Sahagún's scholarly efforts to have the elite set down their previous customs and history furnish the best records we have about Aztec culture. The works affirm the duality already discussed and also throw light on a present-day custom called the *albur*. This is a caustic (though sometimes comical) anti-homosexual verbal duel that was also common among the Aztecs (Edmonson 1974:14). Octavio Paz, one of México's most celebrated contemporary writers described contemporary albur as follows:

> Each of the speakers tried to humiliate his adversary with verbal traps and ingenious linguistic combinations, and the loser is the person who cannot think of a comeback, who has to swallow his opponent's jibes. These jibes are full of aggressive sexual allusions; the loser is possessed, is violated, by the winner, and the spectators laugh and sneer at him. [1961:39–40]

While I have said the Aztecs were prudish in their sex lives outside of ritual activities, I have not really looked into the consequences of being caught having homosexual relations in private. Summarizing Torquemada, Sahagún and others, Bancroft (1886:585) stated that the Aztecs hanged people in México-Tenochitlán for homosexuality, while in nearby Texcoco, the "active" partner was "bound to a stake, completely covered with ashes and so left to die; the entrails of the passive agent were drawn out through his anus, he was then covered with ashes, and wood being added, the pile was ignited."

To summarize the material available for the time of the conquest, homosexuality played an important part in much of the religious life in México, and was commonly accepted in private life in many Mesoamerican cultures as well. However, the prevailing sentiment of the ruling Aztecs outside of ritual was one of sexual rigidity, prudishness, and heavy repression.

Colonial México

The Setting

In the opening years of the 16th century, the Spaniards discovered and conquered Mesoamerica. One of the most dramatic social changes which occurred was the evolution of Mestizo or "Ladino" culture. Miscegenation, acculturation and the melding of beliefs created a social milieu that was neither Spanish nor Indian but forms the core features of modern México.

The Spaniards held a moral viewpoint toward homosexuality which (aside from ritual) paralleled that of the Aztecs. Although homosexuality had been overt and popular in classical antiquity and persisted as such into the Middle Ages in spite of efforts by the Catholic Church and Spanish state to suppress it, Spanish values eventually became homophobic. After the Council of Lateran, in 1179, the Church's punishment for such acts was degradation or confinement for clerics, while Spanish secular punishment was castration and stoning. Then, in 1497, Ferdinand and Isabella decreed burning alive and confiscation of property "irrespective of the station of the culprit" (Lea 1907:362; Murray and Gerard 1984).

In México, after the conquest, all pagan rituals were banished and their rationale discredited. Mestizo culture came to exhibit a melding of Aztec attitudes towards private homosexuality and those of the Spaniards. Indeed, the former Aztec ritual tradition that celebrated homosexuality as communion with the gods was all but lost.

During early Colonial times, when Bishop Zumarraga was the Apostolic Inquisitor of México, "homosexuality, and particularly sodomy, was a prime concern for the Inquisition, and the processors (proceedings) leave no detail of the crime to the reader's imagination" (Greenleaf 1961:108). The usual penalties for homosexuality were "stiff fines, spiritual penances, public humiliation, and floggings." However, homosexuality was tried by the civil courts as well, from whence people were sentenced to the galleys or put to death (p. 132).[3]

---

3. Comparing the records of the Inquisition in different Spanish colonies reveals which sexual activities were most at variance in each instance. In México, though

Homosexual Social Life

At present, the only documents that give a glimpse of homosexual social life during the Colonial period are the records of court proceedings when homosexual scandals occurred. Of such events, a purge that took place in México City between 1656 and 1663 is the best known. An account of this purge is presented by Salvador Novo, México's City's late official historian and a leading intellectual figure of this century. Novo (1972:15) quotes from documents of the time:

> On Tuesday, November 5, 1658, at eleven in the morning, fifteen men were taken from the royal jail of this court; fourteen to be put to death by burning, and the remaining one, because he is a boy, was given two hundred lashes and sold to a brick layer for six years; all of them for having committed the sin of sodomy with one another over many years . . .

According to the court record, "they lived in this city and had nice homes in which they received one another and in which they called one another by the kind of names used in this city by prostitutes."[4] The leader of the group was a mulatto who dressed as an Indian and who used the name "Cotita de la Encarnacion." Cotita began his homosexual career at six years of age and was 40 at the time of his execution. Also executed were his lover, a Mestizo (who was 47), and another man, a Spaniard (very advanced in age), whose name was left blank in the records. The Spaniard was supposedly the facilitator of the group, and they called him "Senora la Grande"—a pun since *grande* means both "great" or "big" and "old." The Spaniard served as a messenger:

> Arranging one day for some and another day for others so that they would be prepared in advance to receive a visit; and after the feast, he put them in their rooms with one another to execute this sin with all levity. He, himself, had sex on all occasions, and at all times and places . . . [Novo 1972:15]

---

homosexuality was frequent, over all, polygamy was the most frequent purported sexual transgression.

4. It is impossible at present to say how long the use of "drag names" has been in practice in Western civilization. In México, they are often created by preceding the woman's name with *la* as in "la Magdalena." This is the form used to denote prostitutes and it is also a way to show deference as in "la Virgin de Guadalupe." Drag names in Mexico are called *Nombres de Batalla* —"battle names."

Referring to the court proceedings, Novo further relates that "Senora la Grande" was considered incorrigible. Once during the case, he was sentenced to two hundred lashes for false testimony. Because of his advanced age, the wife of the Viceroy—then the Duke of Albuquerque—took pity on him and had him sent to the Hospital del Amor de Dios; however, as a result of his amorous adventures with the other patients, he was returned to the courts to finish his trial and be burned with the rest.

Whereas heretics and Jews were burned in the Alameda, now a park near the center of México City, homosexuals were burned in a special burning ground in another part of the city, San Lázaro, because homosexuality was not a form of heresy and thus fell into an ambiguous category of offenses. Therefore, the group was marched to San Lázaro where the officials first garroted them, starting with Cotita de la Encarnacion, and "were done with strangling all of them at eight o'clock that night . . . then they set them afire." Novo states that several hundred people came from the city to watch the event. It should be noted that strangling the victims before burning them was considered an act of mercy. Burning was such terrible agony that it was feared that the prisoners would forsake their faith in God and thus lose their immortal souls. Though the officials were dressed differently from the Aztecs of old, spoke a different language, and worshipped a different god, the public spectacle which transpired was a striking example of cultural melding, or "syncretism" as it is called in anthropology. As Guzmán (1971:44–49) put it:

> Both the Spaniards and the Aztecs, conquering peoples, pursued the ideal of absolute machismo and condemned its antithesis, effeminacy, to a point where the Aztecs tortured effeminate homosexuals. On the other hand, among the less militaristic peoples, it was amply tolerated. The Mexican Mestizo identifies with the Spaniards or with the Aztecs, but never with the "weak" people, or sodomites, and from this, perhaps, comes the cult of machismo and its inevitable counterpart, a permanent fear of becoming homosexual.

Further details of the purge and attitudes of the day are contained in a letter dated 22 August 1662, from the Mexican Inquisition to superiors in Spain, noting that punishments dealt out by the civil government had been ineffective and asking for authority to intervene (after Zumarraga's time, the Mexican Inquisition had been instructed to prosecute only heretics and Jews). The Inquisitors, Doctor don Pedro Medina Rico and Licenciado don Juan de Ortega Montanes wrote:

Very Sovereign Lord: With much pain and sorrow, we must inform Your Highness of the frequency with which the crime of
homosexuality is committed in this city and land, where it seems
that the men, satiated in their sensual appetite for women, go
looking for one another, unrefrained by punishment or fear. For
even though fourteen or fifteen were executed, and another hundred indicted only three or four years ago, during the administration of the Duke of Albuquerque, we have discovered a great
number of people, primarily clergy, who engage in homosexuality
and have passed into bestiality. [Medina 1905:321]

To fortify their request, the Inquisitors cited a list of confessions from
prisoners in the Inquisition's dungeons. One of the more novel confessions is that of Alberto Henriquez, a Franciscan priest, who said he had
sexual relations with "forty men, more or less; three or four mules, and
two or three chickens" (Medina 1905:322).

The purge seems to have ended when the Superiors in Spain wrote
back to México that they did not have papal authority to grant the
jurisdiction the Mexican Holy Office requested, and that the Inquisitors were "not to become involved in these matters or to enter into any
litigation concerning them" (Medina 1905:322).

The End of the Colonial Era

Mexican independence from Spain in 1821 brought an end to the
Inquisition and the kind of homosexual oppression described above.
The intellectual influence of the French Revolution and the brief French
occupation of México (1862–67) resulted in the adoption of the Napoleonic Code. This meant that sexual conduct in private between adults,
whatever their gender, ceased to be a criminal matter. As this change in
law has remained in effect to the present, it merits close consideration.
Mexican legal opinion about homosexuality is summarized by Ramos-
Frias (1966:69–70):

Our legislation does not regard the practice of sexual inversion a
matter of delinquency; other than when homosexuality is realized
through force, moral intimidation, rape, or when it takes place
with a minor. In this case, it may also constitute the crime of
corruption. [Penal Code Section 201]

Further, in matters concerning homosexuality, the Mexican government feels that law should not "invade the terrain of the individual

moral conscience, in order to protect the precious concerns of sexual freedom and security;" and that the law should limit itself "to the minimum ethics indispensable to maintaining society." In limiting itself thus, the Mexican law is "obeying the Latin tradition of indifference concerning these problems." This change of legal attitude was obviously a tremendous improvement for homosexuals over previous Aztec and Spanish ways of dealing with homosexuality, and is considerably more liberal than legislation in much of the United States.

Three Traditions

There appear to be three traditions intertwined by distinct social mores about homosexuality in México today:

1. A tradition of tolerant indifference already visible in Aztec attitudes to other native culture, the Mexican adoption of the Napoleonic Code in the 19th century
2. One of fanatic homophobia already visible in draconian Aztec laws about non-procreative sex and the Spanish Inquisition
3. Acceptance of homosexual behavior and some positive valuation of homosexual roles still evident in some regions of México

Tolerant Indifference

The Aztec and colonial periods have been discussed in sufficient detail to go directly to the legal system of today and its social ramifications. The decriminalization of sodomy that was part of adopting the Napoleonic Code did not grant people the right to be overtly homosexual; for included in the "minimum ethics indispensable to maintaining society" are laws against solicitation and any public behavior that is considered socially deviant or contrary to the folkways and customs of the time. Accordingly, expression and identity must be carefully managed to avoid serious consequences, such as murder, bashing, police detention, blackmail, loss of employment, and more. That some people choose to be offended and scandalized by homosexual conduct or any discussion of homosexuality makes it difficult for establishments, such as community service organizations, coffee shops, bars, restaurants, and baths that must be open to all people. In México, private consensual sex between adults has been legal for more than a century, personal sexual freedom is considered very important, and overt homosexual institutions and most forms of expression are generally repressed. This contrasts markedly to the United States, where private homosexual behavior is often a felony, there is relatively greater freedom to be publicly homosexual, and a variety of books, magazines, and videos representing homosexuality in a positive way are readily available.

Mexicans tend to be homosocial, no matter what their sexual preferences are: men hang out with men, women with women. However, there is also a great deal of mixing of ages, sexes, sexual orientations, and social classes. To many homosexual Mexicans the idea of living in a "gay ghetto" or alone as they see or hear of in the United States is sad and undesirable. Mexicans are by and large very sociable. Over the years and throughout México, I have been in countless informal situations where lesbian, heterosexual and bisexual women, along with homosexual, bisexual, and accepting heterosexual men, visited together in assorted couples or groups at friends' homes. I have had such groups drop in on me occasionally when I have lived alone in México. They often talk openly about their respective romantic and sexual lives. Everyone has seemed quite comfortable and if someone "not in the know" or who was homophobic happened by, the conversation simply changed until that person left. Then, the positive social space for diverse sexualities recurred.

Generally, the Mexican public truly is indifferent to and tolerant of much homosexual behavior. So long as no one is bothered by what is taking place, people can be as homosexual as they wish. However, the moment one individual becomes upset, sanctions can be applied, and serious consequences can ensue for those who set someone else off (Taylor 1986:133).

Tolerance of homosexuality and homosexuals in 1994 includes the following:

1. Allowing the sale of homosexual magazines with erotic, nonsexual photographs in kiosks and department stores of big cities
2. Allowing open, organized political activism, protests and homosexual pride parades
3. Permitting open participation in two of México's three major political parties
4. Inviting homosexuals to take part in public educational television programs and debates
5. Allowing homosexual service organizations, gay bars and an occasional boutique to operate with relatively little police or public harassment in large cities

6. Generally accepting the presence of discreet homosexuals and gathering places throughout the republic or at least allowing homosexuals a marginal subculture with occasional raids, bribes and public crusades.

Fanatic Homophobia

Anywhere in México one can find abundant homophobia and cruelty towards homosexuals. The newspapers are forever reporting homosexual bashings and murders. Almost every homosexual I have ever known there has at least one personal vivid example of violence directed against his or her homosexuality or that of a close friend. Since I began field-work in México in 1961 and now, six of my respondents have been murdered in grisly ways for being homosexual. AIDS has led to an increase of anti-homosexual feelings. For instance, a Guadalajara homo-sexual center that provided AIDS social services was bombed. Several prominent Mexican homosexual activists have been assassinated, and there have been multiple murders of transvestites and effeminate men in Chiapas, Oaxaca, and Sinaloa during the 1990s.

Homosexual Acceptance

Along with the obstacles to homosexuality and the potentially devas-tating homophobia, there are also positive attitudes, including a living oral tradition about historical acceptances of homosexuality. Over the thirty-plus years I have studied homosexuality in México, respondents and friends occasionally have shared with me personal experiences of social acceptance and approval. They also have shared folklore and spec-ulations about what homosexuality was like before the conquest and thoughts of how the past influences the customs of today. I include some of these materials below.

Only a few intellectuals know of the Aztec public orgiastic rites, but quite a few people have heard of group sex among other ancient cul-tures. Many times, homosexual friends have speculated about how the ancients must have met, loved, and had sex. There is even a genre of underground homosexual erotica in which the actors dress in neo-Aztec costumes and make out within sight of some actual ruins.

A few friends have ventured the opinion that the ancients probably looked for partners behind the pyramids near the old canoes that were used as public toilets. They also believe that the steambath or *temescal* must have been a popular place for sex among the Aztecs. Since toilets and steambaths are common places for meeting partners and having sexual encounters now, this may be simply projection. However, the lore of adventurous male sex long ago in such places creates positive feelings and a connectedness to the homosexuality of the past. It is impossible to say how or if positive attitudes toward homosexuality in México of today are connected to ancient ways. It is an important fact that homosexual Mexicans and many non-homosexuals think there are connections.

Another indication of some continuity from pre-conquest homosexuality is that the vulgar term *cuiloni* is still used, and many Mexicans still associate flowers and homosexuality (also noted by Rosenzweig 1973:45). Several lesbian groups chose names from Maya and Nahuatl terms, meaning "women who strew flowers before them as they go." A notorious example of homosexual flowers in the present is "La Xochil," the most prominent transvestite in all of México. Her titles include "Queen of the Queens" and "Empress of all Mexicans." La Xochil is famous throughout México and shows how outrageously homosexual someone can be in the land of machismo. La Xochil began life as an effeminate boy in a small farm town, suffering frequent abuse for effeminacy. Eventually "she" moved to Guadalajara. This was during the late 1930s, a time of great tolerance for homosexuals in México. La Xochil was both young and beautiful. People have told me that she donned a mantilla and the finest ruffled Spanish drag, and became a sensation at the bullfights. It is said that she won so many ears and tails from matadors that the real women became jealous, and fights broke out. Eventually, her presence became such a distraction that she was banned from the bullfights.

She continued her career in México City by opening a chain of bordellos that catered to government officials and rich clients. Many people have told me that she is not a greedy queen (or empress) but helps her poor sisters and their "husbands" both financially and emotionally. She was quite a legend when I first visited México in 1961. Everyone said that her houses and clandestine gay bars were never raided because the police were afraid they would find their bosses inside.

The 1960s were years of unrelenting homosexual repression with frequent police raids, bashings, and murders. However, La Xochil, in the middle of this rein of terror, held a huge "artists" drag ball in one of the most luxurious hotels in downtown México City. Dressed as Cleopatra, she was carried into the hotel on a palanquin by a group of half-naked, muscular "Egyptian" servants and followed by a large retinue of celebrants. Her picture was on the front page of many newspapers and magazines without having been arrested.

La Xochil continues to throw a grand charity ball every year. This is the worst kept secret in México. It takes a great deal of influence either with the poorest drag queens and street hustlers of the city, or being a client of La Xochil's establishments, or having friends who are well connected in high places to get a ticket. I met "Her Highness" and was fortunate enough to attend her 1980 "Señorita Gay de México" contest.[5] It was held in the ruins of an abandoned amphitheater, within sight of "la Casa Rosanda," the official residence of the president of México. Lights for the event were rigged to the batteries of ten idling cars. The celebrants ranged from street people to those clad in evening gowns dripping with jewelry. The straight people had mostly left by 1:00 A.M. and the party really got going. That such a scandalous affair can happen year after year without being raided is not simply a reflection of La Xochil's pull with the government, but also a sign of the tolerance, curiosity, amusement, or indifference of ordinary people who happen to witness the scene.

Although few people I know have read the original sources, many have heard that there was a great deal of homosexuality and bisexuality in both the Gulf and Pacific coastal regions of México before the conquest. They sometimes say that this is why homosexuality is more common and more widely accepted in these regions than in the highlands today. To bolster this perception, a respondent from Veracruz told me that as a child he learned a rustic saying that it is good luck to have a queer in the family: "Es buena suerte de tener un puto en la familia."

I have heard many, many stories of relatives and friends who are accepting of homosexuality. Another respondent from Veracruz told me that he once stayed with a lover in the house of an elderly aunt. It was an adobe hut with walls reaching only part-way to the ceiling. During the night, he and his lover were having sex when they heard a noise. He looked up to see that his aunt had climbed up a ladder and was peering over the wall watching. When she knew that she had been discovered, she egged them on, shouting, "¡Anda que quieren, cabrones!" (Do what you want to do, fuckers) and climbed back down the ladder. They all had a good laugh the next morning.

---

5. I related my experiences of the ball and some of its more flamboyantly dressed participants in Taylor (1981).

On the Pacific coast, I have heard women talk openly about their boyfriends' bisexuality. One woman joked with pride about her boyfriend's sexual vigor, "Es bien mayate, el cabrón" (loosely, he's a good bisexual stud, that fucker). There is also a common joke about one small town on the coast renowned for its bisexuality: "If you drop a peso on the ground, don't bend over to pick it up, unless you want to get fucked in the ass."

In Hermosillo in 1984, I observed that several well-liked *locas* (effeminate homosexuals) daily looked after a group of young boys and adolescents, while their mothers did housework. The lads would go from *loca* to *loca* playing, helping with chores, eating lunch, taking siesta, and having a great time. The mothers joked that the boys were so interested in and jealous of each other that the *locas* rarely got a chance to be alone with any of them. This pattern is well known by Mexicans to exist among the lowland Zapotecs of Oaxaca, where the *muxe*, highly-regarded effeminate homosexual men, also take care of the young males and keep them out of trouble (see Chiñas in this volume.)

While in Hermosillo, a Mexican respondent, who previously had helped me with research in México City and Merida, took me to a favorite place where he liked to find rural sexual partners. Near a small village, about forty kilometers away from the city, there was a series of freshwater lagoons along a river. Villagers went there to bathe and, occasionally, to have sex in the bushes. My friend assured me that the villagers simply ignored what was going on if they chanced to see anything. Wandering along the paths looking for willing bathers, we came upon two young men having sex. They stopped what they were doing, laughed a little self-consciously, and waited for us to pass.

During the period 1961–63 and again in 1970, I conducted fieldwork in rural Chiapas. During long rides over rough dirt roads, the men and women occasionally regaled one another at the front of the bus with gossip about their heterosexual, bisexual, and homosexual exploits, the size and appearance of one another's genitalia, and other intimate details. I was astonished the first time I heard this kind of banter. I asked one of the men I knew whether the stories were true. He assured me that they were. The *campesinos* showed no shame or concern about their behavior, and my personal experience with two different men who took part in such conversations convinced me that the gossip was substantially true.

I also attended several rural weddings and dances in Chiapas where men played music for one another and danced together. Occasionally, when it was dark and they were supposedly "too drunk to know what they were doing," males would go to the bushes to urinate. Spontaneous solitary, mutual, and sometimes group masturbation would occur. On one occasion, a group masturbating was so large (about fifteen) and crowded that the shorter adolescents had to push and wriggle their way between the men just to see what was happening. I very much doubt that any of the participants considered themselves *homosexuales*, since they were not effeminate and were not being anally penetrated. They just enjoyed themselves with each other in the bushes while drunk and celebrating.

Conclusion

The three traditions have co-existed for a long time. They span many cultures and eras, and endure, though it may seem paradoxical that rabid homophobia, indifference, and acceptance can blend so completely in one basically mestizo society. Mexicans seem to have a special ability to thrive in the midst of such contradictions, incongruities, and social paradoxes. Such complexities of social life would be experienced as intolerable chaos by many people. However, such complexity seems to add zest to Mexican interactions. In fact, their great sociability may even depend in great part upon this ability to separate, encompass, and accommodate people of diametrically opposed world views and traditions.

I have stressed throughout this chapter that we can never really know the true history of homosexuality in México. This is a tragedy in one sense, but perhaps not much of a loss in another. I think that the melange of documents, legends, folklore, and contemporary behavior—even the vagueness and uncertainty—serve a much more important function than a simple historical chronicle. They provide new material and the mental space for creative interpretation and reconstruction of Mexican homosexual traditions. In our rush to grasp the new and throw away our pasts, we often fail to understand how extremely important Mexican people feel their ties to antiquity are. It gives them great pleasure and satisfaction to contemplate the past and re-examine their customs and their lives today in order to weave together a meaningful whole: a rich, living tapestry of traditions. The sense of having a special place, of belonging to one's culture, is as vital to Mexican homosexuals as it is to their fellow countrymen. It is in this light that I hope this chapter is of service.

REFERENCES

Bancroft, Hubert H.
    1886 *Native Races of the Pacific States.* Vol. 2. San Francisco: San Francisco
        History Co.
Edmonson, Monroe S.
    1974 *The Work of Sahagún.* Albuquerque: University of New México Press.
Greenleaf, Richard E.
    1961 *Zumárraga and the Mexican Inquisition: 1536–1543.* Richmond, VA:
        William Byrd Press.
Guzmán, Mario
    1971 Los homosexuales en México. *Continedo* (Dec.) 44–54.
Hardoy, Jorgé-Enriquez
    1973 *Pre-Columbian Cities.* New York: Walker.
Hilfrich, Klaus
    1972 Sexualität und Repression in der Kultur der Maya. *Baessler-Archiv* 20:
        138–71.
Idell, Albert
    1956 *The Bernal Diaz Chronicles.* New York: Doubleday.
Keen, Benjamin
    1971 *The Aztec Image in Western Thought.* New Brunswick, NJ: Rutgers Uni-
        versity Press.
Kimball, Geoffrey
    1993 Aztec homosexuality: the textual evidence. *Journal of Homosexuality*
        26(1):7–24.
Kirchoff, Paul
    1952 Mesoamerica. In *Heritage of Conquest.* Sol Tax, ed. Pp. 17–30. Glencoe,
        IL: Free Press.
Lea, Henry C.
    1907 *The History of the Inquisition in Spain.* New York: Macmillan.
Medina, José Toribio
    1905 *Historia del Tribunal del Santo Oficio de la Inquisicion en México.* Santiago:
        Elzeviriana.
Morris, J. B.
    1928 *Five Letters, 1519–1526.* London: Routledge.
Murray, Stephen O., and Kent Gerard
    1984 Renaissance sodomite sub-cultures? In *Among Men/Among Women.* Vol. 1
        Pp. 182–96. University of Amsterdam Sociological Institute.
Novo, Salvador
    1972 *Las Locas, El Sexo, Los Burdeles.* México: Novaro.
Paz, Octavio
    1961 *The Labyrinth of Solitude.* New York: Grove.
Quesada, Noemi
    1974 Erotismo en la religion Azteca. *Revista Universidad de México* 28:16–19.

Ramos-Frias, José A.

    1966 *Estudio Criminológico y Medico-Legal de la Homosexualidad.* México: Virginia.

Requena, Antonio

    1945 Noticias y consideraciones sobre las anormalidades de los aborígenes americanos: sodomía. *Acta Venezolana* 1:43–71. Partly translated as Sodomy among Native American peoples. *Gay Sunshine* 38/39 (1979): 37–39.

Rosenzweig, Jay B.

    1973 *Caló: Gutter Spanish.* New York: Dutton.

Roys, Ralph L.

    1967 *The Book of Chilam Balam of Chumayal.* Norman: University of Oklahoma Press.

Sanders, William, and Barbara Price

    1968 *Mesoamerica.* New York: Random House.

Scholes, France, and R. Roys

    1948 *The Maya Chontal Indians of Acalan-Tixchel.* Washington: Carnegie Institution Publication 560.

Seler, Eduard

    1902 *Codex Vaticanus No. 3773: An Old Mexican Pictorial Manuscript in the Vatican Library.* Berlin and London: A. H. Keane.

Soustelle, Jacques

    1961 *Daily Life of the Aztecs on the Eve of the Spanish Conquest.* Stanford: Stanford University Press.

Taylor, Clark L.

    1981 Ethnographic materials on Mexican male homosexual transvestites. *Anthropological Research Group on Homosexuality Newsletter* 3(1):3–6.

    1986 Mexican male homosexual interaction in public places. *Journal of Homosexuality* 11(3):117–36.

Thompson, J. Eric

    1966 *The Rise and Fall of Maya Civilization.* Norman: University of Oklahoma Press.

    1970 *Maya History and Religion.* Norman: University of Oklahoma Press.

6

Social Attitudes and Sexual Variance in Lima[*]

Manuel Arboleda G.

As in other parts of Latin America, those seeking homosexual encounters begin to drift to Lima's cruising locales *(sitios de ambiente)*[1] shortly after dusk. Although no quantitative study of sexual behavior of the kind pioneered by Kinsey and his associates in the United States exists for Peru, my ongoing observations of my native city show that (1) those who engage in homosexual activities are not solely those labeled as *homosexuales* by themselves or by the majority culture, and (2) although selection of partners involves class and race, expected sex-role preference is a crucial consideration for connections, especially for those lasting longer than one sexual encounter.

The Setting

Although there is a small gay organization (MHOL) that has survived for nearly a decade, social interaction among gay men in Lima occurs mostly in public places. As has been the case since the 1970s, there are only a few separate institutions (bars and discos) catering exclusively

---

[*]An earlier version of this paper was presented at the 1981 annual meeting of the American Sociological Association in Toronto. The author would like to acknowledge helpful comments made on earlier drafts by Barry Adam, Gerald Berreman, Joseph Carrier, Keelung Hong, the late Laud Humphreys, the late Martin Levine, and (on multiple drafts) Stephen Murray.

1. The term *ambiente* has a double meaning: a conception of self-identification and a locale which attracts a critical mass of those interested in homosexual liaisons. The former sense appears to be predominant in México (Taylor 1978); the latter is predominant in Peru.

to gay men. Despite Lima's immense sprawl, those places which serve as *sitios de ambiente* seem to be confined to the downtown section and the modern and cosmopolitan suburb of Miraflores.

In the rapidly deteriorating sections of downtown Lima the nocturnal *ambiente* consists of the Plaza San Martín and the adjacent archways, the heavily trafficked boulevards of La Colmena, the pedestrian mall of the Jirón de la Union, Jirón Ocoña, and a few other *jirones* or streets. Cruising also takes place in some of Lima's most popular cafés, restaurants, some theaters (notably the Tacna and the Plaza), and in two non-gay bathhouses that are frequented by men seeking sex with men, Pizzaro and Fuji. Both are located near the government palace. The one exclusively gay bar downtown, Americo, which opened in 1981, was closed by 1985. Cine Colón is a downtown porno theater that remains a popular trysting place.

In the prestigious coastal suburb of Miraflores, where I lived in 1976, 1978, and parts of the years 1981–85, and have visited briefly every year since then, and where I made most of my observations, men seeking homosocial and/or homosexual interaction assemble in groups in the various shops in or nearby the El Pacifico building, especially in the elegant, sidewalk restaurant Haiti, located in it. In addition to bars and restaurants which come and go, gay men also frequent the nearby (mixed) José Pardo bathhouse and Kennedy Park, situated across the street from Miraflores's main church. All these places are within walking distance of each other. Although these places serve as cruising grounds for those seeking homosexual encounters, they do not (except for the Pardo) function as public locales for sexual activities. Although gay bars and discos do exist in Lima and Miraflores, their operations tend to be ephemeral. Even El Inti, which seemed to be a fixture on the scene, closed after more than two decades (1964–86).

During those two decades, some noticeable changes in gay entertainment occurred. The bars and discos of the 1960s and 1970s maintained mandatory membership fees and identification cards (see Arboleda 1980). In the 1980s and 1990s, exclusivity is less blatantly maintained: anyone who can afford the cover charge can gain admittance. At least one place at any given time will present shows featuring lip-synching of popular recordings. Although female impersonation predominates, some impersonations (by men) of popular male singers occur as well.

In Miraflores, where there has been a long succession of bars, sexual activity in public places is confined to the brush area along the cliffs of the Costa Verde beaches, the parking lots above the beaches, and abandoned buildings. Hotels and motels renting by the hour are not found in Miraflores. Most are situated at the periphery of Lima. Some gay men patronize such hotels, although they are mostly frequented by those culminating heterosexual liaisons. As Patch (1974:315) noted, such establishments frequently charge more for homosexual than for heterosexual pairs.

Private sexual activities within one's own residence is unavailable to most gay men: socioeconomic conditions in Peru, as in the rest of Latin America (Carrier 1976:109; Murray 1980a:7) do not permit males to move away from home until they marry. Such living arrangements clearly affect the sexual activities of the average unmarried Peruvian male, who must gratify his sexual needs somewhere other than where he lives.

In Lima's *ambiente* cruising usually begins with eye contact and continues with standard questions, such as "Do you have a match?" or "Do you have the time?" If the other person is interested, conversation will develop further. At some point during the conversation, questions about role in anal intercourse will be raised: the *punto* (trick) will be asked if he is *activo* or *pasivo*. Although these concepts normally refer to sexual role in anal intercourse, they connote distinct personality constructs as well. In addition to sexual role, those seeking homosexual encounters are also interested in other characteristics, particularly a prospective partner's age. Unlike in the United States, age is positively valued (for both heterosexual and homosexual liaisons). *Pasivos* generally prefer older partners, not just out of respect, but because older partners are more likely to be able to afford to pay for accommodation for sex and for such frills as drinks preceding sex.

Pasivos

Pasivos constitute the "visible majority" in the *ambiente*, because they socialize in observable groups. They are recognized and their members sought out by signs of effeminate behavior or dress. Obvious effeminacy permits others, simultaneously, to find sexual receptacles and to stigmatize them as *maricones*.[2]

---

2. *Maricón* is used to refer to effeminate males. This epithet is widely known outside the *ambiente*. It is by no means the most vulgar term, cf. *rosquette* (a round object with a hole in the center) and *cabro* (goat, which carries a cultural load more like sheep in English, i.e., a fucked-over cuckold rather than a randy fucker).

Pasivos loitering in the park range in age from the early teens to the mid-twenties. Families of those I have interviewed have generally ranged from two to four siblings. Only a few live in Miraflores. Most derive from middle-class families unable to afford to live there.

Although drag queens were and are occasionally seen in the streets of Lima (especially on Avenida Arequipa late in the evening), they rarely appear in the park or anywhere else in Miraflores. Unlike in Brazil, where transvestites may be held in a certain esteem (Landes 1940; Whitam 1979:16; Fry, this volume), those in Peru are only ridiculed. Gay men generally exhibit contempt for transvestites. For instance, one night Martin, a 21-year-old white-collar worker, confronted two transvestites who were loitering in the park. He felt they had no business being in the park dressed as women. One of the transvestites countered that it was his right to dress any way he pleased and ended the exchange by calling Martín a *parquero* (someone who frequents the park rather than the more respectable/commercial parts of the *ambiente*).

Entendidos who patronize cafés are generally older, more affluent, and more group-oriented than the *entendidos* in the park. Most of the café set loathe the park and its denizens. Federico, a young airline employee and a member of the José Pardo bathhouse, described the park *ambiente* in the late-1970s as *maliado,* i.e., having a bad reputation. Kennedy Park's reputation as a social gathering place declined further during the early 1980s, as it increasingly became a hustling ground. As *fletes*—*activos* who exchange their sexual services for the money of older *pasivos*— began to outnumber the effeminate, young *pasivos,* socializing shifted to the El Pacifico area. In the early 1990s Miraflores Mayor Andrade had the park remodeled. Between the remodeling and constant police harassment of suspected loiterers, the hustlers were driven out. For a time after President Alberto Fujimora suspended the constitution and dismissed much of the rest of the government, Kennedy Park was closed altogether.

In public outside the *ambiente, pasivos*—however effeminate they are— carefully avoid disclosing their sexual orientation. This leads to a life full of secrets and multiple roles termed *doble file* (double-edged) in Peru. For example, in 1978 I met Bobby, a 19-year-old student who frequented the park and was very campy while socializing with friends there. But whenever an unexpected, and thus potentially threatening, situation arose, he would yell to his friends, "¡Buse! Buse!"—a cry to behave in a more masculine manner, particularly if a *matacabro* (goat-killer literally, or queer-basher in Anglo parlance) was believed to be nearby.

In general, it is *pasivos* rather than *activos* who have a certain level of gay self-conception and mutual identification. Such awareness is manifested by the increasing adoption of the term *gay* (see Murray and Arboleda 1982) as a self-reference and the concomitant internalization of a gay identity. The terms *gay* or *entendido* are not confined to *pasivos,* nor do all *pasivos* have a gay consciousness, nor accept themselves as gay.

Activos

Except for all being ostentatiously masculine in appearance and public behavior, *activos* are more socially heterogeneous than *pasivos.* The latter seek and endorse the masculine self-image of the former by calling them *hombres* (men), as if they are no different from ordinary males. One way (particularly popular during the late-1970s) to signal one is *activo* is to grow a mustache.

Male sexual activity is accepted in Peruvian society, and a man— even a married man—may engage in homosexual activity so long as he holds everything except his penis aloof from the *ambiente.* A story reported in *El Comercio* (the most prestigious Peruvian daily newspaper) of 4 May 1978 illustrates how a homosexual encounter not involving an effeminate participant is not considered an encounter of *homosexuales:* one night after a party, a 40-year-old male tried to rape a 28-year-old male, who killed the would-be rapist. The newspaper reported this incident as a *violacion del honor sexual.* The image of a masculine 40-year-old was not congruent with the image of the homosexual held in the majority culture and reinforced by sensational press coverage of female impersonators. I witnessed a similar, albeit non-fatal attempt, in which an avowedly heterosexual Peruvian friend did not consider his (failed) attempt to fuck another man was in any way connected to homosexual desire nor an occasion for guilt. These *activos* play their role carefully, so as not to implicate themselves too much with the *ambiente.* They do not cruise with friends and would feel awkward being observed by their friends or convincing them to go cruising together. In any case, prowling alone marks someone in the *ambiente* as an *activo.* As Joselito put it, "What else could he be doing alone?"

Not all *activo* homosexual behavior is oriented towards *pasivos.* For instance, Gus, who was 29 and self-employed, did not engage in heterosexual relationships and had little interaction with women. Despite the fact that his sexual activities were exclusively with men, he denied any homosexual imputation. For him, only *pasivos* are homosexual. While Gus's social network was composed entirely of males, Lorenzo's lover, Lucho, a divorced bank employee, led a double life. Lorenzo was entirely cut off from participation in Lucho's social network. Despite an enduring sexual relationship with a man, Lucho (along with other *activo* informants) considered himself not at all implicated in homosexuality, so long as he remained *activo*.

Although such *activos* may feel internal conflicts about their sexual identity, they do not waver from the public performance of the masculine role. *Activos* consider insertor behavior part of a male's prerogative. Adherence to this belief permits *activos* to gratify sexual needs without compromising a masculine, even heterosexual identity (just as in Mesoamerica: see Carrier 1976:116; Taylor 1978:46; Murray 1980b: 182). *Pasivos* do not challenge the masculine image, whether because they believe it, are afraid of what the consequences of challenge might be, or have fantasy needs of their own met by those acting macho.

Besides de facto approval of *activo* homosexual behavior, masculine Peruvians generally show considerable physical affection for other men without this being viewed as suspect (as it would be in Anglo America). Interestingly, this freedom is inhibited with the *ambiente,* and *entendidos* are self-conscious about touching other men in non-sexual ways.

Modernos

Not fitting the rigid dichotomy of *activos* and *pasivos,* those who are flexible in sexual roles, are labeled *moderno.* This term (analogous to *internacional* in Mesoamerica, see Murray 1980b) may be used to cover *pasivo* role preference by those who are masculine in appearance and in public presentation of self (indeed the term refers more to sexual technique than to a kind of person). This group has not grown as rapidly as the term *gay/gai* has diffused from Anglo North America, so that *gay* is not synonymous with nor a replacement for *moderno. Gay* refers primarily to self-identification in Peru (see Murray and Arboleda 1982).

Social Attitudes

Participants in homosexual encounters are not all the same and do not form a monolithic type. There is variance even within the two types, as well as a folk label for a kind of person transcending sexual role specialization. Nevertheless, Peruvian institutions, including church, school, and mass media uphold and promote a simple dichotomy, in which a *homosexual* dresses in women's clothes, acts femininely, and is exclusively *pasivo* during sex. The psychiatric elaboration of this myth receives considerable publicity. For example, the 26 April 1978 *El Comercio* reported psychiatrist Baltazar Caravedo's speech to a Boy Scout convention in which he warned parents of the dangers of over-protecting children. Other "experts" pretend homosexuality is not a traditional part of indigenous cultures (cf. Villaviciente 1966 with LaBarre 1948 or Arboleda 1981).

Not surprisingly, such "expert" views hamper psychological adjustment. Hector was constantly depressed because he could not find a "cure" for his problem, whereas Cesar had sex with women on several occasions to prove to himself he was not sexually attracted to males. In such an atmosphere of increasingly influential psychiatric moralizing, it is not difficult to understand why only four of my more than sixty informants disclosed their sexual orientation to their families. Of these, two were rejected and evicted from their homes (one was also forced to take male hormones), while the other two endure inconsistent parental tolerance.

Reproduction of Societal Inequalities in
Everyday Peruvian Gay Life

Race

Beside problems inherent in sex-role dichotomies, participants in the *ambiente* often have to confront discriminatory practices derived from the racial, regional, and class inequalities of Peruvian society and replicated within the *ambiente*.

In coastal Lima, where the largest number of *blancos* (light-skinned) are concentrated, and where interethnic interaction is extensive, skin color is important.[3] Dark-skinned men from the highlands are called *serranos* and are subject to *blanco* condescension and outright discrimination. A dialog between Luis, a mestizo youth, and Sandino, a blond

---

3. In the highlands, where more or less everyone is dark-skinned, other indicators are used. See van den Berghe and Primov (1978: 117).

surfer in his late teens is a case in point. Sandino remarked that Luis had "inferior curly hair." Luis did not challenge this slur by arguing that blond hair is no better or worse than dark, curly hair;[4] instead he retorted that Sandino's blondness was artificial, i.e., his hair had been bleached by the sun or from a bottle rather than being hereditary.

Peruvian mass media constantly extol such physical characteristics as fair skin and blond hair as the hallmarks of beauty. For instance, advertisements for the airlines, both Faucett and Aero-Peru, show smiling blondes offering hospitality. Given an aesthetic valuation of light-skinned traits along with the Peruvian lack of enthusiasm for promoting Peru's rich Indian cultural heritage (past and present), it is not surprising to find a low level of racial consciousness and pride among gay men of mestizo or Indian extraction.

Regionalism and Class

"Racial" differences are confounded with regional differences, as darkness-of-skin indicators of the *serrano/costeño* distinction illustrate. Moreover, those born outside the capital city are considered to be provincial *(provincianos)* and—in the absence of markers of class superiority in dress and accoutrements—are presumed inferior to *Limeños*. Outsiders to Miraflores other than light-skinned foreign tourists are automatically treated as *serranos,* especially if they are at all dark-skinned or effeminate.

The class differences separating those patronizing Miraflores's *ambiente* and denizens of downtown Lima cruising locales are startling and lead to interpersonal conflict. Those in Miraflores look down on the scene in Lima as lower-class, and presumptively *provinciano.*[5]

Class discrimination is especially prevalent in the few bars and discos. Mandatory cover-charges and expensive drinks continue to exclude low-income gays. Private membership clubs have disappeared from the scene, but the attitude of some former members lingers. Most of the members of the private clubs were *blancos,* affluent enough to afford the high membership dues and culturally acceptable enough to pass screening interviews for membership or entry. Some of those with entrée refused

---

4. The appropriate response to an insult is another insult, not a serious discussion. See Murray (1979).

5. The irony is that this involves suburbanites looking down at the capital.

to patronize non-private clubs, which they regarded as too *bajo* (lower-class). Others, then and now, slum for sex. Even in the few low-priced restaurants and bars in downtown Lima and in the parks and streets where low-income gay men can socialize and cruise, racial, regional, and class antagonisms reappear.

Collective Action

Concern for discretion combined with cleavages of affiliation in terms of class, race, region, and sexual role create formidable obstacles to collective consciousness and, hence, to collective action. An exception was an unprecedented spontaneous 1978 march composed mostly of transvestites advocating basic human rights for the category *homosexuales* and an end to police harassment. They presented their demands to a congressional workshop drafting a new constitution for the country. Although there are no legal clauses prohibiting homosexual behavior among consenting adults, as in México (Taylor 1978), police harassment of locales frequented by gay men still occurs, sometimes rationalized as attacks on drug trafficking. None of my informants in the late 1970s and early 1980s considered such actions oppressive, especially if directed at flamboyant *bajo* youth. Members of the nascent *Movimiento Homosexual de Lima* by 1985 considered them at least reprehensible. Indeed, MHOL was formed in reaction to a police raid on an elegant middle-class gay club. In 1986 the president of MHOL opened a Miraflores bar, Querelle, where apolitical hard-rock enthusiasts mix with Marxist *salseros*.[6]

In 1983 MHOL drafted a manifesto demanding freedom to lead an alternative lifestyle without discrimination or harassment and sex education aimed at restructuring the mores of Peruvian society. The points of the MHOL manifesto were incorporated as the third article in the platform of the *Izquierda Unida* (United Left) for the 1985 presidential election.[7] The

---

6. [Editor's note] If there is any resemblance to North American gay movement history, Lima's recapitulates the prominence of the Tavern Guild in San Francisco, rather than, say, the New York pattern. See D'Emilio (1983). In Guadalajara, Mexico the leading activist has also been a disco owner (Carrier 1995).

7. Like the Sandinistas in Nicaragua (McCaskell 1981; Adam 1993), IU broke with the usual marxist equation of homosexuality and decadence that has been especially well exemplified in Cuba. See Salas 1979; Murray 1995.

candidate of the IU, Alfonso Barrantes, mayor of Lima, finished second in the contest, although the party gained many seats in both the senate and the chamber of deputies. Thus, a major party publicly endorsed protection for alternative lifestyles, even at a time when the popular press was sensationalizing half a dozen cases of AIDS (or "the gay cancer" as they preferred to call it; see Arboleda 1986).

MHOL recognized the need to educate both the general public and those in the *ambiente* about AIDS and other problems. Indeed, the task of its newsletter, *Conducta Impropia* (first published in 1986), is to challenge the orthodox conservative/Christian views of homosexuality that are dominant in Peruvian society—and not without advocates within the *ambiente*.

REFERENCES

Adam, Barry D.
    1993 In Nicaragua: homosexuality without a gay world. *Journal of Homosexuality* 24:171–81.
Arboleda G., Manuel A.
    1980 Gay life in Lima. *Gay Sunshine* 42:30.
    1981 Representaciones artisticos de actividades homoéroticos en la ceramica Moche. *Boletin de Lima* 16:98–107.
    1986 Peru: gay activism takes hold within a complex multi-ethnic society. *The Advocate* 445 (29 April):29–33.
Carrier, Joseph M.
    1971 Participants in urban Mexican male homosexual encounters. *Archives of Sexual Behavior* 1:279–91.
    1976 Cultural factors affecting urban Mexican male homosexual behavior. *Archives of Sexual Behavior* 5:103–24.
    1995 *Mexican Male Homosexual Encounters*. New York: Columbia University Press.
D'Emilio, John
    1983 *Sexual Politics, Sexual Communities*. Chicago: University of Chicago Press.
LaBarre, Weston
    1948 *The Aymara Indians of the Lake Titicaca Plateau*. American Anthropological Association Memoir 68.
Landes, Ruth
    1940 A cult matriarchate and male homosexuality. *Journal of Abnormal and Social Psychology* 35:386–97.
McCaskell, Tim
    1981 Sex and sandismo. *The Body Politic* 73:19–21.

Murray, Stephen O.

    1979 The art of gay insults. *Anthropological Linguistics* 21:211–23.

    1980a *Latino Homosexuality.* San Francisco: Social Networks.

    1980b Lexical and institutional elaboration: the 'species homosexual' in Guatemala. *Anthropological Linguistics* 22:177–86.

    1995 Heteronormative Cuban sexual policies and resistance to them. *GLQ* 2:in press.

Murray, Stephen O., and Manuel Arboleda G.

    1982 Stigma transformation and relexification in the diffusion of 'gay' in Latin America. American Sociological Association meetings, San Francisco. (Revised version in this volume.)

Patch, Richard W.

    1974 *Serrano* and *criollo*: the confusion of race and class. In *Contemporary Cultures and Societies of Latin America*. D. Heath, ed. New York: Random House.

Salas, Luis

    1979 *Social Control and Deviance in Cuba.* New York: Praeger.

Taylor, Clark L.

    1978 *El Ambiente: Homosexual Social Life in Mexico City.* Ph.D. dissertation, University of California, Berkeley.

van den Berghe, Pierre, and G.P. Primov.

    1977 *Inequality in the Peruvian Andes.* Columbia: University of Missouri Press.

Villaviciente, Victor L.

    1966 *La vida del indigena peruano.* Lima: Barrantes.

Whitam, Frederick L.

    1979 Middle class gay life in São Paulo. *Gay Sunshine* 38/39:16–17. (Reprinted in this volume.)

7

🔥

Two Truths about Costa Rica*

Paul Kutsche

Two sharply distinct models of male homosexuality in Costa Rica are now in print—mine (1983; Kutsche and Page 1991) and that of Jacobo Schifter Sikora, a Costa Rican historian (1989; Schifter and Madrigal 1992; also see Madrigal 1991). This paper will describe both, expanding on my earlier papers; the task of critically comparing them is the subject of another paper, now in preparation.

Mine is a contract model, Schifter's an oppression model. Mine focuses on the large number of men who have sex with other men, whether they define themselves as gay or not, while Schifter's focuses on that portion (a small minority, as he and I agree) whose sex is exclusively or almost exclusively with other men, and who define themselves as gay (a term which was borrowed from English, but is becoming generally accepted in Costa Rica). In the Kutsche model the culture trait underlying all others is that Costa Rica favors sexual expression; Schifter's model is anti-sexual. The next most important part of the sexual structure as I see it is that sex between men is two-layered. The public layer is homophobic, the private layer is quietly permissive and at times even

*Strictly speaking, I never did field research on homosexuality in Costa Rica. My several stays in the country, between 1974 and 1990, were to teach in the program of the Associated Colleges of the Midwest and to collect life histories from rural-to-urban migrants (Kutsche 1994). My data are derived from participation in homosexual activities and from unsystematic conversations with Costa Ricans. ACM and Colorado College faculty research grants funded my visits. I am grateful for their support, to Alison Seyler for patiently and diligently typing what sometimes must have seemed picayune revisions of the manuscript, and to Stephen Murray for critical but encouraging comments. All translations are mine.

favorable to male homosexuality, with the contract operating at the private layer. Perhaps two layers are not enough to construct an accurate model of the Costa Rican valences toward homosexuality: the innermost and private layer is tolerant, as I have said. The second layer is contempt for the *maricón*, the butt of ribald jokes. The third layer is police harassment of gays and lesbians, together with a blind eye toward criminal brutality toward gays and homophobic statements and actions by government officials. The fourth layer consists of ecclesiastical thunder and brimstone against "unnatural behavior," "vice" (a term which in everyday discourse covers a vague multitude of behaviors), and "delinquency." On top of all this is the Napoleonic Code on which Costa Rica laws are based. It treats all sexual possibilities between adult human beings as equally lawful. In Schifter's model Costa Rica is unambiguously homophobic.

Terminology

Discussions of labels, including this one, are labored and pedantic. Nevertheless, labeling is the ethnographic problem, for the ethnographer's task is to find out how the people s/he studies label (define, construct) their cultural universe. Sexual self-labels are changing rapidly in Central America, as Murray and Arboleda illustrate elsewhere in this volume. The change was beginning in the 1980s when I was in Costa Rica. Thus, there are no fixed and satisfactory labels for men who make love to other men.

I never heard *gay* in Spanish, outside university circles, nor did I see *gay* or *gai* in print. The mildly derogatory *loca* was used frequently by homosexuals to refer to others (never to oneself) whose effeminate mannerisms called attention to themselves. The synonymous *maricón* was more likely to be used by heterosexuals. I did not hear the parallel terms which Schifter uses, *travestido* or *travesti*.

The term most frequently used by homosexual men to describe themselves was *de ambiente* (of the ambiance), close to *entendido* (in the know), used elsewhere in Latin America. Those calling themselves *de ambiente* ranged from some who looked and acted masculine (*buga*, though the term is not used frequently) to some who were labeled *loca* by other homosexual men. *Joto,* the invidious term for any male homosexual throughout the Spanish-speaking world, is understood in Costa Rica, but I never heard it volunteered. *Playo* is the Costa Rican equivalent.

In consequence, there is no adequate single term for all Costa Rican men who have sex with other men—no equivalent to the sweeping *gay* in English. In the following section, I mostly use *de ambiente*. I make finer distinctions in the subsection "Categories of Homosexual Identity." Schifter consistently uses *gay* as a Spanish word, so in discussing his alternative model, I reproduce his usage.

The Contract Model

Unwritten, unspoken, yet logically inferred from what informants report, homosexuals and the rest of male society contract for protection in return for service. Many "heterosexuals" have sex with "homosexuals."[1] Behaviorally, that is to say "bisexuals have sex with homosexuals," but straight men find it convenient from time to time to have sex with other men, and those who are *de ambiente* find it exciting to have sex with those they can regard as *hombres de verdad* (real men). Those who do not regard themselves as *hombres de verdad* service those who do. In return, the latter tolerate and at times protect gays, so long as gays don't object when straights utter homophobic remarks in public, and so long as gays stay deeply in the closet and act as straight as they are able in non-sexual situations. This contract gives satisfaction to both sides. It is nevertheless lopsided, because the straight partner gets momentary sexual gratification when he feels the urge (usually as "pitcher" in anal or oral contact, but not so invariably as one might imagine), and also enjoys the public benefit of his heterosexual status; while the *de ambiente* partner gets only the momentary gratification of having sex with *hombres de verdad*, while otherwise he must hide important parts of his identity from the world and often deny them to himself. The contractual relation between this large minority (or is it actually a majority?) of Costa Rican men lies imbedded in male sexual culture, some aspects of which are shared by all men, some of which are peculiar to those who are *de ambiente*.

First of all, a Costa Rican male is a sexual being, and takes his right to sexual activity for granted. His exuberance in his body and its uses was expressed by a 1974 graffito on the wall of the men's changing room at Playa Puntarena: "Yo me baño desnudo, porque yo tengo mucho que

---

1. As argued below, the term "bisexual" makes sense as a self-identifier for some but not all such Costa Ricans.

enseñar y nada que econdir" (I swim naked, because I have much to show and nothing to hide). The asexual morality of the Roman Catholic Church has little impact upon him. Costa Rican culture is sex-positive.

Second, a Costa Rican makes friendships with other males, but rarely with females. A female is a person to transact sexual and family business with, not a confidante. She is also to an extent an adversary in the game of sexual conquest. (A mother is a separate identity entirely.) A Costa Rican man expects himself, in short, to be easy with other males, but not with females, and he spends a lot of his leisure as well as his work time with other males. Consideration of other important shaping features of Costa Rican culture follow:

Form and Anarchy

The tension between rigid form and the ecstasy of anarchy is the fundamental paradigm that I shall use to explain how a *de ambiente* Costa Rican makes his way through his symbolic world.

Form is ancient in Hispanic culture. A reasonable starting point is the heavy order of heaven and of earth of the Hapsburg Dynasty, which established itself in Spain with the Holy Roman Emperor Charles V in 1516, and petered out in childlessness in 1700. It crystallized in the long rein of Philip II (1556–98), who is caricatured in the mystical fiction of Carlos Fuentes's (1975) *Terra Nostra* as death pressing down on Iberian life. That weight of order, that emphasis on the importance of external form, is honored thoroughly and consistently in Costa Rica today.

Anarchy is also ancient—in Spain in the rebelliousness of the Castilian nobility who resented central authority, in the New World in savage competition between *conquistadores*. Only with difficulty did Seville, and later Madrid, rule the captains who conquered land and Indians for the Crown. After fighting was over and the structure of colonial government set up, administrators flouted Spanish and colonial decrees with the sly "Obedezco, pero no cumplo" (I obey, but I do not comply).

The Costa Rican *de ambiente* is heir to both the rigid form and to the anarchy of his ancestors, just as his straight brother is, and the two themes are contrapuntal in his behavior. The most skillful consciously play both tunes in fugues as elaborate as those of Bach. Because form expends less energy than anarchy, more of life is carried on in good form than in wild anarchy, but each is equally important in homoerotic life. The Costa Rican whirls himself like a centrifuge so long as he is making love, always knowing that the harness of social form will restrain him from destruction. Form is not, of course, absolutely fail-safe. Once in a while the harness breaks, and a man whirls himself to insanity; once in a while a man never gets into motion, and he dies from inanition. Carlos Fuentes and Gabriel García Márquez have described both dangers in their novels and short stories, but I cannot point to Costa Rican artists who have written or painted in this vein.

Both anarchy and form, both insanity and inanition, are present in North European cultures, as for instance in William Blake's aphorism "The road of excess leads to the palace of wisdom." How does the Latin version differ, and how does either one shed light on homoerotic cultural styles? By their dictates to the *Tico* in bed. (*Tico* is the Costa Ricans' nickname for themselves.) United States sexual anarchy, especially of the variety seen in the periodical *Fag Rag* and in the occasional short story or novel, is political. It carries the message, implicit or explicit, "Experiment, do anything you can invent, break the barriers, and the world will be permanently changed. The personal is political." Latin sexual anarchy is apolitical. It has been domesticated—or better, it operates within the wide but solid wall of form. The contrapuntal performance that is written in this score is individual, and does not threaten form; it is a performance that baffles and frustrates the foreigner in the cinema or the bath until he comes to recognize the underlying aesthetic structure. A Costa Rican man will be a demonic angel, pushing himself to the limit of sensuality and endurance with one partner or with several partners, in private or with witnesses, not to count coup but to test himself and innovate. When this part of the performance has ended, however, he passes the threshold, which may be the street door of the cinema, the door of the hotel room, or the door to the *cuarto de relax* (cubicle) of the bath, and he is at once a proper buttoned-up gentleman, who greets and speaks with the grace, dignity and impersonality of a Renaissance *caballero*, to the very partners with whom he has just invented new forms of passion. That Costa Rican is not a hypocrite. He is simply acting appropriately, first as a creature of anarchy, second as a carrier of form. He knows both statuses so well he does not need to be conscious of them, and he knows perfectly the role for each status.

Form versus anarchy as a feature of the *Tico* homoerotic ambiance is my construction. A similar statement is made by the Biesanzes, as noted below, but I have not seen it elsewhere. Some of the features that follow are agreed upon to a larger or smaller extent by Schifter and others.

Those will be described more briefly here. Those which diverge will be given more space.

The Family

There is no anonymity in Costa Rica, and *Ticos* do not seem to desire it except for fleeting moments. The entire country, with about the area of West Virginia or the Navajo Nation, contains only three million people, of whom half live in San José. There are only two universities of standing: the University of Costa Rica main campus in San José, and the National University in Heredia. Costa Rica in important respects is like a small town, and there are no secrets in small towns.

Add to small country size the famous strength of the Latin family, at least in the middle and upper classes, and the *ambiente* must be much quieter than gay society in North America or even in Mexico. There was no liberation movement until the late 1980s. All of the middle- and upper-class *de ambiente Ticos* whom I know or have heard about are deeply enmeshed in their families, and all of them put their obligations to their families before all other considerations. (Lower-class *Ticos* may have had to break family ties when they migrated to the city, live in poverty and isolation, and are glad for any association whatever.)

"Do our mothers suspect? Who can keep anything like that from a mother? But you don't say anything, and Mother doesn't either" (Hughes 1985). Within the family the *de ambiente* man wears a transparent mask, to which I shall turn later.

The Discipline of the Day and Patterns of Friendship

Given the strong sense of form, or propriety, and given the small size of Costa Rica and the fact that anonymity can be achieved only with difficulty even in a capital city of one million people, a man greets the day in his own home. Unless he is wealthy enough to live on an estate, he meets several neighbors as soon as he puts his uncombed, unshaven head out of his door. They will be washing their cars, tending their flowers, picking up the newspaper from the lawn, or just scratching themselves in the morning sun. Their wives or mothers, or more rarely they themselves, will go to the bakery to buy the bread and milk or other food for breakfast. That a man, in the capacity of husband or son, should be absent from this domestic scene, would be somewhat scandalous.

Ticos go to work early. Almost everyone is in his office or shop by 8:00 A.M., laborers often by 7:00 A.M. The morning belongs to work, and might be labeled non-sexual. All offices and some other enterprises close for two hours at midday. I do not know to what extent the siesta is defined as a sexual time in Costa Rica; it is so in Mexico, where a joking lore has grown up about it. (Even in puritanical Jackson, Michigan, I have heard factory workers joke about a "nooner.") The early afternoon also belongs to work, although less strictly than the morning. There is nothing irregular about a man who frequents the cafés and cantinas in the afternoon, particularly after about 4:00 P.M.

Late afternoon and evening are free time, both in the sense that they are not dedicated to work, and that, whether he be single or married, a man's time belongs to him and not his family. The social compulsion to eat breakfast at home is nowhere near as strong at supper time. It is in the evening that a man meets those with whom he will enjoy Platonic friendship and sexual adventure, both heterosexual and homosexual, or each alternatively. The schedules of the baths are established accordingly. They open mid-afternoon or early evening, and close around the time the last busses run (about 11:00 P.M.). None is open all night. Bars tend to open earlier than baths, and their clientele and the activity in them changes from day to evening.

All men operate within the same daily discipline. What any man does with his free time is his own business, so long as he supports his family and so long as he is discreet enough not to become publicly obnoxious. A "proper" man seeking other men is therefore not conspicuous. He is flamboyant, if at all, only during the leisure part of the day, when no one has a right to ask where he is, and only inside the walls of establishments which straights would not want to enter.

The friendship and association patterns mentioned above also help give those who are *de ambiente* the freedom to be inconspicuously engaged in homosexual behavior. The *de ambiente* male, as a result of these convenient patterns of time and of association, and as a result of deferring to the superior demands of the family, has no quarrel with society so great as to lead him to make a public call for reform. Just as he conforms to the formal limits set on him by society (including the Church, about which I have little specific information), so society in general tolerates him with reasonably good will so long as he raises no public waves.

One *loca* tells me that tolerance occasionally goes further. In the annual celebration of the black virgin in the old capital city of Cartago,

"Everyone knows," so he says, that the most gorgeous costumes and the most beautiful floats are made by *locas*. Carthaginians honor *locas* for their talents and help them discharge such family obligations as taking care of their children, if any, during the busy season. My informant said that expensive fabrics are imported from Miami and other foreign cities for this celebration, at the personal expense of the men who fashion them. Of course, the fact that these talented men are homosexual is never mentioned in public.

Housing

At the time of my most intense fieldwork, in the 1970s and early 1980s, there were very few apartment houses in San José. Thus, even a man or couple who wanted to live apart from their families of orientation (and few did or dared) would have had a difficult time. The housing shortage conspires to keep homoerotic life casual, sporadic, and unorganized.[2] Steady lovers, as well as cruising males, meet at bars, baths, cinemas, public parks, and the beach. San José has two hotels that rent rooms by the hour and welcome same-sex couples. There is a tradition in the country of groups of friends going off together on weekends and holidays to either coast—most often the Pacific—without families.

Social Class

A cliché of English and sometimes of American society is that the upper and the lower classes have the fun, but the middle class minds the morals and does the work of the nation. That cliché does not apply to Costa Rica.

The upper-class *de ambiente* male is thoroughly enmeshed in his family, and in honoring his family consciously honors the stability of Costa Rican society. It comes before all other considerations. He is, therefore, hyper-discreet. The one aristocratic *de ambiente Tico* whom I know fairly well practices a respectable profession. He says he is sure that several of his colleagues at work know that he is gay, but that none ever discusses it either openly or by allusion. He also says that he is a member of a coterie of thirty or forty *de ambiente* of his social class, who have known

---

2. For elaboration see chapter 2 in this volume.

each other all their lives. They seldom have sex with each other, but they often meet and gossip and dish each other and the rest of their acquaintances. They occasionally spend vacations together at the beach. He never frequents the baths or the more common gay bars, but occasionally patronizes one or two restaurants that are gay-run, whose proprietors are social friends.

The middle-class *de ambiente* male is similar, especially in putting family first. Because he is not quite so conspicuous, he is more free to go to the baths—and, with discretion, to bars. When he is young and a student, he may use the tearooms of the university and elsewhere, or cruise at the beach.

Bars are stratified by class. One of the informants who gave Hughes information for his *Tico Times* story says, "Some [bars] are for the professional class, some for the middle class and some for the workers. 'I wouldn't go there,' said a student of one well-known gay bar in San José. 'It's dangerous. They're rough workers, and if a fight starts you'd be hard pressed to keep out of it'" (Hughes 1985).

The lower–middle class seem to make up the majority of the clientele for most gay bars, and for one of the baths. They also represent a large portion of the customers at the two gay cinemas, which have largely homosexual audiences, but never show gay films. Bruce Lee is a screen favorite, as are other stars who portray violence. Since these cinemas are not at all respectable, their clientele includes few people of high enough social standing to fear being recognized. Otherwise, they are democratic and anonymous.

The lowest-class men are so desperate for survival that they scarcely fit any of the generalizations of this paper. They migrate to San José either because they believe that life is more interesting and abundant in the city, or because they have been squeezed off their land by the impersonal economic force (often multinational corporations) which inexorably transfers title to farmland from subsistence tillers to cash croppers. They arrive in the capital skilled at caring for about fifteen crops and five domestic animals, but marginally literate and commanding absolutely no urban job skills. If they are young and attractive, they often keep hunger away by peddling themselves for a few colones. Is such a man homosexual/gay? That question may not even be profitable to ask. I can comment only that, unlike many North American hustlers, they almost never hide behind a macho facade which says, "I am top man, never bottom man," in the style that John Rechy (1962, 1977) made familiar. Whether needing money or not, Costa Ricans of the lowest class exhibit directness, lack of social mask, and a simple masculinity.

The Church

No one indicated to me that the Church had any influence at all over his behavior, surprising as that may seem. This is not a topic into which I probed.

Categories of Homosexual Identity

The constructionist point of view is the most useful one for describing male-male sex in Costa Rica (cf. Weeks 1981; Parker 1985, 1991), because the term *homosexual* is not a native term at all, nor is *gay*. *Homosexual* is not native in English either, if we can believe Weeks's assertion (1981:82) that "The word . . . itself was not invented until 1869 . . . and did not enter English usage until the 1880s and 1890s . . .". Both terms are only now entering Costa Rican discourse.

We can for analytic purposes isolate three categories of Costa Rican men who enjoy sexual relations with other men, and note what their public images are. The first has no name. It is composed of any male who has sex with another male but identifies himself primarily as a lover of women. He has married a woman, or intends to do so, and has or will have children by her. If one were to ask him to what extent he is a lover of men, he might have to pause for some time to consider his answer (assuming he was willing to search himself for an honest answer), because such a question would not have occurred to him. These men do not consider themselves bisexual; from their point of view, sex with men is not important enough to affect their identity.

The second category is made up of those who label themselves *de ambiente*, which is the nearest native term to *gay*. These men may be exclusively man-lovers or they may make love to both men and women, but they prefer men. They are rather less likely than the first category to marry, but many of them do. A North American gay may deceive himself that these people are gay in his sense, because they make love beautifully, they frequent gay bars and baths, and their conversation has the same tasty seasoning of dishing, indignation, and sensitivity that one becomes accustomed to in North America. What is not simply and straightforwardly "gay" about them is that although they label themselves *de ambiente*, the rest of the world usually has no label for them at all, preferring to take them at face value. The "face" of a man is always masculine if possible, with no public reservations, however many of his friends and relatives may know what he does in bed and with whom.

The Mexican and Chicano poet Alberto Urista (Alurista), upon reading an early draft of this paper, remarked that Latins *de ambiente* wear transparent masks. Some of them have two masks—the straight mask and the gay mask—and change mannerisms to go with each. The mask is not intended to deceive but only to present appropriate appearances, to enable a man to accommodate himself to different environments. Those who see through the mask ordinarily have the courtesy to treat it as if it were opaque.

The first category of men who love men need no mask, because to them men are incidental. The third category, the *loca*, wears no mask because neither a transparent nor an opaque one will hide him (although even at work he subdues his image).

A *loca* or *maricón*, is an effeminate man. His social role is swish. He is often, although not invariably, a drag queen. He is never a permanent transvestite or transsexual. Both in his own eyes and in those of society, his is a separate identity. In Costa Rica as in Spain (cf. Murphy 1984), he is publicly put down, joked about, belittled; but he is not feared or ostracized, and he may become a confidant to women.

In North American terms, the three categories identified here would amount to one that is bisexual and two that are homosexual. In Costa Rica, the first two are not publicly remarked on at all, and the third is not so much homosexual as oriented toward women (that is, it is not so much the *loca's* sexual behavior as his persona that marks him). The paradigm is radically different from the dominant paradigm of North America and Europe when one eliminates that part of Costa Rican discussion that is translated from European psychiatry.

North-South Comparison

Some further comment about these categories may help United States readers to understand how they are distinct from United States "heterosexual," "homosexual," and "bisexual."

Imagine a United States man who desires to make love to another man about whom he is uncertain. If he is open and also impatient, he may blurt out: "Are you gay or straight?" If the question is answered, he will know whether to cut his losses or go for the prize. (The answer may be, "I'm straight, of course. What do you take me for, a queer or something?") In the same situation a Costa Rican would not ask. The question would be meaningless, because except for the *loca* there is no homosexual identity outside of homosexual situations. If the object of his lust did not want to have sex with him, he nevertheless would more likely be flattered than insulted, so long as the invitation was given in private and led to no public social consequences.

If *homosexual* is not a native category, then neither are *pasivo* or *activo*, despite their frequent use in other Spanish-speaking countries. Within the first two man-loving categories, men are very likely to switch from pitcher to catcher in a single night. The feeling seems to be that as a consequence each partner has enjoyed the full range of sexual experience, has engaged all his nerve endings. The *loca* category is behaviorally fixed, at least ideally. His public image says that he always catches, never pitches. (What he does in private is much less predictable.)

A reasonably conscientious North American or Northern European gay is likely, through politics, psychoanalysis, or introspection, to work at bringing his life into a single focus, to be equally "out" in all of his social guises. He may formulate that goal in terms of internal integration, of honesty, of social effectiveness, or in some other way.

The homosexually involved *Tico* has no such compulsion. He neatly but without schizophrenia divides his life according to the rhythm of the day, the week, the time of year, according to the imperatives of family, the limitations of housing, a widely shared view of public propriety. Plenty of time and energy is left over for private activity. He lives by the sexual contract: his sense of what he owes to society is complemented by the tolerance which society shows to him so long as he obeys its public demands, so he seldom has to protect himself against hostile jokes or public opprobrium. Where North American public morality is loud on the topic of sex, where the North American gay may find himself loathing himself either for being homosexual or for hiding it, the Latin male does in private whatever he is moved to do, and Latin public morality is largely quiet on the topic.

The Oppression Model

Jacobo Schifter Sikora seems to say almost the opposite in two book-length accounts: *La Formación de una Contracultura: Homosexualismo y Sida en Costa Rica* (1989) and *Hombres que Aman Hombres*, co-authored with Johnny Madrigal Pana (1992). (Despite the implication of the two titles, the first contains a description of gay life, with only one chapter on AIDS, while the second reports a study of AIDS sponsored by the World Health Organization, with three chapters on gay life authored by Schifter.) I shall précis Schifter's description, with a minimum of analytic commentary.

Schifter offers a no-nonsense factual behavioral approach to what gays do. He uses *gay* as a Spanish term, without comment. He seldom uses either the term *loca* or *maricón*, referring to that category of homosexuals as *travestidos* or the nickname *travestis*, whether they cross-dress or not.

Homosexuals are socially women. Costa Rica is a patriarchal society, in which women are defined as immature and weak, and gays are equated with women. Schifter takes the Marxist view that straight males use homophobia in the same way they use male chauvinism—as an instrument of economic oppression. As employee, the gay Costa Rican is likely to work twice as hard as others, and to decline positions and promotions in order to avoid confrontation. At home, "Gays are the curanderos of the bourgeois Costa Rican family, exploited victims of abuse, their necessities ignored" (Schifter 1989:85). They occupy the margins of society if they cannot hide their identity; if they are rich, they are exposed to blackmail; if poor, to sexual exploitation. Power is not available to either rich or poor. As a result, their values tend to be nihilistic (p. 68).

The social scene is most often the bar scene, "oriented solely toward diversion," politically irresponsible or downright apolitical (Schifter 1989:76). The classic private party is the drag show, an extravaganza in which the actors are "covered with makeup, three-story wigs, and feathers of every color" (Schifter 1989:69). Homosexuals dare not invite their professional colleagues home if they live with lovers, lest it be discovered with whom they live. They drain considerable energy into keeping up a straight front, laughing at homophobic jokes, making empty *piropos* (whispered sexual compliments) to women on the street, and boasting of non-existent heterosexual conquests. They loathe themselves.

Negation

They escape reality as best they can. Experimentation becomes a sexual escape valve to which they become addicted. "They lived for sex, for those ephemeral moments of prohibited pleasure—and as with any pleasant sensation that is intense but of short duration, they sought to repeat it as soon as possible. From this situation stems the addictive and compulsive character of sex for many gays." The obsession with the great orgasm reduced personalities to secondary importance. People measured themselves by inches, physiques acquired obsessive importance, and hedonistic culture was born in Costa Rica (Schifter 1989:87). The compulsive sex of gay *Ticos* is to an extent borrowed from the more general machismo, which dictates that excessive sexual activity is admired in men (Schifter and Madrigal 1992:75).

Schifter includes under "negation" the belief of some gays that "if one knows how to comport oneself, he won't encounter problems." Such people, he says, "simply reject reality" (1989:58). Others negate their homosexuality by a situational schizophrenia, withdrawing from the outside world; these people seldom actually have sex with anyone (p. 59). Some similar men abuse women, using them violently (pp. 60–61), and many gays, for similar reasons, betray each other. The greatest gay-haters are the *locas*. "The way in which they demonstrate this business is to mock all gays, including those who listen [to drag shows in bars, etc.], leaving it very clear that their *quiebres* (body movements) and mannerisms are common to all" (p. 63). Some merely fantasize or wallow in such paranoia as the belief that AIDS was a CIA plot (pp. 64–65).

In Schifter's view, heterosexual activity is not much better. It is a rite of power in Costa Rica as in any patriarchal society. Men try to convince women that the sexual act is an act of love, but there can be no love between the dominator and the dominated. Men in Costa Rica negate women's power, even their existence. Men and women in Costa Rica communicate little; men, whether heterosexual or homosexual, flee from intimacy with women—the former because they cannot love what the patriarchal society teaches them to misprize, the latter because this same society rejects them for their homosexuality (Schifter 1989:88).

Men and men are equally unsuccessful in their search for intimacy. "In patriarchal society, the opportunities for [emotional] expression for a sensitive man are almost nonexistent" (Schifter 1989:69). There are good reasons to think that many, perhaps even a majority, of Costa Rican men experience homoerotic desires (pp. 59–61), but these desires alienate them from each other and lead them into exaggerated homophobic jokes and persecution. Only in certain situations, far from the influence of women—like football, politics, work or drinking—do men permit themselves emotional closeness. "It is not strange that men, when they are alone with each other . . . can touch, embrace, grab each other, protect each other, and communicate. After a few drinks, almost everything is permitted: crying, laughing, confessing, even kissing" (p. 61). After Costa Rica did well in the world soccer competition against Italy in 1990, men did everything noted above plus exposing their genitals in public and flirting outrageously. "It was impressive to observe the quantity of repressed homosexual conduct that there is in the country" (Schifter and Madrigal 1992:60). Nevertheless, real sober intimacy between men is forbidden.

Internalized Homophobia

Negation is very close to internalized homophobia, which Schifter regards as the greatest negation. In this context, as well as describing the phobia of non-gays, he excoriates the administration of Nobel Peace Prize winning President Oscar Arias, "one of the most homophobic in history," which initiated a wave of dismissals of government officials, sometimes authorized by heads of offices who in their own turn were dismissed for the same reason (Schifter and Madrigal 1992:61). This disloyalty, says Schifter, was very much like the betrayal by each other of Jews in concentration camps to save their own skins.

Causes of homophobia by gays themselves include their acceptance of Catholic dogma and of machismo. Schifter (1989:43) believes that the latter derives from Islam. Curiously, Schifter leaves Islam with this passing remark, saying nothing about the complexity of Islamic attitudes toward male homosexuality, which frequently tolerate relations between an older powerful male and an adolescent or post-adolescent boy.

If there were no ideology of domination, more Costa Ricans would turn homosexual, especially women—who are the most exploited and dominated group (Schifter 1989:46). As noted above, even gay men cannot really love other men, because of their own homophobia, and "the act which promised union produces rupture" (p. 89). Alcohol and marijuana contribute to the impersonality of gay sex.

Internalized homophobia is a centerpiece of Schifter's construction, re-examined in each section of the 1992 book and resting on sources drawn from psychoanalysis. The society that puts down gays is the same society that oppresses women, and cannot give up the one domination without giving up the other. However, despite being oppressed by the same patriarchs, gays and lesbians do not unite politically. Many lesbians look at gay men as part of the patriarchy which oppresses them and object to integrating themselves with gay causes. Some gays see lesbians as disloyal because of their adherence to feminist organizations, instead of to lesbian organizations to avoid homophobia (Schifter 1989: 285). Schifter predicts that political separation of the genders will continue.

The damage that internalized homophobia does to gays includes suicides and other acts just short of suicide, the destruction of one's creativity, and obliteration in the work of social scientists of any notice of the creativity of gay Costa Ricans in the development of the nation; in fact, social scientists never mention the theme (Schifter and Madrigal 1992:47).

Housing and Families

Housing is a variable. Not until the 1970s did the construction of apartment houses make it possible for some individuals to rent them and live apart from their families. Schifter waxes playful about the housing shortage: "In the same way in which the writer Virginia Woolf analyzes the lack of 'a room of one's own' for the woman, as the cause of the discrimination she has suffered, one could say that gays can't count on places in which to express themselves as such" (Schifter and Madrigal 1992:81–82). Thus, an independent gay society began to emerge and grow. Still, San José remains so small a city that anonymity is difficult. The beginning of a new gay community "was an opium dream in Costa Rica" (Schifter 1989:75).

The family remains an important part of the calculations of the gay man. "The new emerging class had separated itself a little from its families or origin, but had not broken with them so as to create parallel institutions which serve to protect its members. . . . Gays needed the family in order to work, to invest, to establish businesses or practice professions. Social status continued to be an important passport for survival" (Schifter 1989:75). Some parents accept their gay sons to some extent, mothers more than fathers. Schifter feels that mothers' self-interest sometimes dictates this acceptance: the unmarried gay child is more likely than the straights to stay home and take care of the mother, and she may feel forced to accept his sexual orientation in order to keep his economic support (Schifter and Madrigal 1992:87–89).

Participation of gay males in their families is tense and uneasy for those who cannot hide their gayness. The 1989 book records the history

of gay protest politics, in reaction to raids against both gay and lesbian
bars, initiated by the Ministries of Health, Security and Government in
1987. This movement is headed by an organization of which Schifter
is leader, called "Lucha contra el sida" (fight against AIDS). Schifter
compares the outrage felt by Costa Rican gays against the raids to the
Stonewall Riots in Greenwich Village in 1969.

Patterns of Gay Society

In the AIDS study, Schifter and Madrigal consider prison, bars, bisexuals, "transvestite sex workers," those who have taken consciousness-
raising courses at the National University in Heredia, adolescents, and
those who practice anonymous sex in parks. They also look at how gays
pair themselves.

Prisoners in "La Reforma," the penitentiary in the capital city, divide
themselves into straights and gays (Schifter and Madrigal 1992: chapter
7). (Schifter uses the term *cachero* for active participants in anal sex,
contrary to the Mexican gloss for the same term as a passive, or "one
who catches.") Roles are inflexible. A straight prisoner is not one who
avoids sex with other men, but one who is always active. The gays,
whom he usually refers to as *travestis*, were in most cases homosexual
before coming to prison.

In a similar way, roles in gay pairs outside of prison among older
homosexuals are rigid. The macho *no se abre* as the *loca* of the pair does
(literally "does not open himself," but the term can be taken metaphorically to indicate one who dominates both in bed and out [Schifter
and Madrigal 1992:90]). This complementary pattern fits an under-
developed country well: the macho is a surrogate father, one who is
socially and economically more powerful, and who becomes the protec-
tor of the *travesti*. Violence, which perpetuates the general patriarchal
culture, permeates gay pairs, who communicate more through actions
than through words. Explosions are huge (p. 104). A more modern
pattern, borrowed from other countries and practiced by younger pairs,
is symmetrical rather than complementary. However, Schifter and
Madrigal (1992:95) say that most gay *Ticos* prefer to be passive in
anal sex.

Their discussion of bar and adolescent sex is almost entirely in terms
of statistical likelihood of contracting AIDS, and the description of
anonymous sex is confined to anecdotes about how men meet and how
they have sex. The authors do not interview their informants in suffi-

cient depth to gain a picture of the thinking of men who seek sex anonymously instead of in spaces marked by greater social interaction.

Comparative Literature

To what extent is either of the models consonant with other descriptions of male homosexuality in mestizo and criollo Latin America?[3] Schifter and I are the only scholars who have described the phenomenon in Costa Rica, so far as I know, but the literature for other parts of Latin America is growing.

Comparative evidence for my assertion that Costa Rica (and Latin America) smiles on sex is for the most part indirect, except for Brazil, where Parker's 1991 study makes that point emphatically, and for Whitam and Mathy's discussion of Latin tolerance. "Brazilian tolerance for the homosexual seems to be part of a larger pattern of tolerance for sexuality in general" (1986:141). The tenor of their chapter implies that a pro-sex attitude in a culture almost inevitably correlates with an attitude that favors tolerance of homosexuals, or at least regards sexual orientation as unimportant. Unpublished tourist accounts of the Caribbean contrast such British islands as Jamaica and Barbados—both said to be homophobic through and through and perhaps anti-sexual—with Puerto Rico, a playground for gay and straight tourists, as documented in short stories by the North American fiction writer Richard Hall (1981) and in Oscar Lewis's biography of a poor San Juan family (1966). My undergraduate male students who spend semesters in Costa Rica with the Associated Colleges of the Midwest give me feedback consistent with my pro-sex pro-tolerance-toward-homosexuality description. About half of these students report the following pattern of *Tico* behavior: *Tico* age mates whose appearance and mannerisms label them heterosexual (i.e., not *locas*) approach them sexually; they turn down the approaches courteously, without offensive language; the *Ticos* are not offended or embarrassed; friendly relations proceed without interruption or tension. I take this pattern to indicate that in fact homosexual contacts are a normal part of everyday life, and that those who engage in them are not regarded as a special category so long as they do not make their identities or desires publicly obvious.

---

3. American Indian sexual categories occupy other universes.

The contract model is nowhere explicit in the literature about Latin America, so far as I have discovered, but it characterizes United States prisons, according to a study of a medium-security prison in California. Wooden and Parker say that "Homosexuals and punks are a fact of prison life and are tolerated as long as they keep their place and fit the feminized stereotype. Such acceptance is comparable to the way some black slaves were accepted, and even treated well, in the pre–Civil War South, so long as they kept their place" (1982:19). A contract may also be inferred from Lancaster's (1992) description of Nicaragua, Whitam and Mathy's (1986) comparison of the Anglo Saxon and Latin (and Iberian) erotic traditions. A large number of heterosexual Guatemalan males "use" homosexuals for secondary outlets, and "80 percent of heterosexual males [in Portugal] regularly have such secondary homosexual contact" (1986:134). It would be difficult, though not impossible, for a majority or large minority of heterosexual men to be genuinely homophobic if so many of them are "moving in and out of the homosexual world" (p. 136). Michael Murphy's 1984 work on homosexuals in the Lenten carnival in Seville reports something similar: *locas* are ridiculed but tolerated and protected, while masculine-acting homosexuals are feared and shunned. I believe the contract model is consistent with most of the literature on homosexuality in Latin America.

My form/anarchy tension seemed to me touched with fantasy until I ran across similar language in the Biesanzs' (1982:11) general description of Costa Rica: "Costa Ricans tend to be formalistic and legalistic as well as conservative. . . . At the same time, there is a strong strain of resistance to law, an anarchic, anti-authoritarian tendency that goes along with the belief in individual liberty."

There is nothing explicit that I know of in the literature concerning daily rhythms, but discussions of the behavioral dichotomy between *casa* (house) and *calle* (street) are common in most ethnographies of urban Latin America. Richard Parker delves into convolutions within *calle*, which include temporary inversions of space (1991:101).

The importance of family in determining sexual behavior is also commonplace. Joseph Carrier (1976) says that gays in Guadalajara are reluctant to confront their families. Taylor (1985:133–35) represents Mexican gays as astonished that gringos cut themselves off from the emotional and material support of their families and move to anonymous metropolitan centers. Murray (1987:118–29) devotes a chapter to the strength of family in Guatemala. The housing shortage is discussed in most of the literature as a subcategory of the importance of family; I believe this conflation is appropriate. Kutsche and Schifter agree. So do Carrier (1976) for Guadalajara, Clark Taylor (1985:133–35) for Mexico City, and Murray and Arboleda (in Murray 1987:104) for Lima. The Guatemalan encounters reported by Erskine Lane (1978) are all in the North Americans' hotels or apartments, because their Guatemalan partners live with their families. Murray reports the institution of by-the-hour hotels in other parts of Latin America, some of which charge homosexuals more than heterosexuals. (I do not know whether Costa Rican hourly rates differ, as it never occurred to me to ask.)

Social class is an important shaper of homoerotic life in several Latin countries. Lane's encounters, noted above, are predominantly with lower-class men whose sex with men has no visible impact on their perceptions of themselves as masculine. Winston Leyland's anthologies of Latin fiction (1979, 1983) and an earlier report of my own from San José (Kutsche 1983) say the same thing. John Rechy on Chicano hustlers in Los Angeles (1977) differs in reporting a defensive refusal by the hustler to be a catcher; his masculinity demands that he pitch only. Rechy and Schifter (especially on prisons) are consistent.

The bisexual more rigidly limits himself in Mexico (Carrier 1985) and in the *buga* conception in Nicaragua (Lancaster 1992) than in Costa Rica, according to my model. The easy swing between active and passive and between men and women that my model suggests is consistent with Brazilian sexual behavior, as reported by Parker (1991), Trevisan (1986) and Luiz Mott (personal communications). There is a hint that Mexican bisexuality is not always so rigid, either. In Ceballos Maldonado's novel *Después de todo* (as discussed in Foster's 1991 review of gay works in Latin American fiction), the narrator has a series of young lovers, most of whom abandon him when they reach the normal age to marry. Their "homosexual acts serve as marketable goods that do not impinge on the seller's sexual self-identity" (Foster 1991:104). These were lovers, not tricks of the night, and presumably played a variety of roles. The role rigidity of old-fashioned gay couples in Schifter's model is close to Carrier's. It is also very similar to the Wooden and Parker prison report (1982:145–46).

In my experience, *activo* and *pasivo* are terms that a Costa Rican understands but does not use, and the question "¿Eres activo o pasivo?" which Murray and Arboleda report as a standard part of the introduction of cruising strangers in Guatemala and in Lima (in Murray 1987: 134, 104; this volume; also see Whitam and Mathy 1986:135) is not part of the presentation ritual. Such a dichotomy would fit Schifter's description of the difference between *travestis* and others, but he does not report the question. The homoerotic San José I know is better characterized by role switching between males whose attraction to each other is not usually based on complementary pitching and catching, but more often on the excitement of alternating. I wonder whether those masculine men (simply *hombres* without adjectives) whom Murray and Arboleda report as permitting themselves to show affection for their *maricón* partners (in Murray 1987:108), do not quietly switch roles but decline to talk about it. If gay Costa Rica is in fact exceptional in lacking a rigid separation of roles, the best explanation that occurs to me is its egalitarian democracy, which is unique to the Americas; men who regard themselves as equal to all other men can afford to enjoy sex without worrying about the social consequences of being top or bottom.

As noted, I did not hear the word *gay* from any Costa Rican, except for a few who had lived extensively in the United States or Europe. Schifter uses the term most of the time. Murray and Arboleda (in Murray 1987:130–38) report the rapid diffusion of the term into Latin America during the late 1970s and early 1980s, suggesting that *pasivos* are more likely than *activos* to use it, and that it indicates a shift from acceptance of the ideology of domination to assertion of the right to be homosexual. They also caution against the sloppy equation of terms and concepts from one culture area to another.

Schifter's argument that Costa Rican society treats gays and women as powerless equals, so as to dominate them and use them economically, is an echo of a view occasionally expressed in North American sexual scholarship. Cummings (1991) interprets the sexist imagery in the Rabelasian joking of young Mexican American males described by Limón (1989) as equating passivity with femaleness, denigrating both. Herek (1982) argues that the very terms "heterosexual" and "homosexual" are constructions convenient to industrial capitalism as a way to facilitate the economic exploitation of both gays and women.

The most serious challenge to Kutsche's optimistic and somewhat romantic model of mutual support between gays and straights is implied in Stephen Murray's ironic cautionary "Sleeping with the Natives as a Source of Data." Murray (1991, 1995) holds that foreigners use their own experiences with natives as valid data about what natives experience with each other at their peril:

The meaning to [foreign ethnographers] of what others are doing when they are having sex is not transparent to even the best-

trained, most sympathetic ethnographer. . . . It seems to me very
dangerous to extrapolate from the sexual experiences of a foreigner
in a culture to the ordinary cultural understandings and behaviors
there. . . . The relationship between such data [native-foreigner
sexual interchanges] and native intracultural behavior and thought
is far from obvious. [Murray 1995]

A reasonable buffer against such bias would be observation of what *Ticos*
do with each other sexually. My observation of others in the baths in San
José gives me mild support for my model, although the evidence is far
from decisive.

Most of the comparative literature, would appear to support my
model of tolerance. Some of it implies the two layers of overt homophobia and covert tolerance. Two countries (at least) are exceptions—or
I should better say, "two regimes"—both socialist: Castro's Cuba is
drastically homophobic (e.g., Young 1972, quoted in Whitam and
Mathy 1986: 143–44); Sandinista Nicaragua was unilayered in tolerating homosexuals (my experience is based on visits in 1982 and 1984 and
on several articles in *The Advocate* and *The Body Politic*, listed by Stephen
Foster in Murray 1987:22–23). Castro took the classic Marxist view that
homosexuality is capitalist degeneracy. Why the Sandinistas were pro-
gay I do not know. A government information officer whom I queried
on the topic in 1982 said, naively or ominously (I think the former), "We
have many problems to solve. We haven't got around to that one yet."

Argentina during the military repression of 1976–83 was also as
homophobic as Schifter represents Costa Rica as being. Miller (1992:
182–217) describes a relentless series of persecutions, raids, disap-
pearances, fear, self-hatred and *marginación*. If in fact national attitudes
towards homosexuals are so much alike in one of the most and one of
the least repressive of Latin American countries, then national politics
counts for nothing in understanding homosexuality.

If most scholars agree that Latin American societies are usually more
tolerant of male homosexuality than the United States is, the scholar
who is writing this paper cautions himself that with a few exceptions
these scholars are North American outsiders, who may be falling into
Murray's trap of assuming that intracultural reality is the same as their
own intercultural pleasure.[4] Natives, as reviewed by Foster (1991), have

---

4. Madrigal (1991) faults my description for presenting "aspects of the masculine
homosexual identity of the Costa Rican in a superficial and ambiguous way," espe-

constructed a more complex and far more diachronic picture, from the publication of the Brazilian novel *Bom-Crioulo* in 1895 to the present. Latin gay fiction traces a path from condemnation to tragedy to liberation, which is not basically different from that traced in Europe and North America. The angst that Schifter reports (experiences?) repeats itself in many of these works: the fractured and fractionated self-identities of people who regard themselves as homosexual but not bisexual, and the struggles against public hypocrisy and its damage to private personality. Some of these novelists appear to be taking the heroic role of equating their oppression with that of oppressed citizens in general and of championing all the oppressed. This theme is echoed by Schifter's closing *grito* in the first of his two books: "¡Para obtener poder, sólo el poder!" (1989:287: Power to all the oppressed of Latin America).

AIDS

The Kutsche model keeps to an ethnographic present of 1984: after AIDS had entered Costa Rica but before there was much awareness of its probable impact. After it had to be reckoned with (my 1989–90 sojourn), the fun went out of both form and anarchy so far as sexual activity between men was concerned. In the baths particularly, men became secretive and cautious and mutual masturbation began to replace innovative sexual styles. The grander gestures of formal interaction gave way to timidity and bare acknowledgments. On the streets some men ignored the threat of *el sida,* and some carried condoms, but exuberance diminished whether they did the one or the other. I entered no bars in 1989, so I do not know how much behavior there changed. I am forced to conclude that, while I continue to believe that my form/anarchy model is soundly based in Latin culture, I blew it up bigger than it warranted.

Both of Schifter's books were written after he dedicated himself to "la lucha contra el sida," so it is not easy to see distinctions through his eyes between pre- and post-AIDS behavior among gays. One can infer that the prominence of the drag show has given way to the prominence

---

cially objecting to my assertion that only *locas* have adopted a gay identity, a statement which, he says, "ignores and slanders the efforts which gays make to discover their own [identity]."

of the gay rights rally, that gays affirm themselves more now when the alternative is death than they did when the reward for continued public silence was quiet toleration. The homophobia of the majority of Costa Ricans is more open than before AIDS, he says in 1992: some physicians and many nurses, for instance, at first refused to treat AIDS patients. Schifter implicitly rejects the view that Latin society quietly tolerates homosexuality in its midst.

Ageism

I was a slender 47-year-old when I first visited Costa Rica, 63 during my last visit. My hair had grown much whiter in the meantime, my flesh less firm. The *Tico* reaction to old age during the last visit was more negative than I have usually encountered in the United States. Schifter and Madrigal (1992) state that a frequent pattern between males is for an older, wealthier, more socially powerful man to have a young protégé. Whether the reaction to me at 63 would have been more positive had I fit that slot, I do not know. As a foreigner, I could offer no such protection, short of inviting a young man to accompany me to the United States. This I was not prepared to do. I have seen no discussion of the effects of age on homosexual identity or activity in Latin America in any of the literature, either from an outsider or an insider perspective.

Reconciliation?

Schifter's constructions of male-male sexuality in Costa Rica is a little less contradictory to mine than they appear to be. We are examining different parts of the same elephant. I am looking at the Costa Rican male in the act of having sex with and thinking about other men. I concentrate on the large majority of such men who pass for straight and say little about the small minority who define themselves as *de ambiente* or gay. I seldom went into gay bars. I describe a homoerotic world, but mostly ignore the traditional *ambiente*. Schifter positions himself in the center of that small portion of *Tico* homosexual activity that identifies itself as gay—the *locas*, the *travestidos*—and chronicles their trajectory from self-hatred to affirmation. He describes in minute detail their fight against public opponents and the anguish of their campaign for self-acceptance and for toleration from official public society.

The difference in our "ethnographic presents" also reduces the contradiction between us. I described a contract as of 1984, before either AIDS or the gay rights movement had disrupted long-standing relations between Costa Rican men (see Kutsche and Page 1991:7); Schifter in 1989 and even more Schifter and Madrigal in 1992 concentrate on the late 1980s and early 1990s, when they and others had launched mortal combat to obliterate that contract (one they do not acknowledge and might deny ever existed).

Finally, Schifter's equation "homosexual males equal women in public opinion" opens a large area for reconciliation. Schifter reiterates this theme again and again. Page and I did not consider the question directly, but we made an observation about Costa Rican women that in retrospect looks less casual than when we wrote it:

> Guidelines for women's behavior are changing. Women first entered the professions, and next they are entering politics. Almost inevitably, they will confront the double standard of sexual morality with demands for equality, and they will invade men's private space and times. That confrontation has only barely begun. [1991:13]

If indeed women and homosexual men are functional equivalents in *Tico* ideology, then an actual confrontation by women implies a probable confrontation by *locas*.

Schifter and I read the past of homosexuality in Costa Rica differently: an unrelieved oppression for him, a tacit agreement with benefits (albeit unequal) to both gays and straights for me. For myself, I add the hope that bisexual men, whether they comprise the majority or a large minority of all Costa Rican men, remain secure in their genial polymorphous perversity.

REFERENCES

Biesanz, Richard, Karen and Mavis
    1982 *The Costa Ricans.* Englewood Cliffs, NJ: Prentice-Hall.
Carrier, Joseph M.
    1976 Family attitudes and Mexican male homosexuality. *Urban Life* 5:359–75.

1985   Mexican male bisexuality. *Journal of Homosexuality* 11:75–85.

Cummings, Laura

1991   Carne con limón: reflections on the construction of social harmlessness. *American Ethnologist* 18:370–72.

Foster, David W.

1991   *Gay and Lesbian Themes in Latin American Writing.* Austin: University of Texas Press.

Fuentes, Carlos

1975   *Terra Nostra.* New York: Farrar, Straus, Giroux.

Hall, Richard

1981   *Couplings: A Book of Stories.* San Francisco: Grey Fox Press.

Herek, Gregory M.

1982   Unisexual ideology and erotic hegemony: notes toward a marxist perspective on lesbian and gay oppression. *National Women's Anthropology Newsletter* 16:17–20.

Hughes, Rod

1985   Gay life different here. *Tico Times* (San José, Costa Rica), November 22.

Kutsche, Paul

1983   Situational homosexuality in Costa Rica. *Anthropology Research Group on Homosexuality Newsletter* 4(4):6–13.

1994   *Voices of Migrants.* Gainesville: University Press of Florida.

Kutsche, Paul, and J. Bryan Page

1991   Male sexual identity in Costa Rica. *Latin American Anthropology Review* 3:7–14.

Lancaster, Roger N.

1992   *Life is Hard: Machismo, Danger, and the Intimacy of Power in Nicaragua.* Berkeley: University of California Press.

Lane, Erskine

1978   *Game-Texts: A Guatemalan Journal.* San Francisco: Gay Sunshine Press.

Lewis, Oscar

1966   *La Vida: A Puerto Rican Family in the Culture of Poverty.* New York: Random House.

Leyland, Winston

1979   *Now the Volcano: An Anthology of Latin American Gay Literature.* San Francisco: Gay Sunshine Press.

1983   *My Deep Dark Pain is Love: A Collection of Latin American Gay Fiction.* San Francisco: Gay Sunshine Press.

Limón, José E.

1989   Carne, carnales, and the carnivalesque: bakhtinian batos, disorder, and narrative discourses. *American Ethnologist* 16:471–86.

Madrigal Pana, Johnny

1991   ¿Existe la identidad gay en Costa Rica? *Iconoclasta* 2:19–21.

Miller, Neil

1992   *Out in the World: Gay and Lesbian Life from Buenos Aires to Bangkok.* New York: Random House.

Murphy, Michael D.
1984 Masculinity and selective homophobia: a case from Spain. *Anthropology Research Group on Homosexuality Newsletter* 5(3):6–12.

Murray, Stephen O.
1987 *Male Homosexuality in Central and South America.* San Francisco: Instituto Obregón. (Gai Saber Monograph 5).
1991 Sleeping with the natives as a source of data. *Society of Lesbian and Gay Anthropologists Newsletter* 13:49–51.
1995 Male homosexuality in Guatemala: possible insights and certain confusions of sleeping with the natives as a source of data. To appear in *Lesbian and Gay Fieldwork.* Ellen Lewin and William Leap, eds. Urbana: University of Illinois Press.

Parker, Richard G.
1985 Masculinity, femininity, and homosexuality: on the anthropological interpretation of sexual meaning in Brazil. *Journal of Homosexuality* 11: 155–63.
1991 *Bodies, Pleasures and Passions: Sexual Culture in Contemporary Brazil.* Boston: Beacon Press.

Rechy, John
1962 *City of Night.* New York: Grove Press.
1977 *The Sexual Outlaw.* New York: Dell.

Schifter Sikora, Jacobo
1989 *La Formación de una contracultura: Homosexualismo y sida en Costa Rica.* San José: Ediciones Guayac.

Schifter Sikora, Jacobo, and Johnny Madrigal Pana
1992 *Hombres que Aman Hombres.* San José: Ediciones Ilep-sida.

Taylor, Clark L.
1985 Mexican male homosexual interaction in public contexts. *Journal of Homosexuality* 11:117–36.

Trevisan, Joao Silvério.
1986 *Perverts in Paradise.* London: Gay Men's Press.

Weeks, Jeffrey
1981 Discourse, desire and sexual deviance: some problems in a history of homosexuality. In *The Making of the Modern Homosexual.* Kenneth Plummer, ed. Pp. 76–111. Totowa, NJ: Barnes & Noble.

Whitam, Frederick L., and Robin M. Mathy
1986 *Male Homosexuality in Four Societies: Brazil, Guatemala, the Philippines, and the United States.* New York: Praeger.

Wooden, Wayne S., and Jay Parker
1982 *Men Behind Bars: Sexual Exploitation in Prison.* New York: Plenum Press.

8

Stigma Transformation and Relexifiction
GAY IN LATIN AMERICA*

Stephen O. Murray
Manuel Arboleda G.

The term *gay* diffused rapidly in urban Latin America during the late 1970s and early 1980s, raising the question whether use of the term reflects changes from a gendered to an egalitarian/gay organization of homosexuality. Barry Adam characterized the latter as one in which

(1) people meet and form enduring social networks only because of mutual homosexual interest (2) there is a sense of peoplehood and emerging culture (Murray 1979a; Levine 1979), and (3) there is the possibility of exclusive (non-bisexual) and egalitarian (not role-bound) same-sex relations. [1979:18; also see 1987:6]

In North American cities a shift—albeit one that is not complete even now—has occurred. Formerly, the man who took only the insertor role in homosexual coitus (termed *trade* in the homosexual subculture that preceded *gay community*) was not identified by others and did not identify himself as *homosexual*. Only (some of) those regularly taking an insertee role *(queens)* did.[1] Under the aegis of *gay*—an aggressively stigma-challenging label (Goffman 1963) without the negative connotations of *queer* or *queen*—a shift from what might be considered an exogamous system of sexual exchange in which those identifying them-

---

*Earlier versions of this paper were presented at the 1982 Pacific Sociological Association meetings in San Diego, and the 1982 American Sociological Association meetings in San Francisco. The authors would like to acknowledge the encouragement of the session organizers, Wayne Wooden and William Devall, respectively; and also that of Niyi Akinnaso, Wayne Dynes, John Gumperz, and Amparo Tuson.

1. See Reiss (1961), Humphreys (1975), Murray (1979b, 1981, 1996), Chauncey (1985, 1994).

selves or fantasized by their partners as *straight (trade)* were sought to an endogamous system in which both partners identify themselves as *gay* has occurred in Anglo North America. This change has brought ideal norms closer to patterns of behavior,[2] and ontogeny has recapitulated phylogeny in this transformation to mutual definition by both partners (Miller 1978; Humphreys and Miller 1981).

When the word *gay* was unknown in Latin America, which was as recently as the mid-1970s, homosexual identification was analogous to the pre-gay pattern in Anglo North America: those who only played the *activo* (insertor) role did not consider themselves defined, nor even implicated by such behavior. Neither did their *pasivo* partners. *Activos* were simply *hombres* (men), quite regardless of the sex of the persons who received their phallic thrusts. Even those persons who switched roles tended to identify themselves by one role designation or the other and to attempt to constrain any publicity about the other, although there were terms—*moderno* in Peru and *internacional* in Mesoamerica—for such dichotomy-transcending conduct.[3]

In Lima in 1976 no one used the term *gay*. Only a very few Peruvians who had traveled to Europe or North America knew it. By 1980, however, most informants (self-identified *pasivos* and *activos*) knew the term and preferred it to the previously standard term *entendido* (in the know). Although outside homosexual networks *gay* was an unfamiliar locution, in October 1980 the popular magazine *Gente* ran a cover story entitled "Los Gays Peruanos Son Libres" (Peruvian Gays are Free). The article itself oscillated between linking *gay* with effeminacy and using it in the stigma-challenging sense common in North America. That it was used at all to refer to a group usually invisible in respectable publications and completely stereotyped in tabloids in Latin America (see Taylor 1978; Murray 1980a) was remarkable. By 1982 *gay* had entirely replaced *entendido* as a self-designation. Some used the spelling pronunciation (gai) rather than the phonetic realization borrowed from French or English (i.e., ge[y]).[4]

In Guatemala in 1978 two of five *pasivos* Murray interviewed offered

---

2. See Humphreys (1971, 1979), Murray (1981, 1984, 1996), Weinberg (1978), Wolf 1983).

3. See Murray and Dynes Chapter 13 (this volume).

4. Wooden (1982) reported the other solution to the problem of borrowing a word that is spelled in a way other than the one pronounced, i.e., changing the spelling, in Colombia and Venezuela.

gay as a term for men who chose other men as sexual partners. The three *pasivo* informants who reported not having friends with similar preferences nor any involvement in settings where such persons congregated were not familiar with the term. Both those who identified themselves as *internacional* (and were much-traveled) used *gay* and remarked that the term was achieving ever wider currency in their country. Of the three *activos* from whom Murray elicited lexical data, one did not know the word, one knew it but did not apply it to himself, and one both knew it and applied it to himself.[5]

Borrowed words do not necessarily retain the same meaning they had in the source language. Some of our informants seemed to use *gay* as a fashionable (new and foreign) term that simply replaced *entendido* or *de ambiente* within an unchanged conception of homosexuality. That is, they relexified the pre-existing conceptual order.[6] For others, however, the new word seemed to reflect a new conception of homosexuality, paralleling the stigma transformation involved in replacing *queer* and *homosexual* with *gay* in Anglo North America. Table 8.1 shows which of these models informants varying in (self-reported) role preference held.

Those who answered "No" to the ritualized cruising question, "¿Eres activo o pasivo?" invariably considered those who are *activo* to be *gay*, as well as those who are *pasivo*. For more than a third of those who identified themselves as *activo* and more than half of those who identified themselves as *pasivo* and who were familiar with the word, *gay* was a new word for the already existing conception of homosexuality. Interestingly, those who are stigmatized by this conception are less likely than those who seemingly profit in social esteem by it to embrace the wider conception of who is *gay*. A number of explanations (including false consciousness, covert prestige among the stigmatized, cognitive disso-

---

5. See Murray (1980b) for description of the elicitation procedures and social characteristics of this sample. Subsequent waves of repression in Guatemala prevented return fieldwork as well as driving underground a previously emerging subculture.

6. We interpret Brazilian activist Herbert Daniel's statement "in Brazil there are many words that refer to behaviors and relations between men, many loaded with prejudice and discrimination [but] there is no word that has the value of *gay* in Brazil—that is a word produced by a political movement which took consciousness of its own needs" (quoted in Braiterman 1990:299) to indicate that *gay* has been assimilated to the traditional gender-distinct conception of homosexuality in Brazil, i.e., another lexeme for the sexually receptive "partner." Daniel went on to decry the lack of solidarity among those involved in homosexuality in Brazil and the oppressiveness of active/passive role differentiation.

Table 8.1

Frequency of Conceptions of "un hombre que prefiera los otros hombres"
by Place/Time and Sex Role

Locale/Year of Elicitation Reported Role	Gay Unknown	Only Pasivos are Gay	Activos are Gay	
Guatemala City, 1978				
activo	1	1	1	
pasivo	3	2	0	
internacional	0	0	3	
Lima, 1979				
activo	4	2	2	
pasivo	7	3	1	
Mexico City, 1981–83				
activo	9	6	8	
pasivo	5	3	5	
internacional	0	0	10	
Lima, 1982–83				
activo	0	0	5	
pasivo	2	3	6	
moderno	0	0	4	
Totals				(N)
activo	36%	23	41	(39)
pasivo	43%	28	30	(40)
moderno/internacional	0%	0	100	(17)
late 1970s	50%	27	23	(30)
early 1980s	24%	18	58	(66)

nance and/or ambivalence from heavily involved *activos*) might be proffered, if this pattern holds up for larger samples. Here, we only discuss the more certain change over time observable among both *activos* and *pasivos* rather than tenuous differences by sex role.

Although we claim to have observed change in process,[7] it bears em-

---

7. Structuralist linguistic orthodoxy held that linguistic change is too slow to observe, but Labov (1972) showed that it could. Murray (1981, 1992c) reported generational differences in bounding *gay community* in San Francisco. The example of not merely observing but explaining linguistic change as reflecting significant social change that has particularly influenced the work presented here is Akinnaso's (1980, 1982) work on Yoruba naming.

phasizing that all three models in Table 8.1 represent the conception of some men involved in homosexuality in Latin America. Some still use the old word(s), others have borrowed the word *gay* but simply replaced *entendido* with it in the same slot (relexification); but for some others, *gay* refers to a "new man" who can enact *(estar) pasivo* behavior without being *(ser) un pasivo.*

This change parallels the earlier Anglo North American one (which is presumably the source of prestige for the label *gay*). Nonetheless, some caution is in order before concluding that the development of a stigma-challenging gay community in Anglo North America provides a blueprint of stages for the rest of the world to copy. Although homosexuality in Latin America has been gender-defined, just as it was earlier in Anglo North America, residence patterns, censorship of materials that individual policemen or judges are free to interpret as politically subversive or incitements to vice, the absence of religious pluralism with its concomitant traditions (and freedoms) of voluntary associations, and other factors that may have been crucial to the history of gay institutional elaboration in Anglo North America but are quite different in Latin America (Taylor 1978; Murray 1980a, 1992b; Lacey 1983) may shape different developments to different ends there (and elsewhere). Mexican liberation organizations eschew the term *gay* because their leaders do not consider Anglo gay culture to be what they aspire to emulate. They are also sensitive about "cultural imperialism" from the north and the elitism of expensive local replicas of Anglo gay bars. Moreover, cultures in which homosexuality is age-defined, such as Islamic, Amazonian and Melanesian ones (see Murray 1992, 1994; Herdt 1984) defy any scheme of unilinear evolution to the gay organization of homosexuality even more clearly than the stirrings of change in Latin America.[8]

REFERENCES

Adam, Barry D.
    1979 Reply. *Sociologists Gay Caucus Newsletter* 18:8.
    1987 *The Rise of a Gay and Lesbian Movement.* Boston: Twayne.

---

8. See also Arboleda (1980), Wooden (1982), Kutsche (1983, this volume), Schifter (1990), Lumsden (1991), Adam (1993). Contrast Montero's (1993:24) notice of attempts to displace a gay model with Santiago's (1993:48) confidence that it will in time diffuse everywhere.

1993 In Nicaragua: homosexuality without a gay world. *Journal of Homosexuality* 24:171–81.

Akinnaso, F. Niyi

1980 The sociolinguistic basis of Yoruba personal names. *Anthropological Linguistics* 22:275–304.

1982 Names and naming in cross-cultural perspective. *Names* 30:37–63.

Arboleda, Manuel

1980 Gay life in Lima. *Gay Sunshine* 42:30.

Braiterman, Jared

1990 Fighting AIDS in Brazil. *Gay Community News* 17(39). Quoted from reprinting, pp. 295–307 in S. Likosky, *Coming Out*. New York: Pantheon.

Chauncey, George W., Jr.

1985 Christian brotherhood or sexual perversion? Homosexual identities and the construction of sexual boundaries in the World War One era. *Journal of Social History* 19:189–211.

1994 *Gay New York*. New York: Basic Books.

Goffman, Erving

1963 *Stigma*. Toronto: Prentice-Hall.

Herdt, Gilbert H.

1984 *Ritualized Homosexuality in Melanesia*. Berkeley: University of California Press.

Humphreys, Laud

1971 New styles of homosexual manliness. *Transaction* (March) 38–65.

1975 *Tearoom Trade*. Chicago: Aldine.

1979 Exodus and identity in the gay community. In Levine (1979:134–47).

Humphreys, Laud, and Brian Miller

1981 Satellite cultures. In *Homosexuality*. J. Marmor, ed. Pp. 142–56. New York: Basic Books.

Kutsche, Paul

1983 Situational homosexuality in Costa Rica. *Anthropological Research Group on Homosexuality Newsletter* 4(4):8–13.

Labov, William

1972 *Sociolinguistic Patterns*. Philadelphia: University of Pennsylvania Press.

Lacey, E. A.

1983 *My Deep Dark Pain Is Love*. San Francisco: Gay Sunshine Press.

Levine, Martin P.

1979 *Gay Men*. New York: Harper & Row.

Lumsden, Ian

1991 *Homosexuality, Society and the State in Mexico*. Toronto: Canadian Gay Archives.

Miller, Brian

1978 Adult sexual resocialization. *Alternative Lifestyles* 1:207–33.

Montero, Oscar

1993 Before the parade passes by: Latino queers and national identity. *Radical America* 24(4):15–26.

Murray, Stephen O.
    1979a The institutional elaboration of a quasi-ethnic community. *International Review of Modern Sociology* 9:165–77.
    1979b The art of gay insults. *Anthropological Linguistics* 21: 211–23.
    1980a *Latino Homosexuality*. San Francisco: Social Networks.
    1980b Lexical and institutional elaboration: the 'species homosexual' in Guatemala. *Anthropological Linguistics* 22:177–85.
    1981   Folk models of gay community. *Working Paper of the Language Behavior Research Laboratory* 51.
    1984   *Social Theory, Homosexual Realities*. New York: GAU.
    1992a *Oceanic Homosexualities*. New York: Garland.
    1992b The 'underdevelopment' of gay homosexuality in urban Mesoamerica, Peru and Thailand. In *Modern Homosexualities*. Ken Plummer, ed. Pp. 29–38. London: Routledge.
    1992c Components of *gay community* in San Francisco. In *Gay Culture in America*. G. Herdt, ed. Pp. 107–46. Boston: Beacon.
    1994   *Islamic Homosexualities*. MS.
    1996   *North American Homosexualities*. Chicago: University of Chicago Press.
Reiss, Albert J.
    1961   The social integration of 'queers' and 'peers.' *Social Problems* 9:102–20.
Santiago, Luis
    1993   Twenty years of Puerto Rican gay activism. *Radical America* 25(1): 40–48.
Schifter Sikora, Jacobo
    1990   *La formación de una contracultura: homosexualismo y sida en Costa Rica*. San José, Costa Rica: Guayacán.
Taylor, Clark L.
    1978   *El Ambiente*. Ph.D. thesis, University of California, Berkeley.
Weinberg, Thomas S.
    1978   On 'doing' and 'being' gay. *Journal of Homosexuality* 4:143–56.
Wolf, Deborah G.
    1983   *Growing Older Gay and Lesbian*. MS.
Wooden, Wayne S.
    1982   Cultural antecedents of gay communities in Latin America. Paper presented at the American Sociological Association meetings, San Francisco.

9

Modern Male Homosexuality in México and Peru

Stephen O. Murray

Even before the diffusion of "gay" models, behavior was far less clearly dichotomized than the simple *activo/pasivo* contrast would suggest. Over time (in an individual's sexual "career") or with different partners, behavior(al repertoire) diverged from the ideally clear dichotomy. Thus, Carrier (1976:120–21) noted that while

> there is a low probability that both active and passive anal intercourse are practiced by both participants in a given homosexual encounter . . . a little over forty percent of those playing the anal passive sex role and close to one-fourth of those playing the anal active sex role during their first sustained year, over time, incorporated the other sex role into their sexual repertoire.

In a 1986 sample of 2,400 men tested for HIV-antibodies in Guadalajara, México, 74 percent reported engaging in both insertive and receptive anal intercourse (Vázquez et al. 1988, discussed in Carrier 1989:132). Other studies conducted during the late 1980s of men who have sex with men have also found substantial *internacional/moderno* behavior.

Wisely recognizing that sexual behavior, not sexual identity, transmits HIV, Latin American AIDS researchers have focused on behavior rather than on the degree to which cultural models are internalized as identities. The study by Cáceres et al. (1991) of Lima, Peru is more directly comparable to the pioneering ethnographic studies of Latino male homosexuality in that less than 30 percent of the men in the study were recruited at an HIV-antibody testing site. The sample appears to have been better educated and more middle-class than the national average: 21.8 percent of those in the sample had received some post-secondary education, in contrast to 12.4 percent of Peruvian men in the 1981 census (Wilkie et al. 1992:230). Cáceres et al. (1991:309) coded 58.8 percent of the sample as middle-class and 21.0 percent as upper, and reported that 34.7 percent had salaries more than three times the minimum wage.

Nearly all (97.6 percent) engaged in anal intercourse with men, and 87.9 percent reported participation in fellatio with men. Two-thirds of those who engaged in fellatio and 61.6 percent of those who engaged in anal intercourse were both receptive and insertive. If these men seem *muy moderno*, those seeking HIV-antibody testing in México are even more so.

Probably not coincidentally, they are also more highly educated: in a study from test sites in México's three largest cities (the capital, Guadalajara, Monterey) and three other cities with frequent contacts with non-Mexicans (Merida, Acapulco, and Tijuana),[1] 59.1 percent had some post-secondary education (Izazola-Licea et al. 1991). Circa 1980, only 7.9 percent of Mexican men had some post-secondary education (Wilkie 1992:230). In one from Mexico City, 70 percent had. One would expect higher concentrations of educated men in cities than the national average, and in the capitals (Lima, as well as Mexico City) in contrast to all cities, but these Mexican figures far exceed such an explanation. It seems more reasonable to suppose that there is a connection between education and seeking HIV-antibody testing that vitiates direct extrapolation of the reported sexual behavior in these studies to the population of men who have sex with men in México. Nonetheless, these data show that there is—at the very least—a segment of men concerned about the dangers of HIV-infection, who depart markedly from the traditional cultural schema of *activo/pasivo* distinctions. The departure is more in México City than in the second and third largest cities (comparing Hernandez et al. 1992 with Izazlo-Licea et al. 1991) and more in the three largest cities than in Acapulco, Monterey and Merida (Izazlo-Licea et al. 1992).

Vázquez (1986 data in Carrier 1989) reported seroprevalence rates for Guadalajara *pasivos* of 46.3 percent. In contrast 20.6 percent of the

---

1. Izazlo-Licea et al. (1991:615) characterized the latter three cities as "resorts," which seems to me applicable only to Acapulco. Controlling for insertive-receptive behavior, city, and meeting partners in baths/saunas, they found no statistically significant relationship between reported sexual relationships with foreigners and HIV-antibody status, incidentally (p. 619).

activos and 32.9 percent of the *ambos* were HIV-positive. The 1988 Mexican data analyzed by Izazola-Licea et al. (1991:617) unexpectedly showed those who were only receptive or only insertive to have lower HIV-seroprevalence (3.9 percent and 12.1 percent, respectively) than those who were mostly receptive or mostly insertive (13.3 percent and 18.4 percent, respectively). Those who mixed roles equally had a still higher seroprevalence rate (21.6 percent). This pattern also appeared in the 1988 México City study, with seroprevalence rates of 6 percent for the only receptive, 8 percent for the only insertive, 12.3 percent for the mostly receptive, 24.9 percent for the mostly insertive, and 41.3 percent for those (the plurality) who "practiced both insertive and receptive behavior during half or more of sexual encounters" (Hernandez et al. 1992:886).

The authors of the latter two studies suggest that those who regularly switch roles are drawing on more HIV-infected partner pools (Hernandez et al. 1992:892; Izazola-Licea et al. 1991:619). Hernandez et al. (1992:892) take their data as establishing that mixed-role behavior is as prevalent in México City as in United States cities, so that "the pattern of sexual behavior that has been reported to be normative in Mexico—homosexuals practicing either exclusively insertive or receptive behavior—may in fact be the practice of a minority of individuals."

Although I believe that there is considerable behavioral departure from the rigid role dichotomization of ideal norms in México (the country and especially the capital city), I think it premature to conclude from samples of those seeking HIV-antibody tests that mixed behavior within same-sex sexual encounters is the statistical norm in México. The "modern" gay rejection of role dichotomization clearly exists in México. One can safely say that there are "gay" Mexicans, but whether they constitute the majority of those recurrently involved in same-sex sexual relations, even in the capital, remains open to question. One cannot determine with any certainty the extent of the diffusion of "modern"/"gay" homosexuality from samples of atypically highly educated men who are the ones seeking HIV-antibody tests.

Table 9.1 summarizes the findings of these studies. Hernandez et al. (1992) reported sexual behavior of "bisexuals" (behaviorally defined as men who had sexual relations with women in the six months preceding the study and sex with men since 1979) and "homosexuals" (men who had not had sex with women in the preceding six months and had had sex with men since 1979). Izazola-Licea et al. (1991) split their report of homosexual behavior into two sets of Mexican cities. Neither study

Table 9.1
Attributes of Mexican and Peruvian Men Engaging in Sex with Men

	México City (Hernandez)		México City, Tijuana, Guadalajara (Izazola-Licea)	Acapulco, Monterrey, Merida	Lima, Peru (Cáceres)
Percent aged 30+	37.4		10.9		16.1
Percent with some post-secondary education	70.0		59.1		21.8
Percent married to a woman	5.7		3.3		
	homo-sexual	*bisexual*			
Percent engaging in anal sex with men	92.5	86.3	80.0	71.0	97.6
Percent only insertive	5.9	20.6	11.2	12.7	16.5
Percent only receptive	7.0	4.6	12.5	31.0	26.4
Percent both	87.8	74.8	76.2	56.3	57.0
Mixed, mostly insertive	25.0	33.8	31.2		15.5
Mixed, mostly receptive	15.7	4.6	17.5		22.5
Both, in half or more encounters	47.1	36.2	27.5		18.3
(N)	1759	555	378	328	124

reported demographic attributes separately for these groupings. The percentages below the line in the table are of those who reported anal sex with men (with those reporting mixed receptive and insertive behavior further broken down to predominant patterns).

REFERENCES

Cáceres P., Carlos, Eduardo Gotuzzo, Stephen Wignall, and Miguel Campos
  1991 Sexual behavior and frequency of antibodies to HIV-1 in a group of Peruvian male homosexuals. *Bulletin of the Pan-American Health Organization* 25:306–19.
Carrier, Joseph M.
  1976 Cultural factors affecting urban Mexican homosexual behavior. *Archives of Sexual Behavior* 5:103–24.

1989   Sexual behavior and spread of AIDS in Mexico. *Medical Anthropology* 10:129–42.

Hernandez, M., P. Uribe, S. Gortmake, C. Avila, L. E. De Caso, N. Mueller, and J. Sepulveda
1992   Sexual behavior and status for human immunodeficiency virus type 1 among homosexual and bisexual males in Mexico City. *American Journal of Epidemiology* 135:883–94.

Izazola-Licea, J. A., J. L. Valdespino-Gomez, S. L. Gortmaker, et al.
1991   HIV-1 seropositivity and behavioral and sociological risks among homosexual and bisexual men in six Mexican cities. *Journal of AIDS* 1:614–22.

Vázquez Valls, Eduardo et al.
1988   Prevalence of antibody to HIV in a group of homosexual men in Guadalajara. Paper presented at the International Conference on AIDS in Stockholm.

Wilkie, J. W., B. E. Lorey, and E. Ochoa
1988   *Statistical Abstract of Latin America, Volume 26.* Los Angeles: UCLA Latin America Center.

10

❦

The Image of Gays
in Chicano Prose Fiction

*Karl J. Reinhardt**

Until recently, one of the world's best-kept secrets was that a sizable proportion of men and women find their most significant emotional and physical relationships with members of their own sex. A blatant example of this intentional negligence dealing with Chicano writers can be found in *Literatura Chicana: texto y contexto* (Castaneda et al. 1972:158), in which a selection of John Rechy is given a fourteen-line introduction which does not mention that he is an internationally known gay activist writer. The apparent non-existence of gay Chicanos is not limited to information about creative writers; lesbians and gay men barely exist in social science studies, either—unmentioned, for instance, in *Chicanos: Social and Psychological Perspectives* (Wagner and Haug 1971).

Because of oppression ranging from death penalties, policies of total extermination, limitation of access to professions, housing, and custody of one's own children to parody, derision and scorn; lesbians and gay men have been kept "in the closet." Coming out of that closet is probably the most significant step in the entire life of most gays. The Chicana poet Veronica Cunningham (1976:55) expressed with great simplicity the anguish of forced secrecy followed by the joy of release in this untitled poem in *Festival de flor y canto:*

> when all the yous
> of my poetry
> were really
> she or her

---

*Reprinted with the author's permission from *Explorations in Ethnic Studies* 4(2):41–55.

and
I could never
no I would never
write them
because of some fears
I never even wanted
to see.
how could I have been
that frightened
of sharing
the being
                and
                     me.

This chapter surveys some outstanding pieces of fiction written by men who identify themselves as Chicanos, or who are identified as such by others, and whose writings include homosexual references of one kind or another.[1] Most heterosexual persons well-versed in Chicano literature are unaware of which writers include gay characters in their writings, or of which writers are gay themselves—even among their personal acquaintances. The forced secrecy about homosexuality is perhaps greater among Chicano writers than among others in the United States.

Preoccupation with homosexuality is rampant in Mexican culture— a byproduct of generalized and exaggerated machismo—and this pre-occupation has been passed on into Chicano culture. It manifests itself frequently in very clever conversational give-and-take. The following occurs in Miguel Méndez's significant novel *Peregrinos de Aztlán*. It incorporates at least four disparate styles convincingly manipulated.

¡Epale mariachi! cámbienle, mejor tóquenme la paloma.
No la sabemos.
Entonces tóquenme la culebra.
Que se la toque su abuela. [1974:23][2]

---

1. Most are works regularly used as texts in university courses in Chicano litera-ture. I would like especially to thank Nicolás Kanellos who made available his own expertise and access to his personal library.

2. Superficially this might be translated as follows:

Hey, musicians! Change [tunes]! Play "The Dove" [a well-known song] instead.
We don't know it.
Then play "The Snake" [not a well-known song] for me.
Let your grandmother play it for you.

Such insinuating repartee is constant among men, especially adolescents, within Mexican-Chicano culture. One may hear dozens of such
lines in the course of an evening's conversation among young men. No
male who has grown up in the culture can escape having insinuations
made or learning how to parry back. Yet, such plays on words with
homosexual innuendoes rarely appear in Chicano literature. This is all
the more remarkable in that there is a notable tradition in the Latin
world for authors to write at least one novel about adolescence. Among
Chicano writers, we find Anaya (1972), Galarza (1971), Rivera (1971),
Ulibarrí (1977) and others who have produced works dealing partly or
wholly with growing into adulthood. While none of these authors is
especially notable for a sense of humor, it is still rather amazing that the
clever sexual double entendres are missing.

To a great extent, when homosexuality is mentioned—as opposed to
being central to the theme of the work—reinforcement of heterosexual
stereotyping of gay persons and even physiology is the norm. In *The
Road to Tamazunchale* (Arias 1975:97–98), a hermaphrodite baby is born.
At the father's insistence, the child is sewn up to appear to be male,
even though the *partera* realizes that perhaps the wrong operation is
being performed. In reality, babies born with two sets of external genitalia are so rare that the average practitioner may not see a single case
in an entire career. The mind-versus-body theme is part of the heterosexual stereotype of the homosexual. "A mind trapped in the wrong
body" does occasionally occur, but such people often do not consider
themselves homosexual. Acosta (1972:19) at least understands this in
distinguishing a male-to-female transsexual from a transvestite.

Incidental references, usually unkind to homosexuals, occur frequently
in many pieces of prose fiction. They have nothing to do with the plot,
but simply show that gays are fair game for derision. Again in Acosta's
books, there are passing references to "fancy-assed fags" and similar
derogations (1972:36; also see 1973:101, 103). Reflecting a general deri-

---

The verb "toque(n)" also means "touch." The names of birds and the word for
"little bird" (pajarito) may refer to the penis. "Snake" is an obvious symbol. References
to the moral looseness of an interlocutor's female relatives occur in many popular
expressions. The double meaning, then, is:

Hey, musicians! Change what you are doing and play with my "birdie."
We don't know how.
Then play with my "snake."
Let your grandmother play with it.

sion of effeminacy Hinojosa-Smith (1977:115) has a character defend his right not to have to make a fancy speech by saying "No soy joto, dice. Eso de declamar se lo dejo a ellos" ("I'm no fag. I'll leave the speechmaking to them").

In Méndez (1974:193) we find "Otra [pared que lleva anuncios publicitarios] con el retrato de un joto famoso, que en el cine gringo le hace al cowboy" (another [wall used for posting advertisements] with the picture of a famous faggot who plays cowboys in the gringo movies). And in Navarro (1973:66) "two queens walk by laughing at everything they see with large red eyes . . . Across the street a teenage boy in soiled pink panties stands next to the Salvation Army group singing 'The Coming of the Lamb.'" In none of these quotations, which are typical, are sexual activities mentioned. Gratuitous references to gay males usually present them as identifiable by their public appearance rather than by their sexuality.

The long-abandoned "momma's boy" theory lifts its Freudian head in some of the literature. In Navarro (1973:4–12) an Anglo woman seeks young men to seduce, replacing the son whom she had emotionally smothered and who had died in Korea—by implication the only escape from his mother's over-possessiveness and his own resultant homosexuality. The mother-homosexual son theme occurs in *Autobiography of a Brown Buffalo*: "The tall, pimple-faced man was a mystic of classic proportions, a Mexican fag who'd never gotten over catching his mother with some man in a Salinas grape vineyard where he learned all his Catholicism" (Acosta 1972:18).

Occasional references are made to lesbians, as in Richard Vasquez's (1971:121) *Chicano*, in which a man is asked what has happened to the waitress he had been pursuing:

> Charlie laughed. "Turned out she was a Lesbian. 'Magine that? I didn't know it. That joint she worked in was a dyke hangout. She was knocking down on the bulldykes that came around. I thought it was all tips."

Later in the novel, in a lesbian establishment, "the argument at the rear drew closer to violence, the massive Lesbians screaming the most profane Spanish he'd ever heard at one another" (p. 136).

There are significant, as well as non-pertinent, gay characters in evidence, about which different conclusions can be drawn. Hinojosa-Smith (1977:67–68) draws a minor character: "Al joto que pasaba las pelotas y los guantes le decían la Betty Grable" (The queer who passed out the baseballs and gloves was called Betty Grable). The equipment boy was not appropriately respectful to one of the players, who used that as an excuse to beat up "Betty Grable." This led to the player being expelled for two weeks, "pero de allí en adelante la Betty Grable se portaba mejor" (but from then on, Betty Grable behaved better).

Amid many references to "fags" and "queers," one character in *Brown Buffalo*, José, "my only countryman I'd known in San Francisco," previously mentioned in relation to the "momma's boy" theory, a friend of the narrator, who twice comes to the latter's verbal defense in arguments, was "one of the few homosexuals . . . tolerated" at a straight beer-joint and therefore acceptable to "our holy heterosexual company" (Acosta 1972:46–50). Another gay, who wandered into the establishment, is intentionally burned with a cigarette by the narrator and thrown out. Having witnessed the scene, José lets the beast out of his pockets, emerging from the men's room with his clothes in his hands, causing the narrator to explain, "Except for my cousin Manuel, I have never seen such a long cock" (p. 69). Perhaps, incidentally, this was what had been meant by the description of José as "a mystic of classic proportions" (p. 47). In spite of his long-term friendship with the narrator and his fellow habitués, José is ejected from the bar and from the book: token faggots must keep their place or be banished.

In Villarreal's (1970[1959]:82) *Pocho,* an agnostic, egalitarian Portuguese philosopher, rejected by his aristocratic family settles in California and establishes a platonic mentoring relationship with a boy. Readers learn that Joao Pedro Manoel [*sic.*] Alves, alias Joe Pete Manoel, has had some sort of intimacy with both men and women, but is basically a loner. A young girl, one of his unofficial disciples, becomes pregnant by him. It is concluded from urgings from authorities and townsfolk that Joe Pete had made inappropriate advances to a number of young people, especially boys. While everyone else scornfully maligns Joe Pete, his young male friend can only sit silently and listen. Before trial, Joe Pete went mad and was committed to the Agnews State Hospital for the Insane. Joe Pete was clearly homosexual. If he did seduce and impregnate the girl, he was doing what homosexuals are told they are supposed to do by their families, church, and society.

Torres-Metzger's (1976) *Below the Summit* is an incredible work in which every Anglo is a hypocritical bigot. Readers are told that in Mexico "very few people are concerned with lineage whether of a racial or ethnic kind." The book has a central character named Serveto—a name certainly subject to referential speculation. He is single, an educated, academic Chicano activist, presumably homosexual, perhaps celibate, who is despised for his activism and falsely accused of raping the very sad and lonely Mexican wife of a bigoted Anglo preacher–cutlery salesman, and thus destroyed.

Just as in Hollywood movies of the recent past a woman who went astray or even thought of going astray had to pay for her "sins" and be banished in disgrace, oblivion, or death, so in Chicano fiction homosexuals must pay the price. Not that all that many heterosexuals fare well in these books.

None of the literary examples given so far has homosexuality as the main theme. One novel in this category is Floyd Salas's (1967) *Tattoo the Wicked Cross,* in which the protagonist is destroyed by family and society, a "machote" type brutalized and lost in the world of prison. One obvious reading is that Aaron d'Aragon does not become homosexual by circumstances but would have been in any case, because his relationship with his girlfriend is unconvincing.

The most significant contemporary gay writer is also the most widely recognized Chicano writer, John Rechy. His 1979 novel *Rushes* brings to greater fulfillment his engagement in the male gay world and the devastating effect which the straight world has on the gay. One reviewer said, "Rechy insists that we explore what our lives mean socially, politically, and morally and that we consider the legacy of acts of humiliation and domination for future generations of gays" (Owens 1980:18). Rechy's rage—a word he uses frequently in *The Sexual Outlaw* (1977) derives from the straight world's contempt.

It was mentioned above that the narrator of Acosta's novels had little to do with other Chicanos until he went into politics. Salas's novel is rejected by some as a non-Chicano novel for similar reasons. Rechy's novels show more than accidental avoidance of Chicano homosexuals— with the exception of Rechy himself in his various aliases. In *Numbers* (Rechy 1967), Johnny Rio sets out to see how many sex acts he can provoke by simply being available for a limited time period. Of the dozens of men who take advantage of his availability, not a single one is identified in any way as Chicano. In *Numbers,* as in his other novels, Rechy identifies men, when they remain nameless, in other ways—fat, skinny, blond, tall, short, black, blond, dark ones—but there are no Chicano gays except for the author/narrator.

In summation, gays are presented three ways in the writing discussed:

1. Incidental gay characters not pertinent to the plot are presented derogatorily in their behavior and labels, but their "homosexuality" is social, not sexual
2. Gay characters somehow pertinent to the plot must fail, committing or reportedly committing an unacceptable act, with resultant humiliation, insanity or some other bad end
3. In writings in which homosexuality is central, Chicano characters are excluded from the world described

REFERENCES

Acosta, Oscar Zeta
  1972 *The Autobiography of a Brown Buffalo.* San Francisco: Straight Arrow.
  1973 *Revolt of the Cockroach People.* San Francisco: Straight Arrow.
Anaya, Rudolfo A.
  1972 *Please Me, Ultime.* Berkeley: Tonatiuh International.
Arias, Ron
  1975 *The Road to Tamazunchale.* Reno: West Coast Poetry Review.
Castaneda Shular, Antonia et al., eds.
  1972 *Literatura Chicana: texto y contexto.* Englewood Cliffs, NJ: Prentice-Hall.
Cunningham, Veronica
  1976 *Festival de flor y canto*: Los Angeles: University of Southern California Press.
Galarza, Ernesto
  1971 *Barrio Boy.* South Bend, IN: University of Notre Dame Press.
Hinojosa-Smith, Rolando R.
  1973 *Estampas del Valle y Otras Obras.* Berkeley: Editorial Justa.
  1977 *Generaciones y Semblanzas.* Berkeley: Editorial Justa.
Méndez, Miguel
  1974 *Peregrinos de Aztlán.* Tucson: Editorial Peregrinos.
Navarro, J. L.
  1973 *Blue Day on Main Street.* Berkeley: Quinto Sol.
Owens, E. J.
  1980 Review of Rechy (1979) *Upfront America* (15 Feb.): 18.
Rechy, John
  1967 *Numbers.* New York: Grove Press.
  1977 *The Sexual Outlaw.* New York: Grove Press.
  1979 *Rushes.* New York: Grove Press.
Rivera, Tomás
  1971 *Y no se lo tragó la tierra.* Berkeley: Quinto Sol.
Salas, Floyd
  1967 *Tattoo the Wicked Cross.* New York: Grove Press.

Torres-Metzger, Joseph V.
    1976   *Below the Summit.* Berkeley: Tonatiuh International.
Ulibarrí, Sabine R.
    1977   *Mi Abuela Fumabo Pures.* Berkeley: Quinto Sol.
Vasquez, Richard
    1971   *Chicano.* New York: Avon.
Villarreal, José Antonio
    1970 [1959] *Pocho.* Garden City, NY: Anchor.
Wagner, Nathaniel N., and Marsh J. Haug
    1971   *Chicanos: Social and Psychological Perspectives.* St. Louis: Mosby.

11

🌿

Ethnicity, Homosexuality, and Closetry in Recent Gay Mexican American Fiction in English*

Stephen O. Murray

The past was a thin layer of ash over embers that could still burn.
—MICHAEL NAVA, *How Town* (1990a:14)

Arturo Islas

Arturo Islas's two novels about the Angel family, *The Rain God* (1984) and *Migrant Souls* (1990), continued all three genre conventions that Karl Reinhardt specified in the previous chapter. In the older (than Islas's) generation, Felix had sexual relations with Mexicans, although no particular instance is mentioned. "Fair" in the following might not mean light-skinned: "Constantly on the lookout for the shy and fair god who would land safely on the shore at last, Felix searched for his youth in obscure places on both sides of the river" (1984:115). The men Felix hired and to whom he provided physical exams that focused on checking for hernias and prostate problems (p. 116) were Mexicans, whereas the 18-year-old soldier who kicked him to death when Felix tried to make him was "fair with light-colored eyes" and with no knowledge of Spanish (p. 134).

In the next generation (and next novel), a lesbian niece named Serena has a Boston Irish lover (Mary Margaret Ryan). Her sister (Josie), the only family member to be divorced, had married a local Anglo and the father of her second daughter is Cherokee-French. Miguel Chico,

---

*I was unable to persuade Karl Reinhardt to carry his analysis forward. After I had sent off the book manuscript, an article by Ricardo Ortiz (1993) appeared that insightfully discusses *How Town* (Nava 1990) and Islas's novels along with earlier work by John Rechy from a Barthean perspective.

the gay male of the second generation born in America (El Paso, called Del Sapo in the novels) has no apparent sexual relations with other Mexican Americans. He lives alone in San Francisco at the present time in both novels. Serena is an incidental character. Her sexuality and that of Miguel Chico are not detailed (in contrast to that of Felix in the first novel and that of Josie in the second).

Felix is an important character (at least for two middle chapters in *The Rain God*). Miguel Chico has little plot function in *The Rain God*, but is the central figure of *Migrant Souls*. As the author of a too-close-to-the-truth novel about his family published by a small West Coast publisher (1990:209–10), he is fairly obviously a representation of the author.

Being kicked to death in the desert is far from a pleasant end, but Miguel Chico seems much more tormented than Felix ever was. Drinking oneself to death is slower, but harder on those around one than being murdered is. "Already, in his early teens, he was addicted to guilt," Islas (1990:60) wrote of Miguel Chico. His "cousins accused him of being a sissy" (1984:169), and his father thought that his mother and a servant woman turned him into a *joto*. Miguel Chico "had always felt that his father disliked him for being too delicate, too effeminate. Miguel Grande had consistently refused to acknowledge that his son's feelings and needs might be different from his own" (1984:94). Part of this rigidity (in a man who was a police captain) probably derived from discomfort about Miguel Grande's older brother Felix: "As they grew older, Felix's behavior embarrassed Miguel Grande, and he hoped that the stigma of being *jotos* would not reach past his brother" (1984:87). After Felix has been murdered, Miguel Grande tells Felix's daughter Lena "I don't care what my brother did. I loved the hell out of him" (1984:86), but the omniscient narrator (who is at the very least bears considerable affinity to his son) reports that

> he felt ashamed and frustrated. He had never been able to understand Felix's obsession and did not want to. The thought of touching another man in those ways disgusted him, and his knowledge that Felix enjoyed doing such things had created a barrier between them that neither ever made the effort to overcome. [Islas 1984:87]

This is the interpretation of a gay son (Miguel Chico and/or Arturo Islas). He also notes that "Serena always brought her mother to the family celebrations and left her roommate at home" (1990:217) and

recurrently rails at the conspiracy of silence about heterosexual and homosexual deviations from the ideal of monogamous heterosexual marriage. For instance,

> Josie knew that what she was in the family's eyes was a sinner. Not
> one of her relatives—not even her mother—would have called her
> that to her face, for they were good Catholic people and needed
> mediators to guard them from truths and keep them comfortable.
> [Islas 1990:107]

The first American-born generation considers their elders' refusal to
verbalize sexual affairs hypocritical. Eduviges, the mother of Serena and
Josie, rejects even posthumous recognition of her brother's desires, telling her daughters and Miguel Chico "I don't believe a word of it. There
are no homosexuals" (1990:121). For the immigrant generation, specifically the matriarch Encarción Olmeca Angel (Mama Chona), denial of
sexuality extended to hysterical refusal to attend to the body at all:
"Mama Chona denied the existence of all parts of the body below the
neck, with the exception of her hands" (1990:164) and ignored uterine
problems that prove fatal. Miguel Chico took after her, partly from his
father's demand he not be coddled with doctors early on (1984:86) and
later in delayed detection of intestinal cancer (requiring a colostomy).
Despite the family name, Angel, and the wishes of several of the characters, they are not disembodied. Bodies and desires bring down "plaster
gods."[1] Repression has a high price in both of Islas's novels.

Felix did not seek ongoing homosexual relationships. There is no
evidence that his nephew Miguel Chico did, either. Philandering is the
nature of men in the view of the Angel women and *jotos*. In that Miguel
Grande manages a long-running affair, male homosexual encounters
appear to be more fleeting than heterosexual ones in these two novels.
They also reinforce the view of gender deviance as a correlate or cause of
homosexuality. Childhood effeminacy is recalled for both Felix and for
Miguel Chico.

Serena has a woman's "natural" nesting instinct. She and Meg had
already been together for twelve years when Josie returned to Del Sapo.
Although not a very fully realized character, Serena is given a stereotypical occupation and leisure habits: she is a physical education teacher

---

1. At the end of *The Rain God*, Felix has become that chthonic spirit. At the end of
Migrant Souls, the Catholic saint who is the patroness of his parish church is bidding
Gabriel, the grandson of Mama Chona who became a priest, to dance.

whose interests outside work and *la familia* are bowling and drinking beer (1990:106). Her even shadowier Irish American lover is noted for liking to play golf and to sleep (1990:107).

Michael Nava

In his memoir of his maternal grandfather Michael Nava (1992b:17) suggested that,

> fat, myopic, and brainy, I escaped sissyhood only because of the aggressive gloominess I shared with my grandfather. I was like a cartoon character who walks beneath his own rain cloud, so fiercely unhappy that I deflected the taunts to which I otherwise would have been subject.

In another memoir of growing up in a Mexican barrio of Sacramento, California, Nava (1991:25) recalled an occasion in his childhood (at age six or seven) when he donned a red petticoat and applied makeup "not to transform myself into a girl, but only emulating the one adult in my family [his grandmother] who loved me without condition." Nava (1990b:50) also recalled "my fascination with my cousin's Barbie doll. It was never hard to recruit me to play house, providing I got to choose Barbie's outfits," again adding "I didn't want to be a woman—I just liked their clothes" (1990b:51). Although he "was also a sturdy little boy" involved in masculine pursuits, he recalls, "I felt like a sort of boygirl, I think, even before I knew I was homosexual" (1990b:50). At home with his mother and stepfather constantly bickering, he tried to turn himself to stone and gradually learned to live completely within himself, roaming through the houses of his mother's family. He was not supervised:

> Being everyone's child, I was no one's child. . . . Children barely counted as humans in our tribe. We were more like livestock and our parents' main concern was that the head count at night matched the head count in the morning. [Nava 1991:17]

Like the Angels, the Acuña family "was a matriarchy with my grandmother at its center. My grandfather stood apart, a scowling silent presence" (1991:17). Nava only saw his biological father once (drunk). His

> stepfather showed little paternal interest in me. . . . Practically speaking, I was my mother's child, her favorite. . . . [Even] at five and six, I was aware that my mother's solicitude was due as much

to pity as love. . . . At that early age, in my innermost self, I was no one's child. [Nava 1991:16]

As for Islas (and Miguel Chico), books opened the escape passage from the Mexican tribal village in which Nava grew up.[2] His family encouraged Miguel Chico (and, I presume, Islas) to seek higher education. In Nava's case,

> my love of reading became simply another secret part of me. . . . Like so many other bright children growing up in the inarticulate world of the poor, books fueled my imagination . . . and helped me conceive of a world in which I would not feel so set apart. Yet I do not believe that my brains alone, even aided by my bookish fantasies, would have been enough to escape Gardenland. For this I needed the kind of courage that arises from desperation.
>
> I found this courage in my homosexuality. . . . By the time I was twelve I understood that my fascination [with pictures of nude Greek male sculpture] was rooted in my sexual nature. One day, walking to school, clutching my books to my chest, girl-style, I heard myself say, "I'm a queer."
>
> It was absolutely clear to me that Gardenland could not accommodate this revelation. Gardenland provided the barest of existences for its people. What made it palatable was the knowledge that everyone was about the same, united in ethnicity and poverty and passivity. The only rituals were the rituals of family and family was everything there. But I knew that I was not the same as everyone else. And I was certain that my family, already puzzled by my silent devotion to books, would reject me entirely if it became known exactly what thoughts occupied my silence. [1991: 27–28]

In another memoir, Nava (1990b:50) specified his age when the realization came over him:

> I was twelve. Walking to school one winter morning, I heard myself say, "I'm a queer". . . . For the next five years, until I left home for college, I felt like a foreigner trying to pass as a native

---

2. "Tribal" is Nava's recurrent formulation. One instance is quoted below. Writers are not the best sample to assess the impact of books, being the most likely to have sought escape in them (for another instance, see Arenas (1989:59, not an autobiographical work, incidentally; Arenas's own family constellation was closer to Nava's than Arturo's is, with a fallen woman for a mother and his mother's mother being the center—1993:2–5, 64).

among the people who were my family. . . . I learned early to be cautious about what I disclosed about myself. Consequently, I grew up with the sense that no one in my family really knew me.

As his sexual fantasies focused on male schoolmates, "no one had to tell me to keep these thoughts a secret. . . . Ruthlessly, I dedicated myself to the suppression of any emotion that might give me away" (1990b:51). The feeling of being different, seeking alternative realities in books, and going into internal exile (self-willed autism even) is common in the memories of gay men of diverse ethnicities and class backgrounds. Suffering in silence is a recurrent part of the male role, not just among Chicanos. Memory of self-sacrificing, loving but cowed mothers, paternal contempt, and the mute though reproachful gaze of extended family loom especially large for those in Mexican barrios or Asian immigrant neighborhoods. John Rechy's (1961, 1967, 1977) flight from femininity differs in degree, but not in kind from that of other men (especially, but not only Chicano) wanting men but not wanting to be martyrs to men in the ways their mothers and sisters were and are.

In his mysteries Nava alludes to the nuclear family of his narrator Henry Rios,[3] a Stanford-trained lawyer like Nava, especially dwelling on the violence of the alcoholic father in *The Hidden Law* (1992a).[4] Members of his extended family are not mentioned in the Rios novels. Nor are grandparents.[5] Miguel Chico has a lesbian cousin with whom he is not particularly close. Henry has a lesbian sister, Elena, who is hostile to him. Although these lesbian characters are far from fully imagined and their lovers are even shadowier, they still reduce lesbian invisibility, which is generally considerable in Mexican and Mexican American milieux. Their presence shows that homosexuality does not run just into the males in these families.

---

3. Ortiz (1993:116) relates the name Johnny Rio (in Rechy's 1967 novel *Numbers*) to what is *el rio* in El Paso (i.e., the Rio Grande separating Texas from Mexico). Sacramento, the birthplace of Michael Nava and Henry Rios has two rivers (neither of which is a national border). I would prefer to take the plural as symbolizing the multiple sources of Henry Rios's character—in contrast to "Rechy's unwillingness to explore the 'Mexican' side of his own psyche" (Ortiz 1993:115)—at least in *Numbers* and *The Sexual Outlaw* (it seems to me more salient in *City of Night*).

4. In the first book, Rios says that his father was foreman of a night crew at a Marysville cannery (Nava 1986:91).

5. A multi-generational genealogy is very important to the first book, *The Little Death* (1986), which has a family tree before the title page, but it is that of an elite Anglo family.

Nava (1991:29) recalled "painful, unrequited crushes on male class-mates." In *How Town*, Henry Rios returns to Sacramento (Los Robles) to defend the brother of his prime high school crush, Mark Windsor, who was not just Anglo, but a scion of "local gentry" (1991:8).[6] His law school lover, Grant Hancock, was Anglo. So was Hugh Parris, the almost-client who is murdered in *The Little Death*. The witness who becomes Henry's lover in *Goldenboy*, Josh, is Jewish (also HIV-positive and fourteen years his junior). The relationship that follows Josh's de-cline (in *The Hidden Law*) is with another Anglo. (Lonnie is only ten years younger than Henry.) His few friends are also Anglo (and straight).

There are no Mexican American characters who are not relatives of Henry in *Goldenboy*, no Mexican American characters other than Henry in *A Little Death*. There are a number (mostly servants, but also a policeman who is central to the plot) in *How Town*. In *The Hidden Law* almost all the characters with whom Henry doesn't sleep are Mexican American (including the murdered state senator and the two young men Henry Rios defends).[7] Being Mexican American is not an issue in *Goldenboy*. Returning home in *How Town* brings back old feelings of ethnic discrimination, along with painful reminders that Mark did not accept Henry's homosexuality when he came out to him (after high school). Henry reflects often on the costs of making it in a white world, and other Mexican American characters express their expectation of un-fair treatment in *The Hidden Law*.

Homosexuality and the duplicities and terrors that sustain closetry are the central concerns of *Goldenboy*, and are far from incidental to *A Little Death* (see, especially, pp. 70–71 on his ex's closetry). After Josh comes out to his parents (1988:149–50), Henry "confesses" to him that he never told his parents. Josh asks "Why not?" Henry answers "The easy answer is that they died before I got around to it, but the honest answer is—I was afraid" (1988:154). Henry was 27 years old when his mother died (1990a:3,5). In *The Hidden Law*, Henry tells his therapist that he had to wait until his father was dead before coming out at all (1992a:46). Henry was a 19-year-old sophomore in college

---

6. The real-life model was half-Mexican and tolerant of the 17-year-old Michael Nava's profession of love (see Nava 1990b:51).

7. Rios's secretary and the private investigator he uses are African American. Asian Americans do not appear in Nava's California (the Central Valley, San Francisco, or Los Angeles) with the very brief exception of a maid who plays no part in *The Little Death*.

when his father died.[8] He recalled being surprised that his father was dying:

> "You didn't think he was mortal?"
> "I didn't think he was human. He seemed so big and his fury was bottomless. . . . I was glad he was dying. I thought I'd be free . . . from being afraid of him, from disappointing him, from never measuring up to his idea of what a man should be."
> "Did he know you were gay?"
> "I hardly knew myself at that age.[9] Growing up, I was sensitive and strong-willed. It was a combination that didn't make sense to his notion of being male. He thought I was simply weak and dishonest."
> "And after he died, did that free you?"
> "I live with his judgments of me." [1992a:75–76]

Henry knows that his childhood scarred him. (Michael Nava knows that a somewhat different one scarred him.) Elena likens their childhoods to surviving a concentration camp ("those who once have been tortured go on being tortured"—1990a:12). In therapy in *The Hidden Law* Henry analyzes his relationship with his father. He tries to understand the rage of Mexican American fathers, especially his own:

> Disdained by the majority the people [from a Spanish-speaking village in an Anglo city] were tribal in their outlook and mores. Its cornerstone was the family, and in the family the father ruled, irrevocably and without question. Outside, in the larger world where they labored under the contemptuous eyes of Anglo bosses, the fathers were social and political ciphers. No wonder, then, that in the families they tolerated no dissent from their wives and children. And they drank. They drank to wash down the slights they endured by day and to enlarge small lives which became heroic in alcohol-glazed rumination, but at their cores the fathers knew the full measure of their unimportance, and, so, finally, they drank to quiet the rage.

---

8. This is the same age that he wrote a coming-out love letter to his high-school friend Mark. Nothing indicates the relative timing of his father's death and writing this letter.

9. Cf. Nava (1986:28) "Did you know you were gay when you started law school?"

"I've always known."

I take this as the character's differing self-presentations, not authorial forgetfulness.

But the rage would not be completely calmed. How could it? The church told them their reward would be in the next life, but this is a small consolation for the back-breaking labors of the present, the years of enforced humility. When the rage exploded, they struck out at the only ones over whom they had any power: wives, sons, daughters, particularly the sons in whom they saw their own lost youths. The sons bore the blows and absorbed the rage. It was a recipe for patricide.[10] [1992a:175]

And for second-generation alcohol and drug abuse.

Henry also realizes that he is trying to be the kind of protective father he did not have in his relationship with Josh (and the two young Chicanos who, sequentially, become his clients in what turns out to have been a parricide). Lonnie, an ex-hustler and ex-junkie, is more fully an adult (not to mention eight years older than John was when Henry's relationship with him began, and that much older than Mark was when Henry fell in love with his high school classmate). Without the father-ing aspect, the relationship with Lonnie is less intense.[11]

Henry also realizes that he is very emotionally closed-in. About Mark, he thinks "I had loved so infrequently I felt a debt to those whom I had, for the reprieve from solitude" (1990a:198).[12] Earlier (1986:27) he counted: "Once as an adolescent, twice as an adult, I had been in love." Unlike Miguel Chico, Henry Rios stopped drinking himself to death (at age 33) and committed himself to a lover (at age 36). His creator also owned up to his alcoholism at the same age (1992b:20). It may be that "when I was a child I had worked hard at making myself invisible and I emerged from it without an identity" (1992a:78; cf. the author's similar

---

10. "As he had done in many other ways, my father had died before I could dispatch him" (1992a:47).

11. A relationship with Josh continues, and Henry is certainly not "over" being unable to save Josh from the depredations of HIV. (The AIDS micro-politics are com-plicated and irrelevant here.)

12. The reprieve may have been illusory. Henry recalls that they never said much. "In fact, I never knew what Mark was actually thinking or how he felt. I just assumed that he was as happy to be with me as I was with him" (Nava 1990a:156). In that, until Henry came out (and guardedly came on) to him, Mark felt that "being your friend was the most normal thing I ever did" (1990a:197) and that "I thought you were tough and I respected you for it" (1990a:77), Henry's youthful assumption might have been fairly accurate. Mark's sister-in-law, Sara, tells Henry that she "knew you when you were just a skinny little nothing from the wrong side of town, mooning over Mark like a girl. God, how you embarrassed your sister" (1990a:88).

autobiographical statement quoted above and 1992b:20), but the adult balances several:

> "A gay public figure, a criminal defense lawyer, and a Chicano— you didn't choose the easy road," his friend Terry tells him.
> "I didn't have any choice," he replies.
> "Of course you did," she said, decisively. "You could have stayed closeted and gone for the big money on Montgomery Street [San Francisco] as some huge firm's token minority partner."
> "And drunk myself to death before I was forty. See, no choice."
> [1990a:22]

The still-drinking Henry Rios of the first book was having an identity crisis (1986:3 specifically states this). In the later books he is a recovered alcoholic. Alcoholic Anonymous experiences and contacts are important in *How Town*, and *The Hidden Law* revolves around staff and clients of a recovery house. "Alcoholic" becomes an important identity: up there with Chicano, behind only lawyer and gay[13] (the two master identities in my reading[14]). Like Rios, Nava is very concerned about justice for gay men (see Nava and Dawidoff 1993).

The self-analyses of John Rechy's various narrators and Arturo Islas's alter ego Miguel Chico are often acute, but they are unable to do anything with these analyses. Henry Rios has to some extent come to terms with the anguishes of his past (battling parents, poverty, discrimination, a sexuality he felt was unsharable, and a general sense of isolation).[15] He functions professionally and personally in contrast to the compulsions (sexual or alcoholic) of Rechy's and Islas's gay Mexican American characters. Despite his far-from-forgotten pains and continuing ambivalences, he is a credible Mexican American gay male role

---

13. Nava provided no indication of what Henry did with Hugh or Grant. With Josh and Lonnie only *activo* sexual behavior is mentioned. How Latino are Henry and his adult milieu is open to question, but Henry clearly grew up in a Latino environment (what he calls a Mexican village) and became a gay-identified *activo*, a category of recurrent interest in the rest of this book. Nava (1990b:51) also goes out of his way to specify adolescent fantasies of penetrating, not of being penetrated.

14. Nava (personal communication 26 September, 1994) wrote: "You are correct in your observation that Rios's primary identifications are as a lawyer and a gay man. His ethnic identity is mixed up with his personal history and his family from which he is deeply alienated. A gay Mexican American of his generation (and mine) really was forced to choose between La Raza and his sexual orientation."

15. On the basis of the self-presentation in his non-fiction, Nava has, too (see, especially, 1992b:20). Also see R. A. Rodriguez (1991).

model, the only one I can think of in Mexican American literature.[16] In writing Henry Rios, Michael Nava has left behind all three of the limits on gay Chicano characters that Reinhardt sketched.

REFERENCES

Arenas, Reinaldo
 1989 *Old Rosa*. New York: Grove Press.
 1991 *The Doorman*. New York: Grove Weidenfeld.
 1993 *Before Night Falls*. New York: Viking.
Islas, Arturo
 1984 *The Rain God*. Palo Alto, CA: Alexandrian Press. (Reprinted, New York: Avon, 1991.)
 1990 *Migrant Souls*. New York: William Morrow. (Reprinted, New York: Avon, 1991 [the edition quoted from herein]).
Manrique, Jaime
 1992 *Latin Moon in Manhattan*. New York: St. Martin's Press.
Monteagudo, Jesse G.
 1991 Miami, Florida. In *Hometowns*. John Preston, ed. Pp. 11–20. New York: Dutton.
Muñoz, Elías Miguel
 1989 *Crazy Love*. Houston: Arte Publico Press.

---

16. This could extend to the fiction by gay immigrant writers from elsewhere in Latin America. The misunderstood title character in Reinaldo Arenas's (1989) *The Doorman* is not gay, and a gay couple (one of who is Cuban) in the Manhattan building grossly reinforces the stereotype of sexual insatiability and silliness. Arenas's (1993: 106–7) found the endogamous gay life in the United States tedious in contrast to his adventures with "real men" in Cuba. The successful gay Colombian in Jaime Manrique's (1992) moving, often comic novel *Latin Moon in Manhattan* dies of AIDS. The engaging narrator (who is blessed or cursed with a doting mother and a circle of Colombian would-be patronesses) has not gotten things together either in his career or in relationships. Nito in Muñoz's (1989) *Crazy Love* seems to have his career together and to be making peace with his past, including having been called a *marquita* and gang-raped in Cuba (pp. 15, 19). Nito, like Henry Rios and Miguel Chico, moved away from his family. Geographical distance permitted enough psychic distance to inscribe some of the pains of growing up with fathers whose demands could not be met. Mario, the HIV+ artist in Muñoz's *The Greatest Performance* (1991) has not made peace with his memories of abuse as a child in Cuba, and, particularly not, with his father's rejection (see pp. 35, 67, 123, 134–35). In contrast, in his memoir of growing up "different" (first bookish, later homosexual) in Miami's "Little Havana," Monteagudo (1991:20) writes that he has "made peace with my past. . . . Growing up in Little Havana has made me what I am today, and that can't be all bad." Somewhere in between is Richard Rodriguez's (1992) over-written memoir.

1991   *The Greatest Performance*. Houston: Arte Publico Press.

Nava, Michael

1986   *The Little Death*. Boston: Alyson.

1988   *Golden Boy*. Boston: Alyson.

1990a *How Town*. New York: Harper & Row.

1990b For Chris, wherever he is: a personal memoir of coming out. *Advocate*
562:50–51.

1991   Gardenland, Sacramento, California. In *Hometowns*. John Preston, ed.
Pp. 21–30. New York: Dutton.

1992a *The Hidden Law*. New York: HarperCollins.

1992b Abuelo: my grandfather: Raymond Acuña. In *Member of the Family*.
John Preston, ed. Pp. 15–20. New York: Dutton.

Nava, Michael, and Robert Dawidoff

1993   *Created Equal: Why Gay Rights Matter to America*. New York: St. Martin's Press.

Ortiz, Ricardo L.

1993   Sexuality degree zero: pleasure and power in the novels of John Rechy,
Arturo Islas, and Michael Nava. *Journal of Homosexuality* 26(2/3):111–26.

Rechy, John

1961   *City of Night*. New York: Grove Press.

1967   *Numbers*. New York: Grove Press.

1977   *The Sexual Outlaw*. New York: Grove Press.

Rodriguez, Richard A.

1991   *A Qualitative Study of Identity Development in Gay Chicano Males*. Ph. D.
dissertation (psychology), University of Utah.

Rodriguez, Richard

1992   *Days of Obligation: An Argument with my Mexican Father*. New York:
Viking.

12

Homosexuality and AIDS in Latinos in the United States

AN ANNOTATED BIBLIOGRAPHY

Stephen O. Murray

I thought that AIDS research would probably provide some new insights into Latino homosexuality(ies) in the United States, but I was disappointed both by the quality and the level of insights in the literature. Recurrent findings are somewhat greater (than Anglo or African American gay men) preference for anal over oral intercourse, more bisexuality, greater resistance to condom use, and greater misinformation about HIV transmission. Alas, no one has yet set out to describe or to analyze any Latino homosexuality distinctive to the United States.

Alonso, Ana Maria, and Maria T. Koreck (1988) Silences: 'Hispanics,' AIDS and sexual practices, *Differences* 1:101–24—criticized views of a singular "Hispanic" entity and substituted a "Latino" one that includes urban Nicaragua, rural northern México, and Cuban Mariel refugees, but not Puerto Rico, because the predominant AIDS-risk among New York and New Jersey Puerto Ricans has been needle-injection, whereas phallus-injection has been the predominant AIDS-risk for Miami Cuban Americans and Mexican Americans in the southwestern states (including California). Most of the article expounds the gender-defined cultural model of homosexuality (with *macho* and *joto* as the *activo* and *pasivo* labels) based on vaguely-specified fieldwork in northern México. The authors include no actual data on behavior or beliefs in México or the United States.

Arguelles, Lourdes, and Anne M. Rivero (1988) HIV Infection/AIDS and Latinas in Los Angeles County, *California Sociologist* 11:69–89—asserted that Los Angeles Latina women were much more likely to be infected with HIV by bisexual male partners than by intravenous-drug-using male partners and that "many female partners of bisexual Latinos are forced to engage in anal intercourse" (p. 78, while cautioning that "sex from behind" may not necessarily be anal penetration; Hernandez et al., *American Journal of Epidemiology* 135[1992], p. 891, reported that 92.6 percent of Mexico City bisexuals never had anal sex with women and, presumably, force was not used by all of the other 7.4 percent).

Asencio, Marysol W. (1990) Puerto Rican Adolescents Playing by the Rules, a paper presented at the annual meetings of the American Anthropological Association in New Orleans—discussed New York Puerto Rican street culture, including cross-dressing males who preferred to be referred to as "she," and friendships (but not "too close") between straight youths and butch gay youths (some of whom pretended to be straight).

California AIDS Office (1990) *Monthly Surveillance Reports for State and for Counties of Orange, Los Angeles and San Diego and a Special Breakdown of Latino PWAs* (Sacramento: California AIDS Office), reported per capita Latino case rates inversely proportional to population concentration, and much higher in the San Francisco Bay Area than Los Angeles–Orange counties.

Carballo-Diéguez, Alex (1989) Hispanic culture, gay male culture, and AIDS: counseling implications, *Journal of Counseling & Development* 68:26–30—provided some clinical advice and folk (pop?) linguistics about the difficulties of promoting safe sex among the heterogeneous category "Hispanics." Includes two case studies of HIV+ clients.

Carrier, Joseph M. (1992) Miguel: sexual life history of a gay Mexican American, in *Gay Culture in America*, Gilbert Herdt, ed., pp. 202–24 (Boston: Beacon)—provides a sad, not particularly representative case study of an East Los Angeles Mexican American who began a sexual career with younger Mexican American partners with a younger brother, had sexual relations inside the barrio and outside with Anglo gay men, and drank himself to death at an early age.

Carrier, Joseph M., and J. Raúl Magaña (1992) Use of ethnosexual data on men of Mexican origins for HIV/AIDS prevention programs, in *The Time of AIDS*, Gilbert Herdt and Shirley Lindenbaum, eds., pp. 243–58 (London: Sage)—The extent to which sexual socialization during adolescence was mostly with Mexican Americans or with Anglo Americans is the best predictor of whether a Mexican

American's homosexual behavior tilts toward Anglo American or Mexican homosexuality. Socializing mostly with Anglo American males (either at school or in the neighborhood) increases the likelihood that Mexican Americans will select them as sex partners and will be influenced by and/or adopt their sexual preferences and techniques. A major difference of particular relevance to the spread of HIV is that the available data suggest that Mexican men generally strongly prefer playing either the anal receptive or insertive sexual role and prefer anal intercourse over fellatio. In contrast, Anglos tend to be more sexually versatile, to have more non-steady sexual partners, and to be less focused on anal intercourse. The authors discuss the difficulty of getting HIV-transmission information to *activos* who do not identify themselves as *homosexual*. They also report some Orange County (California) Health Department attempts to use *fotonovelas* to reach a wider audience in prevention education.

Castro, Kenneth G., and Susan B. Manoff (1988) The epidemiology of AIDS in Hispanic adolescents, in *The AIDS Challenge: Prevention Education for Young People*, Marcia Quackenbush and Mary Nelson, eds., (Santa Cruz, CA: Network Publications)—distinguishes intravenous drug use as the New York/New Jersey (Puerto Rican origin) risk behavior from bi-/homo-sexuality in Florida (Cuban origin) and the Southwest (Mexican background).

Ceballos-Capitaine, Alicia, José Szapocnik, Nancy T. Blaney, Robert O. Morgan, Carrie Millon, and Carl Eisdorfer (1990) Ethnicity, emotional distress, stress-related disruption and coping among HIV seropositive gay males, *Hispanic Journal of Behavioral Sciences* 12: 135–52—contrasts 27 Hispanic and 49 non-Hispanic white HIV+ gay men. Although not more stressed overall, Hispanics reported higher severity of stress in daily interactions related to homosexuality than did their non-Hispanic white counterparts. The authors proposed level of acculturation as a possible explanation for the striking similarities along most other psychosocial parameters.

Chu, S-Y, T. A. Peterman, L. S. Doll, J. W. Buehler, and J. W. Curran (1992) AIDS in bisexual men in the United States: epidemiology and transmission to women, *American Journal of Public Health* 82: 220–24—Among 65,389 men with AIDS who reported having had sex with men since 1977, 26 percent indicated bisexual behavior. More Black (41 percent) and Hispanic men (31 percent) than White men (21 percent) reported bisexual behavior. Bisexual men were twice as likely to report intravenous drug use (20 percent) as were homosexual men (9 percent), regardless of race or ethnicity. Among 3,555 women with heterosexually acquired AIDS, 11 percent reported sexual contact with a bisexual man and no other risk factor, although in some states approximately half reported such contact. In 1989, the AIDS rate due to sex with a bisexual man was three and five times higher among Hispanic and Black women, respectively, than among White women.

Cunningham, Ineke (1989) The public controversies of AIDS in Puerto Rico, *Social Science & Medicine* 29:545–53, reviewed articles dealing with AIDS in five Puerto Rican daily newspapers between 1982 and 1988. Incidence rates, control and elementary school education about AIDS were particularly controversial topics.

Doll, Lynda S., F. N. Judson, D. G. Ostrow, P. M. O'Malley, et al. (1990) Sexual behavior before AIDS: the hepatitis B studies of homosexual and bisexual men, *AIDS* 4:1067–73. Data on sexual behavior drawn from samples at STD clinics in Chicago, Denver, Los Angeles, San Francisco, and St. Louis in 1978 showed that white gay/bisexual men had larger numbers of non-steady male sexual partners (whites median 14, blacks 8, Hispanics 10) and engaged in oral-genital sex more frequently than black or Hispanic gay/bisexual men (in 35.8 percent, 25.6 percent, 28 percent of sexual contacts), and were somewhat less likely to engage in anal sex (in 33.4 percent, 38.5 percent, 38.6 percent of sexual contacts).

Forrest, K. A., D. M. Austin, M. I. Valdes, E. G. Fuentes, and S. R. Wilson (1993) Exploring norms and beliefs related to AIDS prevention among California Hispanic men, *Family Planning Perspectives* 25:111–17. A predominantly working-class convenience sample of 75 California Hispanic men aged 18–40 participated in seven focus groups, each with ten-to-twelve participants. They discussed "ethnic factors that might enhance or interfere with AIDS prevention efforts." There were three groups composed of single men, three of married men and one of homosexual and bisexual men. Four groups included only participants born outside the United States. Spanish was the preferred language in five of the groups. Evaluation of the discussions indicated that while AIDS awareness is high among this population, condom use is sporadic. Few participants knew that someone infected with HIV could appear healthy. Many participants thought that casual contact could transmit HIV. The homosexual and bisexual men were more likely to acknowledge that they were at some risk of infection. Most of the heterosexual men did not perceive themselves as being at risk. The participants had ambivalent attitudes toward women who suggested condom use and were often reluctant to initiate condom use themselves. Religion did not seem to play a major role in the men's attitudes about AIDS, sexuality, or condom use.

Hutton, Julia (1992) *Good Sex*, San Francisco: Cleis Press. The one gay Latino sexual autobiography in the volume, "José Antonio" (pp. 18–20), recounted an aim-inhibited adolescent same-sex relationship, subsequent marriage to a woman, and, finally, finding the right man. José Antonio differs from the stereotyped gay Latino patterns in having a "very gay" identity with some bisexual behavior, and in de-emphasizing anal sex and role separation. His comments on the centrality of baby-making to establishing manhood are important for understanding Latino men's condom resistance (in sexual behavior with women).

Lemp, George F., A. M. Hirozawa, D. Givertz, G. N. Nieri, L. Anderson, M. L. Lindegren, R. S. Janssen, and M. Katz (1994) Seroprevalence of HIV and risk behaviors among young homosexual and bisexual men: The San Francisco/Berkeley Young Men's Survey, *Journal of the American Medical Association* 272:449–54—a survey of 425 homosexual and bisexual men aged 17–22 years was recruited from 26 locations during 1992–93. Forty percent of the 95 Latinos had engaged in unprotected anal sex in the six months prior to their interview (compared with 28 percent of Anglos, 38.5 percent of African Americans, and 27 percent of Asian Americans). The Latinos were somewhat more likely to be HIV-positive than the Anglos (9.5 percent in contrast to 8 percent); African Americans were much more likely to be HIV-positive (21 percent). Seventy of the HIV-infected men did not know that they were HIV-seropositive (this was not broken down by race or ethnicity).

Linn, Lawrence S., J. S. Spiegel, W. C. Mathews, B. Leake, et al. (1989) Recent sexual behaviors among homosexual men seeking primary medical care, *Archives of Internal Medicine* 149:2685–90—reported continued high risk (oral or anal) sexual activities by 527 of 823 English-speaking gay or bisexual men seeking primary care at a community-based STD clinic in Los Angeles or from several physicians with sizable proportions of gay patients. With overly aggregated dependent and independent variables, they found that "unsafe" patients were younger, of lower socio-economic status, and more likely to be Latino (and to a lesser extent African American) than Anglo.

Magaña, J. Raúl, and Joseph M. Carrier (1991) Mexican and Mexican-American male sexual behavior and the spread of AIDS in California, *Journal of Sex Research* 28:425–41—attributed higher rates of AIDS in northern California counties in contrast to southern California to greater acculturation to Anglo/gay homosexuality, specifically to sexual versatility in contrast to relatively rigid Latino *activo/pasivo* role dichotomization. The authors did not consider that higher rates of infectivity in pools of potential sexual partners might account for these differences, especially given greater resistance to condom use and enduring preferences for anal intercourse over other sexual behaviors by Mexican Americans.

Marks, G., N. I. Bundek, J. L. Richardson, M. S. Ruiz, N. Maldonado, and H. R. Mason (1992) Self-disclosure of HIV infection: preliminary results from a sample of Hispanic men, *Health Psychology* 11:300–306—examined self-disclosure of HIV infection by 101 seropositive Los Angeles–resident Hispanic men. Disclosure was highly selective. Subjects tended to inform significant others, such as parents, friends, and lovers more than less-significant others, such as employers, landlords, and religious leaders. There was a relatively high rate of disclosure (75 percent) to doctors and dentists who were not treating subjects for HIV-related infections. Gay and bisexual subjects (89 percent of the sample) were more likely to disclose their HIV serostatus to homosexual or bisexual others than to heterosexuals and to inform those who were aware of their sexual orientation. Disclosure increased with severity of disease independently of the length of time since testing seropositive. Self-rated negative changes in appearance correlated with disclosure to less-significant others.

Menendez, B. S., S. Blum, T. P. Singh, and E. Drucker (1993) Trends in AIDS mortality among residents of Puerto Rico and among Puerto Rican immigrants and other Hispanic residents of New York City, 1981–1989, *New York State Journal of Medicine* 93:12–15—contrasted AIDS mortality of residents of Puerto Rico with that of New York City residents identified as either Puerto Rico–born or non–Puerto Rico–born Hispanics. The nine-year-cumulative, age-adjusted AIDS-mortality rate for Puerto Rico–born New-York-City–resident males was five times higher than that of residents of Puerto Rico (702/100,000 versus 141/100,000) and 1.5

times greater than that for other male Hispanic New York City residents (447/100,000).

Morales, Edward S. (1990) HIV infection and Hispanic gay and bisexual men, *Hispanic Journal of Behavioral Sciences* 12:212–22—discussed the psychosocial reality of Hispanic gay and bisexual men, examined the barriers affecting these men in HIV prevention, research, and service delivery systems, and discussed interventions to prevent HIV transmission. Morales cautioned that reported bisexuality may be a function of homosexual stigma (in particular, the Latino cultural equation with effeminacy) rather than an indication of heterosexual behavior: "Many Hispanic men may choose to see themselves as bisexual even though they may live exclusively gay lifestyles" (p. 215).

Murray, Stephen O. (1992) Component of gay community in San Francisco, in *Gay Culture in America*, G. Herdt, ed., pp. 107–46 Boston: Beacon—found San Francisco gay-identified Latinos reported earlier first homosexual experiences than Anglos, but later than African Americans (median ages of 15, 17, 12.5, respectively) and tended to come out at an earlier age (median ages 21, 23, 22.5). Gay identity was less necessary a criterion for inclusion in "gay community" for gay non-whites than for whites: 20 percent of Anglos, 32 percent of Latinos, 33 percent of Asian Americans, and 40 percent of African Americans included men who have sex with men but don't identify themselves as gay or as being part of "the gay community." Differences by generation and ethnicity in migration and coming-out experiences are also discussed.

Preston, John (1991) *Hometowns* New York: Dutton—included analytical reflections on growing up in an unaccepting Cuban-American community in Miami (by Jesse Monteagudo, pp. 11–20) and an unaccepting Mexican American barrio in Sacramento (by Michael Nava, pp. 21–29).

Ramirez J., E. Suarez, G. de la Rosa, M. A. Castro, and M. A. Zimmerman (1994) AIDS knowledge and sexual behavior among Mexican gay and bisexual men, *AIDS Education and Prevention* 6:163–74. Two hundred individuals from Juarez, Mexico (a city across the United States border from El Paso, Texas) were interviewed about their AIDS knowledge, sexual behavior, and condom use. Factory workers and individuals who meet sexual partners in the streets reported more sexual partners than workers in service or professional occupations and those who meet their partners in bars and

discos. Age and number of sexual partners were inversely correlated with using condoms.

Richwald, Gary A., et al. (1988) Sexual activities in bathhouses in Los
Angeles County, *Journal of Sex Research* 25:169–80. Ninety-seven
percent of the 807 men who could speak English leaving Los
Angeles County bathhouses in 1986 were familiar with information on AIDS prevention. Despite this information, 5 percent
reported receptive anal intercourse without a condom. The 10
percent involved in anal intercourse without a condom (this figure
includes insertive as well as receptive; 30 of 84 reported both roles
in the same night) were significantly more likely than those who
did not practice this highest-risk sexual activity to be less than 30
years old, to be Hispanic, never to have attended college, to be
earning less than $20,000 per year, and to have had five or more
male sexual partners in the past month. Unfortunately, monolingual Spanish-speaking men, who constituted five percent of
the sampled population, were not interviewed.

Rotheram-Borus M. J., et al. (1992) Lifetime sexual behaviors among
predominantly minority male runaways and gay/bisexual adolescents in New York City, *Aids Education and Prevention*, Fall Supplement, 34–42—reported lifetime sexual behaviors among two
samples of Black and Hispanic male adolescents in New York City
aged 12 to 18: 59 runaway males in two residential shelters and 60
males attending a community agency (HMI) for gay and bisexual
youths. Ninety-three percent of these youths had engaged in oral,
anal or vaginal intercourse and/or anilingus, with a median of 11.0
female partners among runaway males and a median of 7.0 male
partners among HMI males. For both groups the mean age for
initiating sexual activity was 12.6. Only 13 percent reported consistent condom use. One quarter of the youths reported involvement in prostitution.

Santiago, Luis (1993) Twenty years of Puerto Rican gay activism, *Radical America* 25(1):40–48—discussed the impact of being part of
the United States (and the flow of persons from the island to the
mainland) on incipient gay and AIDS activism in Puerto Rico.
Interviewer Frances Negrón-Muntaner appended a schematic account of lesbian activism on pp. 48–51.

Tori, C. D. (1989) Homosexuality and illegal residency status in relation
to substance abuse and personality traits among Mexican nationals,
Journal of Clinical Psychology 45:814–21—assessed "maladaptive

behavioral and personality reactions to severe stressors" among Mexican homosexual men by comparing substance abuse and Rorschach data obtained from three samples: (a) homosexuals residing illegally in the United States (n = 40), (b) homosexuals living in Mexico (n = 21), and (c) heterosexuals living illegally in the United States (n = 25). Very similar personality structure and substance abuse patterns were found among the participants in the two homosexual groups. As predicted, these men use alcohol or drugs to a greater extent than the heterosexual controls. Rorschach findings indicated that the homosexual subjects were experiencing dysphoric mood and distorted perceptions; they were also having significant difficulties coping with an environment that they considered to be increasingly dangerous.

LATINA LESBIANS IN THE UNITED STATES: A BIBLIOGRAPHY OF RECENT WRITINGS

Alarcón, Norma
  (1993) *Sexuality of Latinas*, Berkeley: Third Woman Press.
Anzaldúa, Gloria
  (1987) *Borderlands/la frontera*. San Francisco: Spinsters.
  (1990) *Making Face, Making Soul/Haciendo caras: Creative and Critical Perspectives by Women of Color,* San Francisco: Aunt Lute.
Arguelles, Lourdes, and B. Ruby Rich
  (1984) Homosexuality, homophobia, and revolutions: notes toward an understanding of Cuban lesbian and gay male experience, *Signs* 9:683–99—touched on Cuban exiles in Puerto Rico, México, Spain, and the mainland United States, but was mostly an attempt to exculpate persecution of "homosexuals" in Castro's Cuba.
de Alba, Alicia Gaspar
  (1993) Tortillerismo: work by Chicana lesbians, *Signs* 18:956–63. Contextualizes Trujillo's (1991) anthology.
Espín, O. M.
  (1984) Cultural and historical influences of sexuality in Hispanic/ Latin women: implications for psychotherapy, in *Pleasure and Danger*, C. Vance, ed., pp. 149–64 Boston: Routledge.
  (1987) Issues in the psychology of Latina lesbians, in *Lesbian Psychologies,* the Boston Lesbian Psychologies Collective, ed., pp. 35–51,

Urbana: University of Illinois Press—outlined similarities between the stage models of lesbian and ethnic identities. The
sixteen Latina lesbians she interviewed preferred to identify as
both Latina and lesbian, rather than as one or the other.

Hidalgo, Hilda A., and Elia Hidalgo Christensen

(1976) The Puerto Rican lesbian and the Puerto Rican community,
Journal of Homosexuality 2:109–21. Despite acute Puerto Rican
stigmatization of them as mannish and repulsive, the authors
contended that more and more Puerto Rican lesbians were coming out of the closet. Also see Hilda Hidalgo, "The Puerto Rican
Lesbian in the United States" in *Women-Identified Women*, Trudy
Darty and Sandee Potter, eds., pp. 105–15, Palo Alto, CA: May-
field, 1984.

Moraga, Cherríe

(1983) *Lo que nuncapaso por sus labios: Love in the War Years*, Boston:
South End Press. In this poetic memoir, Moraga rejects a choice
between her ethnic heritage and her sexual orientation.

(1984) *Giving Up the Ghost*, Los Angeles: West End Press.

Moraga, Cherríe, and Gloria Anzaldúa

(1981) *This Bridge Called My Back: Writings by Radical Women of
Color*, Watertown, MA: Persephone Press. This well-known anthology of fiction, poetry and essays has a wider focus than Latinas or lesbian, specifically, challenging the invisibility of non-
white women.

Silvera, Makeda

(1988) Man royal and sodomites: some thoughts on Afro-
Caribbean lesbians, in *Sight Specific: Lesbians and Representation*,
Lynne Fernie, ed., pp. 36–43, Toronto: A Space.

Trujillo, Carla

(1991) *Chicana Lesbians: The Girls Our Mother Warned Us About*,
Berkeley: Third Woman Press—collected personal reflections
(poems, essays, interviews) by lesbians of Mexican descent, most
of whom were born in the United States.

13

♨

Hispanic Homosexuals

A SPANISH LEXICON*

Stephen O. Murray
Wayne R. Dynes

In the Spanish-speaking cities of both Old and New Worlds, there is a consistent derogation of male effeminacy and a widespread assumption that such effeminacy is the mark of homosexuality. "Mexicans [among others] conceive of homosexuals as a type of person with primary and secondary physical and social characteristics" (Taylor 1978:201), specifically, those of the female role in Hispanic culture. That a masculine presentation of self might mask "passive" homosexuality is unsayable, unthinkable—even to those who have personal experience to contradict the cultural assumptions (see Lacey 1979, 1983).

As recently as the mid-1970s, homosexual identification was analogous to the pre-gay pattern in Anglo North America: those who only played the *activo* (insertor) role did not consider themselves defined, nor even implicated by such behavior. Neither did their *pasivo* partners. Activos were simply *hombres* ("men"—unmarked, or the marked reduplication of *hombre-hombre*), regardless of the sex of the persons who received their phallic thrusts. Even those persons who switched roles tended to identify themselves by one role designation or the other and to attempt to constrain any publicity about the other, although there were terms—*moderno* in Peru and *internacional* in Mesoamerica—for such dichotomy-transcending conduct.

Thereafter (as documented in chapter 8 in this volume by Murray

*Mexican data were a byproduct of Stephen Murray's fieldwork indirectly supported by the National Institute of Mental Health. He discussed Guatemalan data and their elicitation in a 1980 article in *Anthropological Linguistics*. Helpful comments and additional items were suggested by Manuel Arboleda, Brenda Espinosa, Stephen Wayne Foster, Oscar Montero, Luis Paloma, Clark Taylor, David Thompson, and Amparo Tuson.

and Arboleda), the word *gay* diffused rapidly in both Spanish and Latin American cities. As elsewhere in the world (see Murray 1995), the diffusion of North American gay challenges to the traditional stigmatization of homosexual acts and actors has enhanced the popularity of the loan word. When the terms listed below were collected, the homosexual demi-monde mostly reflected the dominant cultural view of homosexuality as unmasculine. Such terms as are known outside that demi-monde *(de ambiente)* continue to be used as derogations. That is, conception of the species *homosexual* in the subculture has broken farther away from the conception in the larger culture.

Any imputation of sexual passivity to a Latino with a masculine self-image continues to be insulting (whether such imputation is apt or not). Such labels are unlikely to perturb those who publicly flout masculine conventions. These are the only ones who can use the terms playfully among each other. The terms for those recurrently taking the active role (a relatively impoverished set of terms) are not insulting, because they affirm—if often grudgingly—someone's culturally approved masculinity. As for the terms indicating a man takes both roles, we have never heard anyone directly addressed with any of them, nor heard them applied to someone both present and within earshot. That they are only applied in the absence of the person to whom they are applied suggests they are viewed as having a dangerous potential for bad feelings or physical attacks. In using terms which might be interpreted as insults, the usual course is avoidance.

Those recurrently involved in the urban homosexual subcultures often use as self-designations the terms that do not mark the active/passive contrast. Some "natives" and those who are only slightly familiar with the subculture may use *gay* to refer only to *pasivos*. So strong is the generative link passive-effeminate-homosexual, that any term, even one usually connoting masculinity, when used to refer to a person whom auditors consider to exemplify any link of this chain, will shift, which is to say that words from one of the non-passive sets below on occasion migrate into the passive set. Passivity is not just a "fuzzy set" (see Murray 1983), but is also a greedy one.

Historical Strata

The following (doubtless incomplete) word list suffices to illustrate the complexity of the accumulated store of Spanish words designating same-sex behavior. Some of the complexity stems from the vast geographic range of the language and the isolation of peripheries from even a semblance of a standardizing center (even within Spain itself, still more within the far-flung former colonies). Much of the complexity derives from the history of the official tongue of imperial Rome, which was subject to an unending barrage of Greek together with more scattered inputs from the Near East. Arabic incursions renewed Near Eastern elements in the languages of the Iberian peninsula. The struggle with Islam gave a particular edge to the Hispanic effort towards self-definition by sharp distinction from the Other (what Devereux and Loeb 1943 termed "antagonistic acculturation"). Inveterate hatred of distinctively Moorish pederasty stoked the fury of the *conquistadores* against New World same-sex customs whenever these were encountered.

We can distinguish a number of layers in the vocabulary limned below.

1. The earliest of these is medieval Christianity forging terms of odium. During this period, Spanish, like other Western European languages received such words as *sodomita* from the story in Genesis 19, and *bujarrón*, reflecting the belief that the Albigensian heretics were sexual nonconformists. In the ensuing fury of the Spanish Inquisition, the favored locution was *pecado nefando* (from the Latin peccatum nefandum): same-sex relations constituted a sin too horrible to be named.

2. The conquest of the New World led to the borrowing of Amerindian words for things and customs unfamiliar in Spain, e.g., *chilntzin* and *cuiloni* from Nahuatl, *guarmilla* from Quechua. Diligent search probably would reveal many words derived from languages that remain in local circulation.

3. The expansion of psychiatry and the appearance of sexology in the late 19th century added some words that achieved international acceptance because of their purportedly scientific character. The most familiar of these are *homosexual* and *invertido*.

4. *Caló* is a distinctive argot used by marginal people throughout the Spanish-speaking area. Some of its terms are of foreign (especially Romany [Gypsy]) origin, while others are produced by mincing and distorting ordinary words. This street language can be entirely opaque even to native speakers of higher-class registers of Spanish. Examples include *coatón*, *lumnio* and *pajabuque*.

5. Recent "modernization" with North American influence and prestige has led to some innovations, the premier example being the word *gay* (sometimes spelled *guei* to preserve the pro-

nunciation). Some homosexual liberation groups have also taken up *lambda* in their names.

As has already been stressed, the driving force of pejorative Spanish lexicon for the domain of male homosexuality is the abandonment of male prestige. Thus, the most frequently used term is *maricón* and its variants, including *maricueca*, *marimari*, possibly *marinero*, *marión* (used by Cervantes), *marquita*, as well as *amaricado*, *amaricondado*, and possibly also *mariposa/mariposón* (butterfly), which may be regarded as a satellite or as an independent word. *Maricón* derives from *marica*, which in the masculine gender has the sense of sissy, and in the feminine magpie (possibly accounting for the common euphemism *pajaro*). Many speakers associate it with the woman's name María: this is the usual folk etymology of the term.

A device deployed in Spanish for altering gender classification is to shift the masculine ending *o* to the feminine *a*, or vice versa as in *puta* to *puto*. Mario easily becomes Maria, Juan Juana, and so on. Ad hoc aspersions are easily available by using incongruous definite articles (e.g., *la general*), or by reclassifying gender, e.g., *soldada* from soldado (soldier).

Animal names—usually those of small defenseless creatures such as *gaillina*, *mariposa*, *pajaro*, or repulsive ones such as *cabron*, *cangrejo*—also derogate homosexuals. A class with no English echo is vegetables, including *apio* and *coliflór*, along with fruits *(mandarina)* and other edible items *(rosquete, tortilla)*. Parallels for all these subtypes can be found in other Western European languages. Only a study of the frequency of use of terms, a study not now within sight, could permit determining any distinctive "Hispanism" of homosexual vocabulary based on greater relative use of particular kinds of metaphors and modes of classification.

In the following word list, after the Spanish term is the closest English equivalent, followed by the locale in which the term has been attested and, occasionally, some etymological suggestions. We have tried to ensure that the list contains only items which have or have had real use. We have excluded nonce expressions and ones that have enjoyed only a brief vogue owing to some passing event or scandal. Stephen Murray has worked primarily by elicitation from contemporary speakers; Wayne Dynes chiefly has consulted written sources. We hope that the resulting combination of methods has produced an adequate sample, ranging from the archaic to the contemporary and from the universal to the local.

I
Terms for those who take the Insertee Sexual Role

Acaponada: one who has been made a *capon* [literally, castrated; figuratively not using male equipment with which he is born; Spain]

aceite: oil [Cuba]

achorongao: fairy [Cuba]

afeminado: effeminate [very common euphemism]

aguacate: voluptuous effeminate man (from Nahuatl word for avocado)

apapayado: from papaya, colloquially used for vulva [Chile]

apio: celery stalk [Seville]

argolla: ring or collar [Venezuela]

badea: lazy one [Ecuador]

[*a la*] *banda alla:* the other group across the border of heterosexuality [Puerto Rico]

bardaje: passive boy [archaic Spain, cf. bardache in French and berdache in English]

blancanieve: Snow White [Spain]

brasilero: Brazilian [Argentina—an ethnopaulism attributing sodomy to opponents, especially rival states as in "Bulgarian" becoming "bugger" in English, *bujarrón* in Spanish]

bufo: buffoon [Argentina] The Standard Spanish term is *brasileño*. Stephens (1989:40) lists *brasilero* as "possible derogatory."

bugato: passive partner in buggery [Dominican Republic]

caballo: mare [México]

cabrito: kid: young, beardless (little goat) [Costa Rica]

cacorro: asshole man [Andes; from *caca*, or *cacharro*, which means a crude clay pot in the Andes, a trinket in Central America, and may be the role complement of *cachero*, possibly from Aymara]

campanero: effeminate man [Guatemala]

canco: fairy [Spain—related to *cancón:* bogeyman?]

cangrejo: crab [Puerto Rico] connoting redness

carne el gancho: meat on the hook [Guatemala]

caucho: from Quechua for rubber [Ecuador]

chachaco: queer—deviant in dress or lacking in respect for conventional standards [Puerto Rico]

chilindrina: drag queen [Guatemala from a popular Mexican television program in which adults dress—mostly cross-dress—as children]

chilintzín: passive homosexual [from Nahuatl]

chingada: one fucked by a *chingón* [México, notably not *chingado*] *chiquito:* anus *(Caló)*

chivo, chivato: kid goat [Peru]

chocollo: passive boy [Andes]

chucheta, chuchón: bitch, pooch from *chucha* (vulva) [Chile]

clavelito: little carnation [obsolescent *Guat*, from dandies' custom of wearing a carnation on their lapel]

coatón: queer [*Caló*] from *coartar* (to limit)

coca culo (from *coca cola*): hot ass [Chile, Peru]

coliflór, colifunto: cauliflower/stupid faggot [Spain]

colmenero: honey drinker/tearoom queen [Argentina]

comilón: big eater/size queen, cocksucker [Argentina]

cuarenta y siete: 47 = *pajaro* [which see] the bird which was the symbol of the Cuban lottery

cuarenta y una: 41 [from a widely publicized police raid on a drag ball in México City on 20 November 1901 in which forty-one people were arrested; a forty-second person was released, allegedly because she was a "real woman," but suspicions were that a close male relative of President Diaz was the forty-second, so *numero cuarenta y dos* means secretly homosexual or one who gets away with behavior that stigmatizes those less well-connected; the terms are still understood in México. See Taylor 1978 for elaboration].

cuiloni: passive [from Nahuatl, not from *culo*]

culero, culo, culón: readily available asshole [Cuba; in Spain *culo* refers to the buttocks, not specifically to the anus]

fina: fine/delicate, pretty boy [Catalonia]

flora: flower/delicate little queen [Spain]

fresco: fresh

gallina: chicken/young queen [widespread]

ganimedes: attractive boy [archaic/literary reference to Ganymede]

ganso: goose [Cuba]

gaviota: sea gull [Colombia]

guallmico, guarmilla: effeminate [Ecuador; from Quechua *guarmi* (woman)]

hueco: empty hole [Guatemala, México]

invertido: invert [pseudo-scientific term of the late 19th century still in occasional "polite" usage]

jano: man-woman [*Caló* from *jana* (woman)]

joto: effeminate [México and points south]

lea: girl[ish man; Cuba 1920s]

lechuza: lettuce [Chile]

leona: effeminate prostitute (Guatemala)

liendra: louse/lowest of the low [whore-house eunuch] [Argentina]

loba: voracious *pasivo* (female wolf)

loca: crazy girl [universal]

lumnio: lit-up/all too available [*Caló*]

machi-hembrado, machi-hembra: man-woman [Caribbean, Andes]

mamadór/mamalón: cocksucker [Puerto Rico]

mandarina: fruit [Colombia]

mandinga: effeminate African American [Caribbean]

madrina: godmother/queen bee of the camp hive

manita caida: limp wrist [México]

mano quebrada: limp wrist [Ecuador; literally "broken hand"]

marchatras: backs onto [México, Argentina]

maricón/marica: queer [universal, possibly derived from the woman's name María via *amarionado* and *amaricado*]

marinero: sailor [used by some as a euphemism for *maricón*; by others to ratify the sexual availability of sailors]

mariposa: butterfly [universal for obvious, flighty queen]

mina{o}: mistress [Argentina]

mostashe-cero: mustard pot [Peru]

mujerero/mujerengo: woman-identified (preferring the company and work considered feminine to masculine endeavors) [Chicano, via *amujerado*]

mula: mule [México]

naguilón: cowardly; from *anagua* (underskirt) [Guatemala]

nena: baby or dearie [a vocative, cf. "Well, Mary!"] [México, Guatemala, Spain]

nuco: owl [Chile]

otro: other/queer [México, Guatemala; the more polite, more common locution is *del otro lado* (from the other side of the street) Guatemala, Venezuela]; cf. Spain's *de la cerca de enfrente* (from the sidewalk on the front); New York Puerto Rican's *a la banda alla* (from the other group); and *izquierda* (left in the sense of the other side)]

pajaro: bird [widespread]

pajubique: ? [*Caló*]

papaya (from *apapayado*): papaya [Andes]

pargo: red snapper [Cuba]

pasivo: passive [universal]

pato: duck/silly, funny-walking [Cuba, México, Puerto Rico]

pederasta: pederast [etymologically it should refer to an *activo* boy lover, in practice it has come to serve as a pseudo-scientific surrogate for *maricón*]

pendejo: pubic hair/dumb faggot [Chicano]

playo: effeminate [Costa Rica]

pollo: chicken [cf. *gallina*, but derived from *pollera* (skirt) by Kany 1960]

puto: one who "takes it up the ass" [universal? masculine form of *puta:* whore, but has less to do with any sexual cash nexus than with the insufficient machismo which is taken as indicating sexual passivity]

raro, rara: queer [Guatemala, México]

redondo: round [Nicaragua; connotes "stupid fucker" in Andes]

reina: queen [universal]

repasado: flamboyant, literally looked-over [Peru]

riñón: effeminate thief [Guatemala], literally kidney

retropulsión: propelled in reverse [Ecuador; cf. *marcha atras*]

rosca: coil ring [Peru; also *rosquette* coiled fritter], a rude term for anus

sarasa: cross-dressing prostitute [Andalusia]

sodomita: sodomite [traditional forensic and ecclesiastical term]

sometico: sodomitic [possibly a corruption of *sodomitico* influenced by *someter* (to submit)]

sucubo: succubus/she-devil [Valencia]

tabla: plank/one who lies immobile and is nailed (*clavando*) [Chicano]

vestida: [cross-]dressed or, more generally, effeminate *pasivo* [México]

violeta: violet [Central America]

zarza: blackberry [Peru]

zurdo: left-handed [Peru]

II
Terms for those who take the Insertor Sexual Role

activo: active [universal]

buey: ox [México] also *burrero*, *burro* (mule)

bufo: buffoon/bugger [Spain]

bujarrón: masculine insertors [derived from bulgarus; Bulgaria was considered the heretical point of origin of sodomy in many languages, including the English "bugger"; there is a drift from *bujarrón* to *bubarrón* among New York Puerto Ricans, and to *bugarrón* among Cuban Americans]

cabrón: male goat/fucker [Cuba, México, a general term for someone who is "muy macho" although, especially in Spain the term is applied to one who is cuckolded, hardly masculinity-enhancing]

cacha: horn of a bull or goat [Peru]

cachero: catcher [Costa Rica]

chapero: hustler [Peru, Bolivia], insertor [Costa Rica]

chichifo{n}: thief/rough trade [Guatemala: someone who rents his body and takes more than what is contracted; in México the thief connotation is not present]

chingón: a hole-stuffer [México; from *chingar* which connotes taking roughly]

chulo: cute boy/trade [Mesoamerica, Central America, Peru—desirable and available for a price]

corchero: plugger [Ecuador; from *corcho* (cork)]

culebro: snake [*Caló*]

gancho: phallic man, literally, hook [Guatemala]

mas-culón: literally, more asshole [Chicano *joto* denigration of the pretenses of the masculine]

mayate: flashy dresser (originally dung beetle from Nahuatl *mayatl*) [Guatemala, México; in Chicano argot the term has come to mean a black pimp]

padrote: Big Daddy (from *padre*) [México]

panas: lovers difficult to distinguish from each other (literally, cluster of breadfruit) [Puerto Rico]

papacito: affectionate term for father/(sugar) daddy [universal for someone who keeps a boy or effeminate adult male]

picadór: an insertor in bullfights [México]

pimpollo: budding, desired youth/trade [Panama]

pipa: tube/a hung hunk [México]

untar: a strong person (literally "without a hole")

vajador: mover-shaker/swinger [México]

vampiro: vampire, hustler [México]

III
Generic Terms and Terms for those
Without Sexual Role Demarcations

ambo: ambisexual (engages in *activo* and *pasivo* behavior) [México]

anormal: abnormal

chapa: trick [rouged spot on the cheeks; or from *chapar* (to suck)] [México, Argentina] *chapero:* hustler [Spain]

cincuenta y cincuenta: fifty-fifty/equal [Chile; cf. the contrast to the North American 69 parallels the anal/oral contrast in sexual practices]

clon: stereotypically masculine man (from American *clone*)

culero, culisto: someone liking anal sex sometimes used for *pasivos*, sometimes for *activos*, but not by the same person [universal]

contestando a dos telefonos: answering two telephones; going both ways [Venezuela]

de ambiente: of the [homosexual] ambience/from that world [Central America]

de ida y vuelta: from here and back again/round-trip ticket [Guatemala]

de onda: of the good waves [increasingly popular term in México during the late 1980s and early 1990s succeeding *de ambiente*]; "Essentially it refers to non-conformity and counterculture," according to Lumsden (1991:60), who also suggests "good vibes" as the sense of "wave" in the idiom.

ficha: poker chip/trick [Guatemala, México]

fresa: literally, strawberry, the Mexican equivalent of the *guppy* (gay urban professional)

hechizo: a made one, i.e., someone who used to present himself as exclusively *activo* but was made into (at least) an *internacional* over time from extensive sexual experience with men

el amor oscuro: dark or crepuscular love [literary euphemism]

entendido: in the know [universal, preferred prior to the 1980s as codeword/self-description]

gay: gay [universal, and increasingly the preferred self-description; sometimes pronounced *gai* rather than *ge*, by those less influenced by the American example]

homosexual: homosexual, although often presumed to be *pasivo* [coined in 1869 in German and diffused to other European languages by the end of the 19th century, especially in medical discourse]

jaladór: swinger [Guatemala; more commonly connotes bisexual in Mexico]

jugando a las cambiadas: playing at [ex]changing; alternating active and passive sexual roles [Puerto Rico]

jugando por los dos equipos: playing on both teams [Chile]

nefendario: nefarious (from *crimen nefandum*, a venerable forensic circumlocution for sodomy) [archaic]

reversible: reversible [Ecuador, from reversible raincoats] *sol y sombra:* sunny and shaded [sides of bullfight stadium] [Valencia, México]

soltero: bachelor [widespread euphemism]

traido: lover [Guatemala]

zorra: literally, possum, for closeted, non-effeminate men [Costa Rica]

IV
Terms for Lesbians

arepera: maker of corncakes [Ecuador from *arepa* (corn cake); cf. *tortillera*]

bucha: female form of butch [Puerto Rico]

cachapera: one who splits something open (here a woman with a dildo) [Chicano]

cochona: sow [Chicano]

hombrecito: little man [México]

jota: lesbian femme [Chicano]

king-konga: lesbian gorilla [Andalusia]

lesbiana: lesbian [universal]

machona: macho woman [Puerto Rico]

machua: macho woman [Puerto Rico]

manflora{o}, manflorico: masculine woman [México, Colombia/Venezuela] Kany (1960:179) proposes a derivation from *hermafrodita;* Chicano folk etymology regards the "man" to be from English, i.e., "man flower" rather than the more likely (given that the word has not been coined recently) "mano" (hand)

maricona: feminine form of *maricón* [Puerto Rico] for women [México]

marimacho/a: macho Maria/dyke [Chicano, Andalusia]

mujerota: aggressive woman

pata: female duck [Puerto Rico]

rara: rare one [Chicano]

safica: Sapphist [literary and obsolescent]

tortillera: [from *hacer una tortilla*, making a tortilla, used for the bodies rubbing against each other throughout Central America]

References

Alonso Tejada, Luis
  1977 *La represion sexual en la Espana de Franco.* Barcelona: Caralt.
Aroz, Xabier
  1987/88 Gayobulario: hablando entre nosotros. *Gay Hotsa* 39:13–16.
Cardin, Alberto
  1984 *Guerreros, chamanes y travestis.* Barcelona: Editora Tusqueta.
Costas Arguedas, José F.
  1967 *Diccionario del Folklore Boliviano.* Sucre: Universidade.
Devereux, George, and Edwin M. Loeb
  1943 Antagonistic acculturation. *American Sociological Review* 8:133–47.
Gallo, Cristino
  1980 *Language of the Puerto Rican Street.* Santurce: Book Service of Puerto Rico.
Kany, Charles E.
  1960 *American-Spanish Euphemisms.* Berkeley: University of California Press.
Krack
  1976 *Tabu Spanish of Mexico.* San Diego: Valcour & Krueger.
Lacey, E. A.
  1979 Latin America. *Gay Sunshine* 40:22–31.
  1983 *My Deep Dark Pain Is Love.* San Francisco: Gay Sunshine Press.
Luján Muñoz, Luis
  1980 Breve estudio el léxico del 'Caló' en Guatemala. *Folklore Americano* 30:99–108.
Lumsden, Ian
  1991 *Homosexuality: Society and State in Mexico.* Toronto: Canadian Gay Archives.
Murray, Stephen O.
  1980 Lexical and institutional elaboration: the 'species homosexual' in Guatemala. *Anthropological Linguistics* 22:177–85.
  1983 Fuzzy sets and abominations. *Man* 18:396–99.
  1995 Stigma transformation and relexification in the international diffusion of 'gay.' To appear in *Beyond the Lavender Lexicon: Gay and Lesbian Language.* William Leap, ed. New York: Gordon & Breach.
Rodriguez Castelo, Hernán
  1979 *Lexico sexual ecuatoriano y latinoamericano.* Quito: Ediciones Libro Mundi.
Roscoe, Will
  1995 'Was We'Wha a homosexual?': Native-American survivance and the two-spirit tradition. GLQ 2:in press.
Rosenzweig, Jay B.
  1973 *Caló: Gutter Spanish.* New York: Dutton.
Schifter, Jacobo, and Johnny Madrigal
  1992 *Hombres que Aman Hombres.* San José, Costa Rica: Ilep-SIDA.

Stephens, Thomas M.

    1989 *Dictionary of Latin American Racial and Ethnic Terminology.* Gainesville: University of Florida Press.

Taylor, Clark L.

    1978 *El Ambiente.* Ph.D. dissertation, University of California, Berkeley.

Valdizán, Hermilio, and Angel Maldonado

    1922 *La Medician Popular Peruana.* Lima: Torres Aguirre.

14

〰

Male Homosexuality and
Afro-Brazilian Possession Cults*

Peter Fry

Writing on the Afro-Brazilian possession cults of Bahia in 1940, Ruth Landes asserted that the majority of male cult leaders and followers "are passive homosexuals of note . . . vagrants and casuals of streets" (1940: 393). Ribeiro (1969:113) reported that in similar cults in Recife "Thirty-four (of 60 cult members) showed various degrees of emotional imbalance and deviant behavior from overt and covert homosexualism to problems of sexual adequacy herewith included alcoholic addiction (*sic*)." Again in 1972, Seth and Ruth Leacock reported that in Belém there was "a widespread belief, both within and without the Batuque religion, that men who wear ritual costumes and dance in public ceremonies are indeed homosexuals" (1972:104). Public opinion in other cities in the North and Northeast of Brazil shares these views, which are not held in Rio de Janeiro (Brown, personal communication), São Paulo (Pressel 1971), and Campinas, where I have been conducting research.

That female homosexuality in the cults is common is hinted by

*I am very grateful to the Universidad de Estudual de Campinas for granting me leave of absence for fieldwork in Belém, to the Ford Foundation for financial assistance for my research in Campinas, to Cruz, Prego, Roman, Sarita, Daniel, Marcos, Reis, Gino, Bene, João in Belém for their friendship and patience, and to Professors Napoleão Figueiredo and Anaiza Vergolino for their help and friendly guidance. I have been fortunate to be able to discuss aspects of this paper with Verena Martinez-Alier, Mariza Correa, Gary Howe, Plinio Dentzien, Ze Luis dos Santos, Sueli Kofes le Ameida, Maria Manuela Carneiro da Cunha, Gilberto and Yvonne Velho, and Leni Silverstain to whom I offer thanks but no blame for what I have written. Special thanks to Rosie Wagstaff for ideas and typing and to Rosemary Lobert Barue, who has done more than she realizes to encourage me. An earlier version of this essay was delivered at the American Anthropological Association meetings in Mexico, D.F., November, 1974.

Ribeiro (1970:129) and the Leacocks (1972), and field reports from Anaiza Vergolino in Belém have confirmed their observations that the cults are generally viewed as haunts of "lesbians, pederasts and prostitutes," while a large part of in-cult gossip and scandal is devoted to supposed sexual idiosyncrasies of cult members. Although Roger Bastide, a recognized authority on the cults, observed that cases of "passive pederasty" were "very common" in certain cult houses in Bahia, he brushed them aside as "pathological cases" (1961:309). It seems likely that male homosexuality and other forms of sexuality defined as deviant by Brazilian dominant cultural values are, in fact, significantly related to the cults in the North and Northeast of Brazil.

Landes, Ribeiro and the Leacocks go little beyond suggesting that the cult houses represent a social niche in which members of a despised social category may achieve high status as successful and respected cult leaders, and in which "homosexuals" may give rein to their "femininity" through association with the predominantly female membership of the cults and through possession by female spirits.[1] I shall argue that in Belém—and probably in other parts of North and Northeastern Brazil—certain males who claim to prefer the sexual company of other males and who are ascribed the status of *bicha* are attracted to the cults not only because they are popularly defined as niches for male homosexuality, but for two other important reasons: first, because both male homosexuality and possession cults are defined as deviant in relation to dominant Brazilian values, and second (following the theoretical leads of Douglas 1966, 1970 and Turner 1969), because to be defined by society as defiling and dangerous is often a positive advantage to those who exercise a profession which deals in magical power: "To have been at the margins is to have been in contact with danger, to have been at a source of power" (Douglas 1966:97).

Research setting

Belém was chosen for the research for two reasons: first, because of the exemplary background work of the Leacocks, and, second, because of the help that Professors Napoleão Figueiredo and Anaiza Vergolino

---

1. Although Roger Bastide, a recognized authority on Brazilian possession cults observed cases of "passive pederasty" were "very common" in certain cult houses in Bahia, he brushed them aside as "pathological" (1961:309).

offered me, both in terms of their own research (Figueiredo, Vergolino and Silva 1967) and in the way of introductions to cult leaders with whom they had established amicable relations over some eight years of research. Although I was only able to spend four and a half weeks in the field, they made it possible to establish excellent relations and to collect sufficient material to begin at least to ask meaningful questions about male homosexuality and the cults.

Basic Properties of Brazilian Possession Cults

The materials from which the ritual, beliefs and social organization of Brazilian possession cults are compounded spring from origins as diverse as European spiritualism as set down by Allen Kardec (Warren 1968 a,b), Amerindian healing cults, astrology, West African religions brought to Brazil by way of the slave trade, and Roman Catholicism. Early studies focused on cultural genealogies of the various forms found in Brazil and resulted in complex classifications (e.g., Carneiro 1964) separating them into more or less "pure," depending on their apparent fidelity to West African forms, although it makes more sense to regard them as local responses to the social structural conditions in which they operate (see Velho 1973).

The cults may be divided into two broad categories: those that follow more or less faithfully the Kardecist tradition and those that approximate more to African and Amerindian forms. The latter are generally referred to as *Afro-Brazilian.* The former tend to be found in the middle classes, while the latter are more commonly associated with the urban poor, even though their magical services may be procured by the wealthy and well-to-do (Fry 1974). Afro-Brazilian cults include Ubanda, Macumba, Zango, Batuque, and Candomblé, but the subtleties of cult nomenclature can only be understood within the specific contexts in that they are employed. The Kardecist cults allow for possession by the spirits of deceased persons in a relatively calm ritual atmosphere without either singing, dancing or drumming, and place considerable emphasis on the doctrine of successive reincarnation, related to an ethic of charity, education, and hard work. Kardecists in general have little respect for the Afro-Brazilian cults, whose association with the poor is metaphorically represented by "undeveloped" spirits that "descend" in the Afro-Brazilian religions, ordered into a para-military hierarchy of legions and *falanges,* each of that is led by an *orixa* of African origin. Orixas are also saints of the Roman Catholic Church, and it is generally agreed that this "syncretism" developed during the colonial period, when slaves concealed their African gods behind the masks of Christian saints.

Under the leadership of the major *orixas* are a host of lesser spirits essential to day-to-day ritual activity: *caboclos, criancas, pretos velhos, baianos, exus, pombagiras,* et al. The popularity of these groups of spirits varies from region to region and from one *terreiro* to another.

Each cult center is led by *mai* or *mae de santo,* who maintains a somewhat autocratic control over the other mediums, or *filhos de santo.* Within the *terreiros* there is considerable competition for recognition among *filhos* and between *filhos* and the cult leader. Ambitious mediums build up prestige over time and, if they are not able to usurp the authority of the cult leader, leave to form their own *terreiros.* The Afro-Brazilian cults, therefore, are in a state of constant expansion, spreading through the landscape rather like an acephalous tribe. Just as competition is rife within cult centers, so is it strong between them, expressed in mutual accusations of *mistificacao* (mystical attack). All centers take elaborate precautions to defend themselves against such attacks. Such a system leads to the maintenance of autonomy on the part of individual cult centers.

Cult centers meet more or less regularly for *seasoes,* or *trabalhos* or *festas,* during which mediums "receive" the spirits relevant to the occasion. With the exception of the most "traditional" Candomblé cults of Bahia, the possessed medium not only dances, but also speaks with clients, giving advice and ritual protection (passes). Theatricality is important and great attention is paid to the mise-en-scene of the seances. Cult houses are elaborately decorated with statues of spirits, paper flags and streamers, silver paper, flashing lights, etc.; the mediums are expected to dress well—the women in long, wide skirts, the men in white singlet and trousers—and they pride themselves in their skills as singers and dancers. The central figure at a seance is supposed to be the *pai* or *mae de santo;* spirits of *filhos* should not attempt to overshadow the spirit of the leader. The ritual normally ends with the departure of the spirits and a closing song, although in Bahia it is not unusual for mediums to remain possessed for hours and in some cases days after the conclusion of the ritual.

For the purposes of this paper it is irrelevant to discuss the psychology and physiology of the trance state; spirit mediumship will be treated as a social role the credibility of that is defined by the actors themselves (see Leacock 1966; Fry 1969; Lewis 1971). Thus, a medium is possessed by a spirit for those who believe he is, and is a fraud for those who do not. It is not uncommon for accusations of fraud to be made against mediums, or for the authenticity of certain instances of supposed possession of recognized mediums to be challenged (such accusations make sense in terms of the micro-political contexts in that they occur, see Velho 1973).

It is important to note that these cults are held in low regard by the majority of Brazilians, especially the relatively wealthy and educated. Negative stereotypes are so strong that, although a large number of middle-class and upper-class persons are faithful clients of the *terreiros,* usually they deny it and visit at times other than during ritual hours. Police repression was reported to be frequent in the past (Rodrigues 1935:18–20; Carneiro 1954:107; Ramos 1934; de Mattos 1938). This is no longer the case: attempts have been made by state and municipal governments to recognize the touristic value of the cults. Nevertheless, negative stereotypes persist. For instance, the *Jornal do Estado de São Paulo,* the recognized voice of bourgeois opinion in São Paulo, described the cults as the haunts of "immorality, crime, and corruption." Herskovits (1966:241) noted that the wider society tended "to derogate African religions as 'superstitions' and place high value on those of European derivation. Such attitudes are bolstered by the association of the Candomblé in the minds of most Brazilians with low socioeconomic status." The wider society classifies the cults as dangerous, and their denizens as marginal, poor, and/or corrupt. Moreover, the cult centers are mostly located either on the geographical margins of the cities or in "solitary places that are difficult to find" (Rodrigues 1935:63)— symbolic representation of the socially marginal positions of the cults.

Earlier Discussion of Male Homosexuality in Cults

Landes (1940:388) claimed that, traditionally, the Afro-Brazilian cults of Bahia were a female domain: "Tradition says baldly that only women are suited by their sex to nurse the deities, and that the service of men is blasphemous and unsexing." She claimed that men only began to emerge as *pais de santo* a generation before 1940 with the rise of a new cult form, the Candomblé de caboclo. This new cult introduced possession by the spirits of Brazilian Indians (called *caboclos* in this context) in addition to possession by the traditional African deities *(orixas).* Landes noted that the new cults "greatly relaxed the restrictions surrounding 'mothers'" (392) and that the rigorous initiation procedures gave way to the upsurge of new cult leaders who had not passed through the lengthy and costly rites. However, the greatest change that Landes observed was the introduction of males as cult leaders. She presented the following table of the sex of cult leaders in the traditional *(nago)* and *caboclo* cults:

Table 14.1
Sex of 1940 Cult Leaders (after Landes)

	Maes *(Mothers)*	Pais *(Fathers)*
Nago	29.9%	4.5%
Caboclo	14.9%	50.7%

N=67
(Source: Landes 1940:393)

Not only were the vast majority of *pais de santo* to be found in the *caboclo* cults, but they were also all under 45 years of age, many in their early twenties. The *pais de santo* were not only young, but, according to Landes, were recruited from the "passive homosexuals" of the Bahian underworld. She affirmed that in Bahia there was a clear distinction between active and passive homosexuals, and that while the latter were universally despised and persecuted, the former "pass unremarked and are very often of importance" (1940:386). Passive homosexuals "solicit on the street in obscene whispers and make themselves conspicuous by mincing with sickening exaggeration, overdoing the falsetto tones, and using women's turns of phrase. All their energies are focused upon arranging the sexual act in that they take the female role" (p. 387).

Landes knew some ten *pais de santo* among whom she distinguished different types. Some like Bernadino (she had no scruples about publishing informants' names)[2] "break their street ties completely and cultivate cult followers who are normal men dazzled by the mystery that surrounds a cult head" (1940:398) and do what they can to "conceal their homosexuality." Others, like João, "retain the old ties along with the new" (p. 398): João is reported to be "quite unashamed, half-mincing in the streets, writing love letters to the men of his heart,

_____

2. [Editor's Note:] In a letter of 16 January 1985, the late Ruth Landes responded that "any name change is transparent to interested parties. Anyway, it was considered honorable practice until a few years ago," serving to acknowledge the contribution of informants to chronicling their culture rather than magnifying the importance of patronizing and pretentious ethnographers.

wearing fancy blouses whose colors and cut set off his fine shoulders and skin—and straightening his hair. Straightened hair, forbidden by Nago, is the symbol of male homosexuals" (p. 396). Landes makes a "bisexual" type of others such as Vava, who, like João, allowed his cult house to be used for amorous encounters, thus "attaining for himself access to the men who visited there originally for heterosexual motives. At the same time he is happily married to an attractive white girl, having been married several times in his 25 years" (p. 397).

Having so described the situation, Landes (1940) offered two parallel interpretations. First, "passive homosexuals" enter the cults in order to act out female roles, and, second, by so doing acquire high status as religious leaders (to compensate for their despised homosexual status). Landes (1940:394) asserted, "They want one thing, for that the Candomblé provides widest opportunity: they want to be women." In cult houses, such men could ritualize their "femininity" in priestly trance and realize their homosexual fantasies under the protection of the cult.

Although Edison Carneiro (1954:142) did not write specifically about male homosexuality, he seems to have shared Landes's views that the Candomblés were a traditionally female preserve, that had only begun to admit men with the introduction of the Candomblé de caboclo. The males who entered "show in the great majority of cases, unequivocal tendencies towards effeminacy . . . They cream their hair, paint their fingernails, powder their faces and are always surrounded by women and conversing with typical feminine volubility" (Carneiro 1954:154–55).

Landes's work did not go uncriticized. Herskovits (1947), reviewing her 1946 book *City of Women,* challenged her thesis that the priestly role in the Candomblés was necessarily reserved only for women. There were fewer men, he claimed, for basically economic reasons. In Brazil, as in Africa, he argued, "It is easier to support a women in the cult house than to withdraw a man from productive labor for months on end" (1947:125). "Moreover," he chided, "Miss Landes overstresses the homosexuality of male priests—there are many 'orthodox' as well as caboclo priests who have no tendency towards inversion" (p. 125); he went on to repeat Ramos's (1942) aspersions of Landes's credentials [that were training by Boas, the same as Herskovits's own].[3] Like Herskovits, Ra-

---

3. Ramos seems to have borne Landes a personal grudge for not making use of his letters of introduction to "various friends, including the authorities and respectable

mos (1942:187) denied that the priestly role was necessarily female, observing that "the best-known cult leaders of the black cult in Bahia, as in other parts of Brazil, are, as it happens, men, as was evident in the two Afro-Brazilian congresses and in the register of African sects of Bahia." Ramos categorically rejected Landes's claims about male homosexuality: "I know myself a few homosexuals *pais de santo,* just as there are a few blacks, mulattos and Indians who are also homosexuals without this having anything to do with defining characteristics of the cult. . . . The presence of homosexuals in the Candomblés has neither religious nor ritual significance, but implies only individual sexual deviance" (Ramos 1942:188, 192). Of course, Landes never claimed that all those who were defined as "passive homosexuals" were members of the Candomblés, nor that all those who were "homosexuals," as neither Ramos nor Landes defined exactly what each meant by the term "homosexual." Ramos's challenge that homosexuality is coincidental in the cults is as impossible to substantiate as Landes's that it isn't. Moreover, Ramos did nothing to challenge Landes's information about the life strategies of the ten *pais de santo* whom she described.

Ribeiro (1969:11) noted that in Recife, as in Bahia, the majority of cult members are female, but found the sex balance more equal among leaders. Whereas Landes had noted that male leaders predominated in the "syncretic" Candomblés de caboclo in Bahia, Ribeiro found male leaders predominating in the "orthodox" cults in Recife:

Table 14.2
Sex of 1969 Cult Leaders (after Ribeiro)

	Maes *(Mothers)*	Pais *(Fathers)*	N
Orthodox	46%	54	(21)
Syncretic	69%	31	(37)

Source: Ribeiro (1969:11)

people who could have helped her in her projected research" (Ramos 1942:184). For illuminating comments on Ramos's attacks on Landes, see Carneiro (1964:227–33) who felt there was "an injustice which has resulted purely from Arthur Ramos's pride and vanity" and that Ramos "read her simple article with ill will and with the intention of discovering how best to sully the scientific and personal reputation of its author, (this) might perhaps eliminate from the Brazilian bibliography on blacks the works of a researcher who spared no efforts to understand them through their religious practices" (p. 227). Also see Landes's 1970 account.

He also noted that at the level of collective representations, there is a relationship between the cults and male homosexuality. "Ten percent of the interviewees gave as reasons for men refraining from participation at these cults the attendance there of homosexuals and the fear of being taken for one of them. Thirteen per cent of the men interviewed thought of participation at the dances as unmanly, and subject to social ridicule, according to the sanctions of traditional Brazilian culture, even though they danced at these same ceremonies" (1969:112). His interpretation of the recruitment of "overt" and "covert" homosexuals, and persons with "thwarted sexual identity" to the cults is similar to Landes's: they enter "to display their mannerisms or to identify with female deities in congeries led by homosexuals" or "they may also be pushed by other complex motivational needs of compensation for the frustrations imposed on them by their positions and interactions within the larger society" (1969:119).

Trying to Interpret Earlier Literature

One of the most serious obstacles to understanding the writings on homosexuality and Brazilian possession cults in terminological confusion, specifically, a failure to distinguish between observers' and actors' categories and between sexual performance and social role, or even between actual and imputed sexual behavior. Thus, when Landes wrote of "passive homosexuals" it is not possible to know whether she referred to persons who always assume the "passive role" in sexual intercourse, those who assume certain "effeminate" mannerisms, or those who are merely imputed to indulge in one of these.

All the authors used the term "homosexual,"[4] but without ethnographic information about the classificatory scheme of the people concerned, it is difficult to assess the findings. Understanding what is classed as "deviant" "requires the thorough study of these definitions and the processes by that they develop and attain legitimacy and taken-for-grantedness" (Becker 1973:207). The remainder of this paper endeavors to do this for Belém.

---

4. Ramos (1942:189, 191) misrepresents Landes as claiming to have observed "ritual homosexuality." She argued homosexuality preceded entrance into the priesthood, not that males coupled with other males out of religious ambition.

Possession Cults in Belém

As elsewhere in Brazil, there is a profusion of terms used to discrimi-
nate between cults and between autonomous rival cult groups. The
most salient criterion for distinguishing cult groups whose meeting
places are termed *searas* from those whose meeting places are termed
terreiros is that only the latter use drums *(tambores)* in their ritual. *Terreiro* rituals are generally much more dynamic and colorful then *seara*
rituals, and the former are commonly associated with male homosexuality, and will, therefore, be the focus here. The cults will be referred
to as Macumba or Candomblé, their members as *macumbeiros*.[5]

Cult groups are autonomous and highly competitive. *Macumbeiros*
form an enormous communication network along that passes information relating to the activities of cult leaders and their followers, on that
basic evaluations are made. Although much of the gossip is malicious
and can be interpreted as expressing conflict, it nevertheless leads to
formulation of common norms and values (cf. Murray 1979). Because
the lines of conflict are cross-cutting, they bolster a certain solidarity
amongst all *macumbeiros* vis-a-vis the wider society (Gluckman 1963;
Vergolino, personal communication). A significant percentage of this
group is devoted to the supposed sexual activities of cult members.

The most important local difference in belief system is the stress
on "carouser spirits" (Leacock 1965) and the important dictum: "A vida
no sento pão tem nada a ver com a vida particular" (The ritual life is
in no way connected to one's private life). The spirits are believed to
interfere with the lives of their hosts only when these latter fail to fulfill
their obligations to them; strictly secular affairs are of no concern to the
spirits (Leacock and Leacock 1972:75).

The socioeconomic background of cult members is difficult to specify. Small numbers of wealthy persons participate in *terreiros* but tend to
consult outside ritual hours. The vast majority of overt *macumbeiros* is
recruited from the urban poor, whose houses in the *bairros* of the city are
made of wood roofed with palm and often built on stilts (because of
frequent flooding). *Terreiros* are generally located in these *bairros,* where

---

5. The term *macumba* is often used in a pejorative sense, almost synonymous with
feiticeiro (sorcerer). Lapassade and Luz (1972) distinguished cults in the center of the
city (Umbanda) from those in the slums (Macumba), and maintained the former
reproduced dominant ideology, while the latter contested it and lacked its sexual
repression.

their adepts live. Leacock and Leacock (1972:123) summarized: "Batuque mediums tend to be poor, over thirty, female of varied physical characteristics, and native to the city." They also noted that in Belém, there are more female than male cult members, attributing this to a "widespread belief both within and without the Batuque religion that men who wear ritual costume and dance in public ceremonies are either effeminate or in most cases homosexuals" (p. 104). The term homosexual in Portuguese is, however, rarely used in the context of the cults. More common are *bicha* (literally, worm), *pederasta*, *fresco* (literally fresh), and *veado* (literally deer). The most commonly used of these is *bicha*, e.g., "If a man gets possessed you can be sure he is a *bicha*: Ninety, no ninety-five percent of *macumbeiros* are *bichas*." To begin to understand the relationship between male homosexuality and *macumba*, it is, thus, first necessary to comprehend the term *bicha*.

The *bicha* role negates that of the "correct" man. A *bicha* is ascribed the "receptor" role (Humphreys 1970) in sexual intercourse with other males, and his general appearance and gestures approximate women's. Those who conform to this ideal type (female in sex and gender roles) are called "real *bichas*" (*bichas mesmo*), *bichonas* (-*ona* is an intensifier), or *bichas depravadas* (depraved). "Real *bichas*" defined themselves and are defined as such on the basis of their social performance, that is supposed to derive directly from their sexual performance (see Lacey 1979). Real bichas usually assume "screen names" *(nomes de tela)* or "war names" *(nomes de guerra)*. They refer to themselves and are referred to as if they were female (with feminine pronouns and adjectives), and assert a preference for sexual relations with "real men" *(homens verdadeiros)*, who maintain their definition as "real men" by taking only the "insertor" role in sexual relations. Humphreys's (1970) terms "insertor" and "receptor" are adequate translations of the Brazilian terms *dar* (give) and *comer* (eat): he who "gives" in a sexual encounter is the receptor (as in "give head" in United States), while he who "eats" is the insertor.

Not all those referred to by others as *bichas* define themselves as such. Accusations of being a *bicha* are often made in situations of conflict, in the manner of witchcraft accusations. The "evidence" that is presented on such occasions usually derives from social performance: *bichas* are supposed to emit diacritical signs, such as how a cigarette is held, or the way legs are crossed, etc., that lead to accusation. These are read as signs that the accused has at some time "given" sexually. Accusations may also be made against individuals who do not show any diacritical signs and who act like "real men." These refer solely to sexual performance and are often made by "real *bichas*" who have claimed to have "eaten" them. Individuals who are labeled *bichas* by others but who do not so define themselves are termed *bichas incubada* (incubating bichas), a term extended also to would-be *bichas*.

According to the ideal norms (behavioral variance from that has already been indicated), the male world of Belém is divided into two distinct categories: those who give *(bichas, veados, frescos)* and those who eat *(homens, machos, garanhoes, fanchoas).* A male is a man until he is accused or proved to have "given," in which case he becomes a *bicha.* Whether or not he becomes a *bicha mesmo* depends on his personal choice to accept the *bicha* role in all its implications, sexual and social. A male who "comes out" *(solta plumas:* releases feathers[6]) and acts out the social role is expected to "give" sexually as well.

The exceptions to this rule, for being considered exceptions, prove it. A young adolescent male who appears to maintain heterosexual relations may "give" from time to time in exchange for cash without being classified a *bicha.* He is instead classed a *panache* (mixed vegetable), but *panache* status is precarious. For a *bicha* to "eat" another male is also considered exceptional, occurring when a real *bicha* finds her supposed man to be a *bicha incubada.* No self-respecting *bicha* would admit to "giving" to another *bicha.* The partner who "eats" in such situations, derives micropolitical advantage thereby. Exceptional also in relation to the ideal model, but nevertheless quite common, are sexual relations between two real *bichas.* Such encounters in that "anything goes" *(scanagem)* and that involve no clear definition of "eater" and "giver" are looked down upon and jokingly referred to as lesbianism. Lesbians are referred to as *lesbicas* or *saboeiros,* that comes from the belief that lesbians do not have wholesome sexual relations: they do not *foder* (fuck), they *fazer* (make soap) or *fazer espuma* (make foam). These terms are extended to sexual relations between two *bichas.* The most humiliating experience for a real *bicha* is to learn that "her man" is, in fact, a *bicha,* i.e., has given, as the following case illustrates.

Jeronimo is a real *bicha* of some 40 years, who lived with "her man," Francisco, until he left Belém with a woman (whom Jeronimo classed a *puta*). Jeronimo's sufferings from Francisco's absence turned to anguish,

---

6. *Solta plumas* suggests the predominance of feathers in carnaval costumes. In the popular imagination *bichas* dominate carnaval, an essentially liminal rite (see De Matta 1973).

when he heard from a *pai de santo* friend that Alberto, who had a reputation for eating *bichas,* had eaten Francisco. Stupefied, Jeronimo could not bring herself to believe the accusation asserting Francisco had always been a man. Before I left Belém, Francisco had heard of the accusations and was preparing to travel to Belém to confront Alberto and defend his reputation as a "real man."

With the possible exception of reference to those who consistently *fazer sabao,* "homosexual" is an inadequate translation. With very few exceptions, males who eat *bichas* are not classed as anything other than real men, differing in no way from men who restrict themselves to "eating" females. The division of the male world into "eaters" and "givers" and the classification of sexual relations in that these two roles are not clearly defined as deviant expresses the dominant heterosexual ideology of the wider society with an expectation of a replication of an absolute male/female dichotomy. Indeed, the same terms are used in relation to heterosexual intercourse and power relations: *comer* is used to refer to taking a piece in chess and to winning aggressively, as when a soccer team "eats" its opponent. *Dar* indicates weakness; the male is supposed to dominate and win the *bicha* in homosexual relations just as he does the women in heterosexual ones.

In sum, while the heterosexual world defines the *bicha* as abnormal, shameful, and even nauseating, because he does not conform to the social and sexual role attributed to males, *bichas* themselves have their own classification in that the roles of "eater" and "giver" of the heterosexual world are replicated, and non-conformity to this dichotomy is disdained as "abnormal."

Having gone some way to understanding the meaning of the category *bicha,* we can return to the public opinion that associates the role *bicha* with that of medium and *pai de santo.* At the level of collective representations the link is indisputable, but whether this corresponds to reality is another matter. It could be argued that since the *bicha* role is essentially an ascribed one, it does not matter whether or not persons defined as *bichas* conform to their ascribed role (following Becker 1973: 14). In this case, it would be sufficient to adopt a similar theoretical position to that adopted in relation to the psychological and physiological reality of trance states.

Given that social networks linking cult members are tightly-knit, and that privacy is difficult to achieve, relatively good fit between gossip and reality seems likely, but the truth of gossip is impossible to ascertain. Whatever the proportion of males ascribed either real *bicha* or incubated *bicha* status in the cults, most people believe *pais de santo* are *bichas*. No one went so far as to say that all those who danced in the *terreiros* were *bichas,* but in two observed instances accusations of being a *bicha* were made solely on the basis of cult participation. One *pai de santo* who defined himself as a *bicha* denied that all cult members were *bichas* on the grounds that "her man," also a medium, was not a *bicha* (i.e., was a real man).

Certainly, many of the most expressive and important *pais de santo* make a point of confirming the label "real *bicha*." Whether or not the proportion is as high as the 80 percent estimate made by the treasurer of the Federation of Afro-Brazilian cults of Para, cannot be known, but as one of young *bicha* who was not a cult member argued, "O povo aumenta mas não inventa" (Public opinion exaggerates but does not invent).

Folk Interpretations

Those who affirmed the majority of cult members were *bichas* were asked why they thought this was the case. Most had initial difficulty in formulating a response, but when pressed put forth suggestions.

Cult members themselves denied that there was any explanation. Like Ramos, they insisted that the presence of *bichas*[7] in the cult bore no essential relationship to the cult. The rule that an individual's saintly life had no relation to private/secular life (already mentioned above) was frequently invoked (see Leacock and Leacock 1972:106). As one *pai de santo* put it, I am a *bicha;* everyone knows that I am a *bicha,* and I have never denied that I am a *bicha.* At the same time, I am a *pai de santo* and was initiated (*feito*) in Bahia. When I have a ritual (*festa*) these things are left aside."

In many *terreiros,* belief in a total separation between saintly and "inner"/private life (*a vida do pecador*) legitimates what appears to an outsider as a considerable degree of sexual freedom. The only restrictions the cult imposes on sexuality are on sexual activity before, during, and after rituals—none at all on the type of sexual activity, or on the gender of the persons involved. Immediately after sexual intercourse, for a period varying from one to three days, partners' bodies are dirty (*sujo*). Anyone with a *corpo sujo* may not enter the *terreiro* on pain of punishment from the

---

7. Henceforth, *bicha* is used as by the informants.

spirits. Rules differ from females to males, for it is believed the former dirty *(sujar)* the latter through sexual intercourse (cf. Amazonian sexual antagonisms). While the male partner may clean *(limpar)* his body by means of ritual bathing before the normal duration of the period of uncleanness is over, the female partner cannot. When asked whether sexual intercourse between a *bicha* and a man also led to bodily uncleanness, informants agreed it did. When asked how—if it was females that made the body unclean—some informants were unable to offer an explanation. Others suggested sexual relations without insertion were not sullying. All agreed that *bichas*—like men and unlike women—could purify their bodies before the end of the prescribed period by bathing.

The fact that feasts in many *terreiros* offer opportunities for sexual encounters to be arranged (a concern to some *maes de santo* aiming to improve the public image of their cult) led some informants to explain that *bichas* are common in cults because of the opportunity provided there to "hunt" *(cacar)* men. By dancing in the cults, *bichas,* who were generally held to like to show themselves off ("A bicha gosta muito de se mostrar"), had sanction for dressing up in fine clothes and competing with other *bichas* ("Cada bicha quer ser maior que a outra") and thereby attracting the "men" present. Although *festas* do attract large publics, some of whom are on the lookout for possible sexual adventures, these are usually arranged by non-participants, rather than by cult members, who have little chance to interact with persons outside the *terreiro.*

Another interpretation given for the presence of *bichas* in the cults was that *bichas* are more artistic than men and women, and are, therefore, better equipped to organize and participate in ritual. One *pai de santo,* who claimed that he would have been a famous transvestite *(transvesti)* if he had not been called by the spirits and who "adores the theater," felt the "real men" did not have the "knack" for dancing for the spirits: "A *pai de santo* must have the knack *(jeito);* if he doesn't it just isn't beautiful. I have a special knack [demonstrating by dancing]. These things give life to the spirit . . . presentation is an art." In fact, the aesthetic side of ritual is regarded as very important. When the qualities of a *terreiro* are judged, the quality of decor, dancing, clothing, food, drink, and hospitality are all taken into account. While this applies to all cult members, it was possible to observe that the *bichas* were in general more extravagantly and expensively dressed, and very often dominated the ritual scene. When possessed by such female "carouser" spirits as Dona Herondina, Dona Mariana, or Dona Jarina, they were notably exuberant and luxuriously clad.

Some people, particularly *bichas,* claimed that many *bichas* entered the cults to be possessed by female spirits, in order to give free rein to their "feminine tendencies." Although males were frequently possessed by female spirits, they were also possessed by male ones. In the case of most *bichas mesmo,* the most important of their possessing spirits, the one they "received" most frequently and for the longest periods was male. It is, however, difficult not to agree with those who felt that some *bichas* especially enjoyed acting as mediums for female spirits. As one commented shortly after a *festa* for Dona Mariana, whom he was to receive, "I am so ugly and Dona Mariana is so beautiful."

Many commentators, both within and without the cults, *bichas* and "real men," claimed that it was not uncommon for the *bichas* to pretend that they were in trance in order to exploit the authority of their spirits for sexual ends. Such "spirits" were referred to as *santos de pegacao* or *santos de fechemento* (saints for picking up or for showing off). As noted earlier, such accusations of false trance are usually made in the context of interpersonal rivalry. I witnessed a *pai de santo,* himself a "real *bicha,*" claiming to be possessed by a male spirit, who agreed to help a *bicha* present arrange a sexual encounter with one of the "men" also present. After the seance was over, another *pai de santo* commented to his friends that it was a clear case of a picking-up spirit, exclaiming, "How could the spirit, who is very macho, mix himself up with arranging sex for a *bicha?*" Another *pai de santo* told me it was very common for males to "receive" female spirits because they wanted to go after men but didn't have the courage to do so on their own, and, therefore, he claimed, used female spirits to mask their personal desires. But as for himself, "I do not know what their game is. Whoever likes me likes me for what I am. There is no need for me to mix my private life with my work, for the simple reason that I am much more of a coquette than any of the caboclos (female spirits) I receive."

These interpretations given by the actors themselves to account for the affinity between *macumba* and *bichas* posit no religious interpretations. No one, for instance, thought the spirits might have a special affinity for *bichas.* Instead, they play on the theme that *bichas* exploit the cults to "show off" or to "hunt men," etc. The only interpretation that suggested any special quality a *bicha* might have that was an advantage to the *pai de santo* role was "artistic"/"theatrical" talents. Not one person suggested that *bichas* entered the cults because they wanted to be women or to be with women. Rather, many opined that *bichas* wanted to be in the cults to be with "men" or to "show off" before other *bichas*.[8]

They were also asked to explain why they were *bichas*, specifically if the cult provided any explanation. Once again, with the exception of one *pai de santo* who said he couldn't give me the explanation because it was a cult secret available only to initiates, those questioned denied any religious explanation. Instead, they saw their sexuality as either a mission *(misao)* or a cross to be borne.[9] The idea that *bicha* status is a mission comes from Kardecist reincarnation beliefs, and carries with it the notion of trial as punishment for behavior in a previous incarnation. Another frequent comment was "every good person has a defect." These replies demonstrate that for the *bichas*, *bicha* etiology was unproblematic, not requiring explanation. At the same time, they echoed dominant heterosexual society's stigmatization, by implying hardship and/or deviance. On closer questioning, however, they indicated they were satisfied with their sexuality.

Bicha status, then, is taken for granted; at most it is a cross to be borne. There is, thus, no motivation for elaborate explanation. We only look for explanations for what is not—for us—obvious and taken for granted.

Analyst Interpretations

The material reported suggests that certain *terreiros* serve as a social niche for a certain number of *bichas* to interact with one another and with non-*bichas* in a congenial setting. The *terreiros* have a daily life of their own interspersed with ritual. The *terreiros* have a small staff who cook, clean and guard the *terreiro* in exchange for food, lodging and pocket money provided by *pai de santo*. Very often these small commu-

---

8. Ribeiro (1969) noted little or no correlation between the sex of patron spirits and the sexuality of their adepts.

9. Those who thought there was a link between such *orixas* as Yansan, Oxum and the androgynous Oxunmare and *bicha* status did not see it as one of cause and effect, but of affinity. Others categorically denied any such link. One *mae de santo* adamantly maintained, "The sexuality of the santos under no hypothesis interferes with the physical integrity of their sons *(filhos)*." Despite this lack of consensus, individuals who are sons of the female *orixas* are often suspected of being *bichas*, and many *bichas* have female *santos* as patrons.

nities contain a number of *bichas* who are out of work or short of money. Some *terreiros* seemed to be sanctuaries for young *bichas* who had problems with their family and had to leave home (cf. *hijras* in India). I observed three cases of young males who left home ostensibly to develop their mediumship but also to escape intolerable family situations. These *bichas* affirmed that family relations improved after their mediumships developed and they attained the prestige of a *pai de santo*. Cult houses, therefore, offer career opportunities to *bichas* in political economic and prestige terms (much as Landes reported for Bahia). Even for those who do not make a career of their calling as mediums, the *terreiro* clearly absorb some young men defined as sexually deviant by their families.[10] In part this is because of a self-fulfilling prophecy. Once the cults have been labeled a locale for *bichas,* "real men" will avoid them for fear of being labeled a *bicha,* while some of those males who have assumed (or thought of assuming) the role will feel attracted to an institution where they expect to be accepted. As the male population of the cults comes to be predominantly recruited among *bichas,* some males might play the *bicha* role to get on in the cult. One informant suggested this: "A man enters the *terreiro*. They talk to him. He goes into a place where they are only *bichas*. In the end, he feels humiliated to be a man." However, all the real *bichas* affirmed that they were *bichas* before they entered the cult, though one might suspect some entered as *bichas incubadas* and changed their strategies to conform when they became full members (and, consciously or not, rewrote their biographies as if they had always been *bichas*).

That *terreiros* are labeled niches for *bichas* still requires explanation. An approach to one requires a closer look at the role of *pai de santo*. The *pai de santo* is essentially a magician-counselor, whose explicitly religious function is to listen to the problems of his clients, provide explanations and offer solutions—whether magical or practical—for them. The whole edifice rests fundamentally on public recognition (cf. Gellner 1969). The success of a *pai de santo* depends upon the continued confidence of his *filhos* in the efficacy of his magic, as evidenced in part by material signs of success. The more cash a *pai de santo* can invest in his *terreiro* and his immediate followers (*filhos de santo),* the more recog-

---

10. A career as a medium/*pai de santo* is clearly not the only option available to poor people with homosexual proclivities. Flight to other cities is possible, but expensive. Other niches include domestic service and prostitution.

nition and political support he can hope to obtain in return. Any leakage of cash outside the circuit diminishes resources available for expenditure on recognition and political support. Marriage and kinship ties oblige a medium to divert resources to non-*terreiro* ends, whereas *pais de santo* not encumbered with such obligations can dedicate all their resources to the cult and their positions within it. In only the rarest circumstances do *bichas* have children. Moreover, their relations to their kinship network are usually tenuous at best, especially if the *bichas* left home to escape or to avoid a crisis at home because of deviant sexuality.

In addition to this exchange aspect, the *bicha pai de santo* has other material advantages over non-*bichas pais* and *maes de santo,* for *bichas* share with women freedom from taboos against cooking and embroidery (both important to the functioning of the *terreiro*) while retaining certain male prerogatives (cf. "berdache"). Socialized as a male, and continuing to interact most intensely with other males, a *pai de santo* will be better equipped than a *mae de santo* to deal with police and officialdom and will probably better be linked to influential figures such as political patrons, doctors, and lawyers. The *bicha pai de santo* is not merely a pale imitation of a woman, as Landes (1940) thought. He is an individual who combines certain key aspects of the "normal" male and female roles, that he can manipulate to his own advantage.

Having suggested ways in which *bicha* status is advantageous to an ambitious cult leader in non-ritual functions, it remains to demonstrate how status as a sexual deviant vis-à-vis the wider society is advantageous for functioning as a magician-counselor.

Advice is normally sought from persons considered well-informed and impartial. Counselors generally occupy positions outside the formal power structure. Uncompromised by alliance to politicians or parties, they can be expected to be impartial. Because they are politically disinterested, such persons can obtain information from all sides of a conflict and become gossip brokers. Since most cases of misfortune that are taken to the *pais de santo* for explanation and cure are believed to be caused by the mystical attacks of enemies, and because *pais de santo* are expected to analyze these problems using the supernatural powers of their spirits or divining apparatus rather than through questioning, they must command a considerable amount of information to be seen as competent. Various symbolic mechanisms for assuring analyses are treated as deriving from an impartial outsider—spirit possession or divinatory techniques such as *jogo de buzios*—but the outsider status of *pais de santo* enhances this.

Pais de santo who also defined themselves as *bichas* are doubly marginal to the wider society. Defined as deviant in sexual terms, they cut themselves off from their kinship networks and thus are outsiders in social structural terms. Not only do they live encapsulated in social networks considered "outside" "normal" (kin-based) society, but they also opt out of the conventional production process: their income is derived from magical services, and these rewards enable them to work exclusively for the saints, that makes them worthy of confidence. Lewis (1971) amassed a remarkable quantity of evidence to show that members in "peripheral" cults are recruited from "peripheral" social categories. Douglas (1966:95) noted, "Though we seek to create order, we do not simply condemn disorder. We recognize that it is destructive to existing patterns, but also that it has potentiality. It symbolizes both danger and power. Ritual recognizes the potency of disorder." Sorcerers, prophets, and healers, she noted, play on the symbols of disorder, associating themselves with those regions of the cosmos defined as "outside" society. "The man who comes back from these inaccessible regions brings with him a power not available to those who have stayed in the control of themselves and of society" (Douglas 1966:95; see also Turner 1969:100). Macumba owes its attributed magical power to its position defined at the margins of society—in the regions of formlessness and *communitas*. Magical power is related to the outside, and easily associated with those who are defined outside in sexual terms, so the link between male homosexuality and the possession cult is not fortuitous, but is due to being classified as both outside, dangerous to existing structures, and endowed with magical powers. Societies classify persons, objects and events into simple, tidy categories. In so doing, they classify that which defies the categorization schema as polluting and dangerous. The magical powers that are believed to inhere in these forbidden areas are the price society pays for its symbolic and social order. "Ins" define nonconformists as "outs" but in so doing furnish them with inherent power that they themselves, cannot have.

One question that arises from such an interpretation is why those who deviate from the correct female role are not also associated with the cult. In fact, public opinion both within and without the cults does associate the cults with *saboeiras, lesbicas, putas,* and *mulheres de programa* (promiscuous women), though to a lesser extent than *bichas,* and a number of male informants conceive a link. A number spontaneously commented on the presence of sexually deviant women. One was explicit: "In the whole of Brazil, and especially in Para and Marangão, if you will research well, it would be difficult to find a *pai* or a *mae de santo* who was wholly correct *(correcta)* sexually. They always have a slip *(dealize)*. The Candomblé was born, you see, in part for homosexuality *(homosexualismo).*" I have little information about what women think about sexual deviancy and the cults, but provisionally would extend the marginality argument to include them.

The remaining, and the most difficult question now can be addressed. If macumba is associated with the margins of society and with persons who are considered marginal, why should sexual categories be so important in Belém in determining what is central and marginal, what is form and what is formless? As was noted at the beginning, the association of sexual deviance with possession in cults is more pronounced in Belém, Recife and Bahia than in the cities of Rio de Janeiro, São Paulo and Campinas. In all these cities the cults are classed as marginal: with the poor and the black at the geographical as well as economic periphery. Only in the North and Northeast do sexual categories assume such importance, however.

Although the whole of Brazil is undergoing rapid change with growing opportunities for social mobility, the rate of change is not uniform throughout the country. Opportunities for social mobility are fewer in the North and Northeast, where wealth and power continue to be ascribed largely by birth. In the southern, industrialized cities, class differences are no longer solely functions of birth, and some breakdown of ascriptive class system is accompanied by erosion of the rigid classification of social roles observed in Belém. Moreover, southern cities are more culturally complex because of the high rate of immigration both from other Brazilian states and from other countries.

In Belém the sexual code is restricted (in the sense of Bernstein 1973): sexual categories are unquestioned and sacred. That roles are defined by birth and gender is taken for granted. In the southern cities, the sexual code is more elaborate—the categories are less rigid and less taken for granted—and while still strong are under attack from all sides as the increase in female employment and changes in attitudes to homosexuality indicate. When classification of what is "correct" is more fluid, "incorrectness" becomes fluid. Where there is no form, there is no formlessness for contrast to it; where there is no structure, there can be no anti-structure.

Just as Bernstein observed a correlation between restricted code and the working class (elaborated code and the middle class), so is the Brazilian sexual code class-linked. Middle-class people in Campinas discuss male homosexuality in terms of psychological theories and social evolution; lower-class informants either refuse to discuss the matter or refer to is simply as a sin. Similarly, the predominantly middle-class possession cults have a highly elaborated theory of male and female homosexuality, represented by the work of Francisco Candi Xavier, medium of the spirit of Emanuel, and one of the foremost leaders of Kardecism in Brazil. In his book *Vida E Sexo* (Life and Sex) the spirit Emanuel notes that there are in all countries "extensive communities of brothers undergoing this kind of experience. They make up many millions of men and women, deserving of attention and respect on an equal footing with that given to heterosexual individuals" (1971:90). Spirits pass, in their various incarnations, through various bodies of both genders, that accounts for an essential bisexuality in all creatures. Homosexuality results when a spirit passes from a male to a female body and vice-versa; such transsexual reincarnations occur as part of the evolutionary process by that the human race will one day achieve perfection.

I do not mean to imply with these final broad comparisons that rigid sexual classification has ended in the southern, industrialized cities [see Whitam's chapter below] nor in the formally educated middle and upper classes, nor, indeed, that an elaborated sexual code implies a greater liberality in regard to various manifestations of human sexuality (psychiatrists such as Bieber use a highly elaborated code!). However, in the light of the high correlation between those defined as sexual deviants in the lower-class possession cults of Belém, Bahia and Recife, and the relative absence of this correlation in Rio de Janeiro, São Paulo, and Campinas, I advance these ideas as working hypotheses in the hope they will lead to further research and subsequent refinement.

REFERENCES

Bastide, Roger
    1961   *O Candomblé de Bahia.* São Paulo: Nacional.
Becker, Howard S.
    1973   *Outsiders.* New York: Free Press.
Bernstein, Basil
    1973   *Class, Codes and Control.* London: Paladin.
Carneiro, Edison
    1948, 1954, 1961, 1967 *Candomblés da Bahia.* Rio de Janeiro: Andes.
    1964   *Ladinos e Crioulos.* Rio de Janeiro: Editora Civilizaçao Brasilieia.

De Matta, Roberto
 1973 Carnaval como um rito de passagem. In *Ensaios de Antropoligia Estrutural.* Roberto de Matta, ed. Rio de Janeiro: Vozes.
De Mattos, D. B.
 1938 As Macumbas em São Paulo. *Revista de Arquivo Municipal* 49:151–60.
Douglas, Mary
 1966 *Purity and Danger.* London: Routledge and Kegan Paul.
 1970 *Natural Symbols.* Baltimore: Penguin.
Figueiredo, Napoleão, and Anaiza Vergolino e Silva
 1967 Alguns elementos novos para o estudo dos Batuques de Belém. *Atas do Simposio sobre a Biota Amazonica* 2:101–12.
Fry, Peter
 1969 *Zezuru Medicine.* Ph.D. dissertation, London University.
 1974 Reflexoes sobre o crescimento de conversão a Umbanda. *Condernos do ISER* 1.
Gellner, Ernest
 1969 *Saints of the Atlas.* London: Weidenfeld.
Gluckman, Max
 1963 Gossip and scandal. *Current Anthropology* 4:307–16.
Herskovits, Melville J.
 1947 Review of Landes (1946). *American Anthropologist* 50:23.
 1966 The social organization of the Candomblé. In the *New World Negro.* Pp. 226–47. Bloomington: Indiana University Press.
Humphreys, Laud
 1970 *Tearoom Trade.* Chicago: Aldine.
Landes, Ruth
 1940 A cult matriarchate and male homosexuality. *Journal of Abnormal and Social Psychology* 35:386–97.
 1946 *The City of Women.* NY: Macmillan.
 1970 A woman anthropologist in Brazil. In *Women in the Field.* P. Golde, ed. Pp. 119–42. Chicago: Aldine.
Lacey, Edward A.
 1979 Latin America. *Gay Sunshine* 40: 22–31.
Lapassade, Georges, and Marco Aurélio Luz
 1972 *O Segredo de Macumba.* Rio de Janeiro: Paz e Tierra.
Seth Leacock
 1965 Fun-loving deities in an Afro-Brazilian cult. *Anthropological Quarterly* 3:94–109.
 1966 Spirit possession as role-enactment in the Batuque. American Anthropological Association meeting.
Leacock, Seth, and Ruth Leacock
 1972 *Spirits of the Deep.* New York: Doublesday.
Lewis, I. M.
 1971 *Ecstatic Religion.* Hammondsworth: Penguin.
Murray, Stephen O.
 1979 The art of gay insults. *Anthropological Linguistics* 21:211–23.

Pressel, Esther J.
    1971 *Umbanda in São Paulo.* Ph.D. dissertation, Ohio State University.
Ramos, Arthur
    1934, 1940 *O Negro Brasileiro.* Rio de Janeiro: Editora Brasileira.
    1942 Pesqueisas estrangeiras sobre or negro brasileiro. In *Aculturação Negra no Brasil.* Arthur Ramos, ed. Rio de Janeiro: Biblioteca Brasileira.
Ribeiro, René
    1969 Personality and the psychosexual adjustment of Afro-Brazilian cult members. *Journal de la Société des Americanistes* 58:109–20.
Rodrigues, Raymundo Nina
    1935 *O Animiscmo Fetichista dos Negros Behianos.* Rio de Janeiro: Civilizacão Brasileira Editora.
Turner, Victor
    1969 *The Ritual Process.* Chicago: Aldine.
Velho, Yvonne M. A.
    1973 *Guerra de Orixá.* M.A. dissertation, Museu Nacional, Rio de Janeiro. (Published by Zahar in Rio de Janeiro, 1975, 1977.)
Warren, D.
    1968a Spiritism in Brazil. *Journal of Inter-American Studies* 10:393–405.
    1968b Portuguese Roots of Brazilian Spiritism. *Luzo-Brazilian Review* 5(2): 3–33.
Xavier, Francisco C.
    1971 *Vida e Sexo.* Editora Espirita Brasileira.

ADDITIONAL REFERENCES TO WORK
ON AFRO-BRAZILIAN RELIGIOS
(STEPHEN O. MURRAY WITH THANKS TO JIM WAFER)

Augras, Monique
    1983 *O Duplo e a Metamorfose: A Identidade Mítica em Comundades Nagô.* Pétropolis: Vozes.
Bascom, William R.
    1972 *Shango in the New World.* Austin, TX: African and Afro-American Research Institute.
Bastide, Roger
    1960 *Les Religions Africaines au Brésil.* Paris: Presses Universitaires de France.
    1971 *African Civilization in the New World.* New York: Harper & Row.
    1978 *The African Religions of Brazil: Toward a Sociology of the Interpenetration of Civilizations.* Baltimore: Johns Hopkins University Press.
Bettencourt, Gastão de
    1947 *Os três santos de junho no folclore brasílico.* Rio de Janeiro: Agir.
Braga, Julio
    1988 *O Jogo de Búzios: Um Estudio de Adivinhação no Candomblé.* São Paulo: Brasiliense.

Brissonnet, Lydie C.
    1988 *The Structuration of Communitas in the Carnaval of Salvador, Bahia.*
    Ph.D. dissertation, Indiana University.
Brown, Diana DeGroat
    1986 *Umbanda: Religion and Politics in Urban Brazil.* Ann Arbor: UMI Re-
    search Press.
Brumana, Fernando Giobellina, and Elda Gonzales Martinez
    1989 *Spirits from the Margin: Umbanda in São Paulo.* Stockholm: Almquist &
    Wiksell.
Cacciatore, Olga G.
    1977 *Dicionário de Cultos Afro-Brasileiros.* Rio de Janeiro: Forense-Univer-
    sitária.
Camargo, C. P. F. de
    1961 *Kardicismo e Umbanda.* São Paulo: Biblioteca Pionera de Ciencias Socias.
Carneiro, Edison
    1940 The structure of African cults in Bahia. *Journal of American Folklore*
    53:271–78.
    1981 *Religioes Negra: Notas de Etnografia Relgiosa.* Rio de Janeiro: Civilizaçao
    Brasileira.
Carvalho, José J.
    1984 *Ritual and Music of the Sango Cults of Recife.* Ph.D. dissertation, Queen's
    University of Belfast.
Cavalcanti, Maria L.
    1983 *O Mundo Invisíval: Cosmologia, Sistema Ritual e Noção de Pessoa no Es-
    piritismo.* Rio de Janeiro: Zahar.
Dantas, Beatriz G.
    1982 Repensando a Puerza Nagô. *Religião e Sociedade* 8:15–20.
Duarte, Ophir M.
    1961 O desenvolvimento das religioes afro-brasileiras em Belém. *Boletim da
    Associação Banco do Brasil* 1(3).
Eduardo, Octavio Da Costa
    1948 *The Negro in Northern Brazil: A Study in Acculturation.* New York:
    American Ethnological Society. (Reprinted, Seattle: University of Wash-
    ington Press, 1966.)
Ferreira, Elmiro M.
    1984 Candomblé-de-Caboclo. In *Encontro de Naçoes-de-Candomblé.* Pp. 59–
    67. Salvador, Bahia: Centro de Estudos Afro-Orientais.
Fontenelle, Aluizio
    1953 *A Umbanda através dos séculos.* Rio de Janeiro: Organização Simoes.
Galvão, Eduardo
    1955 *Santos e Visagens.* São Paulo: Companhia Editora Nacional.
Herskovits, Melville J.
    1943 The Negro in Bahia, Brazil: a problem in method. *American Sociological
    Review* 8:394–404.
    1944 Drums and drummers in Afro-Brazilian cult life. *Musical Quarterly*
    30:477–92.

1955 The social organization of the candomblé. *Proceedings of the International Congress of Americanists* 31: 505–32.

1958 Some economic aspects of the Afrobahian candomblé. *Miscellanea Paul Rivet* 2:227–47.

Herskovits, Melville J., and Frances S. Herskovits

1942 The Negroes of Brazil. *Yale Review* 32:263–79.

Kloppenburg, Boaventura

1961 *A Umbanda no Brasil.* Petrópolis: Editora Vozes Limitada.

Landes, Ruth

1940 Fetish worship in Brazil. *Journal of American Folklore* 53:261–70.

Leacock, Seth

1964 Ceremonial drinking in an Afro-Brazilian cult. *American Anthropologist* 66:344–54.

Lima, Vivaldo da Costa

1977 *A Família-de-Santo nos Candomblés Jeje-Nagôs da Bahia.* Salvador, Bahia: Universidade Federal.

Lody, Raul G.

1975 *Ao Som do Adjá.* Salvador, Bahia: Departamento de Cultura da SMEC.

Maia, Vasconcelos

1985 *ABC do Candomblé.* São Paulo: GRD.

Matory, J. Lorand

1988 Homes montados: homossexualidade e simbolismo da possessao nas religioes Afro-Brailerias. In *Escravidao e Invenção da Liberdade: Estudos sobre o Negro no Brasil.* J. Reis, ed. São Paulo: Brasiliense.

Megenney, W. W.

1989 Sudanic Bantu-Portuguese syncretism in selected chants from Brazilian Umbanda and Candomblé. *Anthropos* 84:363–83.

Monteiro, Duglas Teixeira

1955 A Macumba de Vitória. *Proceedings of the International Congress of Americanists* 31:464–72.

Monteiro, Mario Ypiranga

1961 Festa dos cachorros. *Revista Brasileira de Folclore* 1:29–43.

Moraesribeiro, A.

1990 The Irmandade of the Boa. *International Review of African American Art* 9:44–55.

Mott, Luiz R.

1988 *Escravidão, Homossexualidade e Demonologia.* São Paulo: Icone.

Moura, Carlos E.

1981 *Olóòrisa: Escritos sobre a Religiao dos Orixãs.* São Paulo: Agora.

1987 Candomblé. São Paulo: EMW Editores.

Omari, Mikelle S.

1984 *From the Inside to the Outside: The Art and Ritual of Bahian Candomblé.* Los Angeles: Museum of Cultural History.

1989 The role of the gods in Afro-Brazilian ancestral ritual. *African Arts* 23:54–60.

Pinto T. D. O.

    1991 Making ritual drama: dance, music, and representation in Brazilian Candomblé and Umbanda. *World of Music* 33:70–88.

Prandi, José R.

    1991 *Os Candomblés de São Paulo.* São Paulo: Editora da Universidade de São Paulo.

Pressel, Esther

    1973 Umbanda in São Paulo. In *Religion, Altered States of Consciousness, and Social Change.* E. Bourguignon, ed. Columbus: Ohio State University Press.

    1974 Umbanda trance and possession in São Paulo, Brazil. In *Trance, Healing and Hallucination.* F. Goodman, J. Henney, and E. Pressel, eds. Pp. 113–225. New York: Wiley.

Ribeiro, Carmen

    1983 Religiosidade do 'Indio Brasileiro no Candomblé da Bahia. *Afro-Asia* 14:60–80.

Ribeiro, José

    1985 *O Jogo de Búzios e as Cerimônias Esotéricas dos Cultos Afro-Brasileiros.* Rio de Janeiro: Polo Mágico.

Ribeiro, René

    1952 *Cultos Afrobrasileiros do Recife.* Recife: Instituto Joaquim, Nabuco.

    1955 Novos aspectos do processo de reinterpretaçao nos cultos Afro-Brasileiros do Recife. *Proceedings of the International Congress of Americanists* 31:473–91.

    1956 *Religião e relacoes raciais.* Rio de Janeiro: Ministério da Educaçao Cultura.

    1959 Anãlises socio-psicológico de la posesión en los cultos afrobrasileños. *Acta Neuropsiquiatrica Argentina* 5:249–62.

    1970 Psicopatologia e pesquisa antropologica. *Universitas* 6:123–34.

Rio, João

    1905 *As Religioes de Rio.* Rio de Janeiro: Garneiro.

Santos, Juana Elbein dos

    1977 *Os Nàgò e a Morte: Pàdèm Asèsè e o Culto Égun na Bahia.* Petrópolois: Vozes.

Santos, Juana Elbein dos, and Deoscoredes M. dos Santos

    1981 O Culto dos Ancestrais na Bahia: O Culto Égun. In Moura (1981:153–88).

Scopel, Paulo José

    1983 *Orações e Santos Populares.* Porto Alegre: Escola Superior de Teologia.

Segato, Rita L.

    1984 *A Folk Theory of Personality Types: Gods and Their Symbolic Representation by Members of the Sango Cult in Recife, Brazil.* Ph.D. dissertation, Queen's University of Belfast.

Simpson, George Eaton

    1978 *Black Religions in the New World.* New York: Columbia University Press.

Tocantins, Leandro
  1963 *Santa Maria do Belém do Grão Pará.* Rio de Janeiro: Civilizacão Brasileira.
Trindade. Liana
  1985 *Exu: Poder e Perigo.* São Paulo: Icone.
Verger, Pierre
  1981 Bori, primeira cerimônia de iniciação ao cultos dos 'Orìsa Nàgô na Bahia, Brasil. In Moura (1981:33–51).
Voeks, R.
  1990 Sacred leaves of Brazilian Candomblé. *Geographical Review* 80:118–31.
Wafer, Jim
  1991 *The Taste of Blood: Spirit Possession in Brazilian Candomblé.* Philadelphia: University of Pennsylvania Press.
Walker, S. S.
  1990 Everyday and esoteric reality in the Afro-Brazilian Candomblé. *History of Religions* 30:103–28.
Williams, Paul V. A.
  1979 *Primitive Religion and Healing: A Study of Folk Medicine in Northeast Brazil.* Cambridge: Folklore Society.
Willems, Emilio
  1966 Religious mass movements and social change in Brazil. In *New Perspectives on Brazil.* E. Baklanoff, ed. Pp. 205–32 Nashville: Vanderbilt University Press.
Ziegler, Jean
  1977 *Os Vivos e a Mortes: Uma Sociologia da Morte no Ocidente e na Diáspora Africana no Brasil e seus Mecnaismos Culturais.* Rio de Janeiro: Zahar.

15

The Gay Movement and Human Rights in Brazil*

Luiz Mott

Brazil, the largest and most populous country of South America (with more than 150 million inhabitants) is unique in Latin America in deriving its language and much of its culture from Portugal. It enjoys the international reputation of being the New World country with greatest freedom for homosexuals.[1] Brazilian gays are readily visible in the streets, squares, and places of public accommodation. Historical and cultural factors underlie this phenomenon. The vibrant multi-racial character of Brazil blends large components of indigenous tribes, Africans imported as slaves, and Portuguese colonists. Each had its own homosexual traditions. In recent years, Brazil has also become the most important exporter of transvestites from the third to the first world. Hundreds of transvestite prostitutes—about 70 percent of whom are HIV-positive—occupy the public gardens and streets of Paris and Rome. In Brazil, about half the persons with AIDS are gays and bisexuals.

Despite having so visible a presence of homosexuals in the streets, in the mass media, and in its world-famous carnival, Brazil has only a very tiny gay and lesbian movement. Although there are now forty groups, they muster no more than two hundred engaged militants—in a country in which many millions engage in homosexuality.

The homosexual movement had its beginning in Brazil in the mid-1970s with the foundation of "Somos" (We are) in São Paulo. It was the time of military dictatorship. The generals were fervently anti-commu-

---

*Earlier versions of this paper were presented at La Peña Cultural Center in Berkeley, California, and an Amnesty International forum in San Francisco.

1. In Brazil, "homosexual" refers to both men and women.

nist, but relatively tolerant of pornography and of flamboyantly transvestitic homosexuality. The biggest and most important gay newspaper
in the history of South America, the *Jornal Lampião*, began in 1976. It
helped the formation of several gay groups across Brazil. At the first
Congress of the Brazilian Homosexual Movement in 1980, twenty-two
gay and lesbian groups existed. Most of them disappeared after two or
three years of incipient militance, however. The leadership of those
groups was composed predominantly of young students from universities. They were middle class and influenced to varying degrees by left
and anti-military ideology. The remainder of member of the groups
came from the lower classes and lacked any previous political experience. The reasons for the decline of the Brazilian gay movement from
twenty-two groups in 1980 to only five during most of the 1980s are
complex. They include the scarcity of material support, lack of meeting
places, absence of leadership and a cultural handicap: Brazilians in general are very resistant to political meetings and very alienated from
corporate associations. Homosexuality has not been a crime in Brazil
since 1821. In spite of the generalized homophobia common to all
Christian countries, if a Brazilian is discreetly gay or lesbian or is aggressively transvestite, s/he won't suffer too much discrimination. Like
millions of black Brazilians, Brazilian gays and lesbians tend not to
develop a critical and political awareness and fail to see any need to join
gay groups. There are no gay parades or openly gay politicians, intellectuals, or artists, as there are in the more gay-politicized United States.

Victories of the Brazilian Gay Movement

Surprisingly, in a decade, this small and very poor Brazilian gay
movement obtained important victories for the consolidation of gay and
lesbian human rights, suggesting that even with so small a number of
public followers, active and courageous leaders can obtain important
results.

Grupo Gay da Bahia provides the best example. Founded in 1980 in
Salvador, a city of two-and-a-half million inhabitants that is the capital
of the state of Bahia (with over 15 million inhabitants), the first fight
and first victory for this group was its official registration as a "civil
society" *(sociedad civill)*. This was the first time in Latin America that a
homosexual organization was officially recognized by the government.
The notary public tried to challenge the registration of this unusual

association. However, as neither the Brazilian federal constitution nor the penal code criminalize homosexuality, GGB finally became the first gay organization in Brazil to become legal. Since "legal" in Brazilian colloquial language means "good," the official slogan of the gay movement became "it is legal (good) to be homosexual" (*É legal ser homossexual*).

The second and more laborious victory of the Brazilian gay movement was the fight to annul code 302.0 in the International Classification of Disease (ICD-9) of the World Health Organization. This categorized homosexuality as a treatable illness of "sexual deviance." Our strategy was to obtain the support of the important intellectual and political leaders in our society. In five years of unrelenting battle, first we received approval of five different motions against homophobia, endorsing civil rights of lesbians and gays from the most important scientific associations in Brazil, including the Brazilian Society for the Advancement of Science, and the national societies of anthropology, demography, psychiatry, and social sciences. Very prestigious intellectuals signed our national petition against category 302.0. About one third of the deputies across all Brazil's different parties seconded the motion against homophobia. In the platform of the Workers' Party, one emergent political power in Brazil, there is explicit reference to the need to respect homosexuals and to stop treating homosexuality as a medical or political problem. Several state and municipal councils approved motions supporting our petition. Finally, in February of 1985, the Federal Council of Health abolished code 302.0 in Brazil, eight years in advance of the World Health Organization's striking the category from its list of diseases (in ICD-10).

The third important fight of the Brazilian gay movement has been the attempt to include prohibition of discrimination by reason of sexual orientation in the Constitution of Brazil. In the 1987–88 constitutional assembly, a quarter of the delegates supported our position, but due to concerted pressure of Protestant fundamentalists, we lost.[2] On the other hand, there are laws against discrimination on the basis of sexual orientation in the constitutions of two Brazilian states (Segripe and Mato Grosso) and in seventy-four municipal laws of such important state

---

2. Many leftists, many of whom support gay/lesbian rights, boycotted the 1993 constitutional reform, and inclusion of protection of gay/lesbian rights in the national constitution again failed.

capitals as Salvador, Rio, and São Paulo, and in some small villages, such as Golden America in the state of Bahia. These laws do not yet have penalties specified, and no cases have been adjudicated yet.

Volation of Homosexuals' Human Rights in Brazil

There is a flagrant contradiction inside Brazilian society about the human rights of gay people. First, in the ideology common to other Mediterranean(-derived) cultures, only the *pasivo* is homosexual, while the *ativo* is not. Although we can observe tolerance and even sympathy for homosexuals in some groups—for instance, among Afro-Brazilian religious communities, in which many members, the overwhelming majority of priests, as well as some of the gods are homosexual—on the other side, cruel homophobia is very strong in almost all Brazilian subcultures. It is common to hear sentiments like "Bichas têm mais é que morrer" (Fags must be killed) or "Prefiro ter um filho ladrão ou morto do que viado" (I'd prefer my son to be a thief or dead rather than queer).

Although the transvestite Roberta Close appears on the covers of the most important Brazilian magazines and was elected unanimously the model for Brazilian women, at the same time, the most important newspaper of northern and northeastern Brazil suggests "Keep Salvador clean, kill a queer every day." Contrary to the wishful thinking of foreign observers, discrimination and violence against lesbians and gays is a daily tragedy for millions of homosexuals in this contradictory country. Official regulations of the press forbid discrimination on the basis of sexual orientation, yet in the largest towns, almost every day, gays are insulted in the popular newspapers. Grupo Gay da Bahia has a bulky report of different forms of discrimination against homosexuals in Brazil. Many youths have been expelled from their families after suffering cruel beatings. Lesbian and gay youths have been rejected from schools with the excuse that they would infect healthy colleagues (with the irresistibility of homosexuality). Most must hide their sexual orientation to avoid being excluded in the selection for jobs and promotions. Soldiers and policemen in particular are expelled if their homosexuality is discovered. Then there is the constant persecution by policemen stealing money from transvestites, or sometimes compelling their victims to sexually service them.

Every time that Grupo Gay da Bahia (or any of the other active gay groups) receives a report of such manifestations of homophobia, we write letters of protest to the appropriate authorities, sending copies to the newspapers and to human rights organizations. Happily, sometimes we can celebrate some victories. For instance, an advertisement of a shoestore that had used fag-bashing was censured and further reproduction of the advertisement was forbidden; in another example, an extremely homophobic reporter in Salvador was twice censured by the ethics commission of the reporters' syndicate.

Unfortunately, the most cruel manifestation of homophobia—murder—remains beyond the control of the gay movement. Since its inception, Grupo Gay da Bahia has collected information about violent deaths of lesbians and gay men. This depressing file is terrifying: in the last decade more than a thousand gay men and at least thirty lesbians were murdered in Brazil—one every five days. The real number is surely much higher than the already hideously high number we learn about, because the families of many convince the press not to include scandalous details about the lives and deaths of those murdered for being homosexual. Most of the crimes include extreme violence: castration, burning of the body, hundreds of stab wounds. Only about one in ten of the killers is arrested. The few who are and who go to tribunal frequently claim that they killed the victim because he tried to violate their honor (that is, fuck them). After token penalties, even those who are convicted are free again. Grupo Gay da Bahia regularly denounces the crimes and the lack of judicial concern about fag-killers. The group also sponsors self-defense classes, as well as calling upon the general society to respect human sexual differences.

The support of international gay and lesbian organizations in writing letters of protest, financial aid, and supplying us with materials relating to homosexuality (magazines, videocassettes, posters, cards, etc., which are not readily available in the third world) helps us attract support. We hope that first world people will not stop at defending the rainforests but will join in defending the lives and rights of gay and lesbian Brazilians!

REFERENCES

Aguiar, Flávio
    1979 Homosexualidade e repressão. In *Sexo e Poder*. G. Mantega, ed. São Paulo: Editora Brasiliense.

Aufderheide, Patrica
1973 True confessions: the inquisition and social attitudes in Brazil at the turn of the 17th century. *Luso-Brazilian Review* 10:208–40.
Bastos, José C.
1979 Homossexualidade masculina. *Jornal Brasileiro de Psiquiatria* 28:7–11.
Benedetti, G.
1980 Transexualismo é transvestismo. *Revista Geográfica Universal* 62:87–94.
Bittencourt, Francisco
1981 *A Bicha que ri*. Rio de Janeiro: Esquina Editora.
Bivar, Antonio
1977 Revolução sexual a paulista. *Ele & Ela* 93:50–57; 96:50–52.
Canales, Luis
1981 O homossexualism como pema no moderno teatro Brasileiro. *Luso-Brazilian Review* 18:173–81.
Chinelli, Filipina
1981 Acusação de desvio em uma minoria. In *Desvio é Divergência*. G. Velho, ed. Rio de Janeiro: Zahar Editories.
Daniel, Herbert, and Lela Míccolis
1983 *Jacarés e Lobishomens*. Rio de Janeiro: Achiamé.
De Lamare, Rinaldo
1982 *A Vida de nossos filhos de 2 a 16 anos* Rio de Janeiro: Editoria Bloch.
Dourado, Luiz Angelo
1967 *Homosexualismo masculino é feminino é delinquência*. Rio de Janeiro: Zahar Editora.
Doyle, Iracy
1956 *Contribuição ao Estudo da Homossexualidade Feminina*. Rio de Janeiro: self-published.
Dumbar, J., et al.
1973 Attitudes toward homosexuality among Brazilian and Canadian college students. *Journal of Social Psychology* 90:174–75.
Fabri dos Anjos, Padre Marcio
1980 Homosexualismo: pistas para uma reeducação. *Revista Familia Cristã* 3:43–45.
Faerchtein, Lucila
1982 Homosexualidade masculina. *Jornal Brasileiro de Psiquiatria* 151–65.
Faury, Mara L.
1983 *Uma flor para os malditos: A Homossexualidade na Literatura*. Campinas: Papirus.
Fonseca, Guido
1977 A prostituiçã masculina em São Paulo. *Arquivos da Policia Civil de São Paulo* 30:65–87.
1982 Prostituição masculina. In *História da Prosticuiçao em São Paulo*. São Paulo: Editora Resenha Universitária.
Foster, Robert
1973–74 O sombrio mundo dos amores proibos. *Ele & Ela* 49:28.

Foster, Stephen W.
   1979 Homosexuality and the Inquisition in Brazil: 1591–1592. *Gay Sunshine*
      38/39:17–18.
Fry, Peter
   1982 *Para Inglês ver: Identidade e Política no Cultural Brasileira*. Rio de Janeiro:
      Zahar Editores.
Fry, Peter, and Edward MacRae
   1983 *O que é homossexualidade*. São Paulo: Editora Brasiliense.
Gabriel, Nós-Também
   1982 *Baltazar da Lomba*. Paraíba: João Pessoa.
Gaspar, Maria Dulce
   1985 *Garotes de Programa: Prostituioçao em copacabana e Identidade Social*. Rio
      de Janeiro: Jorge Zahar Editor.
Gauderer, E. C.
   1980 Homossexualidade masculina é lesbianismo. *Medicina de Hoje* (June)
      236–42.
   1984 Homossexualidade masculina e lesbianismo. *Jornal de Pediatria*.
      56:123–25.
Gikovate, Flávio
   1980 *Sexo é amor para jovens*. São Paulo: Editora MG, 212.
      O Instinto Sexual. São Paulo: Editora MG, 124.
Goldkorn, Roberto
   1981 *As melhores piadas de bicha*. São Paulo: Global Editora.
Green, James N.
   1994 The emergence of the Brazilian gay liberation movement, 1977–1981.
      Latin American Perspectives 21:38–55.
Hecker, Paulo
   1979 Que é homossexualismo. *Revista Zero Hora* 23. Homosexualismo em ques-
      tão. Special issue of *Confissoes*. n.d. Curitiba: Grafipar.
Lima, Delcio Monteiro de
   1978 *Comportamento Sexual do Brasileiro*. Rio de Janeiro: Livraria Fracisco Alves.
   1983 *Os Homoeróticos*. Rio de Janeiro: Editoria Francisco Alves.
Lima, Estácio
   1934 *A Inversão sexual feminina*. Bahia: Livraria Científica.
   n.d. *A Inversão dos Sexos*. Rio de Janeiro: Editora Guanabara.
MacRae, Edward
   1982 Os respeitáveis militantes e as bichas loucas. In *Caminhos Cruzados*.
      A. Eulálio, et al., eds. Pp. 99–111. São Paulo: Editora Brasiliense.
Machado, Alberto
   1979 O pensamento duro de um homen da lei. *Revista Jurídica* LEMI 12:4–20.
Mantega, Guido
   1979 *Sexo e Poder*. São Paulo: Editora Brasiliense.
Marra, Heloisa
   1979 Homossexualidade: O que eles querem é pelo que lutam? *Fatos e Fotos*
      17:12–13.

Miccolis, Leila, and Herbert Daniel
1983 *Jacarés e Lobisomens*. Rio de Janeiro: Achiamé.
Misse, Michael
1979 *O estigma do passivo sexual*. Rio de Janeiro: Achiamé.
Moreira, Rita
1980 Lésbicas: O alto preço de uma opçao de vida. *Revista Espacial* 5: 36–39.
Mott, Luiz R. B.
1984 Antropologia, população e sexualidade. *Gente* 1:89–103.
1984 Report from Brazil. *Cabirion/Gay Books Bulletin* 11:14.
1985 Slavery and homosexuality. *Black & White Men Together Quarterly* 24: 10–25.
1985 Homossexuais negros no Brasil e na Africa. In *Os Afro-Brasileiros*. Roberto da Mota, ed. Recife: Editora Mecejana.
1988 *Escravidão, Homossexualidade, e Demonologia*. São Paulo: Icone.
Mott, Luiz, and Aroldo H. F. Assunção
1984 A gay atheist of the XVIIth century. *Gay Atheist League of America Review* 7(2):8–10.
Nanhoum, Jean C.
1967 O homossexualismo visto por um médico. *Revista Vozes* 12:1087–95.
Nava, José
1968 *Uma tragédia anti-florentina*. Belo Horizonte: Imprensa Oficial.
Okita, Hiro
1981 *Homossexualismo: Da opressao a libertação*. São Paulo: Proposta Editorial.
Oliveira, José Lima
1976 Homossexualismo: aspectos éticos no mundo atual. *Arquivos da Policía Civil de São Paulo* 28:28–95.
1979 *Violêncía Presumida*. Bahia: Editora S. A. Artes Gráficas.
Oliveira, Neuza M.
1984 Travesti. *Jornal Maria-Maria* 4:3.
Parker, Richard G.
1987 Acquired Immune Deficiency in urban Brazil. *Medical Anthropology Quarterly* 1:155–75.
1991 *Bodies, Pleasures, and Passions: Sexual Culture in Contemporary Brazil*. Boston: Beacon Press.
Pereira, Armando
1967 *Sexo e Prostituicão*. Rio de Janeiro: Gráfica Record Editora.
Pereira, Carlos A. M.
1979 Desvio e/ou reproducao. In *Textos de Antropologia Social do cotidiano*. Testemunha Ocular. Rio de Janeiro: Editora Tempo Literario.
Pinheiro, Domingo F.
1898 *O Androfilismo*. Bahia: Imprensa Economica.
Perlongher, Nestor.
1987 *O Negócio do Michê: Prostituição Viril em São Paulo*. São Paulo: Brasiliense.
Pires de Almeida, José R.
1906 *Homossexualismo: A Libertinagem no Rio de Janeiro*. Rio de Janeiro: Laemmert Editores.

Ribeiro, Leonídio
  1938 *Homossexualismo e Endocrinlogia*. Rio de Janeiro: Livraria Francisco Alves.
Rodrigues, Armando C., and Luiz M. Paiva
  1976 Transexualismo, transvestismo, homossexualismo. *Arquivos da Policía Civil de São Paulo* 28:7–39.
Santa Indez, Antônio Leal de
  1983 *Hábitoes e Atitudes Sexuasi dos Brasileiros*. São Paulo: Editora Cultrix.
Santos, Roberto
  1931 *Carácteres sexuais neutros e intersexualidade*. Rio de Janeiro: Tipografia Artes Gráficas, 161–86.
Serpa, Fernando
  1975 Androginia. *Ele & Ela* 79:27–34.
Silva, José F. B.
  1959 Aspectos sociólogicos do homosexualismo em São Paulo. *Sociologia* 21: 350–60.
Sinisgalli, Aldo
  1938 Observaçoes sobre hábitos costumes e condições de vida dos homossexuais de São Paulo. *Arquivos da Policía de Identificação* 2:39.
Snoek, Jaime
  1967 Eles também são da nossa estirpe. *Revista Vozes* 9:792–802.
  1967 Emancipação dos homossexuais e valores positivos da homossexualidade. In *Relatorio sobre a II congresso Católico Braileiro de Medicina* (Rio de Janeiro). A. Mattos, ed.
  1982 *Ensaio de Ética Sexual*. São Paulo: Paulinas. Souto Maior, Mário (1980) *Dicionério do Palavrao a termos afins*. Recife: Editora Guararapes.
Sznick, Valdir
  1979 *Aspectos jurídicos de aperçao de mundança de sexo*. São Paulo: Editora Sugestões literáias.
Teixeira, N.
  1966 *Juventude transviada*. Leimeira: Editora Letras da Província.
Trevisan, João S.
  1986 *Perverts in Paradise*. London: Gay Men's Press.
Vainfas, Ronaldo
  1986 *História e Sexualidade no Brasil*. Rio de Janeiro: ediçcoes Graal.
  1989 *Trópico dos Pecados: Moral, Sexualidade, e Inquisição no Brasil*. Rio de Janeiro: Editora Campus.
Varjao, Marilda
  1975 Quase tudo que você sempre quis saber sobre homossexualismo e nunce ousou perguntar. *Manchete* 21:16–19.
Vasconcelos, Naumi
  1973 *Resposta sexual brasileira*. Rio de Janeiro: Paz e Terra.
Whitaker, E. A.
  1938 Contribuição ao estudo dos homossexuais. *Arquivos da sociedade de Medicina Legal e criminologia de São Paulo* 8:217–22.
  1939 Estudo biografico dos homossexuais da capital de São Paulo. *Arquivos da Policía de Identificação* 3:244–62.

Whitam, Frederick L.
    1979 The entendidos: middle class gay life in São Paulo. *Gay Sunshine* 38/39: 16–17. (Revised version in this volume.)
    1991 Childhood cross-gender behavior of homosexual females in Brazil, Peru, the Philippines, and the United States. *Archives of Sexual Behavior* 20:151–70.
Young, Allen
    1972 Gays in Brazil. *Gay Sunshine* 13:4.
    1973 Gay gringo in Brazil. In *The Gay Liberation Book*. Len Richmond and Gary Noguera, eds. Pp. 60–67. San Francisco: Ramparts Press.

16

❧

Os Entendidos

GAY LIFE IN SÃO PAULO IN THE LATE 1970s*

Frederick L. Whitam

The largest gay community in all of Latin America is to be found in São Paulo. In this enormous, noisy city of more than ten million people, the gay presence is more visible than in any other Latin American city. There are, indeed, few cities in North America where so many gay people are to be seen on the streets. Weekdays and nights are fairly quiet, but on weekends, thousands of gay people fill the downtown plazas and avenues—Largo do Arouche, Parca da Republica, Vieira de Carvalho, Avenida Ipiranga, or Praca Roosevelt. The Largo do Arouche, a pleasant plaza filled with flower stalls and sidewalk cafés, safely rivals on a Saturday night such famous promenades as Castro and Christopher Streets. Along all the streets extending out from the radius of Largo do Arouche, thousands of gay men—gay women are much less visible—stroll and cruise or stop to have a beer or eat Esfiha in one of the Arab restaurants that seem to be found at every turn. On weekends virtually every restaurant and café in this section of the city is transformed into a gay restaurant. Knots of three or four gay people crowd these streets, spilling over the curb, sometimes impeding traffic.

Nowhere in Latin America do so many gay people gather in public

---

*This is a revised version of an article which appeared in *Gay Sunshine* 38/39 in 1979. It is included with the permission of Professor Whitam and of Gay Sunshine Press. Although the author felt that AIDS had rendered the chapter of little contemporary relevance, the book's editor felt that the focus here on economic considerations remains quite relevant, though rarely addressed in the burgeoning literature on homosexualities. The title stresses that the chapter's "ethnographic present" is the years before AIDS was identified.

and move about so openly. Nowhere outside, except perhaps in the Copacabana district of Rio de Janeiro, do middle-class gay men walk together in public in groups of two or three or four. Middle-class gays have long done this in large North American cities and groups of lower-class Latin American *bichas* (queens) have long promenaded in public or chattered in clusters on street corners with prostitutes. The public appearance of middle-class gay people is rare in Latin America and is made possible by the growth of large cities and the rapid and widespread movement of young people from the small towns in the interior to large urban areas such as São Paulo, Rio de Janeiro, or Belo Horizonte. The gay Brazilian, unlike his brother in smaller Latin American countries, has at his disposal a number of large cities to which to flee, to hundreds of miles between himself and his family. Even so, the Latin American family casts a long shadow for the Paulista. His relationship with his family is one of the persistent problems of his daily existence.

Anonymity from one's family is more easily achieved in São Paulo than perhaps in any other Latin American city, yet even here it can be a problem. Eduardo, a 23-year-old office worker moved to São Paulo during the late 1970s from a small town 800 miles away in the state of Goias near the border of Mato Grosso. However, shortly after his arrival, the exodus from the interior brought to São Paulo four single cousins who want to share his apartment, arrange dates, or borrow money. Some observers have contended that attitudes toward homosexuality in Latin America are more lenient than in North America. It is certainly true that in most Latin American countries—whose criminal laws are generally derived from the Napoleonic Code—homosexual acts are not criminal acts. It is also true that on the surface, the homosexual is often regarded by heterosexuals as ridiculous rather than criminal. There are, however, strong homophobic elements in Latin American society, especially when it comes to the discovery of homosexuality in one's own family. This homophobia is reflected in the dread of discovery within which the gay Paulista lives. *Casos*, or lovers, whose family live in or near São Paulo are confronted by the delicate decision about living together. Luis and Roberto have been *casos* for five years. They do not, however, live together despite the fact they own an apartment jointly. Each lives apart with his parents during the week. Weekends are spent together making love and entertaining friends.

Religiously, São Paulo's gays tend to be nominally Catholic, somewhat traditional in their views, yet considerably more secularized than both their parents and gays in most other Latin American countries. The emergence of a separate gay church is incomprehensible to them; however, there is considerable interest in "Camdomblé," a religious syncretism of Catholicism and African religions, now enjoying considerable popularity among São Paulo's middle and even upper classes. Camdomblé, outlawed until about 30 years ago, has taken some traditional Catholic saints and given them different names and meanings. The saints of Camdomblé are considerably more earthy than the Catholic saints. Santa Barbara became Iansa, wife of Xaujo, who sometimes changes sex and penetrates her husband, and is the patron *dios* (god) of gays. The rites of Camdomblé are matriarchal in that the person who performs the rites, Babalaorixa, is usually a woman or homosexual. It is said that practically all male Babalaorixa are homosexuals. Pomba Gira, a kind of female devil, embodies the spirit of the prostitute and may be invoked for success in matters of sex. Camdomblé, then, openly accepts the participation of gays and offers African-derived rites to help them with their problems.

Gay "marriages" or similar ceremonies are uncommon; however, there is a Protestant church that allegedly performs gay weddings. Many gays, interestingly enough, wear wedding bands. These are said to be primarily protection against aggressive women or designed to avoid awkward explanations. In some cases, however, the bands are exchanged by male lovers.

The life of the middle-class gay Paulista is austere by American standards. Despite the fact that Paulistas try to make their apartments as attractive as possible, apartments are apt to be small, dark and drab. Kitchens tend to be small, badly lit, often without hot water. Hot showers are more likely to come from an electrical apparatus attached to the shower than from a hot-water tank. Middle-class gays, like Brazil's middle and lower classes in general, are hard-pressed by one of the highest rates of inflation in the world. Food is terribly expensive. A very ordinary lunch in a minimally acceptable restaurant is likely to cost two or three dollars for the entrée alone. By the time a salad, potatoes, and drink are added, a mundane lunch can easily cost the equivalent of five or six U.S. dollars. Paulistas eat out as little as possible, eat frequently with their families, and when they do eat out, it is likely to be at a stand-up snack bar rather than in a restaurant.

While most things are at least as expensive as New York, the Paulista is likely to make one-fourth or one-fifth what his New York counterpart makes. While São Paulo is the financial hub for the prosperous coffee industry that dominates the State of São Paulo, salaries for white-collar jobs are quite low. João has a very good position for his age (24) in one of São Paulo's leading banks, yet cannot live within his income. He makes a gross total 3,539 cruzeiros or about U.S. $240 a month. After social security deductions and deductions for payments on two loans from the bank, he is left with 1,986 cruzeiros or about $135 a month—barely enough to pay for his modest studio apartment in the downtown area. In addition to rent and a $17-a-month maintenance fee, João makes monthly payments on a blue plastic and chrome dining table ($15) and a Grundig stereo system ($40).

Given the state of the Brazilian economy and the basic salaries, it is easy to understand the austerity of gay life in São Paulo. Large parties as known in larger American cities are rare, except among the very affluent. Social life is conservative and centers around small, quiet gatherings of friends. Coffee, tea, and cookies are usually offered, rather than drinks. Well-stocked liquor cabinets are relatively rare. Other drugs are not widely used. Bar life centers on three *boites* (clubs): the Medieval, Nostro Mondo (spelling is Italian rather than Portuguese, for some reason) and Roleta. Actually, it is hardly fair to say that bar life centers on these clubs, because Medieval and Nostro Mondo both demand expensive cover charges—$8 and $10 respectively—and middle-class gays cannot afford to go to these clubs frequently. It would be fairer to say that these clubs serve symbolic purposes. Gays closely follow activities related to these clubs, even when they are not able to attend frequently.

There is more than a little truth in the joke about the "queens who eat bread and water all week to save enough money to go to the clubs on Saturday night." Attendance at the more expensive clubs is usually not spontaneous but may be planned days or weeks in advance, especially on nights when there are shows. The show, a form of cabaret theater rarely seen nowadays in the United States, consists of elaborate dance routines, singing, miming, drag acts, samba, and above all, beautiful and costly costumes derived from the *fantasias* of Carnaval, often designed by São Paulo's leading dress designers. The shows are taken quite seriously by the audience and the casts of fifteen to twenty people, who rehearse arduously for as long as two months and receive a small wage for their performances. The setting for the two-hour show is formal; waiters wear white jackets reservations are necessary, sometimes obtainable only by the layout of an extra 20 cruzeiros. All in all, it is a sensuous and decadent cabaret scene.

Night life in the clubs peaks during Carnaval. Everyone goes to the bars during Carnaval. Even those who never have enough money other times of the year manage the jacked-up prices. During Carnaval the music is exclusively samba. For the Paulista, as for all Brazil, during those four days all the ordinary sounds of the world stop and only the samba can be heard. The gay clubs are jammed and especially conspicuous are the *travestis* (transvestites) in their incredible carnaval *fantasias*. Plans for these elaborate costumes often begin immediately after the preceding carnaval and may cost hundreds or even thousands of dollars. The *travesti* in Brazil occupies an important position in gay life in São Paulo. There are perhaps on the whole no more *travestis,* relatively speaking, in São Paulo than in any North American city of similar size. However, the *travesti,* especially if she is elegant and beautiful, is treated with a degree of respect unknown in the United States. The most desirable of the *travestis* move in upper-class circles and are regarded by straight men as very chic to be seen with Rogeria, Valeria, or Samantha, the most beautiful of São Paulo's *travestis.* Some perform sexual acts for money, often with married men or business executives, receiving as much as 2,000 cruzeiros ($140) a night. (It is said that they are frequently called upon to perform the active role.[1])

The most sensational event of the 1979 Carnaval occurred at the Medieval when Wilza Carla, a very plump comic actress popular with São Paulo's gays, arrived, to their delight, atop an elephant. During Carnaval people who may rarely see each other during the rest of the year dance—sweating, stripping, smashing tables—into a frenzied dawn.

Apart from bar life, probably the most popular entertainment is going to movies which, in contrast to going to bars, is quite inexpensive: a dollar at the fanciest cinemas and half that if one happens to have—as many hard-working young Paulistas do—a student ID card. Good French, Italian, American, and Brazilian films are plentiful. São Paulo is probably the only city outside three or four American cities capable of filling an entire movie house with gays.

Television is popular with those who have sets. There is said to be a large concentration of gays in the television industry. Several years ago a "gay incident" provoked the wrath of the Government and created a public scandal. The controversial show consisted of a panel of a dozen or

---

1. [Editor's note] On this continuing phenomenon see Jared Braiterman, "Beauty in flight: Rio and beyond." *Whorezine* 15(1992):9–11.

so personalities, mostly gay, who acted as judges of entertainers appearing on the show. Interviews were also conducted with well-known dress designers, chefs, and entertainers, some of whom talked openly about being gay. The show became more and more popular as the panel become more and more outrageous: "each one trying to out-*bicha* the other." The axe fell when a guest personality revealed on nationwide TV that he started his homosexual practices in a Catholic school with a priest. The Ministry of Communications forbade the further appearance of open homosexuals and declared that homosexuals would no longer be employed in television.

One of the most exciting bits of gossip that came my way while I was doing fieldwork in Brazil dealt with Mario Gomez, one of Brazil's leading TV actors and, according to many, the "most beautiful man in Brazil." A rumor published in the newspaper *Luta Democratica* stated that Gomez got a carrot lodged in his anus while having sex with another man and had to be taken to the hospital. The rumor swept all Brazil. Many gays, delighted by the rumor, showed sympathy by wearing carrots around their necks. Gomez, who is a top *novela* (soap opera) star and the heart-throb of every housewife in the interior, sued the newspaper for "moral damages."

At the center of the gay Paulista's life are real (not reel) love and sex. As might be expected in such a large city, love and sex have many forms. Many of São Paulo's gays have *casos* and live together quietly, preferably in the downtown area of the city. Some buildings are known to be more or less "gay" (with as many as half the apartments occupied by gay tenants). The sight of lovers or friends living together is treated with the aplomb of New York. Living arrangements are characterized by a considerable degree of personal freedom, and even the drag queen is tolerated in a live-and-let-live atmosphere. A drag queen given to too many "flowers and feathers" to suit her neighbors was recently evicted from an apartment she owned. (It is said that when a queen opens her mouth out come flowers and when she lifts her hand feathers fly all over the place.) While the reaction to the eviction was mostly one of sympathy (many gays own their apartments), the case was generally cited as evidence of the generally tolerant attitude towards gays, because this was the first incident in that a gay was divested of an apartment of that he was the owner. It was viewed as a unique incident without implications for other gays or for the future.

Rio de Janiero, one of the world's great pleasure domes, traditionally has been regarded as the most hedonistic spot in Latin America. The

Carioca is regarded rather disdainfully by Paulistas as lazy, pleasure-seeking and "something of a whore." In fact, there is a relatively large number of *miches* (call-boys) who live in Copacabana with no visible means of support and make themselves available to foreign tourists. Many of these are allegedly *pretos*—blacks or mulattos who are reportedly popular with Germans and Americans. They may have sex strictly for money but more commonly are likely to be taken to dinner at the best restaurants or to dance in Copacabana's best-known gay club, Sota, where a young lady dressed like Carmen Miranda romantically offers fresh roses from her basket for whatever one wants to pay. Despite the Paulista's disdain for the Carioca, Paulistas drive or make the six-hour bus trip to Rio whenever possible, and Rio remains their favorite weekend vacation spot. Also popular are the beach towns to the north and south of Santos, the port city that serves São Paulo. Brazilians, like gays everywhere, like to travel, and many would like to travel to the United States and Europe. Only the most affluent travel outside Brazil, however, because the Brazilian government, in an effort to keep money from going abroad, imposed a compulsory $1000 deposit for anyone leaving the country.

In recent years as the population of São Paulo exceeded that of Rio (10 million to Rio's 8 million), so did the gay population. Paulistas proudly remark that, on any given day, half the population of Rio consists of foreigners and Paulistas. As the population has increased enormously, so has the availability of public meeting places. Presently the possibilities for sex in public places are greater than any city in Latin America and bear considerable resemblance to New York City. Virtually all of the movie theaters in and around Avenida São João and Praca da Republica are "known." Most of the public rest-rooms in the downtown area serve as places for contact. The *rodoviaria* (bus terminal) is especially well-known and is ringed by cheap hotels where documents are not required and any kind of sexual activity is permitted. Such public encounters frequently involve risks for the gay person. The potential sex partner not uncommonly turns assailant, robbing the gay victim at knife-point.

Less risky are numerous saunas, the best known of which is the Aquarius. Here, in one of the few saunas in Latin America operated by gays, one may enjoy all the amenities of a North American gay bathhouse. Bars, saunas and other such places tend to be owned not by gays themselves but by straight businessmen interested solely in profit-making. Ownership by gays tends to be a somewhat delicate affair. In São Paulo, Nostro Mondo is owned and operated by someone widely—

even publicly—known as the "The Condessa" who frequently appears in drag in that club's shows. "The Condessa" has a minor judicial position and is able to own and operate the club by virtue of his family wealth and connections.

For the Paulista with a car, there is a drive-in sexual establishment, where anyone, regardless of sexual orientation, may go to have sex. The customer drives in, parks in a semi-secluded spot, orders drinks from a good-natured car-hop who says something like, "Feel at home, do what you like," while holding his face away from the car, careful not to look inside. Upon leaving, the visitor pays $4 to an attendant who again discreetly avoids looking into the car.

Perhaps the most important place for contacts in a city that is constantly in motion is the streets. While São Paulo in many respects is a walking city (the city also boasts a gleaming new subway), the Paulista loves the automobile. As in many Latin America cities, the car is King. There is considerable cruising in cars in certain downtown areas by both prostitutes in shiny new Brasilias and by gays. There is a particularly well-known spot near the Colegio Caetano de Campos off the Praca Republica widely known as the bus-stop for the "Brazil to Japan" bus. That is, gays stand for hours pretending to be waiting for the bus. They are waiting to be picked up, and the bus to Japan never comes.

Sex itself is characterized by urban promiscuity and anonymity and is prototypically anal, with the general Latin America *activo/pasivo* dichotomy credited in principal. However, while there is considerable discussion of those who only "give ass" and those who only "take ass," Paulistas often ridicule such rigid conceptions of sexual relations. Many have a more flexible sexual repertoire.

As already noted, sexual acts by consenting partners in private are not dealt with in Brazil's criminal codes. Nonetheless, at the discretion of the police, gays are prosecuted for sexual activity in public places, and drag queens appearing in public are rounded up under an *escandalo publico* clause. A much-discussed round-up occurred during the mid-1970s when police using dogs collected *travestis* promenading around the Hilton Hotel (a traditional place for drag queens to be seen during Carnaval) in hopes of meeting affluent foreigners. It was widely believed that the *bichas* were taken to prison to satisfy prisoners clamoring for sex and deprived of women. Sometimes, forty or fifty drag queens are picked up by the police when the jails (police and jailers as well as inmates) need servicing and released after they have sated the "real men."

While there were some discussions about the formation of a gay liberation group, little or no formal organization exists among São Paulo gays. Most gay Paulistas oppose such an organization, considering it a threat to the personal freedom they enjoy. In a relative sense, they feel and are already liberated. As E. A. Lacey noted (in *Gay Sunshine* 40/41[1979]:24), "To the Latin American macho military mind, homosexual practices are not a threat, but rather are regarded as an amusing foible, since homosexuality is not taken seriously. Gay activism, on the other hand, with its accompanying publication, its emphasis on the written word, that Latin Americans take very seriously indeed, and its usual concomitant political libertarianism, could be considered a threat and would be regarded very gravely"—as *bichas* know. Censorship of movies, newspapers, television and theater is widespread. Many books, magazines, and films are denied entry to the country. It is difficult to imagine the emergence of a politically active gay movement in such a climate. There were no gay periodicals during my stay. *Ultima Hora* was widely read by gays. A newspaper dedicated mostly to reporting lightweight news, gossip about TV and movie stars, and reviews of plays and movies, it included a daily column, *Coluna de Meio*, sympathetically reporting gay news from Brazil and elsewhere. Criticism of the government was, however, inconceivable. Although discontent with the government was widespread, nobody talked about it while I was there. Indeed, Paulistas generally were reluctant to express political views in public and resisted inquiries and conversation of politics, presumably out of discretion rather than from any innate lack of interest.

Even though São Paulo gays lacked political organization, they were able to exert some political pressure. In the 1974 congressional elections, a senator known by gays but not by others to be sympathetic to gays and a member of the opposition party, Orestes Quercia, was sent to Brasilia. Gay Paulistas believed their votes provided the margin of victory. He carried heavily gay downtown districts with as much as 95 percent of the votes.

Conclusion

São Paulo, then, has produced a complex and sophisticated gay subculture, bearing considerable resemblances to other urban gay subcultures. Its subculture should not be seen as a copy of others, however. Brazil is an enormous country with its own cultural traditions and symbols, and there is little awareness of what gay life is like in the United States or in Western Europe. While there may have been some exchange of symbols—American gays know Carmen Miranda, and Brazilians, Marilyn Monroe—drag queens in São Paulo do not paint themselves and promenade Avenida Ipiranga because they heard that homosexuals do that sort of thing somewhere else, but because cross-dressing is a recurrent expression of homosexuality. The same social types—drag queens, machos, hustlers, faithful lovers, dancers, and hairdressers—and the same activities—cruising, public sex, camping, becoming lovers, decorating apartments—recur with remarkable regularity in urban gay worlds. Looking at gay life in São Paulo is like looking at American life through a tinted glass: all is different, yet all is the same. These similarities result, not from cultural sharing from place to place, but rather from basic similarities in the nature of human homosexuality, wherever it may be found.

17

Changing Brazilian Constructions of Homosexuality*

Richard G. Parker

The sexual field in Brazilian life must be understood as comprised of multiple subsystems, discourses, and cultural frames of reference that exhibit rather specific social and historical relationships and that exert a central influence in shaping the sexual experience and understandings of different individuals. Responding, perhaps, above all else, to the complex interplay between tradition and modernity in a rapidly changing society, these multiple frames of reference seem often both to contradict and yet at the same time intersect one another, opening up not a single, unique sexual reality, but a set of multiple realities. Nowhere can this multiplicity be seen more clearly than in the case of homosexuality, which, at least in Brazil, must be characterized less as a unitary phenomenon than as a fundamentally diverse one—a case, at the very least, of a variety of somewhat different ho-

*This chapter is excerpted with the permission of Haworth Press from an article entitled "Youth, Identity, and Homosexuality: The Changing Shape of Sexual Life in Contemporary Brazil," originally published in the *Journal of Homosexuality* 17(3/4): 270–85,© Haworth Press, 1990. The author thanks Vagner João Benício de Almeida, Robert Bellah, Stanley Brandes, Roberto De Matta, Alan Dundes, Peter Fry, Paul Kutsche, Ondina Fachel Leal, Rosemary Messick, and Nancy Scheper-Hughes for their helpful discussions of many of the issues examined herein. His field research in Brazil between July and August 1982, August 1983 to July 1984, and July 1987 to August 1986 was made possible by grants from the Tinker Foundation and the Center for Latin American Studies, a Robert H. Lowie Scholarship from the Department of Anthropology, a Traveling Fellowship in International Relations, and a Graduate Humanities Research Grant from the Graduate Division, all at the University of California at Berkeley, as well as a Fulbright Full Grant and a Grant-in-Aid from the Wenner-Gren Foundation for Anthropological Research.

mosexualities rather than of a single, unified homosexuality (Parker 1985, 1987).

I shall try to explicate these rather abstract assertions while paying special attention to the ways in which the particular construction of sexual meanings in Brazil shapes the experience of same-sex sexual interactions there. I also will examine some of the (quite different) ways in which Brazilian systems, at least when compared with our own tradition in the industrialized West, seem to allow perhaps an unusual degree of fluidity or flexibility in the constitution of sexual realities among adolescents. Ultimately, however, I will suggest that the impact of this fluidity or flexibility in opening up the potential for shaping one's own sexual identity is quite clearly strongest for young people in Brazil's larger, more highly modernized and industrialized cities, where, thanks to the contingencies of the current historical moment, a rather unusual wealth of choices seems to characterize the contemporary experience of sexual life.[1]

In seeking some understanding of the experience of homosexuality among young people in Brazil, it is absolutely essential to realize that the very notion of homosexuality itself is, in fact, but a rather recent development. In Brazil, as in the nations of the industrialized West, homosexuality has a history. While a whole set of ideas related to homosexuality (and by extension to heterosexuality as well) has recently taken root in Brazilian culture, these ideas have in fact been imported from the industrialized West—modeled on patterns that had already emerged in Europe and the United States. As relatively recent imports, such notions are far from the only, or even the dominant, way of conceiving the sexual universe in Brazilian culture.

On the contrary, this modern, more highly rationalized way of thinking about sexual life that was originally developed in the West and only later imported to Brazil co-exists there with what is perhaps a far more deeply rooted set of traditional ideas about the nature of things sexual. Such traditional notions can perhaps best be described as a kind of folk

---

1. My central concern here is not the origin of homosexual desires (see Herdt and Stoller 1985), but the ways in which such (pre-existing) desires manifest themselves and play themselves out in specific social settings. I am interested in the various channels that Brazilian society has opened up for such desires, and the ways in which it has sought to organize them culturally, particularly during the crucially important period of adolescence.

model of the sexual universe. They contrast in a number of important ways with more modern notions. This folk model has, until quite recently, served as the central frame of reference that Brazilians have used in articulating and interpreting the significance of their sexual experience (Fry 1982, 1987; Parker 1985, 1987).

Within the folk model of sexual life in Brazil, cultural emphasis seems to have been focused not merely on sexual practices in and of themselves, but on the relationship between sexual practices and gender roles—in particular, on a distinction between masculine *atividade* (activity) and feminine *passividade* (passivity) as central to the organization of sexual reality. It is in terms of this distinction that notions of *macho* (male) and *fêmea* (female), of *masculinidade* (masculinity) and *feminilidade* (femininity), and the like, have typically been organized in Brazil. In daily life, however, these notions have been constructed rather less formally in the discourse of popular culture. They have been less a product of self-conscious reflection than of the implicit values encoded in the language that Brazilians commonly use to speak about the body and its practices, about the combination of bodies, and about the classificatory categories that flow from such combinations.

Perhaps nowhere is this distinction between *atividade* and *passividade* more evident than in the popular language that Brazilians use in describing sexual relations, in verbs such as *comer* (eat) and *dar* (give). *Comer,* for example, is used to describe the male's active penetration of the female during sexual intercourse. It implies a kind of symbolic domination that is typical of Brazil's traditional culture of gender, and can be used as a synonym, in a number of different contexts, for verbs such as *possuir* (possess) or *vencer* (vanquish/conquer). *Dar,* on the other hand, is used to describe the female's passive submission to her male partner, her role of being penetrated during intercourse. Just as *comer* is used to describe various forms of domination through reference to the relations of gender, *dar* can be used to imply submission, subjugation, and passivity in any number of settings. Drawing on these categories (and any number of others that function in precisely the same way), then, the sexual universe is continually structured and restructured, in even the simplest and most common verbal exchanges, along the lines of a rigid hierarchy: a distinction between sexual *atividade* and *passividade* that is translated into relations of power and domination between *machos* and *fêmeas*, between *homems* (men) and *mulheres* (women).

What is particularly important to understand in the present context, however, is not simply the structure of the hierarchy, but the fact that within the traditional context of Brazilian popular culture it has been used to organize and conceptualize sexual relations both between members of the opposite sex and between members of the same sex. The symbolic structure of male/female interactions seems to function in many ways as a kind of model for the organization of same-sex interactions in Brazilian cultures. Within the terms of this model, what is centrally important is perhaps less the shared biological gender of the participants than the social roles that they play out—their *atividade* or *passividade* as sexual partners and social persons. A *homem* who enters into a sexual relationship with another male does not necessarily sacrifice his *masculinidade,* so long as he performs the culturally perceived active, masculine role during sexual intercourse and conducts himself as a male within society. A *mulher* who conforms to her properly passive, feminine sexual and social role will not jeopardize her essential *feminilidade* simply by virtue of occasional (or even ongoing) sexual interactions with other biological females.

The same cannot be said, however, of the errant partners in such sexual exchanges. On the contrary, the male who adopts a passive female posture—whether in sexual or social interaction—almost invariably undercuts his own *masculinidade,* just as a female, in adopting an active, dominating, masculine posture undercuts her *feminilidade.* By upsetting the culturally prescribed fit between biological gender and social gender, both must sacrifice their appropriate categorization as *homem* and *mulher.* The failed *homem* comes to be known as *viado* (from *veado,* deer) or *bicha* (literally, worm or intestinal parasite, but also, instructively, the feminine form of *bicho* or animal, and thus a female animal) due to his inappropriate femininity, while the inadequate *mulher* is known as *sapatão* (literally, big shoe) or even *coturno* (army boot), due to her unacceptable masculinity. Both figures are seen, in a very strong sense, as a failure on both social and biological counts—as unable to realize their biological potential because of inappropriate social behavior, yet equally unable to cross the boundaries of social gender due to inadequate anatomy. Not surprisingly, both are thus subject to some of the most severe stigmatization found anywhere in Brazilian society (see Fry 1982, 1987; Fry and MacRae 1983; Parker 1985, 1987).

Within the framework of this relatively traditional model, then, there exists a fairly explicit cultural construction of same-sex desires and practices. Strikingly, an individual's same-sex object choice seems to be less significant than his or her sexual role, less significant than the connection between anatomical and social gender as played out in terms of *atividade* and *passividade*. Thus, it is hardly surprising that central cultural emphasis in Brazil should traditionally have been given to assuring the *atividade* of *meninos* (little boys) and the passividade of *meninas* (little girls). While average Brazilians are of course unlikely to reflect upon the psychodynamic processes involved in the formation of gender identities, they tend to view the *masculinidade* of the *menino* as constantly threatened by too-close contact with female relatives, and Brazilian men make a rather conscious effort to encourage active, aggressive, masculine behavior on the part of their young male relatives. *Feminilidade*, on the other hand, seems to be seen less as threatened than as threatening—a rather perplexing force, tied to natural rhythms and female reproductivity and in need of almost constant repression. If *masculinidade* must be built, *feminilidade* must be controlled. The *passividade* of the *menina*, no less than the *atividade* of the *menino*, must be encouraged, shaped, and molded by society.

The consequence of the social shaping of active and passive stances among boys and girls becomes fully evident only as children begin to take part in sexual activities. Upon entering adolescence, *rapazes* (boys or young men) who have (or in whom society has) successfully built up an "active" stance in relation to their gender identity are clearly expected to demonstrate and even follow through on their desire for the opposite sex, as are *moças* (girls or young women) who have succeeded in adopting a properly "passive" stance, though the actual activities of adolescent girls continue to be closely guarded and controlled by their male relatives, who are thought to exercise rightfully absolute authority over the sexual powers of their female relatives. As they progress through adolescence and on into full adulthood (most commonly marked in Brazil by marriage), however, these same individuals will not uncommonly also take an interest in sexual play with members of the same sex. Indeed, such play is frequently reported by informants as at least one important part of their early sexual education.

Among *rapazes*, same-sex play and exploration is almost institutionalized through games such as *troca-troca* (turn-taking), in which two (or more) boys take turns, each inserting his penis in his partner's anus. It is perhaps even more obvious in the expression "Homem, para ser homem, tem que dar primeiro"—A man, to be a man, first has to give (in receptive anal intercourse)—often used by older boys seeking to *comer* their slightly younger playmates. And while such practices are perhaps less explicit among groups of *moças*, early sexual play with same-sex partners is cited nearly as frequently by female informants as by males. Such experiences seem relatively widespread, and as a game such as *troca-troca* would indicate, offer participants at least some room to explore both active and passive roles. Assuming that the cultural system has, in fact, successfully carried out its mandate, however, such early adolescent play is quite explicitly not expected to disrupt fundamentally the process of development that will ultimately transform the *rapaz* into an active *homem* and the *moça* into a passive *mulher*.

However, if we have learned anything at all from psychoanalytic theory, it is precisely that cultural systems often fail to carry out their mandate. For the *rapaz* who, for whatever reasons, has failed to acquire a properly active stance, or a *moça* who has been unable to adopt a passive stance, it is in such adolescent sexual play, as well, that psychological dispositions begin to be transformed into a distinct social role. For these individuals, however, the available roles are not the positively sanctioned categories of *homem* and *mulher,* but the stigmatized categories of *bicha* and *sapatão*. Failure to perform properly (i.e., in active/passive terms) in early sexual interactions seems to translate rather rapidly, on the part of these individuals, into an emphasis during all social performances, on the social style of the opposite sex. *Viados* or *bichas,* defined initially in terms of their passive performances during sexual intercourse, rather quickly begin to adopt an exaggerated effeminate style in their more public social interactions as well, just as *sapatões,* defined by their activity, take on many of the most explicit symbols and characteristics of an exaggerated masculinity. They set out upon a life course that is culturally recognized and institutionalized, yet at the same time stigmatized and often even openly oppressed (Fry and MacRae 1983).

Within the context of this traditional, folk model of the sexual universe in Brazil, then, same-sex desires and practices clearly have an important place in the sexual experience of many, if not most, men and women. The specific cultural configuration of such desires and practices is quite different, though, from the Northern modern conception of homosexuality focused on sexual object choice as definitive of sexual identity. On the contrary, within this traditional system, sexual object choice seems unusually fluid or variable, especially during adolescence. One's object choice is clearly less important than what might be described as one's gender role, *atividade* or *passividade*, in organizing or structuring same-sex interactions. The categorical distinctions that shape the experience of both young and old within this system are not those between heterosexuals and homosexuals, but between *homems,* *mulheres, viados,* and *sapatões.* It is perhaps above all else during the sexual experimentation of youth or adolescence that individuals begin to sort themselves out socially within the framework of these categories, transforming private desires into public identities, and develop an understanding of their place within what will rather quickly become a fairly rigid hierarchy of gender that will continue to exert profound influence on them throughout the course of their lives.

While certainly subject to at least some regional variation in terminology and usage, the basic form structure of the folk model of sexual reality described here has been central throughout Brazilian history. As a number of writers have suggested, this model seems to have dominated the sexual landscape in Brazil throughout the 19th and early 20th centuries and continues to function, even today, both in rural areas as well as among the lower classes (many of whom are themselves migrants from the countryside) in Brazil's larger, more modernized and industrialized cities (Fry 1982). Since at least the first decades of the 20th century, however, and increasingly during the course of the past ten to fifteen years, this traditional system has gradually begun to give way to—or, perhaps, more accurately, to co-exist with—a far more rationalized manner of thinking about the nature of things sexual: a model rooted, perhaps above all else, in the conception of modern science and imported to Brazil from Western Europe and the United States.

Introduced in Brazilian culture, at least initially, through the writing of medical doctors, therapists, and psychoanalysts,[2] and translated only gradually into the wider discourse of popular culture, this new medical/ scientific model seems to have marked a fundamental shift in cultural attention or emphasis away from a distinction between active and passive roles as the building blocks of gender hierarchy toward the importance (along European and North American lines) of sexual object choice as central to the definition of the sexual subject. In practical terms, perhaps, its greatest impact has been the creation of a new set of classificatory categories—notions such as *homossexualidade* (homosexuality) and *bissexualidade* (bisexuality)—for mapping out and interpreting the sexual landscape.

By the mid-20th century, these new categories had become central to the medical and scientific discussion of sexual life throughout Brazil, and had been fully incorporated into the language of law and govern-

---

2. See Pires de Almeida (1906), Doyle (1956), and Ribeiro (1938).

ment as well. However, until perhaps the late 1960s or early 1970s, their influence seems to have been limited almost entirely to a small, highly educated elite—the same segment of the Brazilian population that has traditionally maintained contact with and been most influenced by European and North American culture. Restricted to this elite, notions, such as *homossexualidade*—understood not merely as a sexual behavior but as a class of people or even a distinct way of being in the world—had largely failed to penetrate the language of daily life in Brazil. Up until perhaps the 1970s, the system of sexual classifications that is so familiar in Europe and the United States simply failed to play a significant role in Brazilian popular culture or to influence the lives and experiences of the vast majority of Brazilians.[3]

Precisely at the same time that this new conception of same-sex relations was first making itself felt among the elite, a semi-secretive sexual subculture organized around the same-sex preferences and practices was itself beginning to take shape, principally among the popular classes in such large, rapidly industrializing and modernizing cities as Rio de Janeiro and São Paulo. Reproducing the distinction between *atividade* and *passividade* as central to the organization of sexual relations between members of the same sex, and indeed, exaggerating the importance of such distinctions almost to the point of caricature, this subculture seems to have placed less emphasis on a shared identity common to all its participants than on the simple fact of same-sex sexual contacts. It was shared sexual behavior within its protective spaces that seemed to tie the members of this subculture together, rather than some sense of themselves as somehow members of the same sexual species because of this behavior, and the symbolic center of this urban underworld was thus less psychological than spatial: the cafés or bars, the plazas and streets where individuals seeking such sexual contacts were known to meet. Protected, at least up to a point, by the increased anonymity of urban life, a loosely organized, flexible, and constantly shifting sexual community began to take shape in the streets of Brazil's larger cities at the same time that a notion of *homossexualidade* as a distinct mode of sexual being was beginning to form in the saloons and studies of the well-to-do and well-educated.[4]

Thus, throughout the early and mid-20th century, two new models

---

3. See Fry (1982), Fry and MacRae (1983), Parker (1985, 1987), and Trevisan (1986).
4. See Trevisan (1986). Also see Freyre (1981) and Manta (1928).

for the conceptualization and organization of same-sex desires and practices had begun to emerge in Brazil. These two models seem to have contrasted rather sharply both with one another and the traditional model of same-sex interactions available in popular culture. By the late 1960s or early 1970s, however, as a result of developments both within Brazil itself and in the outside world, the histories of these new models began to merge. It was at this point that the Brazilian middle class that had been developing gradually since the end of the 19th century really began to exercise dominant influence in Brazilian society. Always concerned with and sensitive to the latest styles and developments in the so-called developed world, the members of this newly dominant class did not fail to take note of a series of significant changes that had begun to take place in Western Europe and the United States: the emergence of urban gay culture and the gay liberation movement as significant forces in contemporary Western society.

For more conservative Brazilians, as for conservative North Americans or Europeans, such developments were a sign of decadence and decay. For individuals drawn to same-sex relations, and oppressed or stigmatized by the restrictions of Brazil's traditional sexual universe, however, the model offered by gay life in Paris, New York, San Francisco, et al., was in fact profoundly powerful. The notion of *communidade gay* (gay community) organized around an *identidade homossexual* (homosexual identity) or an *identidade gay* (gay identity) rather quickly became, for members of the middle class, a point of convergence where the elite appropriation of modern medical/scientific classifications and the popular reality of a sexual subculture organized around same-sex practices could be brought together and merged, at least up to a certain point. Throughout the 1970s and on into the 1980s, these various currents would continue to flow together and mix, making possible the progressive formation of what is now probably the most visible subculture anywhere outside the industrialized West.[5]

It would be a mistake, however, to view this Brazilian subculture as nothing more than an importation from abroad, a tropical version of the gay community as it exists in Europe or the United States. On the contrary, it has continued to respond in a variety of ways to the particularities of Brazil's own social and cultural context. Perhaps nowhere is

---

5. See Altman (1980), Lacey (1979), MacRae (1982, 1983), Whitam (1979), and Young (1973), in addition to works already recurrently cited.

this more evident than in its reproduction of such traditional categories as *atividade* and *passividade* in a profusion of sexual categories or types. Terms such as *viado*, *bicha*, and *sapatão* are reproduced, and other even finer distinctions are added. Effeminate *bichas*, for instance, are contrasted with *bofes* (studs or hunks), who are characterized in terms of their aggressive masculinity and their active sexual role. The man-like *sapatão* is contrasted with the more feminine *sapatilha* (literally, slipper), roughly like a butch dyke is contrasted to a femme. In the increasingly prominent world of male prostitution (which is, of course, a function not merely of desire, but also of poverty), a sharp distinction is drawn between the *travesti* (transvestite) and the *michê* (hustler, in this context), between an exaggerated feminine figure who clearly prefers a passive sexual role and an almost equally exaggerated masculine figure thought to be generally available for the active role but unwilling to perform the passive one.

A set of active/passive distinctions that is unusually elaborate thus typifies this subculture and clearly emphasizes it specifically Brazilian character. Yet even here, it is important to emphasize just how different this is from the traditional model of the sexual universe that continues to dominate life in rural Brazil. The distinctions that characterize this urban subculture are never seen as absolute. It is part and parcel of the ideology that structures this world that such active/passive oppositions can always be inverted, that *bofes* or *michês* can be convinced to *dar* while *travestis* and *bichas comem*, and so on. The overturning of such categorical distinctions is possible because, unlike the distinctions of traditional culture, these categories are determined and defined from within the subculture itself. While the *viado*, or the *sapatão* in traditional culture are defined from without, stigmatized and labeled by the other members of the wider society, and ultimately excluded from the world of proper *homems* and *mulheres*, here, within this modern subculture, one essentially defines oneself on the basis of one's sexual and erotic preferences and within the community of one's fellows. The company of one's fellows, in turn, provides at least some form of protection from the kinds of hostility and oppression that one might still have to face when confronting the wider social world.

This sense of community comes through perhaps most clearly in the fact that all such elaborate categories can be subsumed under the more general heading of *entendido/a* (one who understands). This more general category had apparently been present for some time within the relatively secretive, almost underground subculture that began to take shape in the early 20th century. It began to be used much more frequently, however, with the great expansion and the increasing visibility of this subculture in the 1970s. At least since that time, it has been used by the members of this subculture themselves as an all-encompassing term referring to anyone who, to whatever extent, participates in—and thus, by extension, knows or understands the nature of—this specific community.

Significantly, then, the term *entendido* applies both to those individuals (again, mostly middle class) who have adopted a strictly homosexual or gay identity based on the model provided by the industrialized West, and to all those who have come to take part in this particular subculture even sporadically, without necessarily limiting themselves to it or defining themselves solely through their relationship to it. In short, it is a category that can apply to individuals who engage exclusively in same-sex interactions, as well as to individuals who engage in sexual relationships with both sexes. Indeed, the *entendido* and *entendida* form almost mirror images of the traditional *homem* and *mulher* (who inevitably engage in relationships with the opposite sex, but who enjoy a certain freedom to interact with members of their own biological sex, as well).

Ultimately, then, what seems to have emerged over the course of the past decade in large urban centers such as Rio or São Paulo—and only to a slightly lesser extent in smaller cities such as Porto Alegre, Recife, or Salvador—is a relatively complex sexual subculture that, while surely woven from Brazilian cloth, nonetheless provides a model for the organization of sexual reality that is clearly very different from the more traditional patterns of Brazilian culture. While this new subculture tends to retain much of the fluidity or flexibility of sexual desire that seemed so typical in traditional culture, it organizes it and links it to the formation of identities in rather different ways, and it clearly offers those individuals whose lives it touches a radically different set of possibilities and choices in the constitution of their own sexual and social lives.

The effects of these changes have surely been felt by Brazilians of all ages, though middle-aged and older individuals who also experienced the patterns of traditional life more deeply are perhaps more consciously aware of the *mudanças* (shifts or changes) that have taken place around (and often within) them. While they may well be less cognizant of such historical dimensions, however, it is a younger generation that has felt the impact of these developments most forcefully, as perhaps nowhere have the rules of the game changed quite so profoundly as for adolescents seeking to shape their own understandings of themselves and of their place within the wider social world.

The experiences of adolescents within this more modern, urban setting are surely not entirely divorced from those of young Brazilians growing up in more traditional settings. On the contrary, even in the most modernized sectors of Brazilian society, the sexual classifications and values of traditional culture are well known and implicitly understood by all. Furthermore, the sexual play of children and young adolescents that seemed so central to the shaping of public identities based on sexual preferences in traditional Brazil continues to be an important part of sexual education and maturation in urban settings. In the more modern context of the cities, however, the significance of such interactions seems rather reduced because of the vastly expanded opportunities for the exploration of one's sexual desires. The existence of a relatively complex and varied subculture where young men and women can begin to explore their own sexuality not only through specific sexual practices, but as part of a much more all-inclusive social experience, has radically transformed the process through which adolescents both shape and understand their own sexual realities.

Almost invariably, it is during adolescence that individuals[6] first come into contact with the *entendido* subculture. One's point of entry into this subculture varies greatly, both from individual to individual, as well as from one social class to another. For boys who come from the urban poor or who have migrated to the cities from the countryside, for instance, some forms of prostitution is a typical rite of passage serving both erotic and financial ends, and the specific streets, plazas, and bars that serve as a focus for male prostitution in any given city provide many lower-class males with their earliest exposure to this new world. For both boys and girls from the middle or upper classes, more expensive clubs or discos and, at least in coastal cities, the gay sections of the beaches, are perhaps more likely settings. Within such more or less protected or protective spaces, same-sex sexual contacts can be initiated and carried out in relative safety, and without much fear of negative social sanction or stigmatization because one's activities are obscured from the view of the wider society. For anyone who experiences same-

---

6. Especially boys. Girls' sexuality continues to be more closely guarded and repressed, even in the cities.

sex desires, then, the appeal of this subculture can hardly be under-estimated.

Thus, the presence of same-sex desires linked to economic need in the case of male prostitution, first draws young women and men to this urban subculture, and same-sex sexual transactions provide the focus for any individual's continued participation within it. Even though this must thus be described as a sexual subculture, a subculture organized first and foremost around a specific set of sexual preferences and prac-tices, there is an ironic sense in which the importance of sex itself is in some ways less absolute here within this subculture than was the case in more traditional settings where no such subculture existed. This is because here, in this urban subculture, sexual conduct becomes linked to an entire social milieu—a community—although certainly not quite as bounded or well-defined a community as those of the industrialized West.

Within this community, a sense of self is built up not only through the meaning attached to one's sexual role (though such meanings do not cease to exist), but through the nature of one's relationships. Perhaps nothing quite so profoundly differentiates the experience of adolescents in contemporary urban Brazil from those in more traditional areas as this shift of emphasis from acts to relations. Within this more modern sexual subculture, ongoing relationships are constructed that may or may not be sexual in nature, but which play a central role in the shaping of social identities.

While these relationships are no doubt as varied as the individuals who form them, for adolescents they nonetheless seem to take shape in at least two significant directions: horizontally and vertically. On the one hand, as young men and women enter the gay subculture, they quickly form friendships with groups of peers roughly their own age, more often than not from the same class background, and almost invari-ably their same sex, who also consider themselves *entendidos/as*. Sexual interaction may take place from time to time between such peer group members, but is generally less significant to the nature of such relation-ships than is a shared sense of comradeship, a shared sense of under-standing and friendship.

At the same time as they are forming these horizontal relationships with their peers, young *entendidas/os* also tend to form vertical relation-ships based on age and class differences: relationships with individuals who are either older, more well-to-do, or (typically) both. Perhaps even more frequently than in the case of horizontal relationships among peers, these vertical relationships begin as sexual relationships, then gradually transform themselves into ongoing and often extremely deep friendships. Such vertical relations tend to be extremely important in initiating younger men and women into the wider world of this subculture, and older individuals are sometimes willing to take on and teach their younger partners almost as if they were apprentices. As it perhaps is to be expected in an extremely hierarchical society such as Brazil, there is often a certain patron/client quality to such relationships as well, with more well-to-do individuals sometimes going out of their way to provide financial support, educational and vocational opportunities, as well as love and friendship, to their younger partners. Thanks to such relationships, and to the sexual subculture, the protected social space that makes them possible, adolescents drawn to same-sex sexual practices in contemporary Brazil inhabit a world that is radically different from that inhabited by their counterparts in more traditional settings, a world in which it is far more possible to shape and reshape one's own identity through both sexual and social interactions with one's fellows. It would be completely incorrect to suggest that this new world is a world without prejudice or social stigma. On the contrary, like the traditional system of sexual meaning itself, traditional prejudices continue to exist, and new ones have certainly evolved as well. However, the ability that young women and men now have actively to shape their own sexual realities, as well as the social world within which these realities will be lived out, surely contrasts quite sharply with that more traditional system of meanings in which the possibilities open to one were largely predetermined and often absolute.

REFERENCES

Altman, Dennis
  1980 Down Rio way. *Christopher Street* 4(8):22–27.
Doyle, Iracy
  1956 *Contribuição ao Estudo da Homossexualidade Feminina*. Rio de Janeiro: LUX.
Freyre, Gilberto
  1981 *Sobrados e mucambos*. Rio de Janeiro: José Olympio. 6th edition.
Fry, Peter
  1982 *Para Inglês ver: Identidade e politica na cultura Brasileira*. Rio de Janeiro: Zahar.

1987 Male homosexuality and Afro-Brazilian possession cults. In *Male Homosexuality in Central and South America.* S. Murray, ed. Pp. 55–71 New York: Gay Academic Union. (Reprinted in this volume.)

Fry, Peter, and Edward MacRae
1983 *O que é homossexualidade.* São Paulo: Editora Brasiliense.

Herdt, Gilbert H., and Robert J. Stoller
1985 Theories of origins of male homosexuality. In *Observing the Erotic Imagination.* R. Stoller, ed. Pp. 104–34 New Haven: Yale University Press.

Lacey, E. A.
1979 Latin America. *Gay Sunshine* 40/41:22–31.

MacRae Edward
1982 Os respeitáveis militantes e as bichas loucas. In *Caminhos Cruzados.* A. Eulálio, ed. Pp. 99–111. São Paulo: Editora Brasiliense.
1983 Em defesa do gueto. *Novos Estudos CEBRAP* 2(1):53–60.

Manta, I.
1928 *A Arte e a Neurose de João do Rio.* Rio de Janeiro: Francisco Alves.

Parker, Richard G.
1985 Masculinity, femininity and homosexuality. *Journal of Homosexuality* 11(3/4):155–63.
1987 Acquired Immune Deficiency in Urban Brazil. *Medical Anthropology Quarterly* 1:155–75.

Pires de Almeida, José R.
1906 *Homossexualismo: A Libertinagem no Rio de Janeiro.* Rio de Janeiro: Leammert Editores.

Ribeiro, Leonídio
1938 *Homossexualismo e Endocronlogia.* Rio de Janeiro: Francisco Alves.

Trevisan, João S.
1986 *Perverts in Paradise.* London: Gay Men's Press.

Whitam, Frederick L.
1979 The entendidos: middle class gay life in São Paulo. *Gay Sunshine* 38/39:16–17. (Reprinted in this volume.)

Young, Allen
1973 Gay gringo in Brazil. In *The Gay Liberation Book.* Len Richmond and Gary Noguera, eds. Pp. 60–67. San Francisco: Ramparts Press.

18

✿

Portugayese

Wayne R. Dynes

Inasmuch as the list offered below is intended only as a preliminary gathering, no attempt at analysis of the Portuguese vocabulary for the semantic field "homosexual" will be attempted here. Two observations are in order, however:

1. As Arlindo Camillo Monteiro remarked in 1922, the Portuguese vocabulary in this realm is very rich, and is probably unsurpassed by any other modern language. This lexical fecundity probably reflects a general tendency, found in both Portugal and Brazil, to a frankness verging sometimes on exhibitionism in discussing sexual matters.

2. Although Spanish and Portuguese share a common Latin origin and a European peninsula, there is relatively little overlap between the two homosexual lexicons. This difference, so much in contrast with the convergence of the general vocabularies of the two languages, is probably to be explained by the particularistic character of all slang. This in turn has two sources: the origin of much slang in a desire to conceal meaning from outsiders, fostering variation; and the fact that slang is generally created by poor and marginal people, who do not travel much.

The following abbreviations are used: Lus. (peninsular Portuguese), NE (Northeast Brazil), S (Southern Brazil). Note that when a geographical designation is given, this does not mean that the term is necessarily restricted to that area, but that it seems to be characteristic of it in so far as the sources allow a determination. Thanks for expert assistance are due to Julio Gomes Viana, João Antonio de S. Mascarenhas, Stephen O. Murray, and Robert W. Howes.

Terms Used for Passive Homosexuals

abemolado: effeminate; from *abemolar,* to soften; also: to mark with a flat
  in music [Synonym: *amaricado*]

abicharar: to become a *bicha,* queen; also: *abichalhado,* effeminate; *abi-
  chalhar,* to act in an effeminate way

abominacão: abomination; from the references in Leviticus often taken to
  refer to homosexuality

acucareiro (Lus.): anus; according to Monteiro (1922), this term (literally,
  "sugar bowl") was a common epithet for a homosexual in Portugal
  in the early years of the century; the same source mentions the
  terms *alfenim, bogueiro bomba, bule, bunda, buzina, caçarola, caixa,
  cifra, clatra, ilho, marmita, orgo, panao, pevide, posterior, quiosque, ra-
  bado, rêgo, retangueiro, sacana, sim senhor, trados, urna, verso, vidrinho
  de cheiro, ze de vestia, zuate*

adamado: effeminate; one who has been made a *dama,* a lady

adelaide (Lus.): an affected, effeminate young man; fop; from a character
  in a Lisbon newspaper serial in the early years of the century

afrescalhado: effeminate; from fresco; variant: *afrescado*

ambissex(u)o: hermaphrodite

amaricado: effeminate; from *maricas,* etc.; also: *amaricarse,* to become
  effeminate, pansify oneself

amelia (Lus.): effeminate; from the woman's forename; cf. *adelaide*

amulherado: effeminate; womanized; from *mulher,* woman; variant: *Amul-
  herengado*; there are also verbs: *amulherarse, amulherengarse*

amunhecar: to drop on all fours ready for anal penetration

anca de vaca (S): effeminate (literally, "rump of a cow")

androgino: androgyne

aqualirado (NE): effeminate

as de copas (Lus.): faggot; from the slang meaning "buttocks" (literally,
  "ace of hearts")

baitola (NE): pansy

bicha: queen; probably the most common vernacular term for (passive)
  homosexual in Brazil; the standard meaning of *bicho* is "worm,
  bug, or small animal." *Bicha* may also mean a female prostitute.
  Ultimately the word derives from the Latin *bestia,* by which it is
  connected with the French *biche,* doe, an interesting link because
  the commonest synonym for bicha is *veado,* deer; ariants: *bicha
  louca, bicharona; bichona*

bonecola: fop; conceited man (literally, puppet, doll); can also mean "pretty woman," "penis," and "prostitute"

borboleta: fairy (literally, butterfly; cf. Spanish *mariposa*); the meanings "vagina" and "prostitute" are also found

cabaço: virgin; note the expressions "X tirou o cabaço de Y" (X took out Y's hymen), *"tirar o cabaco do cu"* (to insert the penis into the anus of someone who had never before been fucked that way)

canoinha: (Maranhão) cunt (literally, "vulva")

catamita: catamite; a learned word from the Latin *catamitus*

chibateiro (NE): cocksucker; from *chiba,* penis

chimba (NE): faggot

coisinha: little cunt; diminutive of *coisa,* "thing," employed as a euphemistic term for vulva

congrio (S; Rio): faggot; from *congria,* whore

corujona (S): invert; augmentative of *coruja,* owl; may also mean an ugly old woman, thus closely paralleling "faggot"

cudeburro (S; Rio): faggot (literally, "donkey's anus")

cudechupeta: faggot (literally, "anus," "opening" or a "sucking tube")

cuzeiro (NE): invert (literally, "anusist")

desmunhecado: limp wrist (literally, "amputated")

domador de serpentes: "snake charmer" (*serpente* = penis)

efeminado: effeminate

entendido: expert; in the know; aware person; the most common polite term used by Brazilian homosexuals to describe themselves

enxuto: pansy; from *enxuta,* shapely woman

femeo: invert; from *femea,* whore

florzinha: little flower

fodidincul: fuckee; a term with medieval antecedents (literally, "fucked in the ass"); contrasts with *fodincul,* fucker

fraliqueiro: mollycoddle; the sense is one who clings to his mother's apron or skirt

frango: invert; from *franga,* young woman

fresco: fresh one; also: *frescura,* fresco ways or manners; faggotry

fronha (S): fairy (literally, "pillowcase" or "pillow")

frouxo: weakling; sissy. *Frouxo* is a common adjectival meaning "weak, lazy, vacillating"; cf. Spanish *flojo*

fruta, fruita, frutão: fruit; may also mean "vulva"

fufa (Lus.): fairy

goriba (NE): pansy

guaxebo (S; Rio): old queen

guei, gay: gay; North American borrowing, usage tending to reflect some importation of concepts, though often incomplete. Increasingly common.

gunga: fairy; may also mean "child's [i.e., little] penis," "little prick"

homen puto: fairy (literally, "whoreman"); also: *homem efeminado;* used by itself, *homem* means "(real) man," and by extension, "trade" or "active homosexual" passing for straight

incubada: incubus

invertido: invert; this international word was diffused from Italy, where it was launched in a scholarly article published by Arrigo Tamassia in 1878; in romance languages, the term is perceived as a noun, adjective, and past participle (the latter suggesting, though often only subliminally, that something or someone has inverted the individual); also *inversão sexual*

janeco: pretty man with homosexual tendencies

jilo: fruit juice

locru (NE): faggot.

lolo: fairy; may also mean: buttocks, anus, child's penis

louca: crazy queen; compare French *folle,* Spanish *loca*

lourico (S): faggot

lumio: faggot; from *lumia,* whore

maninelo: effeminate; also: fool; Related to *maninho,* barren, sterile

mais para la do que para ca: that way (literally, "more there than here")

maricas, marico, maricao: effeminate; the cognate of Spanish *maricón,* though much less common. Diminutive: *mariquinho;* cf. also *maricagem,* effeminate ways

marinelo: effeminate (perhaps a blend of *maninelo* and *maricas*)

mariquinha: little Maria (old-fashioned Brazilian term [Penteado 1979: 240])

marisco: faggot (literally, "shellfish"); influenced by *maricas*

marreco (S): invert; from *marreca,* knowing girl

meiacomoda: faggot (literally, "comfortable stocking")

membeca (NE): sissy; from a Tupi word meaning "soft"/"tender"

miloca (S): faggot

mosqueiro: faggot; from a slang term meaning anus (literally, "fly trap")

nãometoques: haughty effeminate (literally, "don't touch me")

narisco: Narcissus; conceited pretty boy

neutro: effeminate; neuter

panasca: fairy; also: vagina

paneirinha: effeminate (literally, "little basket")

paneleiro (Lus.): invert

panila (Lus.): fairy

passivo: passive; one regarded as taking the woman's role in sexual relations

patrona: grande dame (literally, "patroness")

pecego, pecegote (Lus.): faggot

peito de egua: effeminate (literally, "whore's tits")

perequete (NE): elegant pansy

perobo: faggot; tiresome person

petisco (S): invert; also: desired woman

pintoso: obvious one; someone who, by his effeminate manners, can be easily detected as a homosexual

pisaleve: delicate man; light stepper; also: *pisaflores.*

pita: fairy

puto: male prostitute (literally); can be used for any male homosexual thought to be promiscuous; the learned word is *prostituto*

quartão (NE): invert; also: strong woman; virago

rabo (Lus.) faggot (literally, "tail")

ramiasco (Lus.): invert

refrigerado (S; Rio): effeminate (*fresco*)

roto (Lus.): ragamuffin, urchin (literally, "broken")

salsinha: sissy (literally, "parsley")

saltamoita (NE): fairy (literally, "breakjumper")

saltaposinhas: effeminate, especially one with an eccentric walk (literally, "puddle jumper")

samicas: effeminate

socratico, amor socratico: Socratic love, a learned term used by Monteiro, who contrasts it with *amor safico*, lesbian love

sune: invert

terceiro sexo: third sex; now largely obsolete, this concept had considerably international diffusion owing in part to the fact that it was favored for a time by the German homosexual rights movement

tobeiro: ass man; from *toba, tobi,* anus

travesti: cross-dresser; transvestite

tres-vezes-oito: "three times eight"; variant of *vinte-e-quatro* (see below)

tripulante (S): faggot (literally, "crew member;"/"sailor")

trucas (Lus.): trick

vaca noca (NE): faggot; from *vaca* (easy woman; literally, "cow") and *nova* (new)

vagalume (NE): swish (literally, "firefly")

veado: faggot/queer (literally, "deer"); in Brazil, this term vies in popularity with *bicha*, which also has the primary designation of an animal; both are offensive, *veado* somewhat more so; associated with *vinte-e-quatro* (see below); also: *veaderrimo,* superfaggot; and *veadagem,* faggotry, typical manners and conduct of faggots

ventilado: effeminate; perhaps from *ventilar,* to fan

vint-e-quatro: "twenty-four"; corresponds to the category *veado* (deer; faggot) in the game of *bicho;* it is said that some Brazilians try to avoid using the expression "twenty-four," substituting "three times eight" *(tres-vezes-oito),* which itself has become suspect

xibungue, xibungo: fairy; perhaps from *xiba,* vulva

zinho (NE): effeminate; from *zinha,* girl

Terms Used Primarily for the Active Homosexual, or Indeterminate

besouro: active; bugger

boche: "husband"; masculine-appearing man who is perceived as taking the active role in a homosexual relationship

bode/bofe: stud; an active straight or straight-looking man who screws passive gay men, often for money

efebo: attractive adolescent (ephebe; from Greek), who is probably available

enrustido/a: the male (female) homosexual who tries to pass; a closet case

faça de bainha: active and passive (literally, "penis of vagina")

fanchono: faggot; an old word (since the 16th century); perhaps from the French diminutive *fanchon,* France; also: *afanchonado*

fodincul: active; fucker; medieval term

ganimedes: attractive young man; originally a proper name: Ganymede, the favorite of Zeus

gilete: active and passive; from Gillette double-edged razor blades which cut on both sides

gorgota (S; Rio): active

gregorio (NE): active; may also mean penis (Lus.)

homem: (real) man; according to context it can mean straight, trade, or the active homosexual in a couple

homossexual: homosexual; an international term, introduced through medical and psychiatric writings, but now very widely used; also: *homossexualismo,* homosexuality *lulu:* homosexual child

miche: homosexual prostitute who plays the active or passive role according to his patrons' wishes

panache: mixed vegetables (versatile)

pederasta: pederast; etymologically, this term should refer to the active, but (as in French and Spanish) it tends to be used for both active and passive, or simply be restricted to the latter; popular usage tends to restrict it to the last sense

peão: trade (literally, "farm hand"/"peon")

qualira (NE): masculine homosexual

sodomita: sodomite; derived from a medieval Latin word for the legendary inhabitants of the Biblical city, the destruction of which is recorded in Genesis 18:19; also *sodomia, sodomitismo* (nouns), *sodomico, sodomitico, sodomitigo* (adjectives), and *sodomizar* (verb)

Terms Used for Lesbians

fanchona: dyke; this is the feminine form of *fanchono* (see above); like other terms of this kind it can be confusing: the *fanchona* can be the female counterpart of the faggot, or it can mean a feminized or stereotypical faggot; generally speaking, however, Portuguese speakers do not tend to conceptualize the lesbian as the counterpart of the male homosexual. This parallelism is itself essentially a product of the introduction of the overarching category "homosexual," which has only been partially received in Portugal and Brazil

fressureira: lesbian; from *fressura,* lesbianism; the pluck—literally "guts"— of slaughtered animals

mariarapaz (Lus.): tomboy

pratilheira (Lus.): lesbian

quartosexo: fourth sex; often more specifically a woman who lives in a coupled relationship with another

rocadeira: lesbian; variant: *rocadinho;* cf. *rocinha* (vulva)

sabão, saboeiros: lesbianism practiced by mutual manual stimulation (literally, "make soap")

safica, safista: Saphist; this international term refers to the ancient Greek poet of the island of Lesbos

sapatão: butch dyke (literally, "big shoe")

tribade: lesbian; a learned term from the Greek *tribas*

REFERENCES

Almeida, Horácio de
   1980 *Dicionário de termos eróticos e afins.* Rio de Janeiro: Civilizacão Brasileiro.
Fock, Nina
   1981 *Dicionário Sexual.* Curtiba: Grafipar.
Monteiro, Arlindo Camillo.
   1922 *Amor safico e socratico.* Lisbon: privately printed.
Penteado, Darcy
   1979 Snow White revisited. In *Now the Volcano,* W. Leyland and E. Lane, eds. Pp. 237–53. San Francisco: Gay Sunshine Press.
Rasmussen, Kenneth W.
   1971 *Brazilian Portuguese Words and Phrases for Certain Aspecty of Love and Parts of the Body.* Ph.D. dissertation, University of Wisconsin, Madison.
Silva, Aguinaldo
   1975 *Primeira carta aos andróginos.* Rio de Janeiro: Pallas.
Souto Maior, Mario
   1980 *Dicionário de palavrao e termos afins.* Recife: Guararapes.

19

❦

"Sentimental Effusions"
of Genital Contact in Amazonia

Stephen O. Murray

In Northwest Amazonia, as in Melanesia (see Herdt 1982[1]), initiation, more than marriage,[2] is the central passage from the asexual world of childhood to the sexual world of adulthood, and from a particular family to being a member of society. According to Stephen Hugh-Jones (1979:110),

> From an outsider's point of view, one of the most noticeable manifestations of this is the incidence of joking sexual play among initiated but unmarried men . . . Missionaries working in the Piraparana are frequently shocked by the apparent homosexual behavior of Indian men. However, the Barasana distinguish between this playful sexual activity and serious male homosexuality. This play, rather than coming from a frustration of 'normal' desire, is itself seen as being normal behavior between 'brothers-in-law' and expressed their close, affectionate, and supportive relationship.

---

1. Gilbert Herdt also called my attention to the Hugh-Jones books; Wayne Dynes to Gregor's.

2. Christine Hugh-Jones (1979:160) did not consider marriage a significant event in the typical life-cycle, because,

> Marriage was described as an event in another domain—that of kinship and inter-group relations [the classic Lévi-Strauss position]. Although there is a sense in which marriage is obviously a life-cycle event, it is not ritualized like birth, menstruation, Yurpary rites and death. The physiological possibility of a new generation has already been ritually recognized in initiation.

In most of these tribes, chiefs monopolized women. The impossibility of obtaining a wife recurrently led to substituting young boy "wives" in African societies and also to sexual use of younger boys by men and by older boys in Islamic societies (Murray and Roscoe 1996).

He further averred, "Such play does not entail sexual satisfaction." He did not explain how he concluded that. Claude Lévi-Strauss, who had reported "reciprocal sexual services" by classificatory "brothers-in law" among the Nambikwara in 1943 (p. 407; also see 1948a:95–96, 1948c: 366) suggested (in a personal communication cited by Hugh-Jones) that "it appears to provide unmarried men with an outlet for sentimental effusions." Lévi-Strauss (1974:313) also remarked, "It remains an open question whether the partners achieve complete satisfaction or restrict themselves to sentimental demonstrations, accompanied by caresses, similar to the demonstrations and caresses characteristic of conjugal relationships." Reading this "clarification," I wonder whether it was Lévi-Strauss who defined homosexuality out of the possibility of "complete satisfaction" and also whether "conjugal relationships" exclude ejaculations. Although maintaining that "the brother is acting as a temporary substitute" for his sister (1974:314), he admitted, "On reaching adulthood, the brothers-in-law continue to express their feelings quite openly" (p. 314).

Stephen Hugh-Jones (1979:110) reported, "A young man will often lie in a hammock with his 'brother-in-law,' nuzzling him, fondling his penis, and talking quietly, often about sexual exploits with women." Christine Hugh-Jones (1979:160) similarly noted, "Boys approaching initiation are sometimes involved in homosexual teasing which takes place in hammocks in public: this play is most common between initiated but unmarried youths from separate exogamous groups."[3]

One is left wondering if fondled penises on occasion produce effusions more tangible than "sentimental," as they have been reported to do elsewhere in the world, especially among young men who, having little sexual experience and few approved sexual outlets, are "given over to personal display" and to talking about real or fantasized sexual exploits. Similarly, one wonders how Altaschuler (1964:231) could have been so sure that the young Cayapa boys he saw wrapped around each other on the floor or sharing hammocks confined themselves to "homo-eroticism" in contrast to "homosexuality."[4]

Murphy (1955:82–83) challenged Lévi-Strauss's (1948b:337) inter-

---

3. This suggests marriage is more important than her statement quoted in note 2 indicates.

4. His credibility is further reduced by the argument based on Bieber that there could not be the "innovation" of homosexual intercourse, because homosexual behavior is based on feelings of inadequacy, and those who feel inadequate cannot innovate.

pretation of Buell Quain's fieldnotes on the Trumai Indians. Murphy maintained that liaisons cannot be predicted along the lines of marriage rules; indeed, that a boy might seduce his own father. In general, the boys made the advances to the men. In contrast, among the Yanomamo, "Some of the teen-age males have homosexual affairs with each other. [There, too,] the females of their own age are usually married" (Chagnon 1977:76). In his 1967 dissertation, Chagnon wrote, "Most unmarried young men were having homosexual relations with each other but no stigma was attached to this behavior. In fact, most of these bachelors joked about it and simulated copulation with each other in public" (1967:62–63; note the contrast of "some" and "most").

Alves da Silva (1962:181) attested public mutual masturbation by Tucano boys, although officially, homosexuality only occurs in the initiation rites for pubescent boys (p. 380). Karsch-Haack (1975:428–29) read a source not available to me (Martius 1863) as reporting Tupi shaman (pa'yé) disciples receiving magical power by being inseminated by their teacher.

Nimuenadju and Lowie (1938) reported formalized, intense, but apparently non-sexual friendships among another Gê tribe, the Ramko'kamekra. Wagley's 1939 salvage anthropology of the Tapirape, a Southern Amazon tribe with a Tupi-Guarani rather than Gê language (who were therefore likely pushed from the coast rather than being traditionally jungle dwellers prior to 1500), included stories

> of males in the past who had allowed themselves to be used in anal intercourse by other men. They were treated as favorites by the men, who took them along on hunting trips. There were no men alive in 1939–40 with such a reputation [there were only 187 Tapirape people alive by then]. Kamairaho gave me the names of five men whom he had known during his lifetime or about whom his father had told him "had holes." Some of these men were married to women, he said, but at night in the *takana* [men's house] they allowed other men to "eat them" (have anal intercourse). His father told him of one man who took a woman's name and did women's work . . . Older men had said that the "man-woman" had died because she was pregnant. "Her stomach was swollen but there was no womb to allow the child to be born." None of my informants had ever heard of a woman who had taken the male role or who preferred sex with another female. [Wagley 1977:160]

Even during the lifetime of Kamairaho's father, there were not very many Tapirape. Thus, five is a considerable number to have been known to be sexually receptive. There is nothing to indicate that these five were younger or judged to be less masculine than their partners; married men, of course, were judged fully adult. In any case. I do not know of any reports of Gê tribes with a "man-woman." The acceptance of male sexual receptivity without such a role among the Tapirape is as notable as the memory of a gender-crosser.

Gregor (1985) added a muddled account of conceptions of homosexuality as (1) inconceivable, (2) situational, and (3) forgotten for the Mehinaku of the Xingu River. The evidence for inconceivable is the lack of a "term for the role of homosexual." As usual with such assertions, Gregor's is not accompanied by explanation of what role it was he attempted to elicit by what means. The basis for "situational," the second line of defense (whether Gregor's or Mehinakus'), is that young men from other villages "consorted with the white man [because] they wanted gifts. They had no sexual interest in him whatsoever. Admittedly, they were foolish to have participated, but no man really desires homosexual relations" (p. 60). This rationalization (and its possible shaping by acculturative pressures) was passed on without comment by a Freudian ethnographer! In relating a myth about a man who got pregnant from having sex with his friend, he only commented on the lack of elaboration in the tale. Gregor concluded his muddled account of Mehinaku conceptions by relating

> one historical instance . . . of a Mehinaku who, though uninfluenced by perverted [one does not know if this is supposed to be the Mehinaku view or is Gregor's own] outsiders, stepped beyond the boundaries of the masculine role. Tenejumine, "Slightly a Woman," as this person is referred to today, died more than forty-five years ago . . . grew up to assume the dress and role of a woman . . . [and] all agree that he formed special relationships with a few of the men that resembled those of lovers. The men, it is said, would get into the same hammock as Slightly a Woman and "pretend" to engage in sex play. [1985:61]

To preserve tribal honor, Tenejumine's partners were attributed the same rationalization used now (i.e., when Gregor was in the field): they only wanted presents. Gregor was struck that memories of Tenejumine were not clearer, though Tenejumine was two generations removed from Gregor's informants, who were not even descended from him.

In an earlier, less Freudian ethnography, Gregor (1977: 254) had written, "The villagers tolerate sexual deviance. Girls who experiment in lesbian affairs or men who participate in homosexual encounters are regarded as extremely foolish, but no one would directly interfere." There, he also more calmly discussed the "mutability of gender" in Mehinaku myth and ritual.

Soares de Souza (1851 [1587]: 316) asserted the Tupinamba were "addicted to sodomy and do not consider it a shame . . . In the bush some offer themselves to all who want them."

In the upper Amazon, Tessman (1930:361) found, that

> while there are no homosexuals with masculine tendencies, there are some with extreme effeminacy. My informants knew of two such instances. One of them wears woman's clothing . . . [The other] wears man's clothing, but likes to do all the work that is generally done by women. He asked one member of our expedition to address him with a woman's name and not with his masculine name. He lives with a settler and prostitutes himself as the passive partner to the settler's workers. He pays his lovers. He never practices active sexual intercourse.[5]

Paul Fejos's (1948:106–7) ethnography of a Uitoto-speaking tribe, included a description of a Yagua dandy. Either this description or personal communications led Ford and Beach (1951) to code Witoto as a tolerant-to-homosexuality culture. There is also a stray reference in Holmberg (1950:169) to a man-woman among the Siriono of Eastern Bolivia. Among the depopulated Wachipaeri, Lyon (1984:258) reported one enduring homosexual relationship.

A more extended description of widespread homosexual play and of fairly enduring but "open" relationships in northwestern Amazonia was provided by Sorenson (1984:184–88). He wrote, "Young men sit around enticingly sedate and formal in all their finery, or form troupes of panpipe-playing dancers." Occasional sex is regarded as expectable behavior among friends: "One is marked as nonfriendly—enemy—if he does not join, especially in the youth age group (roughly 15–35). . . . Homosexual activity is limited neither to within an age group nor to unmarried men" (1984:185). Moreover, intervillage homosexuality is encouraged and some "best friends" relationships develop. That the

---

5. Nimuendaju (1948:718) wrote that among the Tucuna, "there are no vestiges of homosexuality, as claimed by Tessman (1930:563)."

"best friend" is more likely later to marry a sister of his "best friend" is implied in what Sorenson wrote (1984:189).[6]

Beyond the peripheries of what is considered "Amazonia," there are reports that do not attempt to argue away the sexual components of gender variance. Kirchoff (1948:486) wrote that homosexual relations were very common and publicly condoned among tribes north of the Orinoco River. He also mentioned male homosexuality farther west among the Llanos (1948:467). In north-central Venezuela, at the time of Spanish conquest (which they vigorously resisted during the late 16th century), some Caracas, Teque and other tribesmen fit all the attributes of the berdache role: i.e, "some men in these tribes were sexual inverts. They wore their hair shoulder length, were sodomists, practiced transvestism, avoided going to war, and carried on traditional tasks of women, such as spinning and weaving" (Hernández de Alba 1948:478).

Wilbert (1972) attested that among the Warao, who live in the Orinoco delta, male transvestites sometimes lived in union with other men. Hill et al. (1956:29) wrote about one 40ish Warao transvestite who did women's work and another man "married" to three men younger than he. Turrado Moreno (1945:296) attested a Warao lexeme for the transvestite role, *tiraguina*.

Bolinder (1925:114) and Reichel-Dolmatoff (1951:290) noted male homosexuality among the Cagaba Kogi of Colombia. The men of the neighboring Goajiro had (have?) a considerable reputation as lovers of men. Some men dressed as women and did women's work (Bolinder 1925:114, 1957:61; Armstrong and Métraux 1948:379).

Far to the south, Métraux (1946:324) used the term "berdache" for such behavior, including explicit sexualization of the role, among at least one of the northeastern tribes of the inland Gran Chaco plains: "Berdaches were very common among the Mbayá. They dressed and spoke like women, pretended to menstruate and engaged in feminine activities. They were regarded as the prostitutes of the village."

Some of the denials that homosexual behavior among "my people" is "really homosexuality" say more about the observer than the observed. Pierre Clastres's (1974, 1977) trivialization of Guayakí homosexuality to "erotic play" provides an instance (Goldberg 1991:52–54, 1992:189–93). With no apparent native warrant, Clastres (1974:91) was very eager

---

6. See Murray (1992:5–12) on kinship constraints on boy partners being the same as on possible wives in aboriginal Australia and Melanesia.

to exculpate the male partners of the band's effeminate "sodomite" as "more bawdiness than perversion." This contrast is not any clearer than Altaschuler's 'homoeroticism' versus 'homosexuality.' In his cogent critique of Clastres's anxieties about sexuality and gender (and marked misogyny), Goldberg (1992:282,n.15) went too far in claiming that "Clastres does not want to admit the possibility of indigenous homosexuality." Clastres can justly be accused of trying to limit "indigenous homosexuality" to the feminine man and of failing to report Guayakí views of what hunters copulating with the "sodomite" were doing, what they or others said about that conduct, or even what they called it and/ or called those doing it. However, in contrast to many anthropologists' ellision of sexual receptivity from "berdache" roles, Clastres (1974:90) made the sexual role clear by calling Krembegi a "sodomite" (also "homosexual" and "pederast"[7]) and, most importantly, by adding a native label for his role[8] in terms of sexual practice: "he was a *kyrypy-meno* (anus-make love)."[9]

In other cases (Werner 1985:130–31; and to some degree Gregor 1985), denials of observable homosexuality come from natives. In such cases, it is difficult to know whether the concern that imputations of accepting homosexuality will stigmatize their tribe is the result of Western acculturation (at least to the extent of knowing about Christian disapproval

---

7. Contrary to Goldberg (1992:191), Clastres applied "unconscious invert" to speculations about Krembegi's earlier life, not to the time of Clastres's fieldwork. Nonetheless, in a single paragraph, Clastres managed two very loaded European labels and a native one. He also worked into the same paragraph the archaic psychiatric "invert" as a hypothetical etiology and the stereotype of the "artistic" homosexual. His Krembegi is another "berdache" who does women's work better than biological women. As in other accounts, Clastres did not make clear whether this is a native or the alien's judgment.

8. I take the copula as warrant that the anal receptivity was the basis for a recognized role. I would not assume there are no other Guayakí terms for other aspects than that and Krembegi's lack of hunting luck *(pané)*. Kremebegi was one of two *pané*. Clastres elaborated on their differences, and Goldberg questioned Clastres's analysis of their relative inclusion into "male" and "female" categories.

9. Métraux and Baldus (1946) did not mention such a role. However, they began by noting the sketchiness of records for them to synthesize: "The elusive Guayakí who roam the forest of eastern Paraguay represent one of the least-known tribes of South America" (p. 435). Their description of sex differences in tonsure and ornamentation (p. 439) also does not fit easily with Clastres's analysis of what was feminine in Krembegi's appearance, but they seem to be writing of the Guayakí two or more centuries earlier than Clastres's fieldwork.

of sexual and gender variance) or of more venerable ("aboriginal") cultural concerns. Lack of evidence, and even denials (whether from with natives or from missionaries or anthropologists identified with or at least concerned about "my people") do not prove absence. Records of indigenous sexual conduct have been—and continue to be—distorted by the anxieties and prejudices of those inscribing behavior and culture.

REFERENCES

Alves da Silva, Alcionilio Brüzzi
  1962 *A Civilicacao Indigena do Uaupés*. São Paulo: Centro de Pesquisos de Iauraté.
Altaschuler, Milton
  1964 *The Cayapa*. Ph.D. dissertation, University of Minnesota.
Armstrong, John M., and Alfred Métraux
  1948 Goajiro. *Handbook of South American Indians* 4:379.
Bolinder, Gustaf
  1925 *Die Indianer der Trapishen*. Stuttgart: Strecker und Schroder. Translated as *Indians on Horseback*, London: D. Dobson, 1957.
Chagnon, Napoleon A.
  1967 *Yanomamo Warfare, Social Organization and Marriage Alliance*. Ph.D. dissertation, University of Michigan.
  1977 *Yanomamo*. New York: Holt & Rinehart.
Clastres, Pierre
  1972 *Chronique des Indiens Guayaki*. Paris: Plon.
  1974 *La Société contre l'état*. Paris: Éditions de Minuit.
  1977 The bow and the basket. In *Society Against the State*, pp. 83–107. New York: Urizen Books. (Translation of Clastres 1974.)
Fejos, Paul
  1948 *Ethnography of Yagua*. Viking Fund Publication in Anthropology 1.
Ford, Clellan, and Frank Beach
  1951 *Patterns of Sexual Behavior*. New York: Harper & Row.
Goldberg, Jonathan
  1991 Sodomy in the new world: Anthropologies old and new. *Social Text* 29:45–56. (Incorporated in Goldberg (1992:179–93.)
  1992 *Sodometries*. Stanford, CA: Stanford University Press.
Gregor, Thomas
  1977 *Mehinaku*. Chicago: University of Chicago Press.
  1985 *Anxious Pleasures: The Sexual Life of an Amazonian People*. Chicago: University of Chicago Press.
Hernández de Alba, Gregorio
  1948 The tribes of north central Venezuela. *Handbook of South American Indians* 4:475–79.

Herdt, Gilbert H.
    1982 *Rituals of Manhood*. Berkeley: University of California Press.
Hill, George W., et al.
    1956 *Los Guarao del Delta Amacuro*. Caracas: Universidad Central de Venezuela.
Holmberg, Alan R.
    1950 *Nomads of the Long Bow: The Siriono of Eastern Bolivia*. New York: American Museum of Science.
Hugh-Jones, Christine
    1979 *From the Milk River*. New York: Cambridge University of Press.
Hugh-Jones, Stephen
    1979 *The Palm and the Pleiades*. New York: Cambridge University of Press.
Karsch-Haack, Ferdinand
    1911 *Das gleichgeschlechtliche Leben der Naturvölker*. Munich: E. Reinhardt. (Facsimile edition, New York: Arno Press, 1975.)
Kirchoff, Paul
    1948 The tribes north of the Orinoco River. *Handbook of South American Indians* 5:486.
Lévi-Strauss, Claude
    1943 Social uses of kinship terms among Brazilian Indians. *American Anthropologist* 45:395–401.
    1948a La vie familiale et sociale des Indiens Nambikwara. *Journal de la Société des Americanistes de Paris* 37:75–96.
    1948b Tribes of Upper Xingu. *Handbook of South American Indians* 3:321–48.
    1948c The Nambicuara. *Handbook of South American Indians* 3:361–70.
    1974 [1955] *Tristes Tropiques*. New York: Atheneum.
Lyon, Patricia J.
    1984 Changes in Wachipaeri marriage patterns. *Illinois Studies in Anthropologist* 14:248.
Martius, Karl Friedrich Philipp von
    1863 *Beiträge zur Ethnographie und Sprachenkunde Südamerika's, zumal Brasiliean*. Leipzig: F. Fleischer. (See Spix and Martius 1824.)
Métraux, Alfred
    1946 Ethnography of the Chaco. *Handbook of South American Indians* 1:197–370.
Métraux, Alfred, and Herbert Baldus
    1946 The Guayakí. *Handbook of South American Indians* 1:435–44.
Murphy, Robert F., and Buell Quain
    1955 The Trumai Indians of Central Brazil. *American Ethnological Society Monograph* 24.
Murray, Stephen O.
    1992 *Oceanic Homosexualities*. New York: Garland.
Murray, Stephen O., and Will Roscoe
    1996 *Islamic Homosexualities*. New York: New York University Press.
    In press. *African Homosexualities*.
Nimuenadju, Curt
    1948 The Tucuna. *Handbook of South American Indians* 3:713–27.

Nimuenadju, Curt, and Robert H. Lowie
    1938 The social structure of the Ramko'kamekra (Canella). *American Anthropologist* 40:51–74.
Reichel-Dolmatoff, Gerardo
    1951 *Los Kogi.* Bogotá: Iqueima.
Quain, Buell
    n.d. *The Trumai.* MS (cited by Lévi-Strauss 1948b:337).
Soares de Souza, Gabriel
    1851 [1587] Tratado descriptivo do Brazil em 1587. *Instituto Histórico e Geográfico do Brazil Revista* 14.
Sorenson, Arthur P.
    1984 Linguistic exogamy and personal choice in the Northwest Amazon. *Illinois Studies in Anthropology* 14:180–93.
Spix, Johann Baptist von, and Karl Friedrich Philipp von Martius
    1824 *Travels in Brazil . . . 1817–1820.* London: H. E. Lloyd.
Tessman, Gunter
    1930 *Die Indianer Nordost-Perus.* Hamburg: de Gruyter.
Turrado Moreno, Angel
    1945 *Etnógrafia de los Indios Guaraunos.* Caracas: Vargas.
Wagley, Charles
    1977 *Welcome of Tears.* New York: Oxford University Press.
Werner, Dennis
    1984 *Amazon Journey.* New York: Praeger.
Wilbert, Johannes
    1972 *Survivors of Eldorado.* New York: Praeger.

20

🌿

Mistaking Fantasy for Ethnography*

Stephen O. Murray

Informal communication among experts usually ensures that dubious work is ignored. So long as suspect results are not built upon nor are enshrined as established knowledge, experts feel no need to pillory them in public (Barnes 1972:287; Murray 1980, 1984). "Ignoring what is regarded as non-science is standard operating procedure in all scientific disciplines. Only when suspect work is taken sufficiently seriously by some scientists is any need for public discussion felt," as I wrote of another case of purported ethnography (Murray 1979:191; see de Mille 1976, 1980; Murray 1981).

Tobias Schneebaum's (1969, 1970) account of homosexuality and cannibalism in which he said that he had participated during 1956 among a heretofore undescribed Amazonian tribe provides another case in which the informal professional dismissal of specialists needs to be made explicit, since psychologists and sociologists in search of vivid examples of extreme cultural variability have taken it for authentic ethnography. Schneebaum's account provided the major example of culture-wide homosexual preference—"in which all the men in an entire tribe maintain an ongoing predominant homosexuality"—in Tripp's (1975:64) widely diffused (and for the most part sensible) book. It was also taken as exemplary by Mehan and Wood (1975:27–

*An earlier version of this chapter appeared in the *Anthropologists' Research Group on Homosexuality Newsletter* 2, 3 (1979):4–5. A German version appeared as "Ein homoerotisches Phantásien—Ethnographisch mißdeutet." In *Authentizität und Betrug in der Ethnologie.* H-P Duerr, ed. Pp. 58–62 (Frankfurt: Suhrkamp, 1987). The encouragement and assistance of Richard de Mille are gratefully acknowledged.

31),[1] and by Sir Kenneth Dover in his magisterial account of pederasty in ancient Athens (1978:100).

Schneebaum (1970:17) himself was careful to note, "There will be no pretense of objectivity here." Moreover, he added a further disclaimer to the paperback edition of *Keep the River on Your Right*—"This book is not an attempt at an anthropological account of a tribe"—(1970:viii), and has reiterated the subjectivity of his writing (1979, 1980).

Anthropologists concerned with Upper Amazonia did not take Schneebaum's fantasies seriously. *Keep the River on Your Right* was not reviewed in the *American Anthropologist* and has not been cited by anthropologists as a valid report of an Amazonian culture or of plausible conduct of any existing human group. An expert on Amazonia, Napoleon Chagnon (1969:12), unequivocally stated, "What he described in this work can only be taken as a highly fictionalized account, a gross and inappropriate vilification." Since this judgment was reproduced in the 1969 *Book Review Digest,* it was readily available to anyone made suspicious enough by the unusualness of what Schneebaum "described" (or by the ripeness of his prose), to check whether the book was taken seriously by anthropologists. T. R. Moore, an anthropologist who studied the same tribe with which Schneebaum stayed, reported:

> *Keep the River on Your Right* is neither an ethnological study nor an accurate factual account, as Schneebaum himself makes clear. . . . There is no evidence for Amarakaeri cannibalism. . . . The character Schneebaum calls "Manolo" and reports beheaded and probably cannibalized [in 1956] was living in Ayacucho in the early 1960s. The sleeping arrangements and homosexual practices Schneebaum describes are not part of the Amarakaeri tradition. [quoted in de Mille 1980:74; also see Moore 1980]

Travelers' reports predating scientific study of cultures cannot be ignored, but such reports must be examined critically—especially when they include explicit disclaimers such as those made by Schneebaum and when what they contain is wholly at variance with what is known

---

1. That both of what are regarded as exemplary ethnographies by the explicators of the "reality" of ethnomethodology are fiction fits perfectly with "Agnes" duping Garfinkel in the original *Studies in Ethnomethodology.* While Garfinkel (1967) could not be sufficiently bothered by mere newer or more plausible information to change his chapter, his psychiatric collaborator, Stoller (1968), frankly acknowledged his earlier misdiagnosis.

about neighboring cultures and are embedded in what seems to be wish fulfillment.[2]

Biases about homosexuality are rife in what has been published about Amazonia. As the previous chapter showed, much of the "scientific" literature on aboriginal tribes systematically obfuscates homosexual relations. Instead of arguing away homosexuality, Schneebaum projected his fantasies on a little-known tribe, exaggerating the extent of their dedication to it.

REFERENCES

Barnes, Barry
　　1972 *Sociology of Science.* Baltimore: Penguin.
Chagnon, Napoleon A.
　　1969 Love among the cannibals. *Book World* 3(38):12.
de Mille, Richard
　　1976, 1978 *Castaneda's Journey.* Santa Barbara: Capra.
　　1980 *The Don Juan Papers.* Santa Barbara: Ross-Erikson. (Second edition, Belmont, CA: Wadsworth, 1989.)
Dover, Kenneth J.
　　1978 *Greek Homosexuality.* Cambridge: Harvard University Press.
Garfinkel, Harold
　　1967 *Studies in Ethnomethodology.* Toronto: Prentice-Hall.
Mehan, Hugh, and Houston Wood
　　1975 *The Reality of Ethnomethodology.* New York: Wiley.
Moore, T. R.
　　1980 *The White Peace of Madre de Dios.* Ph.D. dissertation, New School for Social Research.
Murray, Stephen O.
　　1979 The scientific reception of Castaneda. *Contemporary Sociology* 8:189–95.
　　1980 The invisibility of scientific scorn. In de Mille (1980:188–202)
　　1981 Die ethnoromantische Versuchung. In *Der Wissenschaftler und das Irrationale.* H-P Duerr, ed. Pp. 377–85. Frankfurt: Syndikat.
　　1984 Fauler zauber in der Südsee. *Psycholgie Heute* 3(11):68–72.

---

2. Similar skepticism is in order for Schneebaum's (1984:47) claim that in Western New Guinea among the Asmat, "All children are allowed to play with each other sexually. It's considered normal. As the boys get older, they continue the sexual relationship with their *mbai,* as the male friend is called. . . . This is a lifelong relationship . . . between men of the same age group," a claim elaborated in Schneebaum (1987).

Schneebaum, Tobias
  1969, 1970 *Keep the River on Your Right*. New York: Grove Press.
  1979 *Wild Man*. New York: Viking.
  1980 Realities loved and unloved. In de Mille (1980:91–93).
  1984 Interview by Steve Abbott. *The Advocate* 396:44–50.
  1987 *Where the Spirits Dwell*. New York: St. Martin's Press.
Stoller, Robert J.
  1968 A further contribution to the study of gender identity. *International Journal of Psychoanalysis* 49:364–69.
Tripp, C. A.
  1975 *The Homosexual Matrix*. New York: Signet.

ADDITIONAL REFERENCES TO HOMOSEXUALITY IN INDIGENOUS SOUTH AMERICA

(suggested by Stephen Wayne Foster, David F. Greenberg, and Luiz Mott)

Beals, Carleton
  1967 Latin America: Sex life in. In *Encyclopedia of Sexual Behavior*. A. Ellis and A. Abarbanel, eds. Pp. 599–613.
Becker, Raymond de
  1964 *The Other Face of Love*. New York: Grove Press. Pp. 84–87
Carpenter, Edward
  1914 *Intermediate Types among Primitive Folk*. London: Allen & Unwin. Pp. 33–37, 70–71, 168.
Dumont, Jean-Paul
  1976 *Under the Rainbow: Nature and Supernature among the Panara Indians*. Austin: University of Texas Press. P. 114.
Fernandes, Florestan
  1963 *Organizacao Social dos Tupinamba*. São Paulo: Difusao Duropeia do Livro.
Frederici, Georg
  1925 *Die Amazonen Amerikas*. Leipzig: Verlag von Simmel.
Freyre, Gilberto
  1956 *The Masters and the Slaves*. New York: Putnam. Pp. 33, 117–23, 149.
Giel, R.
  1990 Tropical tribades: a report on homosexuality and lesbian relationships in Surinam. *Bijdragen tot de Taal- Land- en Volkenkunde* 115:311–15.
Goldman, Irving
  1963 *The Cubeo Indians of the Northwest Amazon. Illinois Studies in Anthropology*. 2:181.
Guerra, Francisco
  1971 *The Pre-Columbian Mind*. New York: Seminar Press, Pp. 26–27, 34, 45, 222–29.
Guppy, Nicholas
  1958 *Wai-Wai* London: Murray. P. 244.

Hemming, John
    1978 *Red Gold.* London: Macmillan. P. 391.
Henry, Jules
    1941 *Jungle People: A Kaingang Tribe of the Highlands of Brazil.* New York: J. J.
    Augustin. Pp. 18–19.
Karsch-Haack, Ferdinand
    1911 *Das gleichgeschlechtliche Leben der Naturvölker.* Munich: Reinhardt. (New
    York: Arno, 1975).
Kracke, Ward H.
    1978 *Force and Persuasion: Leadership in an Amazonian Society.* Chicago: University of Chicago Press.
Lucena Salmoral, Manuel
    1969 Bardaje en una tribu Guanhibo del tomo. *Revista Colombiana de antropología* 14:261–66.
Magalhaes de Gandavo, Pedro de
    1922 *The Histories of Brazil.* New York: Cortes Society. II:89–90, 173.
Maybury-Lewis, David
    1967 *Akwe.* Oxford: Clarendon Press. P. 82.
Nash, June
    1969 *We Eat the Mines and the Mines Eat Us.* New York: Columbia University Press. P. 141.
Nimuendajú, Curt
    1946 *The Eastern Timbira.* Berkeley: University of California Press. P. 122.
    1952 *The Tikuna.* Berkeley: University of California Press.
Norwood, Victor G. C.
    1964 *Jungle Life in Guiana.* London: R. Hale. P. 142.
Reichel-Dolmatoff, Gerardo
    1971 *Amazonian Cosmos.* Chicago: University of Chicago Press.
    1975 *The Shaman and the Jaguar.* Philadelphia: Temple University Press. Pp. 105–7.
Rodrigues do Prado, Francisco
    1839 Historia dos Indios Cavaleiros ou Nacao Guaicuru no ano de 1795. *Revista do Instituto Historico e Geografico do Brasil* 1:32–33.
Steinen, Karl von den
    1915 Entre os borores do Brasil Central. *Revista do Instituto Historico e Geografico Brasilero* 78:473.
Wagley, Charles, and Eduardo Galvao
    1949 *The Tenetehara Indians of Brazil.* New York: Columbia University Press. P. 96.
Wavrin, Robert
    1948 *Les Indiens sauvages de l'Amerique de Sud: vie sociale.* Paris: Payot. Pp. 112–94.
Westmarck, Edward
    1931 [1908] Homosexual love. In *The Making of Man.* V. Calverton, ed. Pp. 534–63. New York: Modern Library.
Wilbert, Johanne, and Karin Simoneau
    1984 *Folk Literature of the Gê Indians.* Los Angeles: UCLA Latin American Center.

21

〜

South American West Coast
Indigenous Homosexualities*

Stephen O. Murray

"Sodomites" in Pre-Inka Cultures

The Inka civilization and those conquered by and absorbed into it lacked writing. Therefore, what is known about earlier societies derives either from archaeological excavation or from chronicles of the conquerors' conquerors, the Spanish. According to them, the northwestern coast of South America was notorious for "shameless and open sodomy." In *Chronicles*, written between 1539 and 1553, the conquistador historian Pedro Cieza de Léon's mentioned that, near Guayaquíl, Popayán men "pride themselves greatly on sodomy." He added (but did not explain what this meant) that they were "religiously inclined to it" (1959:293). He also noted men on the island of Puná "indulging in the abominable sin" (p. 313).

Cieza quoted Father Domingo de Santo Tomás's accounts of punishing male temple prostitutes in Chincha (south of modern Lima near Pisco on the coast) and in Conchucos (near Huánuco in a highland valley) during the years of the conquest (p. 314). Cieza judged the Inkas and other mountain peoples *(serraños),* specifically including the Colla (the conquistadors' label for the Aymara others living on the high plateau *(collao)* generally) and Tarma, free of the nefarious sins so common on the coast, especially in what had been the Chimú empire (see Rowe 1948), conquered by the Inkas less than a half century before the arrival of the Spaniards (Cieza 1959:277). That the Tarma lived in the province of Conchucos wherein Cieza reported Santo Tomás punishing a male

---

*An earlier version of this section appeared in the *Society of Lesbian and Gay Anthropologists Newsletter* 11,2 (June 1989):15–19. Manuel Arboleda encouraged my interest in Cieza de Leon, while discouraging paying any attention to what Garcilaso de Vega wrote.

temple prostitute makes Cieza's statement that the Indians of the province of Tarma "are free of the sin of sodomy" (p. 113) puzzling, unless he meant that the Spanish had eliminated it. Pedro Pizzaro is the only chronicler who claimed that Cuzco's nobility ever engaged in sodomy (during times of drunken celebrations, in the precincts of Inka grave-sites, called *huacas*).

From their use of an insult, "Asta Huaylas," which he translated as "May Huayla men run after you" (p. 113), Cieza inferred that in the neighboring (to the west) province of Huaylas "in olden times there must have been some given to this grave sin," presumably as penetrators. Later equation of homosexuality with passivity has led to this being read as indicating the Huaylas wanted to be sodomized. However, I think the position of the chaser and the potency of the threat suggest that the Huayla men aimed to penetrate others.

Drawing on what he had heard as a child in Peru from his Inka relatives, Garcilaso de la Vega wrote *Commentarios Reales* (between 1586 and 1612, i.e., half a century after the Spanish conquest). In it, he imaginatively syncretized Counter-Reformation Catholicism with how he thought an Inka theocracy must have operated. For Garcilaso, a major commonality was a shared abhorrence of sodomy. He stressed that before the arrival of the Spanish, his Inka ancestors had attempted to extirpate sodomites. Of the Yungas, a coastal people, Garcilaso wrote that, before Inkas subdued them, they had prostitutes available for sodomy "in their temples, because the Devil persuaded them that their gods delighted in such people" (1966:14). This seems to indicate that there was a sacred role for sodomites in the coastal tribes the Inkas conquered. In contrast, Garcilaso stressed, sodomy was "so hated by the Inkas and their people that the very name was odious to them and they never uttered it" (p. 162). This formulation seems to be a projection of "the sin not named among Christians." This seems especially likely in that Garcilaso could not have known directly what words were in common use more than a century earlier.

Attributions of sodomy to particular tribes or areas conquered by Inka armies is more reliable than the resemblances Garcilaso adduced between Catholic and Inka cosmology. The practice of sodomy was not attributed to all conquered tribes. Open practice of sodomy was attributed to still fewer. Therefore, charges of sodomy do not appear to have been a general-purpose rationale for South American conquests, although they were certainly a part of justifying conquest within a Christian cosmology (see Roscoe 1991:170–76). One should not assume that sodomy only occurred in the areas in which Garcilaso or conquistador accounts explicitly mentioned it. However, one can accept that it was recognized rather than invented in those areas that were mentioned.

According to Garcilaso, the tenth Inka, Tupa Inka Yupanqui, who reigned from 1471 until 1493, vigorously persecuted sodomites. His general, Auqui Tatu, allegedly burned alive in the public square all those for whom there was even circumstantial evidence of sodomy in the [H]acarí valley. He also threatened to burn down whole towns if anyone else engaged in sodomy (1966 [1609]:162). Again in Chincha, Garcilaso claimed that Yupanqui burned alive large numbers, pulling down their houses and any trees they had planted (p. 335). Unlike Cieza, Garcilaso attributed sodomy to the Tarma and Pumpu. He followed Cieza in mentioning the notorious and (embarrassingly) *serraño* sodomites of Callejon de Huaylas, and the curse "Asta Huaylas." Brundage (1967:187) asserted that "transvestic homosexuality was a prominent feature of the life of the Yauyos [in the vicinity of modern Lima] . . . [They had] public houses with men dressed as women and painted their faces."

Yupanqui's son, Huayna Capac, who reigned from 1493–1525, appears to have been less zealous in attempting to extirpate sodomy from the lands he added to the Inka empire. He merely "bade" the people of Tumbez to give up sodomy. Garcilaso did not record any measures taken against the Manta, who he said "practiced sodomy more openly and shamelessly than all the other tribes" (1966 [1609]: 559, 561).[1]

The giants of Santa Elena, also purportedly practiced open/public sodomy. Their legend fascinated the conquistadors, especially since large bones (probably mastodon bones) were found in the area. At least according to Garcilaso, this all-male race was destroyed in a fire while everyone was engaged in a society-wide orgy of sodomy (1966 [1609]: 562–63). This is clearly a Spanish version of the destruction of Sodom. In the indigenous myth, "a youth shining like the sun" descended from the sky and fought against the oppressors of the Indians, throwing flames that drove them into a valley where they were all finally killed, and where what were believed to be their bones were found by a Spanish captain in 1543 (Zarate 1968 [1555]:34). There is no mention of sodomy at all in this earlier account.

In addition to mention of sodomy in the chronicles, archaeological

---

1. Murra (1946:805) mentioned a Manta myth of the origin of an all-male world.

excavations have produced evidence of coastal homosexuality, especially Moche ceramics.[2]

Before turning to the south of what was the Inka empire, mention should be made of a northeastern extension of Andean culture, the Lache (of the Timotean language family) living on the slopes of the Nevado de Chita (in Colombia):

> almost certainly through the neighbors and friends the [Chibchan-speaking] Arawakan Caquetío, publicly recognized male homo-sexuals, whom they married and buried as if they were women. Women who bore five male children consecutively were permitted to rear one as a woman. [Métraux and Kirchhoff 1948:363]

Inferences from Aymara Lexicon

Without specifying the source for attribution (possibly Garcilaso?), Brundage (1967:187) claimed that the Aymara-speaking "Lupacas who lived on the shores of Lake Chucuito had an established practice of homosexualism and sodomy" in the 16th century. Modern anthropologists have also attributed tolerance for male and female homosexuality to the Aymara on the basis of vocabulary relating to masculine women, effeminate (castrated?) men, and fellatio in an early 17th century dictionary. Although there are no published reports of homosexual behavior or roles among 20th-century Aymara,[3] most of the vocabulary recorded then has survived.

Neither of the two major attempts at depth psychology of Aymara culture by 20th-century American anthropologists (Tschopik 1951:167; LaBarre 1948:131–33) included any evidence of Aymara homosexuality from their own fieldwork. Both instead appealed to an early–17th-century Jesuit missionary dictionary to evidence conceptions three and a half centuries later. Although such a course can hardly be recommended as safe methodology, many of the words Bertonio included in his dictionary can be correlated to modern Aymara terms. Even more

---

2. See Arboleda (1981); Geberhard (1970); Hocquenghem (1986); Larco-Hoyle (1965); Posnansky (1925); Wassermann-San Blas (1938).

3. After citing three early Spanish reports of cross-dressing and "the abominable sin" *(pecado abominable)* Bandelier (1910:146,n.76) wrote: "My inquiries on this point were always answered in the negative, and I never observed anything that led me to suspect that such a habit might exist at the present time" (in contrast to his familiarity with its "open practice" in turn-of-the-century New Mexico pueblos).

might be if the early orthographies were more transparent and/or consistent.

Now as then, *mako* or *mank'a* means "eat testicles" and *allu mank'a* means "eat penis." Among the terms for effeminate men, *k'ewa* is fairly obviously *keulla*. *K'ewsa-Keussa* and *cutit chacha* continues to refer to a man who speaks like a woman, and *marmija* is plausible for cross-dressing (*marmi* means woman).[4] If LaBarre is right that *huaussa* meant castrated (so that *ipa huassa* is a father's sister fashioned out of a father's brother), it has been replaced by *irsuna* and *k'orakana*, neither of which can conceivably be Spanish replacements for an earlier indigenous term. Nevertheless, the kin specification for a homosexual role is intriguing enough to merit further efforts to decode *ipa huaussa*.[5]

There are Aymara terms for masculine-acting women. (Typically of most cultures) no conception of commonality between effeminate men and masculine women is apparent in Aymara lexicon. The following are said to be equivalent to marimacho in Spanish: *orkoch*, *wac'u chachacu*, and the unmarked *chachacu*.

While contemporary Aymara seem to conceive gender-variant (or gender-crossing) roles, expressions Bertonio glossed as "male with male sinning" that no longer (seem to) relate to sex suggest the possibility of age-graded homosexuality alongside berdache-like relations in pre-conquest Aymara. *Chacha pura* might be glossed "among the pretty, young boys." *Yok'alla* is a pre-pubescent boy, but what he is among in *yocalla pura hochachasitha* is obscure to me. Similarly, what *vel* represents phonologically in a language with no "v" or "b" sound is mystifying.

That these lexical sets have not disappeared is important, because missionary dictionaries are an unreliable basis for inferences about the absence of homosexual roles and behavior (see Murray and Arboleda 1985), and also because the other sources LaBarre (1948: 134) used to support his contention that male homosexuality is "well-doc-

---

4. If Bertonio's *ccacha* is *k'achu* and applied to a man, it would mean "womanly," but elsewhere (e.g., *macco* for *mako*) Bertonio seems to have used *cc* for unaspirated (cf. *keussa* in Bertonio for what we would now represent *k'ewsa*), so this is a dubious derivation.

5. If *huaussa* has been reduced to *wasa* (bachelor), we might have the metaphor that an unmarried father's brother might as well be a woman, but it seems to me more likely to be a Freudian anthropologist than the Aymara who interpreted a sister to be a castrated brother and took this as an expression of Aymara sexual antagonism.

umented for this region" are to coastal not to altiplano Peruvian cultures.[6]

Between the Aymara and the Araucanians

Hardly anything is known about the social structures and cosmologies of the indigenous peoples who lived between the Aymara and the Araucanians (such as the Atacameno, Chango, Lipe, and the Chilean Diaguita), whose cultures did not survive for 20th-century fieldwork and whose populations were not as large and concentrated as those on the northwest coast of South America, due to the extremely inhospitable climate and terrain. Late marriage ages for the Argentine Diaguita probably indicate elaborate initiation rites, but nothing is known of their content, homosexual or otherwise.

Among the semi-acculturated (cholofied) indigenes of contemporary Bolivia, Nash (1969:141) wrote, "Only men can dance the role of the *chinas*, or seductresses who are the consorts of the devil, since the obscene gestures required would make the role too much for a woman to overcome after Carnival, I was told. The role often attracts men with homosexual tendencies, like Tito, who can find in the Carnival an acceptable outlet."

Araucanian Third-(and Fourth-?) Gender Shamans

A number of observers (e.g., Métraux 1946: 324; Steward 1946: 723) were struck by the similarities between the tambourine-centered curing ceremonies of cross-dressing male shamans in the far north Pacific (see Bogoras 1901; Murray 1992:293–352) and in southwestern South America. Even the most speculative trans-Pacific navigation claims have posited east-west travel, without adding the immense north-south distances. Thus, the parallel berdache/shaman roles have been regarded as independent invention rather than diffusion. Araucanian (also known as Mapuche) territory (south of Santiago in Chile, extending into Ar-

---

6. This includes the one LaBarre marked "?Aymara" in which Garcilaso seems to me to be drawing on Cieza de Leon, who was generally Garcilaso's source of information on non-Inka groups, although Cieza (section CI) reported of the Colla that they "abhorred the nefarious sin" (*aborrecian el pecado nefando*). Kauffman-Doig (1979:78–79) alleged a phallic cult in the area. Even if his strained interpretation were true, the cult would not necessarily substantiate sacralized homosexuality, however.

gentina) is not even contiguous to other South American groups sharing the trait of spirit possession (Bourguignon 1968).

Métraux (1942; 1967:181–84) reviewed a number of 17th- through 19th-century accounts of transvestitic shamans living with the young men of southern tribes. The accounts (at least as recounted by Métraux and echoed by Cooper 1946:750) prefigure the special niche/role Devereux (1937) made for the (North American) Mojave berdache: delicately constituted non-warriors in a culture focused on warfare take a culturally validated role with special powers. Male Araucanian shamans were individuals "more than a little aberrant." Among the predisposing/explanatory features noted were epilepsy, nervous/hysterical/emotional/feminine temperaments, St. Vitus Dance, and blindness, as well as the native's own explanation: calls to serve by a spirit and active recruitment by already recognized shamans.

Métraux (1967:182) suggested that prejudices of the clergy and the creole population may have indirectly influenced a reaction against effeminate male shamans *(machi)*, although it is not clear whether Métraux was referring to influences of the original conquistadores or influences after the final pacification of the Araucanians in the 1880s. Over the course of the first half of the twentieth century, male homosexuality allegedly remained frequent among the Araucanians (Hilger 1957:68, 128, 249—all three references appear to rely on assurancesof one non-Araucanian informant), but fieldwork done around mid-century found most *machis* to be women. Titiev (1951:115–17) wrote, explaining Araucanians' historical views with his own understanding of gender non-conformity,

> Many years ago the office was generally held by men and it is practically certain that they were abnormal, at least with respect to sexual conduct. Some of them may have been true hermaphrodites, the rest were berdaches or transvestites, and widespread indulgence in sodomy and pederasty were common. There then followed a period when the post of machi might be filled by a man or a woman, and at this stage sexual irregularity is less frequently charged, particularly in regard to female practitioners. At present, male machis are rare, and some sexual irregularity is still associated with them [a photograph of a male *machi* and his two male assistants is plate IX]. Certainly, they wear feminine clothes while performing their duties, and it is not unlikely they are homosexuals . . . The great majority of contemporary machis are women who seem to be sexually normal. They marry, bear children, care

for their households, and follow the usual feminine occupations, except when engaged in professional activities. A suggestion of homosexuality is revealed in their relations with novices and assistants. . . . The novice goes to live with her tutor for a period of a year or more, during which they work and sleep together. Whether or not they actually enjoy homosexual relations is uncertain.

The first extended Spanish account of the Araucanians, by their "happy captive" Francisco Núñez de Piñeda y Bascuñán (1924 [1663]: 159; 1977 [1663]:58,83) included descriptions of passive homosexual curers *(hueye)* who cross-dressed (wearing a blanket instead of breeches), wore their hair long and loose (like Araucanian women), and whose profession was highly respected by both men and women.[7] The Irish Jesuit Thomas Falkner (1774:117) wrote:

> The wizards are of both sexes. The male wizards are obliged (as it were) to leave their sex, and to dress themselves in female apparel, and are not permitted to marry, though the female ones or witches may. They are generally chosen for this office when they are children, and a preference is always shewn to those, who at that early time of life discover an effeminate disposition. They are cloathed very early in female attire, and presented with the drum and rattles belonging to the profession they are to follow.
>
> They who are seized with fits of the falling sickness, or the chorea Sancti Viti, are immediately selected for this employment, as chosen by the demons themselves; whom they suppose to possess them, and to cause all those convultions and distortions common in epileptic paroxysms.

Relying especially on another very early report (Ovalle 1646 [1961]) that there were female *machi*, Faron (1964:153) challenged other anthropologists' reading of 17th–19th-century observations of Araucanian life:

> Simply because male shamans were transvestites does not mean that there were no female shamans . . . [n]or that they were outnumbered by men. . . . The shift from a male-dominated profession, at some vague period prior to the middle of the 18th

---

7. Much of *El Cautiverio Feliz* involves the author recounting having politely warded off the advances of Araucanian women. Although Núñez regularly slept with young men, he did not record any assaults on his Christian chastity by them or by any *hueye*.

century, to the contemporary dominance by females is actually unsubstantiated.

Nonetheless, Faron provided an explanation for a decreasing function for male *machi*, viz. that the only distinctively male function of *machi* was forecasting the outcome of military actions (1964:154). The final pacification of the Araucanians in the late 19th century would certainly have obliterated this part of the role.

After noting "there has never been a *machi* who was considered fully masculine" (1964:152), Faron suggested that the husbands of *machi* are not particularly masculine:

> It seems that machi take the initiative in arranging marriage for themselves, marrying their choice of subservient males, selecting one who is not a member of a traditional wife-receiving group, in a ceremony that does not involve the custom of brideprice and the sets of rights and obligations surrounding the traditional linkage of two patrilineal descent groups. With regard to patterns of inheritance, marriage, and residence, then, machi seem to operate outside the traditional structure of Mapuche social relationships. [Faron 1964:155]

Faron's is one of the few accounts by anthropologists of any culture in which the husband of the third-sex man is regarded as less than fully masculine, whether or not this is the Araucanians' own view.

More common is the attribution of special powers to those in liminal roles. The power, which is a part of gender non-conformity for female as well as for male *machi*, is inextricably bound up with social distance. "As outsiders without linkage to ancestral spirits [particularly local ones], female shamans are precisely those persons in whose hands supernatural power is safest" (Faron 1964:156). "Male machi tend to live uxorilocally if they marry at all, and if not married seem to stray from their natal reservation" (Faron 1964:155). This neo-Durkheimian stress on sacred distance (compare chapter 14 in this volume; also concerned with a culture in which changing sex ratios of cult practitioners have been controversial) undercuts the special niche explanation (implicit in Métraux's accounts). Faron (1964) contested the bases for claims of changes in the sex ratio of machi, but none of the ethnographers of the Araucanians attempted to argue away homosexuality (as in Amazonian cases discussed in chapter 19). All the Araucanian fieldwork discussed here (including Faron's, which was done between 1952 and 1954) was done before the abolition of reservations in 1960 and the subsequent upheavals of Chile's governments; fresh fieldwork has not been possible.[8]

REFERENCES

Arboleda Grieve, Manuel A.
    1981   Representaciones artisticas de actividades homoeroticas en la ceramica moche. *Boletin de Lima* 16:98–107.
Bandelier, Adolph Francis Alphonse
    1910   *The Islands of Titicaca and Koati.* New York: The Hispanic Society of America. (Reprinted, New York: Kraus, 1969.)
Bertonio, Ludovico
    1612   *Vocabulario de la Lengua Aymara.* Lupaca: Iuli. (Reprinted, Leipzig: Julio Platzmann, 1879.)
Bogoras, Waldemar
    1901   Chukchi of Northeast Asia. *American Anthropologist* 6:340–62.
Bourguignon, Erika
    1968   World distribution and patterns of possession states. In *Trance and Possession States.* R. Price, ed. Pp. 3–34. Montréal: R. M. Bucke.
Brundage, Burr Cartwright
    1967   *Lords of Cuzco.* Norman: University of Oklahoma Press.
Cieza de Léon, Pedro
    1959   [1553] *The Incas.* Norman: University of Oklahoma Press.
Cooper, John M.
    1946   The Araucanians. *Handbook of South American Indians* 2:687–760.
Degarrod, Lydia N.
    1993   Politics, patriarchy and female shamanism among the Mapuche of Chile, 1881–1931. Paper presented at the annual meeting of the American Anthropological Association in Washington, D.C.
Devereux, George
    1937   Institutionalized homosexuality of the Mohave. *Human Biology* 9: 498–527.
Garcilaso de la Vega
    1966   [1609] *The Royal Commentaries.* Austin: University of Texas Press.
Falkner, Thomas
    1774   *A Description of Patagonia and the Adjoining Parts of South America.* London: C. Pugh. (Facsimile edition with notes by Arthur Neumann, Chicago: Armann & Armann, 1935.)
Faron, Louis C.
    1964   *Hawks of the Sun.* Pittsburgh: University of Pittsburgh Press.

---

8. An interesting ethnohistory of female shamans, who were blamed by some for the defeat by the Chilean army in 1881, was presented by Degarrod (1993). For the more general context see Latcham (1924).

Flornoy, Bertrand
  1956 *The World of the Incas.* New York: Vanguard.
Geberhard, Paul H.
  1970 Sexual motifs in prehistoric Peruvian ceramics. In *Studies in Erotic Art.*
    T. Bowie, et. al, eds. Pp. 109–69. New York: Basic Books.
Hilger, M. Iñez
  1957 *Araucanian Child Life and Its Cultural Background. Smithsonian Miscella-
    neous Collection* 133.
Hocquenghem, Anne-Marie
  1986 Les representations erotiques Mochicas et l'ordre Andin. *Bulletin de
    l'Institut Francais D'Études Andines* 15:35–47.
Kauffman-Doig, Federico
  1979 *Sexual Behavior in Ancient Peru.* Lima: Kompaktos.
LaBarre, Weston
  1948 *The Aymara Indians of the Lake Titicaca Plateau. American Anthropologi-
    cal Association Memoir* 68.
Larco-Hoyle, Rafael
  1965 *Checan: Essays on Erotic Elements in Peruvian Art.* Geneva: Nagel.
Latcham, Ricardo E.
  1924 *La organizacion social y las creencias religiosas de los antiguos araucanos.*
    Santiago: Cervantes.
Métraux, Alfred
  1942 Le shamanisme araucan. *Revista del Instituto de Antropologia Universidad
    Nacional de Tucuman* 2:309–62.
  1946 Ethnography of the Chaco. *Handbook of South American Indians* 1:137–
    370.
  1967 *Réligions et magies indiennes d'Amerique du Sud.* Paris: Gallimard.
Métraux, Alfred, and Paul Kirchhoff
  1948 The northeastern extension of Andean cultures. *Handbook of South
    American Indians* 4:349–68.
Murra, John
  1946 The historic tribes of Ecuador. *Handbook of South American Indians*
    2:785–822.
Murray, Stephen O.
  1992 *Oceanic Homosexualities.* New York: Garland.
Murray, Stephen O., and Manuel A. Arboleda G.
  1985 The dangers of lexical inference I: Maori homosexuality. *Journal of
    Homosexuality* 12:121–29.
Nash, June
  1969 *We Eat the Mines and the Mines Eat Us.* New York: Columbia University
    Press.
Núñez de Piñeda y Bascuñán, Francisco
  1974 [1663] *Cautivero Feliz, y Razón de las Guerras Dilatadas del Reino de
    Chille.* Santiago: Zig-Zag. (Translated by William Atkinson as *The Happy
    Captive,* London: Folio Society, 1977.)
Ovalle, Alonso de
  1646 *Historica relacion del Reyno de Chile.* Rome: F. Caualli. (Spanish version

published by Zig-Zag, 1961 in Santiago; an English version of the first five of the six parts was published in 1703 by A. & J. Churchill, London).

Pizzarro, Pedro

1986 [1571] *Relacion del Descubrimiento y Conquista de los Reinos del Peru*. Lima: Pontificia Universidad Catolica.

Posnansky, Arthur

1925 Die erotischen Keramiken der Mochicas und deren Beziehungen zu oksipital-deformierten Schendeln. *Abhandlungen zur Anthropologie, Ethnologie und Urgeschichte* 2:67–74.

Roscoe, Will

1991 *The Zuni Man-Woman*. Albuquerque: University of New Mexico Press.

Rowe, John H.

1948 The Kingdom of Chimor. *Acta America* 6.

Steward, Julian H.

1946 South American cultures. *Handbook of South American Indians* 5:669–723.

Titiev, Mischa

1951 *Araucanian Culture in Transition*. Ann Arbor: University of Michigan Press.

Tschopik, Harry

1951 *The Aymara of Chucuito, Peru. Anthropological Papers of the American Museum of Natural History* 44.

Wassermann-San Blas, Bruno K.

1938 *Ceramicas de antiguo Peru de la Coleccion Wassermann-San Blas*. Buenos Aires: Casa Jacobo Peuser.

Zarate, Augustin de

1968 [1555] *The Discovery and Conquest of Peru*. Middlesex: Penguin.

ADDITIONAL REFERENCES TO HOMOSEXUALITY IN ARGENTINA, COLOMBIA, AND PERU

Ardila, Ruben

1985 La homosexualidad en Colombia. *Acta psyquitrica y psicologica de America Latina* 31:191–210. Ardila reports prevalence of homosexual behavior—at least one leading to orgasm—among university students (28 percent for males, 13 Percent for females in Bogotá), and a survey of 100 Colombian male homosexuals (38 percent also reporting that they enjoyed heterosexual relations; 24 percent reported not being committed to homosexuality). 5 percent perceived themselves as isolated; 11 percent had moderate to severe depression; 53 percent considered themselves somewhat to very effeminate.

Bao, Daniel

1993 *Invertidos sexuales, tortileras*, and *maricas machos*: the construction of homosexuality in Buenos Aires, Argentina, 1900–1950. *Journal of Homosexuality* 24:183–219. Reviewing the writings of an early 20th-century psychiatrist (Francisco de Veyga), a lawyer (Eusebio Gómez), and a playwright (José Castillo Gonzales), Bao discusses evidence of a transvestite subculture, the view of a distinct species *(especie desecta),* and one queen's poetic standard offer to perform fellatio (p. 200).

Calancha, Antonio de la
    1639 *Crónica moralizada del orden de San Augustín den el Perú.* Barcelona: Pedro Lacavallería. 1:571–79.
Castañeda de Nágera, Pedro de
    1838 *Relation du voyage de Cibola.* Paris: A. Bertrand. Pp. 150–56.
Castillo González, José
    1957 [1914] *Los Invertidos.* Buenos Aires: Carro de Tespis. Play discussed by Bao 1993.
Denegri, Marco Aurelio
    1966 Birth control in Peru. *Sexology* 32:421–24.
    1967 Prostitution in Old Peru. *Sexology* 33:853–55.
Fernández de Piedrahita, Lucas
    1942 *La Historia general de las conquistas de Nuevo Reino de Granada.* Bogotá: ABC. Pp. 25–26, 86.
Flornoy, Bertrand
    1956 *The World of the Inca.* New York: Vanguard Press. Pp. 128–29, 170.
Friede, Juan
    1955–60 *Documentos ineditos para la historia de Colombia.* Bogotá: Academia Colombiana de Historia. III:271; IV:95; X:334.
Gómez, Eusebio
    1908 *La Mala Vida en Buenos Aires.* Buenos Aires: Juan Roldan. See Bao 1993 on his account of the antics of inverts.
Jamandreau, Paco
    1975 La Cabeza Contra el Suelo: Memorias. Buenos Aires: Flor. Bao (1993: 218) notes that throughout his autobiography Jamandreau distinguishes *maricones* (effeminate, bitchy men who dress as women) from *homosexuales* (masculine men who dress as women.)
Jauregui, Carlos Luis
    1987 *La Homosexualidad en la Argentina.* Buenos Aires: Ediciones Tarso.
McCaskell, Tim
    1980 Gay life in Colombia. *Body Politic* 68:19–21.
Majia-Xesspe, Toribio
    1962 Sex Life in Ancient Peru. *Sexology* 29:102–6.
Montesinos, Fernando
    1882 *Memoria antiguas, historiales y politicas del Peru.* Madrid: Ginesta.
Moore, Sally Falk
    1958 *Power and Property in Inca Peru.* New York: Columbia University Press.
Stein, William W.
    1961 *Hualcan: Life in the Highlands of Peru.* Ithaca, NY: Cornell University Press. P. 181 notes that Quechua *estancia* studied, "The topic of sexual deviance is also a cause for humor. Both male and female, passive and active, cases were known. The ephithet *we.ne* (passive male partner) is used frequently, and perhaps there are more accusations of homosexual practices

than actual cases. Two cases of male partners who lived together were reported, although one of these 'marriages' was broken by death some years ago. A female case was reported as having existed in another *estancia* of the district. These individuals were the butts of joking but apparently managed to maintain their relations."

Tessmann, Guenter

    1920 *Die Indianer Nordost-Perus.* Hamburg: Friedrichsen. P. 563.

Valdizán, Hermilio and Angel Maldonado

    1922 *La Medicina popular peruana.* Lima: Torres Aguirre. Pp. 310–30.

Villavicencio, Victor L.

    1942 *La vida sexual del inigeno peruano.* Lima: Barrantes 73–77.

Von Hagen, Victor W.

    1965 *The Desert Kingdoms of Peru.* Greenwich, CT: New York Graphic Society.

22

🍃

Isthmus Zapotec Attitudes
toward Sex and Gender Anomalies*
Beverly N. Chiñas

The Zapotecs of the Isthmus of Tehuantepac in the southern Mexican
state of Oaxaca have long been known in Mexican lore for their tolerance of gender and sex preference variations. San Juan Evangelista, the
village in which I have conducted field research intermittently since
1966, is a typical peasant community. Most men earn the bulk of their
livelihood by farming small plots of land with small-scale irrigation
almost certainly in use prior to the Spanish conquest (Torres 1958
[1580]), while the women raise pigs and chickens and process various
foods for local and regional markets. Zapotec is the everyday language. Most people now can communicate with outsiders in the national language (Spanish), although in the 1960 census 43 percent
were monolingual Zapotec speakers, the highest rate of any Isthmus
community.

Isthmus Zapotecs hold contrasting attitudes about sex and gender.
On the one hand, there are the Catholic ideals of virgin brides and
women's honor that remain very much a part of the ideal culture that
Isthmus Zapotecs carry in their minds and which families strive to
maintain. On the other hand, there is an unusual degree of openness
and acceptance of gender/sex "deviations." Isthmus Zapotecs deal with gen-

*An earlier version of this chapter was presented at the 1988 American Anthro-
pological Association meeting in Phoenix, Arizona. It incorporates material from
Chiñas (1985) and has been incorporated into the ninth chapter of the second edition
of my book *The Isthmus Zapotecs,* © Holt, Rinehart and Winston, 1991. Some of my
research in Oaxaca has been supported by grants from the National Endowment for
the Humanities and the Wenner-Gren Foundation.

293

der and sex preference variations daily, often within their immediate
families. Like a mild physical abnormality, sex/gender variation is discussed openly in third-person terms, but is usually politely avoided in
first- or second-person conversation.

Muxe, persons who appear to be predominantly male but display
certain feminine characteristics are highly visible in Isthmus Zapotec
populations.[1] They fill a third-gender role between men and women,
taking some of the characteristics of both. Although they are perceived
to be different from the general heterosexual male population, they are
neither devalued nor discriminated against in their communities.[2] Isthmus Zapotecs have been dominated by Roman Catholic ideology for
more than four centuries. Mestizos, especially mestizo police, occasionally harass and even persecute *muxe* boys, but Zapotec parents (especially mothers and other women) are quick to defend them and their
rights to "be themselves," because, as they put it, "God made them that
way." I have never heard an Isthmus Zapotec suggest that a *muxe* chose
to become a *muxe.* The idea of choosing gender or of choosing sexual
orientation—the two of which are not distinguished by the Isthmus
Zapotecs—is as ludicrous as suggesting that one can choose one's skin
color.

Women feel especially close to and trustful of non-related *muxe* (in
contrast to non-related heterosexual men) and often address them directly as *niña* (little girl) in non-public contexts. *Muxe* so addressed
seemed to consider *niña* a term of endearment.

Young boys are sometimes identified as *muxe* by the community as
early as their third year. They gradually become aware of this identification as they grow up. Little boys are tentatively identified as *muxe* by
family and community if they prefer playing house and playing with
dolls with little girls, if they imitate their mothers more than their
fathers, or if they prefer dressing up in girls' clothing. Some boys who
displayed few of these characteristics in childhood nonetheless become

---

1. I have never heard even a rumor of hermaphroditism in San Juan.

2. Campbell (1990), who worked in a much larger community and focused on
political actions, disputes my conclusions about the lack of discrimination. Our con-
flicting data come from different segments of the population and were collected in
different social contexts. I spoke mainly with women and with men within family
settings. Campbell collected much of his data from all-male groups in political
meetings and cantinas. The gender of the fieldworker, the gender of informants, and
the physical setting of data-gathering influence results.

muxe around the time of puberty. Others who acted "girlish" when small cast off such behavior in their teens and become indistinguishable from their non-*muxe* brothers: they go on to marry and to sire children. Much more research would be needed to account for final outcomes on the basis of childhood indicators.

Unlike the *hijra* of India (Nanda 1990), *muxe* are rarely mistreated or criticized by their family in attempts to inhibit their femininity. Therefore, they tend to remain within their natal family into adulthood. As is common for young literate men, they may eventually leave to take a job outside the area. If they remain in the community, they may or may not enter a heterosexual marriage. If they do, the married couple will live with the parents of one or the other partner for a few years. Like the *hijra*, *muxe* are conceived as being engaged in prostitution, although I am not at all sure that many are.

Isthmus Zapotec believe that *muxe* are the brightest and most gifted children. In my observation, many young *muxe* fit the stereotype, but others evidence no special talents or superior intellect. Parents often consider them the best bet for educating beyond the level of other children in the family. Not all proto-*muxe* but only those who continue to show superior academic performance will be kept in school beyond the sixth grade. Most families cannot afford to educate all of their children even that far.

Some *muxe* do certain kinds of "women's work," particularly embroidering women's fiesta costumes, sewing items of women's clothing, decorating home altars, and drawing designs for embroidery. These are all means of earning money. Others do traditional "men's work," such as making silver and gold jewelry. Besides being thought to be exceptionally intelligent, *muxe* have a reputation for having artistic abilities. The "women's work" they do is said to be done more artistically and with greater care than when women do it.

Nowadays, *muxe* often find white-collar jobs in banks, government offices, and businesses—jobs that traditionally have been viewed as "men's work" in Mexican culture, although by the 1990s women also filled some of these white-collar positions. *Muxe* have recently become heavily involved in local politics, even to the point of being elected president of some *municipios* (see below).

In private, young adult *muxe* sometimes wear mestizo-style women's dress. On occasion, they wear cosmetics and such feminine items as high-heeled pumps, neither used traditionally by Zapotec women. Their hair is cut in the male style, but usually is combed in a more feminine way.[3] Their mode of dress is predominantly male, consisting of men's trousers and shirts, although *muxe* usually take more care about fit, quality of fabric, and tailoring than most masculine/heterosexual men do. Sometimes, they wear gold earrings or necklaces and have gold-coin buttons made for their shirts. *Muxe* do not wear jewelry or makeup when working at white-collar jobs.

In contrast to "berdache" in many indigenous North American cultures (Williams 1986; Roscoe 1987, 1988a,b, 1991; Murray 1992: 341–52) and northeastern Asian ones (Murray 1992:293–340), *muxe* have no special religious roles today, although it is possible that they did in former times. They are in no way excluded from community religious rites either. In the folk Catholicism practiced today, adult married *muxe* participate as men. They are not barred from sponsoring public fiestas, a major avenue to prestige, nor are they prohibited from participating fully in any of the other rites appropriate for men.

Young *muxe* are permitted certain public behavior at the fiestas not appropriate for men, such as couple-dancing with women and with each other. Heterosexual men do not dance in couples with either sex, performing only traditional dances such as the *Zanduga,* a dance in which men and women circle each other without touching. Women, though, dance together in close bodily contact, just as it is natural and expected that women show much public affection toward one another. At fiestas it is considered very unseemly for a woman not to dance with her sisters, female first cousins, mothers, and comadres. Isthmus Zapotec culture allows both women and men more freedom to express affection in public for persons of the same sex than does Anglo North American culture. I could not detect any sexual innuendos in such behavior. Elderly men walk down the street hand-in-hand, as do women of all ages and relationships. Women also stand with arms entwined in public, a gesture expressing friendship and sisterly affection.

Young *muxe* may dance with women—most often their mothers, sisters, or cousins—just as though they were women. They also dance with other *muxe.* In the context of fiesta dancing, then, *muxe* may take the role of women, but not the costume. The same individual does not

---

3. At the time of my 1966–67 fieldwork "more feminine ways" included bangs or "spit-curls" in front of the ears. In 1990 I saw one *muxe* with flowing, longer than shoulder-length hair that was bleached red.

take the men's ritual role and dance in the women's role on the same occasion, nor even in the same life phase.

Homosexual and bisexual men solicit sexual relations with *muxe* (as well as with other homosexuals and with non-*muxe* boys). However, being *muxe* does not necessarily correlate with homosexual preference. Although the Isthmus Zapotec lack separate terms, there is no inevitable connection between transvestism and homosexuality. Moreover, as in many other societies, including the United States, there are a number of homosexual males who are invisible because their public behavior is indistinguishable from that of heterosexual males.

It is not surprising to the Isthmus Zapotec that some *muxe* marry and raise families. Many do so, in which case they are viewed and treated the same as other husbands/fathers. Married *muxe* tend to put aside the more blatant symbols of the third sex and strive for a male image. Parenthood is considered the highest of life's achievements. Perhaps the expectation and encouragement of *muxe* to marry is another indication of the general cultural gender equality of the region (see Chiñas 1973, 1991). No informant suggested to me that marriage was encouraged as a gentle way to try to get a *muxe* on the male pathway.

In dress, behavior, and choice of occupation, *muxe* do not follow the pattern of either males or females, combining elements of both.

Marimachas

There are also a few Zapotec women who are masculine in behavior. Referred to by the Spanish word *marimachas,* they are not culturally recognized as essentially different from other women, although they appear physically more masculine and sometimes display hostile, aggressive behavior resembling Latino men. They neither dress differently from other women nor do they use different hairstyles. What seems to identify them in the community is their physically more masculine appearance and behavior and their preference for masculine work, even though only one *marimacha* known to me has taken a man's occupation full-time: a woman in her sixties who had returned to the pueblo after many years was self-employed chauffeuring a public conveyance for hire.

Marimacha women are not nearly as visible as *muxe* men. It is my impression that they are considerably fewer in number in the pueblo than *muxe*. Zapotec culture does not consider them a separate gender category, nor do the *marimachas* themselves.

Bisexuality

Bisexuality among both men and women may be more common than exclusive homosexuality. Zapotecs are as tolerant of bisexuality as they are of transvestism and homosexuality. Persons with both homosexual and heterosexual predilections almost always marry and raise families. It is often only late in life that the community becomes aware that an individual "has turned homosexual." Over the twenty-plus years I have worked in San Juan, several prominent citizens with grown children have left their opposite-sex mates to live with partners of the same sex. This may lead to some whispering for a short while, but no real ostracism. This is not to say that they condone such a course. Tolerating and approving are not the same.

Same-Sex Couples[4]

Persons who publicly form same-sex couples seemingly experience little change in their community life. They continue to attend fiestas as before, fulfilling the fiesta behavior expectations of their sex. This is particularly easy to do because there are virtually no heterosexual couple interactions in religious contexts. Genders are always seated in different places at religious festivals and have different roles and duties throughout. Heterosexual couples often do not even attend fiestas as a couple but as individual representatives of their households, one or the other attending as appropriate.

Lesbian couples seem to occur about as frequently as male homosexual couples. Of the several I have known, most had been married to a man and raised a family before becoming publicly lesbian. I observed no outright ostracism of lesbian couples, although it is my impression that they are seen as a bit more scandalous than male-male couples, perhaps because women are believed and expected to be morally superior to men. In one case, the 18-year-old unmarried heterosexual daughter of a mother who had turned lesbian went to live with her godmother because the lesbian home was no longer considered a proper environment for the virgin daughter. I do not know who made

---

4. I do not know of a Zapotec word for same-sex couples. I have heard the Spanish "amantes" (lovers) used.

the decision. Especially if she was being courted, it may have been the daughter's.

How frequently married women become involved in lesbian relationships without leaving their male spouses is unknown. It is probably more common than those who opt to live as a couple, as for male homosexuals. In 1982 there were rumors of a suspected lesbian relationship developing between neighbor women. One was married with a husband and small children. The other had been abandoned by her husband and left with children several years earlier. In this case, the "macho" partner was said to be the still-married wife who was also about ten years younger than her neighbor.

Younger, unmarried women may become involved in lesbian relationships on occasion, although this seems to be much rarer than the involvement of older, married women. In the single case of which I have knowledge, the unmarried eldest daughter of a close friend and informant left her mother's home and took up residence in another barrio with her older lesbian lover. The daughter was then 25 years old, not yet beyond the expected age of heterosexual marriage, which might have been a factor in her mother's consternation. The daughter's action proved so upsetting to the mother that relations between the two broke off in bitterness. A reconciliation of sorts occurred a year later, and the daughter continues to live with her lesbian partner a decade later, visiting her natal family on infrequent occasions.

In the past there were occasional male-*muxe* common-law marriages. The most famous case occurred some years before my first visit to the area and was related to me by several people in 1966–67. A man had been widowed and left with a large family of small children. Instead of remarrying, he took in a *muxe* who acted as surrogate mother to the children, doing all the woman's work, such as making tortillas, cooking, laundering clothes, and shopping. At least posthumously, people spoke admiringly of the sacrifices he made as a mother-substitute, telling me that "every one of those children got an education and was sent to school clean and well fed." This couple lived together for the remainder of their lives.

Muxe, Economic and Political Changes

In recent years, *muxe* in San Juan have begun to take an increasingly dominant role in local politics. At least one has been elected *presidente* of the *municipio*, and involvement at various lesser levels has increased since my original fieldwork there. This increasing political involvement is probably indirectly related to the economic changes beginning in the 1980s.

Several trends converged. All over Mexico, men in their thirties and forties became local political leaders. Part of the reason for this is demographic and part is due to the higher education level of younger Mexican men in comparison with their fathers, and concomitant greater ease and familiarity with the national language (Spanish) and (probably more importantly) with the institutions and institutional manners of the nation.[5]

The fact that *muxe* tend to be better educated than the average gives them an advantage in seeking office. Also, since most of them do not marry and establish families as early as other males (if at all), they continue to live in their natal homes. Therefore, they have less economic pressure than their brothers who have young families growing in size to support. Thus, they have more time and energy that does not need to be devoted to earning income, enabling them to cultivate political alliances. The cultural definition of them as more capable and intelligent than their agemates and their relative freedom to focus on political activity enhance their chances of being elected to office.

Conclusions

Research on gender and sexual variation is still far from a stage where definitive statements about causes can be offered, but a few tentative suggestions seem appropriate. Although no attempt has been made to establish the incidence of sex/gender variability in San Juan, it appears higher in the Isthmus Zapotec population than among other indigenous populations in Mexico. Rymph (1974) found 6 percent of the males in one Isthmus Zapotec community in the early 1970s to be *muxe*. In contrast, Selby (1974:41) asserted that among the highland Zapotec, "the division between men and women is so clear, so absolute, so well marked, and so unquestioned that the mere thought of engaging in homosexuality is foreign to them. Sexual activity is only defined for intersex relations." He did not mention transvestism, but it would seem that he would have included it as "unthinkable" (unlexicalized).

Among the Isthmus Zapotec, *muxe* "run in families." In one family,

---

5. Roscoe (1988b, 1991) discussed comparable Zuni and Navajo instances.

five of six sons are *muxe*. The sixth—a middle-aged father of seven children—exhibits mildly effeminate behavior. Isthmus Zapotecs themselves believe that these sex/gender anomalies have a genetic base. Nonetheless, they recognize considerable variation in the age at which boys exhibit *muxe* traits. While some boys may be tentatively identified as *muxe* as young as age three, others give little or no indication of being *muxe* until after puberty. Moreover, some boys identified early as *muxe* and displaying very effeminate behavior in their pre-pubescent years turn into heterosexual adults, outwardly at least, at or soon after reaching puberty. People take a wait-and-see attitude about ultimate outcomes.

The generally benign and tolerant attitudes of Isthmus Zapotecs for all types of gender and sexual variation do not discourage young people following whatever path they are inclined to take. From their simple lifestyle and low level of formal education, some might consider the Isthmus Zapotecs an unsophisticated people, yet we could all learn from their open-minded and accepting attitudes about sex/gender variations.

REFERENCES

Chiñas, Beverly Newbold

    1973, 1991 *The Isthmus Zapotecs: Women's Roles in Cultural Context.* New York: Holt.

    1985 Isthmus Zapotec 'berdache.' *Anthropological Research Group on Homosexuality Newsletter* 7(2):1–4.

Murray, Stephen O.

    1992 *Oceanic Homosexualities.* New York: Garland.

Nanda, Serena

    1990 *Neither Man Nor Woman: The Hijras of India.* Belmont, CA: Wadsworth.

Roscoe, Will

    1987 Bibliography of berdache and alternative gender roles among North American Indians. *Journal of Homosexuality* 14:81–171.

    1988a *Living the Spirit: A Gay American Indian Anthology.* New York: St. Martin's Press.

    1988b We'wha and Klah: the American Indian berdache as artist and priest. *American Indian Quarterly* 12:127–50.

    1991 *The Zuni Man-Woman.* Albuquerque: University of New Mexico Press.

Rymph, David

    1974 Cross-sex behavior in an Isthmus Zapotec village. Paper presented at the American Anthropological Association meeting in Mexico City.

Selby, Henry A.

    1974 *Zapotec Deviance.* Austin: University of Texas Press.

Torres de Lagunas, Juan de
    1958 [1580] *Descripción de Teguantepec*. México: Vargas Rea.
Williams, Walter L.
    1986 *The Spirit and the Flesh*. Boston: Beacon Press.

ADDITIONAL REFERENCES TO HOMOSEXUALITY IN INDIGENOUS MESOAMERICA
(STEPHEN O. MURRAY)

Beals, Ralph L.
    1945 The contemporary culture of the Cahita Indians. *Bureau of American Ethnology Bulletin* 142:82.
    1946 *Cheran: A Sierra Tarascan Village*. Washington: U.S. Government Printing Office. P. 177.
    1952 *The Comparative Ethnology of Northern México Before 1750*. Los Angeles: University of California Press. P. 205.
Blaffer, Sarah C.
    1972 *The Black Man of Zinacantán*. Austin: University of Texas Press. P. 8.
Blair, Doniphan
    1985 Gay men in Nicaragua. *Advocate* 422:48, 51.
Bricker, Victoria R.
    1973 *Ritual Humor in Highland Chiapas*. Austin: University of Texas Press.
Clavígero, Francisco Saverio
    1780–81 *Historia antigua del Mexico*. London: Ackermann. IV:195–200. (2 vol. ed., Xalapa: Universidad Veracruzana, 1985).
Gossen, Gary H.
    1974 *Chamula in the World of the Sun*. Cambridge: Harvard University Press. Pp. 99–105.
Griffen, William B.
    1959 *Notes on the Seri Indian Culture, Sonora, México*. Gainesville: University of Florida Press. P. 33.
Hidalgo, Mariana
    1979 *La vida amorosa en el México antiguo*. México: Editorial Diana. Pp. 69–81.
Hilfrich, Klaus
    1972 Sexualität und Repression in der Kultur des Maya. *Baessler-Archiv* 20:139–71.
Parsons, Elsie Clews
    1936 *Mitla*. Chicago: University of Chicago Press. Pp. 437, 506.
Romoli, Kathleen
    1953 *Balboa of Darien*. Garden City, NJ: Doubleday. Pp. 55, 157, 217.
Royce, Anya P.
    1987 Masculinity and femininity in elaborated movement systems. In *Masculinity/Femininity*. J. Reinisch, et al., eds. Pp. 339–42. Oxford University Press.
Thompson, John Eric
    1970 *Maya History and Religion*. Norman: University of Oklahoma Press. Pp. 21, 46, 286.

Contributors

STEPHEN O. MURRAY earned a Ph.D. in sociology from the University of Toronto and is the author of *Social Theory/Homosexual Realities*, *Oceanic Homosexualities*, and the forthcoming *North American Homosexualities* and several books on the history of social science. He is director of Instituto Obregón in San Francisco.

BEVERLY NEWBOLD CHIÑAS earned a Ph.D. in anthropology from UCLA. She is the author of *The Isthmus Zapotec* and *La Zandunga*. She is a professor of anthropology at Chico State University.

MANUEL ARBOLEDA GRIEVE is a native of Lima and a doctoral candidate in anthropology at the University of California at Berkeley. He is the author of *Inca Cuzco*.

WAYNE DYNES earned a Ph.D. in art history from New York University and is a professor at Hunter College, CUNY. Formerly editor of *Gay Books Bulletin*, he is the author of *Homolexis*, and of *Homosexuality: A Research Guide*, and editor of *The Encyclopedia of Homosexuality*.

PETER FRY earned a Ph.D. in anthropology from Cambridge University and currently works for the Ford Foundation in Rio de Janeiro. He is the author of *Spirits of Protest*, editor of *Para Inglês ver* and coauthor of *O que é homossexualidade*.

PAUL KUTSCHE earned a Ph.D. in anthropology from the University of Pennsylvania. He is the author of *Canõnes, Values, Crisis, and Survival in a Northern New Mexico Village* and *Voices of Migrants: Rural-Urban Migration in Costa Rica*. He is professor emeritus of Colorado College.

LUIZ MOTT earned a Ph.D. in anthropology from São Paulo University. He is a professor of anthropology at the University of Bahia, founder of Grupo Gay de Bahia, and author of *O Lesbianismo no Brasil, O Sexo Proibido* among a host of other published works.

RICHARD G. PARKER earned a Ph.D. in anthropology from the University of California Berkeley and is the author of *Bodies, Pleasures and Passions.* He currently works for the Ford Foundation in Rio de Janeiro.

KARL J. REINHARDT earned a Ph.D. in Romance languages from the University of Texas at Austin and is a professor of Spanish at the University of Houston.

CLARK L. TAYLOR earned a Ph.D. in anthropology from the University of California at Berkeley. He is coordinator of the San Francisco Community College District AIDS Education Office and a professor at the Institute for Advanced Studies in Sexuality in San Francisco.

FREDERICK L. WHITAM earned a Ph.D. in sociology from Indiana University and is a professor of sociology at Arizona State University. He is co-author of *Male Homosexuality in Four Societies*.